ISSUE 124 ————————————

bamboo ridge

45th Anniversary | **JOURNAL OF HAWAI'I LITERATURE AND ARTS**

ISBN 978-1-943756-10-0

This is issue #124 of *Bamboo Ridge,*
Journal of Hawai'i Literature and Arts (ISSN #0733-0308).

Published by Bamboo Ridge Press

Printed in the United States of America

Bamboo Ridge Press is a member of the Community of
Literary Magazines and Presses (CLMP).

Guest Editors: Eric Chock and Darrell H. Y. Lum
Editor: Juliet S. Kono
Managing Editor: Joy Kobayashi-Cintrón
Copyeditors: Normie Salvador, Gail N. Harada, and Milton Kimura
Business Manager: Wing Tek Lum
Typesetting and book design: Misty-Lynn Sanico
Photo: *Abunai!* by Darrell H. Y. Lum
Cover art and design: Nāpunakō Sanico

Bamboo Ridge Press is a nonprofit, tax-exempt corporation formed in 1978
to foster the appreciation, understanding, and creation of literary, visual, and
performing arts by, for, or about Hawai'i's people. The organization is funded
by book sales, subscriptions, and individual donors, with support from the
Poetry Foundation and the Community of Literary Magazines and Presses
(CLMP). This publication was made possible in part by the Atherton Family
Foundation.

Bamboo Ridge is published twice a year.
For orders, subscription information, back issues,
and to purchase books contact:

Bamboo Ridge Press
P.O. Box 61781, Honolulu, Hawai'i 96839-1781
808.626.1481
read@bambooridge.org
www.bambooridge.org

— REFLECTIONS —

From the Editors

Whew! Why did we agree to edit the 45th anniversary issue? I had forgotten how much work it is to be an editor. Kudos to all those who have done the "grunt" work since we left in 2014. Special thanks to Juliet Kono who stepped in as editor after we retired, to our managing editor who claims to be the "barely managing" editor and wishes to remain unnamed, to copy editor Normie Salvador, and to book designer Misty Sanico for shepherding each issue until it gets into the hands of readers. Thanks especially to Gail Harada who was here from the start (and continues to contribute) and to Wing Tek Lum, who calls himself the Bamboo Ridge bookkeeper but is really the fiscal guru who tsked-tsked our complete lack of financial acumen at the beginning: $5 a year for four issues, postage included!

Who knew that when Eric and I played pinochle on Friday nights in the 1970s, chewing on the idea of a literary magazine between shuffling and dealing—imagining how it would look and feel, how we could get all the creative writers we knew from classes at UH and from community readings to send something to us—that literary could mean LOCAL.

As Eric describes the process, there's no real magic involved: reading, deciding, a little arm wrestling. It is exciting though to read submissions that are fresh, inventive, and surprising. From new writers and from some old friends.

We did it the old-fashioned way. The stack of mailed submissions was shoved into a Liberty House paper bag left on each other's front porch like an orphan hoping to get adopted. It has been replaced by electronic Liberty House bags, each one filled with the hard work of writers who had the courage to submit their work to us. Hence these 400+ pages. We think it all belongs in *Bamboo Ridge*.

The founding of Bamboo Ridge came at around the same time as an ethnic writers conference in 1978 called *Talk Story: Our Voices in*

Literature and Song; Hawai'i's Ethnic American Writers Conference,
organized by Marie Hara, Arnold Hiura, and Stephen Sumida. The
event was instrumental in bringing together Hawai'i writers who had
been working in isolation, as well as learning about Hawai'i's literary
history that dated back to the early 1900s—a history of literature that
was readily available but largely ignored in schools and by scholars. It
was our turn to read and learn from the writers who had come before
us, and to distinguish ourselves from visiting Asian American
mainland writers. The *Talk Story* motto was "words bind, words set
free" and it has, in part, continued to guide Bamboo Ridge.

We hope Bamboo Ridge continues to do that for all of us:
discover, read, enjoy, and celebrate our literature.

— Darrell H. Y. Lum

***

It was difficult in the time of COVID to meet for editing. In the
olden days, the two of us would often meet at Darrell's office, since I
didn't have one, or, since Darrell worked on campus at UH, maybe in
a meeting room he'd reserved. A few times, we tried a café or
restaurant nearby at lunch. Once we tried a meeting room in the
library. Later, we'd often meet at Wing Tek's office. But during
COVID we never met in person at all.

We read submissions electronically, separately at home, then met
by phone. Although we no longer made physical piles, we tried to
follow the same practice that had served us all those years—the three-
pile method: yes, no, maybe.

One of the beauties of the method is to have a lot of overlap in
the "yes" and "no" piles, those we were sure we wanted or sure we
did not want. We'd have stronger feelings about those and could
usually/often argue the other into agreement.

But if this did not immediately result in accord, it'd go into the
"maybe" pile. This was the difficult pile, where we had to come up
with reasons we wanted or did not want to publish something, and
those reasons could vary, and minds could change, there might be
some waffling, or maybe flashes of new insight.

The detailed explanation of how we got through all the "maybe"
piles over the years would take far too long and we are too old to even
attempt that. You'll just have to imagine what we'd say, the faces
we'd make at each other, the table pounding and "uh-huh" and

"hmmm" and eyeballing and moments of silence or "I guess I'll have to trust you on that." And sometimes we'd just run out of time and have to set a new date to meet again.

It's been a great 45 years. Thanks for coming along for the ride and seeing us through.

— Eric Chock

***

Imagine Hawai'i without Bamboo Ridge Press: the unheard voices, the unexplored narratives, the underappreciated local culture. Eric Chock and Darrell Lum gave voice to the many writers who have appeared over the decades in the publication itself. But even more importantly, they gave structure and substance to the idea that Hawai'i has a distinctive culture worthy of expression. They gave local writers the impetus and the courage to be themselves but also to speak in whatever voice they wished even if that voice was not "local" under the common definition. For all the writers who have appeared in *Bamboo Ridge*, there are many more who were just encouraged by its existence to speak and write. Bamboo Ridge is the spring that became a stream that created a muliwai, rich with mixing, before reaching the ocean. At this time of celebration and reflection, my gratitude to the founders and all who have contributed is deep and abiding. Mahalo nui loa.

— Juliet S. Kono

ATTENTION:

The following pages contain works of literary mischief.

Stories and poems herein may be disruptive, subversive,
provocative, transformative, addictive, creative . . .
and all the best adjectives that end in -ive or other suffixes.

SARA BACKER

Hong Kong 1990

The plane nosedives, *holy crap*,
but no one else panics. I later learn
Kai Tak Airport is famous for its death

drop landing. Christmas Eve, a shopping throng
on Nathan Street intensifies into a crazed swarm
rushing to the docks. A girl trips and falls.

I scream. The muscle of the crowd compresses,
lifts me off my feet. No choice but to board
the ferry. Three days in my hotel room, I lie in bed

and drink cheap beer, watch Jackie Chan movies
on TV, decompressing from my job in Japan
and worrying about the girl.

Men in gray suits talk on boxy cell phones while laborers
on flimsy scaffolds risk their lives for pay. Tea and rice
served on pavement in dirty cups a block away

from thousand-dollar five-star steak houses. Inside this
cocktail of money and danger, everyone speaks
about the coming *handover*. The end of British rule.

The narrow beach is mucky and cold, but the lights
on the dhows at night glitter in choppy water
and at the top of the tram, the high and windy

hill gathers mist into ghosts. Perhaps the mist-ghosts guided
me to the tiny shop with painted scrolls. I buy one
in the Sung style. Five people look across a clouded gulf

to admire a steep waterfall. I think the man in pink robes
could be Li Po. Thirty years later, the poet is still
in my room and I am still on their precipice in deep fog

SARA BACKER

Alone in Paris Twice

My solo December—living on onion soup
and the Musée D'Orsay. Constantly
cold, I drew sketches in a blank book.

Years later with a man, I felt fettered—in line
at the Louvre while he fussed with maps.

Though acrophobic, I followed his spiral
up 387 stone steps to the top of Notre Dame.
I broke down, shaking, embarrassing him.

The boat tour leveled us. Someone complained
c'est du fromage touristique. I laughed.

To be in Paris, but not *in* Paris—on the Seine,
drifting under bridge after bridge, lights reflected
in river dapple and in my glass of wine.

He didn't understand that I could ride this river
forever. He couldn't wait to get off.

SARA BACKER

Gingko

The sun ignites small yellow leaves,
little fans fluttering
covering the sidewalk up the steep hill.

In Japan "*ginko*" means "*bank.*"
Not a bank of trees, but paper
backed by silver and gold.

I was never more alone than in Japan.
I carried a pad of red ink to stamp
my name and deposit my paycheck.

What is money without friends
who could understand me?
But I had friends.

Sparrows on my laundry line.
An enormous wasp that zoomed
around me when I stepped outside.

My red bicycle with no gears.
Wild hydrangeas, white radishes,
a snail on my balcony. *(Hi, Issa!)*

The billboard every morning
in English: THINK TOMORROW
making it okay not to think today.

To watch gingko leaves quiver
is enough.
The path is golden.

AMITA BASU

The City

My friend who lives in New York City emailed me that, while she was walking her dogs yesterday, she heard a ruckus. Gunshots, screaming and running, silence, then sirens. A man one street over had started shooting strangers. My friend's sons were away at school, same neighbourhood. She described the steps she'd taken to discover whether they were alright, step by rational step. Her coherence amazed me. It amazes me every time an eyewitness—to terrorist attacks or forest fires, calm or upset—talks on television coherently, salvaging sense from the abyss. I sympathised with my friend, but wondered how anyone could live in that crazy USA, where every day someone starts shooting strangers. Here in Bangalore, I wouldn't know where to get a gun if I wanted to kill someone, or myself, which I do sometimes. Since I wasn't currently feeling murderous or suicidal, I felt smug about living where it's hard to get guns.

Make me, God, like the paper napkin, with which the artist-cum-writer wiped the gravy off her lips, painted carefully raspberry, to match the stones in her silver chandelier earrings. The artist-cum-writer used to be a model, used to be, your time is short, hurry, make the most. Her ears sagged with six decades of statement earrings. But her breasts probably sagged no more than mine already at 34. For she'd preserved herself, no high-impact aerobics to make the face sag, make the breasts sag prematurely. She'd come to our casual lunch fashionably dressed, like in the 1980s when she confronted the world from ramp ends and magazine covers. She was still svelte, except a little tummy, which it would be unseemly to lack at 65. She'd had several shows of her mixed-media art, won copywriting awards, published several books, and had many lovers. All these achievements she'd told me about, soon after we met, making with her words a cushion for her bottom, the more comfortably to sit opposite me. I've achieved nothing, but I'm still young, my potential vast, needing to be cushioned against, so my new friend kept listing her achievements for my judgment, shoving them onto the scales against the weight of her years. Books published, awards certified, lovers photographed, life journalled, still nothing would ever be enough, still playing catch-up with time, still her eyes scanned my as-yet-unwrinkled skin and my as-yet-unsagging triceps, as she wiped from her raspberry lips the gravy from her half-portion of chicken keema which, now, she pushed away unfinished, and wiped her hands on the paper napkin, though her hands were already clean. Make me, God, like the paper napkin, preserving the world's oily chins and lipstick-smeared cheeks, preserving strangers' fingerprints, recording without ego and with fidelity lunch-hour accidents, happy-hour spills—so that, when it's all over, the detectives may examine my sticky layers for clues to the final mystery: the mystery of human unhappiness.

Can you make me, God, a napkin? I've never believed in you, still sometimes I pray to you. For some things are so important that I wish someone were listening. It was the people's wishes that made you, God, back when the sea surged black with mystery. But I live in the aftertimes. I yearn only for the next ready-to-eat plastic-wrapped chicken biryani. My sea surges only with microplastics, white, disintegrating into white foam. My wishes are too degenerate to make you, God, can make at best a mountain-tall plastic snowman, a Thermocol plate stuffed in its cheeks, an ersatz Buddha smile, a Chelsea grin. That I could make. But that they wouldn't call God, they'd call What.

And feeling smug that, unlike my friend in NYC, who'd narrowly escaped being shot by Who knows whom, What knows why, I sit in the autorickshaw, going home from meeting the writer-cum-artist. The driver swings the fifty-pound vehicle across the road, racing traffic lights, wedging us into the four square feet between a city-bus and an SUV, either of which could swallow us, a one-bite snack. Autorickshaws have no walls, so I perch on the little seat's centre, putting between myself and the swerving, speeding traffic one more inch of life. Revving his diesel engine, hurtling down the dozen meters of clear road before the next traffic jam, the driver brakes always last-second, last-inch before a collision. So, behind him, I "brake" on time for him: dig my toes into the floor, we're going to crash into this truck's giant wheels, brake, driver, brake, for What's sake—and, voilà, he feels me braking the floor, at the last second the brakes screech, we lurch.

Why don't I ask him to slow down?

He'd obey. Briefly, before insidiously speeding up again, cleverly defying me, daring death. Still, I could ask him.

I don't. You see, he's blasting music on the radio. The speakers behind me throb with lyrics in old-world Urdu, sung largo, each line repeated two dozen times: this self-indulgent baritone has all the time in the world, his angst luxuriating, a love song, the yearning pulling at my heartstrings, though I've never been in love, for it's 2022, and love obsolesced along with USB 2.0s. But the music says otherwise, says love is good, love is here, everything will be alright. I let the music lull me. I don't ask my auto-driver to slow down. For I'm not really afraid, I couldn't have a road accident. Not me. Lacking courage to speak up, I survey the auto, seeking vindication for not speaking up. The windshield is spiderweb-cracked: he's just had an accident, he'll be careful now. He's driving fast, but not recklessly: he does always brake at the last second. He's not endangering me, just getting me there fast.

And who wouldn't want to get there fast? There, wherever I'm going. Look at the traffic! Even on a Saturday afternoon. Cars and cars and cars and cars, weaving speeding screeching. Motorbikes and motorbikes and motorbikes and motorbikes, weaving between SUVs, shortcutting over rubble piles, mounting the few fragments of sewer-gaping pavement that Bangalore's got left, crossing the road's median to overtake traffic, crossing quickly before the cars rushing down the other way, honking warning, come.

On motorbikes, and in cars, autorickshaws, and buses, sit the passengers, still as sheep on the final truck, uncurious where we're all going. Maybe we'll get there, or maybe we'll have an accident, at least then we'd get time off work. The drivers' eyes glint, watching the traffic monitor's countdown, red on black, watching the seconds tick away, gone forever, every second piling up more to catch up on. Driving all day on these streets, three traffic jams per kilometre, everybody speeding, vehicles materialising from What knows where to fondle your fenders, you must always be on, on alert, on cocaine, just to survive.

And the heat! All morning the sun struggled to break through the dusty air, through the dust that is the air, dust from metro construction, dust from hillocks of burning rubbish, burning is how we dispose of plastic, rubber, paper, rotten radishes, dust from the condo complexes towering over the suburbs, where last year stood a shale hill covered in scrub, scrub that had spent aeons crumbling the shale into red soil. You can still see the hill's guts between the condo complex and the mega-mall. The scrub is gone, the hill's round climbable boulders are gone, the slow red soil is gone, they've carved up the hill from all sides, like a turkey. Its jagged bones and shapeless guts stand spilling stone-dust into the air. All morning the sun fought the dust, and the autorickshaw driver inhaled it, and at 2 p.m. the sun won the battle. Now the sun roasts us, in the thick polyester suits they sent us from NYC, via China, which we donned, like good sheep, sheep roasting in clothes made for Europe on India's slowly revolving spit.

Driving a truck all day through traffic, dust, heat, riding a motorbike as a Delhivery man, Swiggy food-deliveryman, Dunzo or UrbanClap domestic-chores man, or the teacher who's spent all day talking at primary-school students, every student leering at his smartphone under the desk, or the clerk who's spent all day pushing papers, now sitting sheeplike in the bus behind the red-eyed driver, counting the days till he or she can buy a car—can you blame them for wanting to get there, wherever, right now? Can you blame my poor autorickshaw driver for endangering my life? Everybody drives this way. He has no choice. For, however many me-me-monuments Modi may erect, India's a poor country, life's cheap, thus the suicidal driving, diesel's too expensive to squander it driving safe. Another war is raging, global supply-chains disrupted, diesel is sprinting up the charts, up like the space rocket into regions unknown. Brave space rocket! Don't crash.

If you want to live, there's never a choice. When my American friend drives down a highway, they've got a maximum speed limit and a minimum, but the other drivers want her to drive at the maximum, above the maximum, a blur in the nanosecond-shutter-speed traffic-cameras. She used to try to drive safe, at the minimum speed limit. But another car rear-ended her, chastising her. Holding us up, we don't have all day. But they're rich in America, at least those people speeding down the highway are, roaring cars, purring engines, throbbing music. So they must have some other ailment, not poverty, that's causing their suicidal driving. Go as fast as you can, don't you dare slow down. If you want to live, there's never a choice.

This one autorickshaw trip, from one part of south Bangalore to another, six kilometres away, has already taken 130 minutes, we're not there yet. What with the cost of diesel, the cost of living, the driver must make What knows how many trips per day to scrape by. And to fund his cigarette addiction, second-hand chain-smoke vacuumed into my lungs. Well, cigarettes are better than alcohol, which is the leading addiction among autorickshaw drivers, the leading cause of their wives' deaths. He had to drop out of school, he says, and from the way he steers and the way he talks—thinking metres ahead, anticipating other drivers' moves, not easy, for nobody sees these lane markings, they're purely ornamental, anybody can swerve anywhere any minute, and we race past other vehicles almost colliding but never colliding, decelerating with the hair's-breadth precision of action-movie choreography—you can tell he's got a good brain, reflexes like an owl hunting at witching hour. An intelligent man, spending all day shuttling through this heat, dust, and methamphetamine honking, through this death-circus traffic in which he has no choice but to participate—can you blame him for driving suicidally? So I reason, sedating myself with empathy, for I haven't the courage to ask him to drive slowly, for I don't really believe I'll die in a road accident, for it's me. So I brake the auto's floor with my feet, that'll help, I'm sure, if we smash into something, I check to see if I'm in the centre of the auto's skeletal frame, I clutch the frame two-handed, I listen to the Urdu baritone singing of love. On the auto's speakers the bass is on max and the beat pounds, loud but slow, coaxing my heartbeat slow, slow, all the time in the world.

On motorbikes and in cars and behind the glass windows of restaurants sit people gossiping about their friends' failed fertility treatments, their colleagues' questionable clothing choices, and how many crores their own new flat cost them. They don't say 'Crore,' they say 'Cr,' misabbreviating one-syllable 'Crore' into two-syllable 'see-are,' so as not to sound boastful. It costs 'one-see-are,' that's ten million rupees to my American friend, to get away from the city, live in peace and green. Then fifty lakhs for a big air-conditioned car to zoom back into the city for work, and fifty thousand a month on diesel. Diesel is the new gold, diesel half-combusted thickening the air, sweetness in our nostrils, stuck on the streets hour after hour, nausea in our skulls at day's end. So then you order mint chicken, delivered to your doorstep in stylish plastic bowls, for your body knows mint cures nausea, and the chicken comes along for the ride, comes along on the Zomato deliveryman's speeding weaving motorbike, for, if he's a minute late, you get your money back.

In cars and in restaurants, vomiting words, stuffing their faces, sit thin people and fat people. Lots of fat people. India has the world's biggest population of malnourished humans, but 60% of us are overweight; watch out USA, we're catching up to you in gross tonnage. French fries and ice cream, burgers and mithai, fried chicken and mutton biryani, every second step, and discounts galore. The restaurants are all air-conditioned, gotta be, for Bangalore had a paradise climate, but then everyone came here and the trees went and the buildings came and the forests went and the roads came, now you must have air-conditioning to get any work done, to get any sleep slept, get ahead, and if you don't get ahead you'll lose your livelihood; it's that simple, never a choice. They have central air-conditioning in these condo complexes, twenty towers per complex, twenty floors per tower, actually nineteen, for there's no '13,' NYC said 13 was bad, and only six flats per floor, so that everybody gets a good view. Good views, the giant hoardings promise, and 80% open space, hundreds of metres of concrete jogging track gleaming white, imported palms, new-and-improved flowers, designer swimming pools, all buffering India's one-see-are persons behind their climate-controlled windows from the traffic speeding and the dead-mountain dust swirling past the tall walls.

I pretend to despise these alienated euphemising snobs in their one-see-are eyries. Truth is, if I had one-see-are, I'd be in there quicker than a rabid dog's canines in your calf. The city's become unliveable, too hot dusty noisy crowded, bring me some alienation please, on a one-see-are silver platter, mow down the shale mountain, grind it into cement to build me up, no, fool, not this shale mountain, this one's in my penthouse view, paid for and protected, go find another.

My auto's stuck in traffic before one condo complex's gate. I watch the fat green garden pipes drenching the thick poolside turf, overflowing onto the jogging track. The swimming-pool glisters full and blue. I think of my maidservant, in India everyone middle-middle-class and above has a maidservant, you knew that, I hope she won't pass this way, won't see the swimming-pool. For my maidservant has no running water. She waits every Sunday for the water-tanker, and fights with her neighbours to fill her house with water for the week, water in plastic jugs, steel jars, tin cans, water for drinking, bathing, cooking, clothes-washing, shit-flushing, handwashing, for in her shack-strewn neighbourhood, the water pipes became in 2018 purely ornamental. There was once a pond beside her house, but that's dried up. I hope she'll never see this swimming-pool, full of water, empty of people, feeding the parched air.

We're off again. I survey the deliverymen motorbikers, searching for my maidservant's son. His job is riding a motorbike around town, delivering Amazon parcels, parcels shipped from who knows where, ordered by who knows whom, ordered not even who himself remembers why. I wonder if this is him, weaving between these eighteen-wheelers. If he goes fast enough, a little faster, works night and day, he'll get rich. There's nothing to do but work: his colleagues change every few months, cycling between Amazon, Swiggy, Zomato, seeking that secret perfect job. He laughs at them—his mother taught him about the rolling stone, taught him to stick it out— and keeps to himself, keeps on the roads all day, for his goal waits at the end of this long straight road, out of sight, it's true, but definitely there. Towards that goal he speeds, while his mother overeats. My maidservant's so fat, she barely fits with the mop through my doorway. American television on their smartphones tells them they can do anything, rags to riches. Do they know America is lying? Is that why he speeds, risking his neck, determined to get wherever, now or never, is that why she overeats? He's had two accidents, and she's had her gallbladder out, and sticks herself with insulin thrice a day. She works all day, eats all evening, there's nothing to do but work and eat: her family are all back in the village, where the ruined farmers are hanging themselves.

Fellow Indian, away up there in your penthouse, buffered behind thirty metres of imported greenery, in your tower so high, behind your windows so shut—what has frightened you so, that you hide away up there? When you're driving, and a motorbike parked on the street's other side suddenly wheels across into your path, and you miss pancaking it by a second, you're startled, you honk in protest, lament, India will never be a civilised country. But you speed and weave with the best of them, seatbelted in your SUV. You speed home, scurry up your tower, stuff yourself with a porterhouse steak from Via Milano, bury your head in the dead cow's womb, and in Netflix. Wealth does not buffer you from the malady, for the malady is in the air, contagious as COVID, it finds you even if you never step into the day's record-breaking heat, even if the weather's only the numbers on your iPhone's forecast app, even if your jetsetting job leaves you never time to read about the war, famine, ice sheets collapsing. Up in your tower, still the common malady finds you, in diabetes depression rage alcoholism domestic violence embolic stroke anxiety deep vein thrombosis lung cancer suicide insomnia obesity suicidal driving.

The auto drops me off. I pay him what he asks. Such acrobatics deserve either a medal or jail. But suicidal driving isn't a crime in India; if I complained, traffic police would laugh me off, and Ola would assure me, my feedback is very valuable. I could chastise the driver myself. I can't be bothered. Now that I've disembarked his auto, his suicide-murder driving is not my problem. I walk away, shaken from the thrill ride I didn't sign up for. I tell myself it's alright, I could never have been killed. But my motto feels hollow, the bottom drops out of my smugness, and I realise that, like my friend in NYC, I, too, take my life into my hands whenever I walk out the door. I sit down on the foot-high pavement. My body feels life's horror, but my mind is still valiantly thinking, chattering, avoiding confronting, everything's alright.

If I am like my friend, then the mass shooter is like my auto-driver. Hurrying to get where we're all going, determined to get there on his own terms. If there must be a collision, better that it's you who does the colliding, better than sitting there obeying the rules, driving safe, waiting to be collided into. If only the mass shooter had sat around instead, eating fried chicken, listening to those languid songs of love, the baritone would've told him: don't hurry, my friend, there's time for everything. There was time for love when the world was beautiful.

I sit on the pavement, nostrils quivering, sniffing the tandoori chicken, with which the students streaming from the colleges are compensating for their day's travails, up before dawn studying preening commuting yawning through class after-school part-time job commuting again. Sitting here, I want to tell the mass shooter to eat chicken, fried or tandoori, whatever he wants, as much as he wants, and lay down his arms. But I can't. For I see now that every autorickshaw I sit in is a gun, and every driver is a gunner, except his victims would be only himself and me—for, whatever vehicle an autorickshaw might run into, it's us that'll be pancaked, the gun will misfire back on the shooter. My autorickshaw driver is the shooter, and I'm the mother or friend or teacher of the mass-shooter-to-be, and I sit back, humming along to the music, thinking: yes, he's a little disturbed, a little rash, but it'll be fine, he won't really go mad and shoot me, not my son, not my auto-driver, not me. And anyway he's not my problem, I've got to get there, wherever, got my job to rush to, to do God knows what, What knows why. The sea isn't going to fill itself with Thermocol, mine's a one-megaton-Thermocol job, that's one-em-tee-tee.

I want to ask my elderly artist-cum-writer friend why she goes on about her wrinkled skin, why when we try on clothes she sucks in her little tummy, why she tells me she needs to resume running. She has lived, and loved, and made of her living and her loving, pictures and books that speak to strangers. She has earned her years, she's interesting, as every elderly person ought to be, ought to have had the chance to become. Still she wants smooth skin and taut triceps, still she wants to outrun time. Still her output of achievements doesn't match her input of years: the equation always stringent, the scales every day more uneven. On this road, down which she's rushing, other drivers began hours ago, other artists began years ago, brilliant young artists, and svelte older artists. She's always playing catchup. So she wants to do more, to weigh less, achieve more, look younger, to feel for one second that she's caught up with time.

Make me, God, like the paper napkin, with which the artist-cum-writer—but no, but she threw away the napkin. Napkins don't last. You can't absorb all the world's shit and stay sane. You'll go off the deep end, shoot strangers, drive rashly, kill yourself. Make me, then, God, like the marble disc instead, which was our tabletop, over which I sat with the artist-cum-writer, chatting, under our elbows the marble hot and getting hotter, marble hard and strong, smooth and blind.

May God make us all marble, blind to our own malaise. May What keep dribbling into our mouths, upturned like nestlings', fast cars, slow songs, preloaded guns, food-at-your-doorstep-in-five-minutes, please-tip-your-deliveryman, brand-new content, and scrub-covered shale mountains to turn into mountains of gravel to build Bangalore's coolest new condo complex, one-see-are, see-see-are, see us vanishing into the clouds. May What keep us nodding along to the music, sucking our thumbs, as we race our eighteen-wheelers down the smog-shrouded dust-coffined highway, visibility zero at midday in an Indian midsummer, the sun trying to fight through, the prince trying to fight through the brambles to awaken Sleeping Beauty. May What keep us sleeping, keep away the evil prince who wants to awaken us. What forbid! For if we woke up, if we stopped racing, stopped eating, stopped shooting, binge-watching, gossiping, binge-shopping, humming along, if we opened our eyes, we'd go mad.

I've got to get home, email my friend in NYC my own near-death everyday experience, vivid but casual, get to bed, rinse and repeat tomorrow. So I get up from the pavement and rush down the road. Let's all get there, wherever, immediately—or not at all, that wouldn't be so bad. Of course one doesn't really think about death, one never really thinks about anything, but really, that wouldn't be so bad, it'd be better than slowing down. For wherever we're going isn't worth getting there slowly, doesn't deserve one extra minute, but does deserve every hair's-breadth escape from speeding trucks and mass shooters. Those're just friendly little jolts to keep you awake.

Beauty and romance and leisure, the things to love, are going and gone. Anger is our only fuel now. Meanwhile there's music to hum along to, food to swallow, strangers to shoot, fellow autorickshaws to race, any sound, any taste, any sensation in which to curl up, shut our eyes and suck our thumbs, curl up in the womb again, to hide away from our panic and our pain.

Hand-Washed

My mother keeps nagging me to remodel our kitchen. Because I wash each dish by hand. Because she can't stand to see her daughter washing the dishes every day. My mother keeps on nagging. Because our utensil drawers have no runners and drop splinters into the pots and pans below. My sticky foot soles smile back. Adorned with bitter metallic.

Once, just once, I saw her cry. Sitting on a hotel bed. I understand why she felt that way. I, too, want to be loved. Because she isn't the only one who eats dead wood around here. See the chips along the front edge of my teeth? I never wanted to be perfect.

At the family reunion, my cousins all shared a story in remembrance of Nai Nai. But I had no stories. I only met my grandmother once, a long time ago, when I was a little girl with pale skin and glossy black hair. I wore a hand-sewn ruffled-lace dress and could only speak English. My mother scolded me for playing outside. Because torn clothes and dark skin should only be for peasants.

I remember staying up late. Listening to the sounds of the kitchen being cleaned. Every night—a symphony. Clicking chopsticks shoved in the back of the silverware drawer. The clank of ceramic saucers against teacups—stacked high into the cupboard. These sounds were the whispering fleece, blanketing me, speaking every word she never said out loud.

SALLY-JO KEALA-O-ĀNUENUE BOWMAN

The Signers

I sit in the U.S. National Archives
in cold March light from tall north windows
with gloved and gentle hand
touch signatures on a desperate petition
ten thousand eight hundred ninety-one
women signing for their homeland a century ago

Picture brown hands dipping pens in wells of ink
wetting purple indelible pencils with their tongues

Imagine my grandmother standing in line
in long white ruffled muʻumuʻu
waiting to sign in brown-ink perfect penmanship
Mary Elemakule age 20

Hold these frail pages, a ream of women
daring to say to the great United States
"We earnestly protest against the annexation"

I finger companion forms signed by ten thousand men
their shouting voices caught on legal sheets in matching folders
all told, with yet a third petition, the signers number
three-fourths of the subjects of our Hawaiian Kingdom

Handle every single sheet of women's names
straightening the edges, tidying the stack
as if cleaning a grave and laying a hand-strung flower lei
on new-cut grass beside the headstone

I weep for the bravery of all these women
their husbands, fathers, brothers, sons
facing a surging behemoth of greed
chorused voices could slow but never halt

I wonder if on December 9, 1897
the date petitions were read in the U.S. Senate
winds blew so cold and biting as this March day
I sit at my lone oak table in library silence
tracing spirits in signatory script

WENDIE BURBRIDGE

The Cave Man

I pulled Ryan out of the cave entrance and wrapped my hands around the wound in his neck. I told him with my eyes that it would be okay, just hold on, Mule was on his way. In the moonlight, I thought I could see Ryan's blue irises go midnight. He tried to talk and I shook my head to tell him not to. Save his energy. Don't think about giving up.

Don't you even think about dying, man.

It was silent speak, one we had mastered early in our SEAL training. I felt his blood-wet hand grasp my wrist, and then Mule was immediately next to us, the medkit open at Ryan's shoulder. Mule tried to stop the gusher, but as he packed the wound with gauze, he turned his head to make eye contact with me, and I knew Ryan was not long for this world.

I glanced past Ryan at the caves behind his body and felt the darkness gape back at us. The mouth of the cave's entrance screaming at us to get away, to go home, to go back from where we came from. I turned my gaze back to my two buddies and let the smell of blood keep me focused and sharp. I chased out all other thoughts and worked on keeping Ryan's life in my sights.

***

Ever since we arrived in Afghanistan, unceremoniously dumped in what looked exactly like what Mule called "the middle of bumfuck Egypt," all I really could think about were the caves. The red rocks that butterflied out into gothic-style arches in the Afghani caves were so different from the ones I explored as a kid growing up in Hawai'i. During Christmas break, Mom and Pop would take me to visit my mom's sister, Aunty Elizabeth, and her husband, Uncle Joel, who lived directly over the Kaumana Caves in Hilo. The Kaumana Caves were dark lava tubes, left behind by Madam Pele, the Hawaiian goddess of fire. She was a jealous god and the legends Pop told were endless, filled with hidden bones and sacred resting places. Even in the black Afghani night, I could see the same black-and-gray speckled walls of the caves I had known since I was a boy.

I tried to push the image of the lava tubes out of my mind as I came to the Comm Tent. In the dusty haze of the late evening, it was sometimes difficult to find my way in the makeshift base camp set up only a few weeks before. I walked ten paces and was inside before I could have been spotted by anyone. Dropping my helmet next to the rest of my gear, I sat in front of a darkened laptop and moved the mouse to power it on.

As the screen flickered, I thought about sending a quick email to Pop as I remembered the first time he took me through the lava tubes at Volcanoes National Park. Mom never liked going down into the caves. Too dark, too slippery, too dangerous, she said. Pop and I would leave her topside and spend hours investigating the dark with only one flashlight and a cheap disposable camera. I remembered taking picture after picture of what looked like black ropes of lava cake batter dripping onto a red earth floor. My pudgy seven-year-old hand looked like a white starfish against an inky bed of coral.

As I tried to shake my memory out of my mind, I looked down at my hand on the gray mouse and wondered if my seven-year-old self would have imagined the kind of caves we would be exploring twenty years later. Outside the tent, I heard someone call me.

"Trog? Get outta there, will you? You'll never get a connection now. Screw it. Let's get some z's, man." I looked at my watch. It was 2100, time for a buddy check. My friend and fellow Lieutenant Mark Mueller, SEAL call sign "Mule," stepped into the tent and looked at me in the blue-gray light from the monitor. He was a brute of a man, from Kansas, his Jayhawk tattoo bold on his right forearm. Mule was my best friend; I owed him two lives and a sister if I had one.

We had not spoken since we returned to base camp. Mule had gone to shower and I had headed to the Comm Tent. I should have gone to shower too, I thought to myself. I was covered in sand and dirt. And Ryan's blood.

I nodded at Mule, not speaking, knowing he was right. I shut down the computer.

"Sure, man, let's hit the rack," I said, scrubbing my hand over my face. I was done for the night and I didn't want to think of Ryan. Not this moment when I knew his body was lying in a morgue in Kabul, waiting to go home.

Mule didn't answer as he waited for me. I picked up my M4 and my helmet and Mule and I headed out into the camp. Maybe after some sleep, I could send a decent email to his mom. Let her know his SEAL brothers were there for her. For whatever. Whenever.

Mule was quiet. He kicked small stones as we walked across the base to our makeshift rack. I knew we were both thinking about Ryan. Mule had taken it the hardest after we put him on the chopper to Kabul.

"Hey, Trog?"

"What, Mule?"

"You remember Mrs. Ryan's shitty cookies?" he said, not looking at me.

"Yeah, man, I remember those god-awful cookies. Chocolate chip rocks, more like it." I laughed. We were silent, thinking about all the shit we gave Ryan for his mother's attempt at cooking. His mother lovingly sent her son a care package every week during BUD/S and we nearly broke all of our teeth trying her cookies. Other mothers and wives sent care packages, and we all shared, devouring anything from home. Ryan got the most grief about his care packages because they were always filled with terrible cookies. But we ate them, and she kept sending them. We were always grudgingly grateful.

"I guess it's like your mom sending the fish that smelled like your gym socks," Mule said.

I knew he would have eaten all my dried cuttlefish if I had let him. I laughed.

"Mule, you tell that shit comment to my mom's face the next time you see her. I dare you," I said, chuckling. I wanted him to stop thinking about Ryan. I knew it bugged him, and he didn't want to talk about it—much. He didn't respond to my dare. I heard the exhaustion in his voice as he spoke.

"Jesus, Kaholo." Mule paused. "Ryan was a good guy."

I nodded. When we were serious, we often dropped the nicknames and used the names our mothers gave us. Mule knew my real first name, and he was the only one who said it right. For a Kansas boy, his Hawaiian was pretty good.

But I knew what he didn't want to say. That he was glad it hadn't been one of us.

When we got to our tent, Mule sat on his cot on the left side, his gear stacked in ready order, unlike my own. I flipped on my diode light and sat on the thin blanket I had draped over my makeshift cot. I dumped my helmet into my pack and laid my M4 across my knees to clean. Nothing was worse than sand in a weapon. I needed to be ready to go. Ready to move. At any time.

"Mule," I said. He was lying on his cot, not doing anything. His weapon was already cleaned, his radio checked, new MRE's were in his pack. Mule was always ready. Shoot, communicate, and move, that was our SEAL motto. Not to whine like a baby. I continued to speak into the darkness.

"He was gone before we got to him, you know that, don't you?" I said, as easily as I could to my large friend. Even though Mule was the biggest and strongest of our BUD/S class, and would gladly strip the skin off of anyone who threatened his brothers, he was by far the softest-hearted.

"I wish I had gotten to him before those fuckers did." Mule put an arm over his eyes. It was always odd when he swore; it was like a blonde, blue-eyed Bamm-Bamm saying the f-word at Dino.

"Me too, Mark. Me too." I listened to the wind whip against the tent. I knew that the sun would be up soon and the mission would continue without Ryan. But Mule and I would be in it, like the first day we got to Afghanistan. Like it had always been since we first helped each other push a Yokohama bunker up a sandy dune in Coronado the first day of BUD/S, and like it would be every day until one of us was placed in a chopper and sent to Kabul. Like we did today with our brother.

***

It was night again. Twenty-four hours since Mule and I had said farewell to our fallen buddy. I had not thought of Ryan until we circled the cave the scouts had mapped for us. We had spent the day in a small village filled with women, children, and old men, and had of course found little more than "peaceful farmers." Farmers who had RPGs, other ammunition, and weapons hidden in their mud huts. The medics had taken care of the ill and the injured, we shared cigarettes with the old men, candy and small toys with the kids, and we had fixed broken doors and tables for the women. All PR to gain their trust. A few men told us that some of the Taliban leaders might be using one of the caves as a hideout. We hoped our target, Sattar Sadozai, would be there. All of our intel pointed us toward the village, so we deduced he would be nearby. The caves were the only place he could wait us out.

Come nightfall, we were there, silent as we could be, ready to search for Sadozai. We did not use choppers, so there was no warning to anyone using the cave as a refuge.

"Trog. Mule. Move out." Captain Fagenbush gave us the order. His voice came over our headsets and I nodded at Mule before taking the lead toward the cave.

"Roger that." I always went in first. Just like a troglodyte. Used to living in the dark. The unblinking darkness of a cave. The comfort of it all.

The cave looked almost royal as I entered it, my night vision giving me the feeling that green aliens reigned within its magnificent chert-covered walls. When Pop took me the first time to the Kaumana Caves, we had seen what looked like white icing decorating the ebony lava. I saw my first petroglyph in those caves, my first evidence of my ancestors. My caves were nothing like these. Mine were sacred. Kings may have lived here, but gods lived in mine.

My weapon was drawn; Mule was five paces behind me, the rest of the team close behind him. Our early reconnaissance team, three snipers who had moved ahead to find the cave right after the mission brief, messaged back that it was all clear. No one had emerged from the cave since our search of the village. A perfect place to sit and wait. Or so we thought.

"Trog?" I heard Mule's voice in my ears and hit the comm button. "Anything?" Mule was speaking low and quietly and I copied in turn.

"Negative, nothing as far as I can see, but I can't see much, man." I got no response from him, not that it was needed. I inched further in, my senses heightened. My nose filled with the scent of onions and the moldy dampness of the cave. My eyes covered the cave walls, looking for shadows more than anything else. Shadows meant people. The cave could hide many secrets and also reveal all to those who looked carefully, those who knew what to look for. I used my night vision scope on my weapon to see what was ahead of me. I lost focus for a second and heard my father's voice in my ears.

"Kaholo, when you head into a cave, you want to have a good light, and you always want to pay attention to what is above you," Pop said as we entered the lava tube. I was seven and both afraid and excited about the seemingly endless dark in front of me. It was love at first sight. I knew we would find treasures I had only dreamt of in the blanket fort I had built over my bed.

"Why should I look up, Poppa?" I had asked, feeling as if my father would bestow on me a large piece of wisdom I had to remember.

"Because, buddy, you don't want to hit your head." Poppa moved his palm off of his forehead and it was then that I saw the blood from a small gash a few inches above his eye. He had hit it on a low overhang and the black lava cut open his skin. *"People don't ever look up. They look at their feet, they look straight ahead, but never up. A sailor always looks up."* He was smiling, so I knew his cut would be okay. He just wanted me to remember to look up.

So I did.

That was when I saw the shadow.

***

I don't remember what Mule said into my ears, but I moved quicker than I thought possible. I heard a shot and my instinct kicked in. I felt a smattering of rocks slice into my cheek and my adrenaline surged.

"Move, son!" I heard my father shouting in my head.

I moved fast to the side, tucking myself behind a flying buttress of rock covered in flowstone. I took one quick shot at the shadow and heard my father again in my head.

"Kaholo, look up! Shine your light up. What did I tell you, son?" I felt my sides for my SabreLite. I found it but didn't fish it out. I needed my hands to use my weapon. I could hear shooting along with my father's angry voice scolding me. I flipped my night vision goggles on and saw the shadow directly ahead of me.

The shadow had a weapon. And it was firing on us. Game on.

I shifted down the side of the cave rock to my knees and shot at the spark of light flashing from the deep darkness of the cave. I didn't stop shooting until the bursts coming at us ended and my father's voice in my head stopped screaming.

It was Mule who spoke first. I heard his voice, tightened by excitement and fear.

"Trog? Fuck! What's your twenty?"

I sank to my feet, breathing hard, my weapon in my hands.

"Mule, I think I killed him," I said. I swallowed hard.

"Trog, we're moving in." Mule's voice was back to business.

"Affirmative, Mule, let's do this." I heard their boots tromping toward me and stood up, ready to see who I had killed and what other secrets the cave held. Whatever we found, I readied myself to see the face of the third man I had ever killed in my life. That I knew of for sure. I was sure I'd probably killed more, but they had all been faceless and far away.

"Kaholo, be careful as you crawl through." I heard Pop again as Mule and I belly-crawled on the Afghani cave floor. My arm hit something and I stopped. I felt Mule hit my leg and he stopped too. We were patient, listening for any other signs of movement.

"Now, son, what you have here is something you don't want to touch."

"Why, Poppa? Is it bad?"

"No, it's just very special."

"Like treasure?"

"Yep, like a treasure. Only, we don't disturb this kind of treasure. We leave it where we find it, and we don't tell anyone we saw it. Affirmative?"

"Ah-ffirmative."

The bones stayed where they were in the lava tube. Pop didn't even say anything to Mom about seeing them, wrapped in decrepit kapa, turning to dust as we hid them behind chips of lava and stones. Mom had told my haole father about the sanctity of Hawaiian bones, and Pop had great respect for his wife's native culture. His son's birth culture. We took out what we carried in and we never came out with anything extra.

But this time, when I exited this cave, a different cave than the ones I loved in Hilo, I would be carrying something extra. Something very special to someone. They were bones, but they were still covered in flesh.

***

I dropped the body at Captain Fagenbush's feet and held my breath as he pulled the *keffiyeh* off his head. The face of the young man was ordinary, like that of any Afghani farmer. Sunbaked, cracked with dirt, a face old before its time. Fagenbush searched the man's clothing and spoke, not looking at me.

"Weapon?" he said.

"None, sir," I said. Fagenbush looked up. I knew what that meant. I needed to find a weapon. I couldn't have shot an unarmed man.

"He was firing on us, sir!" Mule said.

"No shit, Lieutenant, I heard the fire, but we need the evidence or we'll have a major clusterfuck on our hands." Fagenbush stood and pointed an index finger at me. "You understand me, Lieutenant Troy?" he looked at me with stern eyes. He said my name like I was fresh out of boat school, and like my father did when he didn't want a problem. Lieutenant Kaholo Troy, son of Lia and Chief Donald Troy, United States Navy SEAL, retired.

"Aye aye, sir," I responded, and turned on my heel. I didn't want the captain to look at me like that again. Like my father. *Kaholo, did you hear me?*

I heard Mule following me, as Fagenbush radioed orders to the snipers. We were going back to the cave. I needed to find a weapon near where the body fell. And maybe some intel. This time we didn't go in quietly. By now, the entire village knew where we were, and soon we would have more to deal with, than the dead Pashtun at the feet of my commanding officer. I flipped my night vision over my eyes and moved into the opening.

My fingers gripped my M4 and I moved quickly along the cave floor, following the disturbed dirt path we had left behind. Mule didn't make any sound. As I watched the path, he watched ahead for movement and shadows. When he whistled, our signal to stop, I was surprised.

"Something ahead, Trog. two o'clock. Shadow." I looked up ahead. I saw nothing.

"*Kaholo, let me tell you a story,*" I heard my father's voice again. And I wondered why I was remembering him so vividly. Was it the cave?

"*This is an old story. Grandpa told it to me when I was about your age. It's about two sailors. One was a very young sailor and he was very scared of storms. And the other was an older sailor, who had been at sea a very long time.*"

"*Longer than you, Poppa?*"

"*Longer than me, son.*"

Mule shined his light down the cave to where he had seen the shadow. I took off my night vision goggles and turned on my SabreLite.

"*It was the younger sailor's job to fix the sails. So one night, during a very big storm, the older sailor ordered the younger sailor to climb the mast and do what he was trained to do. The young sailor got halfway up, looked down at the old sailor, and got dizzy and sick.*"

I saw it. A shadow, moving a hundred yards ahead. Mule hit my shoulder in triumph and we cut the lights. The cave plunged into darkness. Night vision helped me to see again and we moved forward toward the shadow.

"The old sailor was standing on the deck and he knew that the younger sailor was scared. He shouted up to him, "Look up, son, look up!" And the young sailor looked up, he saw what he had to do, and he kept climbing up the mast."

The shadow moved again. I pulled my M4 up and wrapped my finger around the trigger.

"What happened, Poppa?"

"Well, the younger sailor got up the mast and fixed the sail."

The shadow got longer, and I could see that the person was hidden behind one of the buttresses that had shielded me earlier from gunfire. I let the M4 greet the shadow first.

"He completed his mission, Kaholo. He did what he had to do. But the story is about looking ahead, not back."

"Trog, don't shoot!" I heard Mule yell and felt his hand on my arm, pulling the M4 down, just as I was about to pull on the trigger.

And that's when I heard the crying. I stiffened my fingers, and let my arms down. Mule lifted his light and shined it toward where my gun had been pointed. Two little boys sat behind the rock buttress, their hands stuffed in their mouths, desperately trying not to make a noise. They were so little, both under five or six years. Their eyes were big and focused on our guns.

Mule picked both boys up in his large arms and spoke with his soft kind voice.

"Nothing to cry about here, boys. You're going to be just fine." As Mule stood up, he banged his forehead on a piece of overhang.

"The story is also about looking up, Poppa. Right?"

"Yes, Kaholo, looking ahead and up."

I heard movement behind me and turned. I looked up and saw the glint of metal flash above me. I lifted my M4 and fired. I had found the gun we had been searching for. I did not listen as the boys wailed in agony. I did not take my finger off the trigger until their mother's body dropped down from the cave ceiling. I did not hear anything but Poppa's voice screaming in my ears.

Look up, Kaholo, look up.

These Days

Most of us had seen it before we heard about it from Sami. She had pulled into the parking lot of Lum's (Her family's shop) at 5 a.m. like she normally did every day except Tuesdays to find a huge cartoon phallus spray painted in neon green below the shop's sign. The tag beside it was indiscernible. "Who the hell?" we asked.

Although the shop's location (45 minutes to North Shore; 30 minutes to town; 15 to Kāneʻohe), attracted locals, military, and tourists alike looking to buy Spam musubi (2 for $3.00), cheap beer (12 pack of Coors $12.99), and the service (Aloha) you couldn't get at the 7-Eleven down the road, most of Kahaluʻu had known the family since small kid time and would never think to do something like that. Some of the older folks could even tell you what the sign had read before the sun and salt wind had faded it to just Lum's (Lum's Dairy, Lum's Gas and General, Lum's Grocery). Some still remembered when they stocked bait, boots, and bowls of beef stew. All of us had a story to tell about Papa Lum, Sami's grandfather who had taken it over after his father had sold the dairy's land; Dede, her mother who never hesitated to stock Mr. Takata's jerky or Jackie Dumadag's lumpia; or Captain, her father who used to drive the fireboat when there still was one.

Some of us wanted to blame the graffiti on the houseless who caught crabs from the nearby bridge, but we all knew that, for the most part, they never bothered anyone but themselves. And Sami? She laughed for a whole minute, leaving it there for three days until Ms. Meheula, seeing it while driving her kids to school, called to complain. "Let me tell you, traffic is bad enough without that conversation."

***

Sami grew up pedaling grocery orders to neighbors on her bicycle, but running the store wasn't her first choice. It wasn't necessarily the work but the monotony of it. Plus, no matter the sweat she put in, anytime she suggested a change, like a credit card machine (You seen the fees? We going have to raise our prices) or stocking the ube cheesecake tarts that her friend Lei could hook the store up with ($5 for one?! Who like that?), she was voted down, so she dreamt of other things. Since a little girl, watching Lori Fung's gold medal win at the 1984 Olympics, she had wanted to be a champion in rhythmic gymnastics (Ribbon dancing, can you believe?). For her ninth birthday, she begged Captain to buy her the Sasaki ribbon set from the hobby store in the mall (Lavender rayon ribbon, fiberglass stick with the white rubber grip, Made in Japan, FIG and JGA approved), then spent the whole day in front of the store making flicks, circles, and swirls while the passing traffic stared in awe or confusion, thinking she looked like one of those tube men flailing in front of the Toyota dealership.

Many of us didn't get it and talked to Captain about the AYSO tryouts and girls' basketball, but he wasn't bothered. "Her life," he said to those of us who brought it up, and he kept saying that when she decided to stay home for college (against their wishes) instead of accepting a scholarship to the University of Oregon (Go Ducks!) because she knew her parents needed help with the store. Same as it had always been. Family is family even if they only saw her BA in business (Summa cum laude!) as an opportunity to boast rather than grounds for her suggestions. But she found ways to engage her passion, taking classes at a dance studio downtown and stocking the counter with her own goodies when working shifts by herself.

Then the pandemic hit, Captain catching it in the first wave, spending months on a breathing machine, and passing a few days before he was supposed to go home. Dede a short time after. We called to express our condolences (Damn this disease) and share stories (You remember when . . .). We blanketed the front of the shop in carnations, birds of paradise, and roses. We cried with her in the aisles between stacks of corned beef hash and rows of flour.

"What do you think's going to happen?" We asked each other, knowing it was her chance to be free of the place or to change it completely. "What do you think she's going to do?"

But most of us, especially those who were closest to the family, already knew.

"Whatever she wants to do," we supposed.

***

But she surprised us all when she kept the store open, continuing to stock anything and everything that she knew was sold out everywhere else. We'd stop in to say hello and to pick up toilet paper and crack seed. When people started losing their jobs, she wrote out

IOUs on receipt paper and started a food pantry out of the back of the store. "Pay what you can, take what you need."

"Is she crazy?" one of the new neighbors asked. A haole guy telecommuting from Missouri outbid the Reyes's son so he could work with a view. Considering how business-minded Sami was, it was strange to see. Even a few of us were worried the shop might close, yet the register was never short (Or she never said so) and the prices remained the same.

We guessed that's why even Missouri was stunned that someone would go and disrespect the storefront. "I'll take care of it," he said, making plans to buy the paint. When we heard that, we called him up to talk about another possibility.

***

The next Tuesday, Uncle Miles spoke with his (Kinda) famous nephew, a muralist who made magic out of the walls all over town. As discussed, Missouri pitched in for the paint and a handful of us helped prime the surface while Miles' nephew sketched out the design. Then we watched him turn the eyesore into a UV green squid with dark blue flecks in honor of the ahupuaʻa the store straddled (Waiheʻe) and Captain's famous squid lūʻau that he used to sell (A local favorite). When Sami showed up to the shop the next day, we were excited for her reaction.

"What you think?"

She walked up to it, the squid, a flash of brilliance against the flat white (The same color it had been since the street it fronted was cracked mud) and smiled.

***

Of course, no one expected how popular the mural would be. It was less than a week before the small shop became a destination for selfies and hipsters (From Waikīkī to Kailua). The mural spread along with #Lums, #localstyle, and #squidgame (No one was really sure what the latter was about). Lum's Yelp! page started blowing up with reviews (From 4 reviews to 254, all 5 stars with a few exceptions) mentioning the *quaint, hometown feel of the store* and the rather *standoffish* owner (One of the exceptions), *an Asian aunty who looks like she's got a lot of stories to tell but no time to tell them.* Business was flourishing as Ms. Meheula's son Brandon (The kid likes to read) said when he walked in to grab a blue Powerade and a bag of chips but left because the line wrapped back to the paper plates.

You'd think Sami would be happy about it, but without her parents, she was opening and closing the store herself and working through her meals. When Hawaii News Now called to ask about filming a five-minute spot for their *Sunrise* morning show, she hung up before they could finish their pitch. She even kicked out a Karen who complained that the tako poke didn't have enough fish. Kaleo Reyes even heard her swear at a customer who asked if she would take a picture with their phone (You fricking kidding me?).

We figured things would quiet down. Return to normal. Hype is, as Brandon says, "transitory" (See da kine). But two months and still Sami could barely keep up. Worse, food trucks started showing up across the street. Some of us started asking if we could sell lychee and mango in the parking lot (Can cut you in). Then, one Saturday in the middle of July, Guy Hagi forecasting a high of 89 degrees and plenty of sunshine all week, Elani Teixeria showed up to grab a shave ice and found the barn doors locked. No sign, no nothing. He called the store. No answer.

One of her neighbors said she saw Sami and asked her why the store was closed, but she didn't want to get into it. Still, when a few days stretched into one week, then into two, people talked. Kim, a property vulture (i.e., a real estate agent), wondered if she was considering closing the store or selling the land (It's a prime location). We asked one of Sami's good friends from business school, Natalie Lau, but she didn't know, and Marcus's boy told everyone that he had seen Sami ribbon dancing in the garage one morning. Then, Ms. Meheula saw her truck in the driveway and decided to pop in, but she wasn't home or didn't want to answer. Through the picture window, she could see the place was empty, and that was it, we thought.

***

Without Lum's, we had no choice really. We made the trek to Times, Safeway, CVS (Longs), and Walgreens to pay double the price. We hauled it an hour both ways to Sam's and Costco. We smiled at strangers in line. We talked story with the cashiers while they watched us bag our groceries or asked us to swipe our cards again. We tried to quell our taste for pickled mango with the packaged stuff from the crack seed store by the mall. We traded shave ice for Slurpees. We laughed by ourselves. And when one of us brought up Lum's, we traded memories (Like when Jonathan Castillo met his girlfriend reaching for the same can of SPAM, or when Dede caught Marcy Shimabukuro sampling a fresh batch of li-hing strawberry belts and sampled them with her) because it felt like that's all we had left of the place. That and an empty building on the side of the road. In a year, they might turn it into a McDonald's (Or God forbid, a Chick-fil-A).

***

But some of us held on to hope. A month after the store closed, Natalie ended up having lunch with Sami at Masa and Joyce. It took some digging, but finally she admitted the store was just too overwhelming, and who could blame her (I mean, it's just her, you know?).

When the news spread, we figured, maybe she'd reopen it if she had some help. So, Brandon, done with the SATs and looking to make some money before college, walked over to Sami's and taped his resumé (Basically his name, address, and a list of neighbors/references) on the door so she would see it. Others followed suit, thinking it would convince her. Eventually, the entire door was paper, but when she saw it, she just pulled them all down and let herself in.

Uncle Miles, thinking that his first mural idea was a hit, contracted another. This time, he tried to get everyone involved (Let's show her what this shop really means). Twenty of us came out on a Sunday morning to paint bags of lūʻau leaf and trails of cartoon kakimochi, caricatures of neighbors talking story, Dede's crazy aprons and kind smile, Captain's firefighter hat and slick beard (Eh, is that Sean Connery?). Brandon lectured everyone on perspective and the Rule of Thirds while Ms. Meheula directed. The Reyeses brought chili and mac salad, even offering Missouri a bowl. When they were done, Natalie drove Sami down to the store. Her response? "The tourists will like it."

But that was it.

Then things got worse. The Monday before Labor Day, Ms. Meheula was driving home from hula and saw someone on the side of the shop. She called Uncle Miles (Of course) whose other nephew Wade happened to be a cop. When he got there, the person was gone and with them the sign that hung above the store.

***

It wasn't Sami though. When she found out, she was just as surprised as any of us. "But," she told Natalie. "Maybe it's an omen. I mean, it was my parents' store and with them gone, I don't know. Maybe it's time."

Kim talked to her about her options (Sell or lease it out). We volunteered to help with the cleaning and the maintenance, trimming the overgrowth and making sure all the wiring was up to code. Rather than sell what was left, she opened the doors and handed out whatever people wanted. She kept the photos of neighbors (Whoa, look you), family that were pinned up next to the cash register, and the first dollar she found framed in the back room. She packed Papa Lum's old ledger (Handwritten) and a love note Dede wrote to the Captain when they first took over the store. She gave away what recipes she could find. The beef stew and the tako poke. Someone's notecard with careful instructions for manju. It took a few weeks, but eventually Lum's was just an empty space, just a building. Kim called, she had someone interested in seeing the place.

So, Sami drove out to meet them, but when she got there, the parking lot was empty except for Kim's car and, leaning against the door, the stolen sign. "Lum's" painted over and "Sami's" in its place, a ribbon of violet crossing under it in flicks, circles, and swirls. The same indiscernible tag from before. Kim couldn't see her face, but she didn't have to. She reached out and traced the ribbon. Then stepped back and took it all in.

A month later, some of us were still grumbling about the store closing and how things not the same (These days). That's what they always said, adding "these days" like they were any different than the other days or the days before. Of course, we all knew it didn't matter anyway. Who we are, the community, that was what mattered most, and Sami, well, it was her life (Whatever makes her happy).

Then, that summer, out of nowhere, Ms. Meheula saw a delivery van pull up to the back of the store. What they were unloading, she didn't see. "Was Sami there?" She didn't know, but a week after that, the lights were on, and the doors were open, a familiar name hanging above the door.

Dottie

Math before Punahou was about using calculations in real life situations, like drawing stray Hawaiʻi Kai cats into a fictional family pyramid. One hundred forty-four feral cats bred over a couple years due to one unspayed female. In 6th grade, kids at Punahou were already using *pi* to calculate the circumference and area of a circle and knew the equation for the volume of a sphere. When I thought about calculating perimeters, areas, and lengths, all I saw were cats. I never broke a C in 7th grade algebra.

By the beginning of 8th grade, they placed me in Mrs. Foster's math class, and my C's were nearing D's. She taught geometry in what I first thought were costumes. Her outfits matched the shiny exterior of her vintage convertible, which all sparkled in the afternoon heat as she left campus. My attention went up, but not my grades.

One afternoon, Mrs. Foster faced the blackboard, writing out more rules for solving equations. Then she stopped, mid-formula. I watched the white tassels on the back of her vest come to a halt. She set the chalk down, swiveled her boots and faced the class. After a dramatic pause she brushed her hands clean.

"I'll tell you what I'm gonna do," she said in her Southern accent. "I want all of you to take and retake every math test until you get an A. But you'll only pass when you have an A and understand how to solve every problem."

I could see some nodding and smiling in my periphery. I'm sure my classmates were thinking what I was thinking. Easy A.

"Everyone got it?"

We looked at each other and I saw two guys roll their eyes, like Mrs. Foster's age, outfits, and mainland ways finally scrambled her brain. But we all gave our approval.

She clearly wasn't local, but today I actually admired Mrs. Foster's attire. While other teachers wore muʻumuʻu and aloha shirts, Mrs. Foster wore a purple cowgirl hat, purple mini skirt, and a white leather tasseled and sequined vest over a long-sleeved, purple collared shirt. All that purple and shining jewelry on a white-haired 70-year-old.

When the lecture was over, Mrs. Foster walked up to my desk in her tall, purple leather cowboy boots. She bent down carefully in her mini skirt and tilted her hat up to look into my eyes.

"What do you think about my rule?"

Mrs. Foster's gaze was thoughtful, as if she saw someone greater than myself inside my denim shorts and Bongo T-shirt. I felt like I was 8 years old and at Disneyland again, except now I was meeting Minnie Mouse in a middle school classroom in Hawai'i. Mrs. Foster's light blue eyes were done up with dark mascara and dabs of midnight purple on her lids. The desks were in rows of six, facing the blackboard. My classmates had their heads down and pencils moving. I smelled fresh sheets of binder paper continuously shifting under the scratch of graphite as the Hawaiian sun kept piercing through the high window, trying to dissolve the artificial lights. A false eyelash sat on the floor.

I gave her an easy smile.

"Your rule makes this better," I said.

Many of my classmates thought she'd just gotten old, that she didn't care what people thought of her anymore. *She can break the rules*, they'd say, *and give us whatever we want*. What I wanted was to understand how to form and solve equations. I needed the freedom to fail and to forget about calculating stray cats.

"That's what I love to hear." She hit my desk with her right hand and I heard her rings clink. "You just keep asking those questions." She stood up, tipped her purple hat toward me with a smile, and went to another student.

Her name was Dottie. Dottie Foster.

In high school, my best friend Erin told me Mrs. Foster had called her house twice, asking for her mother. Erin mimicked her soft but stern Southern accent, "Mrs. Nakamura, Erin did not do her homework!" And we laughed. No other teacher would call a student's home. Mrs. Foster gave us every opportunity to make mistakes without consequences, as long as we completed homework, took the tests, and asked questions. No other teacher did what she did.

Mrs. Foster didn't eat SPAM musubis, mac salad, malasadas, or chicken katsu. She lifted weights in the weight room after school with the students and lunched on green salads. Her radiant, white skin showed no signs of discoloration or sun spots. I was more likely to run into her at a Saturday farmers' market in a silk-lined sun hat than while putting down my towel at Kaimana Beach. She'd been living in Hawai'i for years, probably decades, but she still looked like a visitor.

It was easy to laugh and sling judgments at the ways of "mainlanders." Being born and raised in Hawai'i meant inheriting a forgetfulness that most of my classmates and myself were descendants of visitors who'd stayed. Mrs. Foster's disinterest in assuming local ways seemed unnatural to my 13-year-old mind. Her vitality and critical thinking were essential to her individuality. Even the value she put on failure inspired questions I didn't yet have words for.

Math started becoming solid, test after test, one equation after another. Mistakes were no longer disappointing or left unexamined. There was now a door open within myself to paths of understanding.

Yes, I got an A in geometry and in every math class that followed. Yes, my grades across all subjects rose to consistent A's. But learning how I learned became more important than letter grades.

Whenever I have a problem I can't solve, I still hear the voice of that white-haired Southern woman, as if she were dipping her chin to look straight into my eyes, saying, "You just keep asking those questions."

I never saw a hint of Hawai'i on Mrs. Foster's body, but everything she gave was aloha.

JACEY CHOY

How to Make Sang Ssam

It's hard to know the right
name for a dish sometimes,
and it's hard to sift through
memories to come up with

the correct moment when you
learned how to make it, so
what I know is ssam sah, but
maybe it was sang ssam, or

ssam sang, because it was
my father who taught me
about ssam sah, standing in
the kitchen telling me about

his mother, my grandmother,
who sometimes ate ssam sah
when she was growing up in
Korea as a young girl, finding

a single lettuce leaf, crisp and
green, scooping hot rice into
the middle, putting in a little
meat, if they had any, and a bit

of gochujang, red chili pepper
paste, except when my father
showed me how to make it,
he got out a can of sardines,

opened the can with the key
attached under the bottom,
rolled open the top, and put
the whole can into a small

pot on the stove, adding some
shoyu, garlic, ginger, stirring it
around while he laughed and
told stories of eating ssam sah

as a boy, a snack between
meals, grandma laughing, her
eyes sparkling, her laughter

like a song, and me, standing
there, a baby bird, waiting in
the kitchen, waiting to be fed.

JACEY CHOY

How to Pick Mangoes

First you must have a
Hayden mango tree, large
ripened orbs that hang in
thick glossy green leaves,

an emerald tree studded
with orange, red, yellow
jewels, some just within
your reach, but others high

above your head, so high
that when you look up
you can't see the fruit at the
very top, your eyes squinting in

the hot sun, and you swear
under your breath asking why
your father can't do this,
can't be here to pick the

mangoes from the tree
that he planted when he
and your mother moved
into the house, the tree

he was so excited to have
that he dug a deep ditch
around the trunk after he put
it in the ground, then got

a jar of honey and filled the
ditch with the sweet syrup, .
while your mother stood,
eyes wide, scolding your father

for wasting food, for pouring,
golden honey into the ground,
until she finally shook her head
and went into the house,

your dad laughing, his eyes
shining, saying he was going
to have the sweetest mangoes
around, and you stop swearing,

you know he was right, and you
just wish he was here with you,
that he hadn't left town, left the
family, left you.

SUE COWING

I'd Have Found That Iceberg

Coco's Coffee Shop, all orange and brown Formica,
its yellow menus laminated against change.
They'd offered The Devil on Horseback there
for years, and the same people had ordered it.

But someone came in I knew from old headlines.
Someone who brought home Olympic gold
and cruised on his tanker like a bird
from Sans Souci to the Royal Hawaiian back in the days
when surfing was all salt ocean and real wood
and you had to go see for yourself if the waves were good.

His hair stone white, his skin kukui brown.
No finer arrangement of molecules
had ever graced that place. The Duke sat down
and signaled the waitress with his eyes.
He'd have the corned beef, yes, but could the salad
be of iceberg, cut with the sharpest knife?

Sorry sir, our salads are Manoa lettuce here.
You don't have iceberg? *No.*
She waited, glanced around.
He knew just what he wanted. So did I—

those crisp green leaves, releasing cool
sweet water from their crunchy cells and not
some limp green doily for canned pears.

I have two fantasies. In one,
I've just been shopping, have in my bag
a head of iceberg that I bring to the waitress on the sly,
no charge. Or I *am* the waitress and I answer
Certainly Mr. Kahanamoku, glide to the swinging door,
dash past the startled fry-cooks to my car,
drive anywhere to get that lettuce.

Once back, I slice the head myself
and bring it in, say *Sorry to take so long*.
He smiles his pleasure and my little waitress sins
just float away. I'd have found that iceberg
somehow, somewhere. For the Duke.

SUE COWING

Dawn Moment

Just before daybreak, chubby low gray clouds
almost obscure Koko Head and the Crater,
while higher, tattered ones get set to shine.
Both sky and the reflecting bay below
an oddly arctic shade of steel-gray-blue.
A man wades out, pulling his little raft
of fishing gear behind like a portable shrine.
A dove, walking along the shore, calls,
"Take your time, take your time," and yet
this moment, like all moments, will soon be gone.
Never mind. Another one always comes along—
in less than a minute.

SUE COWING

Getting an Idea

Sit completely quiet at the edge
of an empty-looking tide pool,
thinking of nowhere else,
even your shadow not moving.
Sit there long enough like this and the pool
will come alive, with little damselfish
and banded shrimp darting out
from the crevices, trusting you

to be no more to them than a rock.
Ideas are tide pool creatures
bursting with life, but easily startled
back into their hiding places.

Be a rock.

SUE COWING

Kalama Flow

Seaward from the volcano's quarried memory
a wide plain extends, then come dunes
with their sprawling shawls of pāʻū-o-hiʻiaka,
a smooth expanse of sand, and, at the water's edge,
a rubble of dull flat black
that swallows light, or doesn't let it in.

The waves' perpetual *shhhhhh*
dulls my ear. Lava rock's porous blackness
muffles the drumming of surf, the whoops
of children playing out of sight.
Makes me wonder if I'm deaf, or if
a film is rolling with the sound turned off.

It's only thirty steps from where I am
to enter water, but jagged aʻā
would shred my feet to seaweed first.
I'd need the ocean's liquid toes
to cross these rocks and not be worn away.

We're morning glory sending runners out
across the hot white sand,
putting out pale blue flowers,
rooting against the wind.
But sand can't hold.
Water carries it. Lava buries it.

When all the would-be waders in the world are gone,
this lava too will be black sand, and still
the great-great-great-great-grand-
descendants of this pāʻū-o-hiʻiaka
will approach, but not quite reach, the water.

LEANNE DUNIC

Ambush Predator

Twenty-eight thousand meters
Below, a habitat
That wants to crush us

There, a blobfish is not a blob
But a gelatinous-skinned sculpin
Fortified by pressure

They know how to survive a world
We cannot

They reserve energy
To protect the next generation
To ambush a crab

    A greedy trawl
Hauls upward
To a pressure drop

Anatomy displaced
Its collapsed, tissue-damaged body
Awarded "The Ugliest Fish"

Their miraculous actuality
A curiosity more than
A life
    de formed

We wave our nets, crude creatures
Displacing others until *place*
Is no longer

39 Days Later: Periodical Rearrangement

I look up from a book about logos and letterheads
to see a store clerk tidying the magazine section.
Deftly he flips through the racks, drops drop-cards to the floor,
moves a lone copy of *Card Creations* from behind
a stack of *Rubber Stamper* and places it
at the front of the line of its brothers.
He throws *Wine & Spirits* to the floor, for it belongs
in another section, and soon
it is joined by journals for cat-lovers, astronomers, and home
decorators.

When copies of one title are spread too far apart
so that identical *P*'s repeat themselves in a stutter
until *Painting* is finally spat out
across the top of a watercolored scarecrow harvesting pumpkins,
a practiced pinch lines them up again so
all the scarecrows and future jack-o'-lanterns are stacked neatly,
like jacks and queens in a deck of cards
and when files of different titles are too close together,
with the opposite motion he fans apart *Woodwork,*
Wood, and *Woodsmith*
and each is visible for any who'd know the difference.

He moves along the racks and down the aisle
a trail of subscription cards in his wake
gathering homeless issues and returning them to their places,
which he knows by heart like a mailman on a familiar street.

I wonder what I'd pay for him to sort through
what she's left me with—
kitchen utensils and CDs,
T-shirts, coat hangers, and
half-used-up baking ingredients in large, zippered plastic bags;

I want to ask if he'll help me separate and stack the birthday cards,
the long phone calls,

the smell of her hair, Christmas Eve in Nashville.
And when a backpack-wearing college girl in platform sandals
tosses an unpurchased magazine
wherever it happens to land, leaving
it to obscure one-half of *Spa Finder*
and he waits until she's gone before he corrects the flaw
without a sigh or shake of the head,
I ask myself why I insist
on making things so complicated.

SHARLA JANE AIALANI FOSTER

Choke Flowers

I nevah know how tings gon' end up fo' me afta school, but leaning 'gainst one wall in da middle of nowea while trying fo' catch my breat' wit' one fricken blood stain on my shirt dat look like it getting biggah? Fuck, didn't tink would be dis.

Dis time las' yea' I was one high school senior goin' fo' lunch wen Magic Mike wen' stop me. He da Army guy at school but ev'rybody call 'im "Magic Mike" fo' some reason. He ask wat I gon' do afta graduation an' I tol' him I jus' like graduate first, y'know? Don' know 'bout afta. He wen say he was da same in school, jus' tryin' fo' graduate, and den he wen' join da Army. I figgah he jus' tryin' get me fo' join 'cause dat guy wen' speak wit' *ev'rybody*. Ev'rybody he talk to he tol' 'em 'bout da Army. But all good, he not pushy or nahting; he say hi wen we walk by an' let us hang out in 'is office during break. We cool off in the AC an' he tell us 'bout da places he go, like Japan, Germany. Braddah had some good stories. He even tol' us 'bout da time him and some friends got busted 'cause dey still hangin' wen' dey show up fo' work—an' dey no get fired! Too good dat.

Graduation day came an' I remembah I get choke leis. Choke, like no can see. Get choke money, too. Choke ev'ryting. Was nice. Nevah know wat gon' do tomorrow or da day afta', but I remembah dat day ev'ryone stay happy and cryin' at da same time. My moms an' dad hug me an' say dey proud o' me fo' graduating—get plenty cousins das why, who nevah finish and my braddah wen' drop out, too. He work County, so not like he one bum or someting. I neva wen' Project Grad, just me an' some friends hanging out, grillin', talking any kine shit. Always good fun wit' dem.

Magic Mike wen' give ev'rybody his card "just in case." I nevah tink nahting 'til I seen 'um in my wallet latah. Shoulda trown 'em away but I nevah. I just tought "Eh, nevah know." Not like anyone else give me dey card. During dah summah aftah graduation, I seen 'im at da gas station down da road. He laugh and ask if I stalking him or someting. I laugh too an' tol' 'im he da one stalking me, I tink. I live dea, not him. He got serious an' ask if I wen' tink 'bout joining and I tol' 'im I don' know wat da Army can do dat da County no can. He shook 'is head and tol' me stop by da office and he gon' show me wat da Army can give me. Wen I tol' 'im school stay closed he say da card he wen' give me get da main office address and he be dea all summah.

So, I go check 'um out.

Not like I *like* be in da Army or anyting, I just nevah know what else fo' do. I need one job, my parents said. If I only gon' surf I need fo' get paid for it, and I no like work County even if my braddah say get opening. Too much dramas jus' from wat he say. Magic Mike tol' me I can get a good job wit' da Army, an' dey train me, so why not? I get good pay, travel 'round da world, so I figure I try. Can do *someting* wit' my life, right?

Wen I wen' tell my parents I wen' sign up—ho, you tink I wen tell 'em I hāpai or someting. Dey nevah had nahting fo' say, just look at me fo' a bit befoa my faddah wen' ask "You shuah?" When I say yeah, he jus' nod and say "Kay" and walked out. My mom stayed quiet doh, and I tink she wen' cry in her room so I nevah see her. My aunty wen' call us at night and say my dad stay drinking wit' her an' uncle dem and wen' tol' ev'ryone I gon' go Army. Ho, dat wen' start da whole ting 'bout how stupid I am and no can trust da military and stuff. Ev'rybody get one opinion an' tink I no can have one, too. So all da moa I figgah I gon' go, right?

I slide down da wall, groaning; fucking ting *hurts*. My hand stay wet, too, now. I look 'round but can only hear yellin' and shooting. Not da way I expec' to see da world. My dad prolly have plenty fo' say if he seen me now. Da weeks before I left doh, he nevah have much fo' say.

Wen I wen' finish training I wen' go back home fo' visit. Ev'ryone stay happy fo' see me but nevah get leis like grad time, jus' hello's and hugs. Get cookout, at least. My faddah hug me hard but still nevah say much. My maddah at least say "Welcome home" and I tink dis time she wen' cry 'cause she happy. I tol' dem 'bout training and da drill sergeant dat sound like Unko Joe, but not as loud. Dey tol' me how ev'ryone stay, who hāpai, who foolin' around, who get in trouble. Same ol' tings, I realized. Same ol' tings from grade school an' high school an' now. Nuttin' change. 'Cept me.

Afta I lef' I still Facetimed ev'ryone. I showed dem da base and some people I knew. It ain't home, but ain't no place like Hawai'i so, y'know. I tol' 'em the food s'okay but I miss da Sunday imu and dey wen' laugh wen I wen' grumble dat da mac salad taste diff'ren' ovah hea. I made shuah to send money wit' each paycheck fo' help my parents, even if dey said no need. Not like I need it, I get food and bed fo' free. Christmas time came an' I nevah go home but I wen' call. My maddah sounded happy, even my faddah wen' wish me Merry Christmas, but my maddah said she wen' watch da news and dey was talking 'bout all da troops goin' Afghanistan. Wen she wen' ask if I gon' go I jus' laughed an' said "Nah, why send me wen dey get guys ovah dea already?" I nevah tol' 'em we was gon' deploy. We wen' ship out a mont' latah.

An' now I'm hea. Hot, dis place. And nuts. Only been a few weeks an' already in da middle of one gun fight. Crazy. Was suppose to check out one school, make sure ev'ryone stay safe but we nevah know was one trap. No kids, no school, just guys dat no like us hea. I get hit tryin' fo' duck. So stupid. I tink ev'ryone else stay hiding behind diff'rent walls 'cause I no can see 'em.

Fuck. Ho, dat last explosion hurt and was just da boom I feel. Yeah, see da world. Army Strong. Das some BS. Working County sounding bettah an' bettah right now. Fuckin' guy. I nevah seen 'im aftah I got sworn in, he prob'ly at da school, sharin' stories again. He not gon' tell 'em dey could end up hea, I bet. Make it sound like dey gon' go Florida or Japan, not frickin' Afghanistan.

Few mo' explosions latah and I ready fo' quit. My fingahs stay red 'cause I tryin' fo' stop da bleeding. No help, my jacket stay red, too, already. Don' know what wen' hit me, if was one bullet or someting else, but I too tired fo' tink.

Shoulda jus' stay home. Stay safe. Be one bum, even.

I hear more yelling. English, at least. Maybe we winning.

Da noise soft now, like dey moving away. Good, can rest a little bit before I get up.

Nevah like be one hero. Jus' like do someting. *Be* someting.

I laugh 'cause now I tink I dead but I nevah sign up fo' die.

I bet goin' get choke flowers wen' I go home dis time.

JUDITH GRAHAM

The Ruins At Māhukona

There is a particular smell of kiawe that is haunting. It is a smell that lingers along the dry coasts of the Island of Hawai'i, sometimes mixed in the mind with the smell of urine. Not altogether favorable but once you are used to it, a welcome smell. The tree grows where no others will, where the rainfall may be only seven inches a year, as with the "red desert" soils of Kawaihae. The trees may be barren for months waiting for rain, then suddenly green. The leaves are feathery and delicate, and make a lacework when they fall among rocks and soil that has the composition of dust and of the past. You will find them nestled, most green, in scattered groves alongshore, touching some hidden underwater spring. Here too are found ruins of a former culture not yet redone by the modern age. It seems unlikely that resort hotels will come here although it is said that they will. And the trade wind blows, shaking the branches. Kiawe make a creaking sound when disturbed, and the thorns of the branches are a self-protective device, one reason that even cattle won't touch them.

The trees may surround a seldom-frequented picnic area and have been here since the early twentieth century, introduced first at dry Kīholo where Hawaiian sweet potato patches once flourished. If they fall near shore, and they often do, being shallow rooted, the trunk and branches after a time take on the gray look of old bones touching the tide as it comes in, fallen over lava rock and the white remains of coral tossed up.

In certain places like one I recall near Māhukona, kiawe is a sentry for Hawaiian rock walls and burial niches, caves marked by perhaps a single shell. Or if the grave has been opened, a flurry, lying on the ground, of white leho shells, broken, called by experts midden, evidence of old habitation. In the hot sun which comes on early in the morning, the stone mound burials rise disguised by feather grass, giving the past a soft unobtrusive quality. These ruins do not proclaim themselves. They have not been subject to walkways, tours, and brochures that in their exploitation make the scene so ugly. These things may come but for now the kiawe tree still finds the place hospitable. It is not a tree that one would want to preserve.

It is not the ruins, I am saying, that give a mysterious effect, but the protector trees that seem to guard these places with a thick tangle of wood bodies, heightening the value of what is difficult to reach.

Or you might happen upon a large construction, a wall enclosing an area perhaps seventy-five feet in length and as wide. The wall, smoothly vertical with well placed stones of varying sizes, is the height of a man. Was it used to keep men out or to shelter them? This is not clear. A platform within the construct at its highest place suggests an altar. It is a fact that these sacrificial altars touted by missionaries as evidence of unspeakable native evils were less prevalent than their literature suggests. The platform is not smooth any longer. Its floor is pocketed with yellow kiawe scurf.

In this walled place the air is dank and the dead branches on the floor many. The trees here are old and therefore large. To this region few in the last century came. As the old time Hawaiians of good family will tell you, this was a forbidden place. Here lived still wild Hawaiians, those who resented the incoming culture and continued to live by canoe and by the sea. This place was forbidden to nicer Hawaiian children almost a century ago. This was an eddy of the old civilization, overlaid with a froth of resentment.

The nearby smaller mounds have neatly made compartments, caches, that archaeologists call cupboards. The neatly made boxes, like some slight but careful Egyptian tomb hid within the mound, are only visible because some have been opened and entered. Midden is scattered about. But now there is no trace of cloth or bone or artifact. Where did these go? Perhaps some are now as far away as Honolulu where such things scarcely exist except in glass cases. There the tapa might look moldy. In its day, it was subtly colored and fresh. Hawaiian tapa had a fine blue; some tapa designs recall sea urchins and tiny tidal creatures moving across the cloth in regular patterns. Now the impression is browner—no doubt a primitive civilization. The natives found shelter in, and gave birth in, caves. The more frequent habitation was the rush house resembling a large haystack. These dotted this shore before the white man, and the shading kiawe, came. Plovers still visit seasonally and seasonally also whales offshore, their large black backs breaking the ocean's level.

The Babcocks were a traditional missionary family, reaching the Hawaiian Islands in 1844. Less than a century later family holdings were considerable. In those days a white person did well, and early missionary families ingratiated themselves with the Hawaiian chiefs, and provided many services to them, such that either land grants were available as gifts, or when the land of the islands became accessible for purchase in 1850, they were able to buy at prices sometimes less than a dollar an acre. Nearly 100,000 acres changed missionary hands before the century closed, and some family groups, who incorporated, held this amount singly. The finer families were removed from the backbreaking labor of plantation life, usually performed by Asian immigrants, but reaped most of the fruits of their labor.

Jerome Babcock was a thin man with a hooked nose and in later life a handsome shock of white hair. His wife Emmeline, a stern and conscientious woman who grew more so as she aged, was an honored helpmeet but afforded Jerome few of the other pleasures of marital life. Their seven children, not all of whom lived, were the fruit of such moments. Babcock, after a time, did not so much sense the deprivation to his manhood as come to the realization that this should be the way for all men. He was by nature lusty. He did not condemn himself, but did not recognize this and may have pontificated more fiercely at those around him, dusky of hue, the bronze race they had once called them in earlier, more romantic times, who fornicated. And for this they were severely punished. Unmarried pregnant women did work upon the roads—not at Babcock's insistence to be sure, and privately he felt this to be inhumane; but he did not stint with vituperation upon this most loathsome of bodily tendencies. His wife Emmeline looked in her tiny dimity purity as if he had never touched her, and he seldom had.

Lecturing on occasion in the open air and later in handsomely constructed Congregational churches paneled in koa, with limestone and coral walls nearly two feet thick, he might thunder: And the Lord God has told His children, now is the moment for repentance. Cease evil. Thou listening know well of which I speak. (Babcock was not always grammatical.) I speak of fornication. And so on. And adultery. And the white eyes would look up at him under an array of bedraggled bonnets, rags that wretches in mainland cities in the nineteenth century might have worn. But Babcock knew that, despite the extreme temptations, which beset this Hawaiian flesh, some of these folk sincerely sought Christ. He taught of Christ as a shining example of manly purity, as perhaps a white example. Babcock believed that some of his words sank deep in the Hawaiian soul and would bring a change there. So that the older he became, the handsomer, the more elegant and the more love-starved his nature. This gave him a fineness, almost a French appearance.

Many years later much to his surprise, Babcock had not taken form as an angel on God's right-hand side or even in an outer ring of heaven, but was to be found haunting a palm grove at Lāhainā, Maui, this in the era of vast tourist expansion. Babcock had missed the full fruition of the sugar plantation era; it remained a black blot in his mind. After his late demise in 1905 he had not, so to speak, found himself, except briefly, until he found himself in the palm grove. His wife Emmeline was by his side.

They were denizens of a technicolor spirit world, could pass through trees if they cared to and could have traveled the length of Maui if they cared to, but Babcock did not. He wore his spiritual garb lightly and for a time had been sincerely confused as to what had happened to him. But when he could no longer see his shadow, and when he spoke to those living who walked through the grove on an afternoon, or perhaps a camper who spent the night, he noted that they could not see or hear him. From these things he concluded that he was indeed a spirit. Perhaps he was one of those whom the Hawaiian historian Samuel Kamakau had foretold would wander in the wiliwili grove of Crisscross, he hoped not forever.

There was still a fineness about Babcock's temperament but his mind endlessly dwelt on those he had not been able to convert and endlessly turned over what he would argue if he had the opportunity again to spread the gospel.

Light among the trees, the gentle palm fronds crackling as the wind blew were a comfort. His wife's face, upturned in a listening pose, though he no longer needed to speak to her, was a comfort. In this bright realm her face took now a rosy hue, now greenish, depending on temperament. Babcock slept as others did, and woke, but no longer ate. His slight frame retained its familiar sharp outline in his wife's spiritual eye. Babcock did not know how long such conditions customarily persisted.

At the floor of the grove he could now stare untroubled for hours but increasingly restless. Perhaps he had not given up his wish to use rhetoric or his wish to denounce bodily life.

It occurred that he might yet find a convert lover, and it was after several attempts to hug those living who passed through the region— which gave them a sudden constricted feeling and so they left quickly, or not so quickly if they did not take their intuitions seriously—that a susceptible young man did enter the grove, and on this person Babcock fastened with real success.

This tall young man, thinner than Babcock himself and with many aspirations, felt Babcock's hug and did not leave. To Babcock's astonishment, after the hug he himself seemed to remain associated with the thin young man and might not have been able to free himself, though he did not try. He caught Emmeline with a piercing blow to her hovering sensibility and brought her in train. Tentatively he began a few words and found that the young man heard him. Babcock had now found a host and an ear for his fine gray form.

Rob had a mind that would fasten at the easiest and first instance on what engaged it, with apparent serious intention. He had had a stern father who frequently condemned him. Babcock's voice was thus familiar, and at first wondering at the technicolor realm opening around him and listening to half-caught phrases from the Bible, he thought that God might have selected him. At first it was with great optimism that he felt Babcock's hug and that he sat abruptly down to let happen to him what might, in Lāhainā, Maui, formerly a whaling port with a busy commerce in rum and prostitution.

In the spaces where Robert walked, the light was always slightly brighter than elsewhere and he walked a great deal. Others might have said he was unhappy—his frame seemed so, trudging the road, and occasionally he looked crazed—but he himself would have said all this was more than compensated for by moments of grace when the kiawe rose before him shining, when his earthen bed could be smelt. He walked at night and slept now in a palm grove on the island of Hawai'i not far from the place of ruins but never specifically there. His body was brown and his light blue eyes had the look of the ocean, which he stayed near. He lived on fruit, not solely but when at his best. He had become still thinner, Babcock encouraging him to eat what was pure and to prepare himself.

To prepare himself for what, Robert did not know, but he was guided now, never alone, by the God spirit as he understood it, in truth by Babcock who came to his consciousness most often at evening and to criticize. The faults Babcock could find were innumerable, and when Robert fell from grace he always knew, because the voice of endless carping would begin. In moments of rebellion Robert wanted a lawyer—give me a lawyer.

Since acquiring Babcock he could no longer at purest moments seek to provide his own food, but his food must come to him provided by God. Rob knew well that in fact he would be guided where a bunch of bananas had ripened or where a casual friend would buy him a meal or offer small change. Sometimes he clung to the defiled clairvoyant powers he possessed. At other times he would be hungry or nervous, would want to take a job and earn money. But Babcock would not let him rest until he had quit any of these jobs, which he always did suddenly, the construction or handyman work he had managed to pick up. Sometimes he smelt noticeably.

In moments of grace the air shimmered for him in spans and he saw every bird—the small finches that had gone wild here, the owl looking at him like the face of God, or the bright white butterflies that lived in dry places. Then the road before him did not seem long. He walked at night past rolling hills of thinly veneered lava under a deep blue-black sky.

Robert hated Babcock's sterner voice, the tones that spoke only of his son—he only thinks of his son (Jesus), that's all he thinks about, Robert said once in exasperation aloud (to a woman, who looked at him oddly), but he himself had not released the hope that he was a second son if only he could live more purely. The region was still rural, and Robert was lost in the transient flux, which is the predecessor of expensive development.

If he acquired a jacket or shirt or even a ten-dollar bill, Babcock might order him to throw it away, and most likely he would, dropping it by the side of the road in anguish because the bill was all that stood between him and going hungry.

His days were long and there were for him no days of the week. His territory was a fifteen-mile stretch of coastline, and he never overtly hitchhiked but was often picked up by those who had come to know him a little and who became concerned, such that conversation among these acquaintances might run to, How's Rob? Oh, I saw him at breakfast yesterday, he was looking good (happily!), he's working.

Rob's speech had a driven quality, bursts of enthusiasm, clinging to any thread passersby offered, talk of dolphins or football or how good running is for the body. Rob needed shoelaces and accepted a ride to get them but he could not run far. He could walk patiently for many hours.

He had a sense of Hawaiian moʻo though he would not have known what to call them. He could see the falseness in others and he knew intuitively when it would be acceptable to stay a day or two at a friend's house in a papaya grove. His face flattened with chastisement and elongated. His dangling fingers and long legs splayed as he tried to express himself, but he scarcely mentioned to others his haunting and did not think of it as such. He dated the significance of his life from the time two years before in the palm grove on Maui. A fluke, a fluke, that I should have gone there, he exclaimed. And he wanted to leave and work in Alaska but Babcock refused and Rob argued and argued with his God to no avail. Personally he was aware that he not only had been chosen by God, but had seen Mary (this was Emmeline, the quieter partner). He became increasingly jealous of Babcock's solicitude for his "son."

When asked (by the same woman who had given him an odd look) if the spirit had hugged him, he exclaimed excitedly, That's it, that's exactly it! They were sitting in the darkening night near the lapping ocean water beside his palm grove. When asked how it felt he said, Imagine, being embraced by God! He sensed that Babcock was at the grove and would wait for him, but if he tried avoidance by staying in the next district for too many days, then sure enough, there was the condemning voice seeming to come from inside his own head or slightly above or between his eyes. He began to think he could never be free and could never be alone. I want to be alone, I want to be master of my fate, he rebuked his master. Yet he liked well the heightened effect of colors in this universe that he had acquired since Maui, and the sense of pervading grace Babcock sometimes vouchsafed. He continued to purify himself, was institutionalized once and afterwards was taken by a friend to a physician where he received sedatives. He paced for hours under these sedatives. A cloud had descended, the scene was decidedly dull, no voices and no colors. He could barely bring words up from the depths of his throat, and all the kiawe leaves, previously sparkling gold, lay like corpses under his feet. It was as if sludge were shortly to overwhelm his mind. He wanted again the gleaming vistas, the hearty breaths that were God's air, not lassitude, and would never take the pills again.

Nearing three years, although he felt he had grown, although his body he knew was special and pure now, a chosen manhood, although he felt some pride in his self-reliance, not needing clothing or a home or even a tent, yet he noticed others looking askance, felt he could never benefit his aging mother in another state, which project was becoming a fixation that Babcock would not rid him of, and in short longed for the normal life. At times his bones ached and periodic infections weakened him. A gift of several shirts had been thrown by the wayside. His red slacks, the garment he had owned longest, seemed acceptable, never in question. He must also, and this was the fiercest taboo, never touch himself, and prospects for sleeping with a woman, though it was a time of easy sex, eluded him. He was most beaten when he wanted this most and had not the honesty (for which he railed at himself) to acknowledge this subject openly to Babcock. His sense that one day he would be seen by the world as the shining second coming diminished, and his guilt for not caring for his elderly mother (this he did bring up; Babcock would not hear of him leaving the state; the one time he had tried was the time he had been institutionalized, when he cried from a wheelchair where he was strapped, I want a lawyer, I want a lawyer) preyed on his attention. After three years it occurred that he had been possessed, and he wore a cross about his neck on the advice of one of his rides, but it had not helped. He began to hear of other talismans, but with a kind of anguish as he looked at the shining beauty of the world, he cried from deep within, how could I, who am special and blessed, not meet the standards of my Maker? He told himself repeatedly, and he had to remind himself, that he must be worthy of the scarlet gift, but he was becoming increasingly weary and unkempt.

Did you see Rob, said one, He was filthy. And the owl, the 'aumakua, flew past on silent wings one evening as he walked near the place of Hawaiian ruins by the water at Māhukona. He looked at the sloping land waiting to receive him and decided to sleep in this place. It was dusk and (for which he could expect rebuke) he had shared a bottle of wine with a friend not long before. He felt restful and wanted to stop.

It was with a smile, although none were there to see, that Robert ambled down the dusty road serviceable for four-wheel drive vehicles. Families enjoyed picnics by the water along this coast, where the children could play in tide pools among the pretty pebbles. Yet this particular entrance was rarely used, the road so bumpy, and the shoreline barred from entry by a chain-link fence, an absentee landlord. Robert felt alone and comforted. Small birds rose in flocks into the still warm evening air and preceded him. The grasses murmured. The trade winds had returned twice this day.

It was not far to the shore and the road seemed smooth to a veteran walker with wine thoughts stirring the brain. The smell of kiawe came up. To his right he could see a low dark shape, a rock wall. He was familiar with them. And then another. He thought, this is an archaeological trove. It made him happy to use, even for his pleasure alone, special words. By Jove a trove! And he slipped past the edge of the chain-link fence.

He planned to eat oranges and part of a loaf of bread and then sleep near the sound of the ocean. On the makai side of the fence, the walls rose more thickly. They caught even an inebriated eye and were lit in places by the sun as it sank amid a splendor of bud-like clouds. He tramped through one large walled area, splintering twigs as he went, and wondered at the height and straight edge of the construction, but as the air darkened and young kiawe sprouted up everywhere before his path, he hiked near the water's edge and lay down on a sharp declivity of water-washed pebbles. He laid out his bag and fell asleep. It was a star-filled night. The wine had been good to him. Not once had he expected and not once had he heard the admonishing voice. He spent a blank night and would have not the least memory of it when he awoke early to hike out for his morning coffee at a Japanese store several miles away.

Babcock's alertness had increased even as they moved down the rutted road; there was a smell to this place that hinted of the last century and seemed dear to him. On the other side of the chain-link fence, which he conveniently and debonairly passed through, he was astonished at the habitation remains, all the old stones. The great width of walls, two or three feet, old, and the dankness that might have repelled others was to him like wine.

He could see shimmering above the corners of the ruined places the ghostlike forms of earlier inhabitants, who in turn gave no appearance of seeing him. By the small compartments, opened, he saw children, as if veiled, as if not awake to the technicolor world he customarily experienced, and without expression. Large men moved about the canoe house, silently intent, wearing cast-off broadcloth, the remnant of a paniolo's scarlet bandanna at the neck. Canoes could not be seen by Babcock, but they seemed to see them and to lug this and that here and there. By the water was a woman; her features seemed to Babcock part Chinese and recalled the pretty Hawaiian wife of the Chinese shopkeeper at Mākena, Maui, with whom, God help him, he had once been intimate. Babcock did not harangue Robert this night because he had lost all interest in him. And it came to his understanding that these people did not know they were dead. These did not know they were dead. As it was a lost, querying experience he had once had, he recognized it. And because in former times he had been a literate man with even an anthropological bent, he surmised they were those who had leapt from the leaping place (in the Hawaiian system), whether a cliff or the branches of the great breadfruit tree, into Pō, and had not been welcomed. Into darkness, Pō, and had not been welcomed.

Babcock's training rose in him, whole new sermons that could be advanced in this field. He saw a family of rough Hawaiians gathered around, beginning to listen, their eyes opening to show the white and a gleam of intelligence. He ruffed up the back of his neck and smoothed down the black shirtwaist in which, lamentably, he had been buried. As darkness came over the place, Babcock peered here and there at the long bones that had once lain in this mound burial; the halo remained. Through the grasses he could detect more of these mounds, which reassured him that he would have not one family only but a string of coastal inhabitants, like the pearls of his wife's necklace—whom he had, incidentally, altogether forgotten.

To these denizens who in truth did not know they were dead, neither Robert nor Babcock registered. In the morning Robert packed his bedroll neatly, felt a joy at heart and wanted to be on the road to catch the early resort workers driving past. In the morning, however, these hostile Hawaiians did become aware of Babcock through a bright illusion that numerous of them perceived independently and in unison. It was a vision of a white, expressionless face with a hooked nose breaking through clods of earth, as if some white man had been buried in a shallow grave near their place and now rose up to meet them. The hair was brown and the dark earth falling away from the fair skin seemed to go on and on, like a dream image that does not leave. While motorboats began to sound offshore—early Japanese fishermen—they awoke to this illusion. And as a group, with strength, they rushed it and throttled it.

NYC, August 6, 2019

On August 3, 2019, nine people were killed and twenty-seven others were wounded by a gunman in Dayton, Ohio. On August 4, 2019, twenty-two people were killed and twenty-six others were wounded at a Walmart in El Paso, Texas.

A low rumbling
then a crescendo of running footsteps
interrupts Scout's last speech in *To Kill a Mockingbird*
in the Shubert Theatre on 44th Street
The actors onstage are looking past us
What's that noise coming from the lobby?
The stage empties
What's going on?
Everyone's standing up
Then we hear "There's a shooter!"
Pandemonium erupts
If a white supremacist were to target a play
this would be it
I'm a tourist from Hawai'i in the Big Apple
visiting a good friend from high school days
and I'm trapped in a nightmare
far away from home
I drop to the ground
yell at my friend to get down
Thud, thump, noise splinters
I crawl fast but the people in front of me
seem to move slow motion
Thuds, thumps,
cacophony of panic
We reach the end of the row
run for the exit
then stop
What if the shooter is outside?
In the small group gathered near the exit to the street,
a man looks at his phone and says,
"No shooter. NYPD says it was motorcycle backfire
outside the theatre."

Someone else says, "Everyone's on edge."
My friend lost her handbag
We go back inside to look for it
Chair backs and seats dangle broken at odd angles
We find her bag intact among the wreckage.

Outside on the street, people are sobbing
Trampled papers, cups, signs litter the sidewalk
Someone lost a shoe
Miscellaneous debris is scattered
in the wake of the stampeding crowd
that flooded Broadway and Times Square

I am thousands of miles away,
a continent and an ocean
too far from home.

GAIL N. HARADA

Orchid Near the Door

I didn't know what kind of orchid plant was in the pot near my front door. It had a pseudobulb, so in case the plant was still alive, I watered it a little a few times a week. Months later, two leaves sprouted and grew into thick leaves. Then something emerged from the base of a leaf. A curled bright pink inflorescence started to push itself out of its sheath. When the orchid bloomed, I saw it was a cattleya. The pedicel was bent, so the flower bowed its lovely face down toward the ground. Should I stake it to hold the flower up? I let it be.

The color orchid is not just purple. It is the color of cattleya orchids.

My father's father raised orchids. My mother's father built houses and buildings.

Clutter of memories
Not puzzle pieces that fit
Just fragments, impressions,
Shape and shadow

My memory of 1970s Chinatown at night includes the Orchid Ballroom neon sign glowing the vivid color of the frilled lip of a cattleya orchid above Tin Tin Chop Suey. But who can rely on memory?

I asked some friends if they remembered the Orchid Ballroom sign on Maunakea Street, but none of them did or even knew there were still taxi-dance halls in the seventies. They all remembered eating at Tin Tin Chop Suey.

Back then I knew the Orchid Ballroom was a taxi-dance hall, and I was curious about it. I didn't think it was dangerous, but it didn't feel quite right to go there alone at night, and I would have felt like an outsider. I wish I had walked up those stairs. My friend mentioned my question about the Orchid Ballroom sign to her husband, and though he didn't remember the sign, he and his best friend went there a couple times in the seventies for the live music—the band played kachi kachi and love songs. And the best friend danced a couple songs with a girl. Some of the girls were college students. Most of the customers were old Filipino men. It wasn't very crowded.

In postwar Honolulu, soldiers and sailors also patronized the taxi-dance halls. A ticket bought a minute or two of dancing, and the band might play nonstop, changing tempo and starting a new song to mark the dance time bought by a ticket. Some dance halls would ring a bell to mark the dance time. A whole song could be 3 or 4 bells long. When the band started a new song or the bell rang to mark the end of the dance time bought by a ticket, the man had to give the dance hostess another ticket to continue dancing with her.

My friend's husband doesn't remember a bell at the Orchid Ballroom when he went there in the seventies.

Taxi-dancers could do ballroom dancing, including foxtrot and cha-cha.

We were required to learn how to box step foxtrot and cha-cha in PE class in seventh or eighth grade. It was called "social dancing." Box step foxtrot: one-two-three-four, one-two-three-four. Cha-cha: one-two, cha-cha-cha; one-two, cha-cha-cha.

In the early seventies, plans for Chinatown redevelopment determined that some old buildings not designated as historic would be demolished to make way for new buildings. Old-time businesses and residents would be displaced. Where could they go? Activists, business owners, residents, government officials, developers, and politicians got embroiled in protests, meetings, hearings. People Against Chinatown Evictions pushed for affordable housing for residents who wanted to continue living in Chinatown. Third Arm ran a free medical clinic on Pauahi Street.

Names float up
Surface after such a long time
Pulled up in the net of memory.

The Palace Ballroom, Tin Tin Chop Suey, and the Orchid Ballroom were in one of the buildings slated for redevelopment demolition.

The Palace Ballroom was the oldest taxi-dance hall in Chinatown.

Tin Tin Chop Suey was popular with downtown workers for lunch and was the Chinese restaurant to go to after midnight.

In a 1965 *Honolulu Star-Bulletin* classified ad, the Orchid Ballroom claimed to be the "busiest ballroom in town." Dance hostesses could gross up to $250 for thirty hours a week, and transportation was offered.

In the seventies, a dance ticket was fifty cents (twenty-five cents went to the dance hostess). Coffee with a girl might be a minimum five dollars plus the cost of the coffee.

In the seventies, the Orchid Ballroom was used for workshops and public meetings about Chinatown redevelopment, including an all-day conference in summer 1977.

I don't know when the Orchid Ballroom closed.

Tin Tin Chop Suey closed its doors for the last time at 3 a.m. in February 1985.

The Palace Ballroom closed in late 1984. It was a place for the regulars to see their friends and maybe dance. The last night at the Palace Ballroom was not crowded. The few regulars—mostly old Filipino men. The few remaining dancers. The band. The last song.

But the Palace Ballroom wasn't the last taxi-dance hall in Chinatown; Benny's Dance Land on Hotel Street was. It was open 7 p.m. to midnight. According to a 1996 *Honolulu Advertiser* classified ad for Benny's Dance Land, dancers could earn $85 to $100 a night commission. By the 1990s, a dance ticket cost five dollars for five minutes instead of fifty cents for a minute. Most of the dancers were college students or military wives. Benny's Dance Hall included a restaurant where the owner cooked Filipino food, and the customers could hang out and talk story. There was a pool table too. Eventually the dance hall had to switch from live bands to music tapes because the musicians got too old or passed away. But some of the customers, mostly old Filipino men, still danced. It was somewhere to have fun, relax, and see friends. No fights or trouble. Benny's Dance Hall closed in 1999.

Time and place
memories woven
stories lost and found

Who remembers People Against Chinatown Eviction? Who remembers Third Arm? Who remembers the Aloha Hotel protest? Who remembers who lived at Pauahi Hale and stayed after it was renovated? Who remembers the old buildings being razed and new structures rising in their places? Who remembers who got keys to affordable units in the Smith-Beretania Apartments? Who remembers the residents turned activists? Who remembers Chinatown of that time? Who is watching Chinatown now?

Since the seventies, there have been three tiger years—1986, 1998, and 2010. This year, 2022, is the year of the tiger. The tiger's roar is so powerful it paralyzes other animals, but it's not what people can hear that paralyzes. It's what we might feel but cannot hear—low frequency infrasounds passing through us.

I drive through Chinatown looking at people, buildings, signs. People are celebrating Chinese New Year, and Maunakea Street is busy. There's a long line of people waiting outside Sing Cheong Yuan Bakery, probably to buy gau and New Year good-luck candied vegetables and fruits—lotus root, winter squash, kumquat, coconut. Everyone is wearing masks in this time of Covid.

A young rooster appeared in my front yard last week. He has glossy black feathers. He is sleek and slim like teenagers can be, curious and unafraid. Quick. When he crosses the street, he has the good sense to run like crazy before any car can hit him.

A new cat has appeared in the neighborhood. It is the color of smoke and never crosses to my side of the street. I don't know where it goes.

My friend's daughter's dog has idiopathic old dog disease.

The cattleya orchid plant has one flower, six leaves, and two more pseudobulbs.

Spirit Rocks

Part One

It was taking longer than it should for sister-in-law Maya to get her kids ready for the drive to Hilo airport after a weeklong family visit. Lost socks, missing underwear, bathroom emergencies, and a stubbed and bloody toe, the usual things when you travel with kids. Still, it seemed to be taking longer this time: Find one lost sock and a shirt goes missing. Find the shirt and Brother goes missing. Find Brother and get the car loaded, and the battery is dead. Jumper cables to the pickup and, finally, they're on their way. But still nobody was happy.

"Stop picking on me."

"I'm not. Don't touch me."

"You're on my side."

"Brother! Sister! Stop it right now!"

They got to the airport late and jostled their way through boarding and seating. Maya sat between Brother and Sister to keep them separated. But when were they gonna take off? It was a warm day, and the A/C was not on. Who knew why? Wasn't it time to leave? Wasn't it past time to leave? Finally, the captain announces that there was a maintenance delay but that they would be going soon. Sorry about the A/C.

Eventually they close the doors and taxi toward the runway behind two other planes waiting for takeoff. Waiting. Still waiting.

"Have they got the A/C on?"

"Sounds like it."

"Doesn't feel like it."

They finally get airborne and enter an especially turbulent sky toward Honolulu. A prolonged holding pattern before landing and a baggage mixup on the carousel slow them down still more. A Wilson Tunnel tie-up results in their limping home after dark, dazed and bedraggled.

"Pile your stuff in the living room," Maya says. "I'll start a wash after you guys go to bed. Hey, what's that?" she asks Brother. "Where'd you get that rock?" Dark and roughly polished by time, the lava sphere is about baseball-size.

"Just a rock I found."

"Where did you find it? At Uncle's? In Hilo?"

"Yeah, well I didn't break it off or dig it up."

"From Uncle's?"

"He got it from Uncle's backyard," Sister says. "By the fence."

"Give it here," Maya says, holding out her hand. "You guys have cereal for dinner, then go straight to bed. School tomorrow."

"Where are you going?"

"To the airport. This rock is going back to Uncle's."

Her mission to return the rock to its Big Island home is unimpeded by weather, traffic, or mechanical breakdown, Uncle meets her at the Hilo airport, and she makes it back home a little past midnight. The bad luck cycle has been stopped in its tracks, no real harm done. Some locals shiver at the possible consequences of not returning that fragment of Earth's crust to its rightful location, its home according to Pele. Apparently.

I can see why part-Hawaiian Maya and her children, Island people to the core, might believe such things. Maybe such things can happen to Island people, but would they happen to me, an outsider, a haole? Doesn't my other-ness immunize me against such superstitious beliefs and from the consequences of such beliefs, real or imagined? I kinda thought so, though I had no intention of putting it to the test. But what if "it," whatever "it" is, decided to put me to the test? What do I mean, "What if?" Here's how it happened.

Part Two

Hawai'i has been my home since 1966. While I've spent significant time visiting friends and family around Puget Sound where I grew up, none of those visits were in spring, and I missed being part of that magical season. Things hadn't lined up to favor a springtime trip until the end of the century. My mom was nearing the end of her long tenure on Hood Canal, Daughter Two would be on spring break at Western in Bellingham, and I would be on spring break from the Lab School. Teachers don't make much money, but, like students, they get spring breaks. This should be a good one.

Everything about it was positive, the way schedules lined up to put me in the right place with the right people at the right time. The air was briskly warming, the sky clear, the sun bright. Mom's yard was bustling and buzzing with life, color, fragrance. When was the last time I'd seen trilliums blooming, alders and maples in full bud, spring robins, chipmunks? On the beach, small crabs scrambled in the rocks, and at low tide, clams and oysters invited harvest. Gulls screeched, wheeled, probed.

On a worn scrap of plywood in the weeds near the top of the rock bulkhead lay an assortment of what my nephew called his "mud babies." My untrained eye sees a form of sedimentary cohesion, a kind of sandstone composed of very small particles. He mostly collected them at low tide out near mid-channel. Usually flat, they formed unpredictable patterns like weighty, rounded-off snowflakes. I liked knowing he'd spent happy hours capturing mud babies on Grandma's beach.

Other aspects of my visit were equally ideal. The drive to and from Bellingham took me through brightly fresh vegetation, and I rolled down the windows on Mom's trusty Tempo, even on I-5. Everything felt good. Daughter Two and I went hiking and exploring Boundary Bay and Bellingham town for food and fun. We lucked into three great films: *High Fidelity*, *Ghost Dog*, and *American Beauty*. Everything was great. All smiles from both of us the whole time.

Back at Mom's, I find two friends from high school who, like me, have developed a taste for single-malt Scotch, and we spend a muzzy afternoon tasting, toasting, and reliving those thrilling days of yesteryear. Manly handshakes and smiles all around when we break up. "Until next time," we vow. "South Kitsap Wolves," we laugh.

The afternoon before I leave, I hike on over to the Potters, long-time neighbors and Mom's closest friends. Dirk and Maureen were locally famous for their dedication to a spartan diet of iced screwdrivers and shared, chain-smoked Marlboros. And for their warm hospitality and neighborliness.

A comfortable couple of hundred yards' walk by beach or highway, their house was always neat and clean, belying some popular assumptions about alcoholic haze and clutter. The Potters were responsible. They took care of business. They prospered and shared, were valued friends in tune with their natural environment and social obligations. Nearing seventy, the question was how long could they keep it up?

"Screwdriver or Bloody Mary?"

"Whatever you're having."

"I'm learning to alternate days. Yesterday we hailed Mary. Today we screw the driver."

"You should be so lucky," Maureen says from the kitchen.

I face Dirk catty-corner in the living room overlooking Hood Canal with the Olympic Mountains looming white on the horizon. We sip our way through two drinks apiece, making small talk about Hawai'i and Mexico, where they have vacationed. "Slowing down," Dirk says with a small grimace. "I'll make seventy this year." His large-knuckled left hand grips the frosty glass with nonchalance as he squints against the smoke rising from the cigarette in his right hand. The size of his large hands is exaggerated by his lean frame. It is not a healthy lean-ness. His skin color is not good. He kind of vibrates, a low-grade version of the shakes.

"I'm not that far behind you," I offer.

"Your mom's doing well."

"Thanks to neighbors like you."

He's losing steam, so I finish my second glass and get up to leave. He struggles to his feet, leaving a darkly wet patch on the chair cushion. I try to give no sign that I've noticed, we shake hands, I hug Maureen, and that's it. All smiles, of course. "When you coming back to Hawai'i?"

"We keep talking about it," Maureen says.

"Any day now," Dirk adds.

"Let us know," I say.

Later I tell Mom I don't think Dirk's doing very well. "It's the smoking," she says. "They both smoke too much."

Monday morning while I'm waiting for my ride to Sea-Tac, I take a last walk on the beach, giving Nephew's mud baby collection a bit more scrutiny as I pass by. The tide is halfway out as I walk slowly from end to end of Mom's beach, absorbing and absorbed by the smells and sounds of nature in Northwest spring, its feel, its touch.

Or its look. Looking at me! What? What's that in the gravel? No doubt about it, something's in there. Some being? What we seem to have here is a small, three-part geological being sculpted delicately by nature to represent, I don't know, universal life? It's a mud baby, of course, but uncannily un-coarse in its appearance. Three perfectly proportioned discs molded large-medium-small, bottom-to-top. Smooth. Rounded. Dark but not black. Richly lustrous.

The top disc, the small one, the head, has a face. The face is very distinct, proportional, located in the exact center of the disc. It seems emotive, but just what message it sends is unclear, fraught with subtle changes from one look to the next.

It's fascinating. I'd love to just drop it in my pocket and carry it home to Hawai'i with me. I think about sister-in-law Maya in Kahalu'u and the rock she returned to Hilo. But that was a Hawaiian belief involving Hawaiian geology and mythology. Anyway, I wouldn't be taking a rock FROM Hawai'i, I'd be taking a rock TO Hawai'i. Big diff, right, Pele? But, no, I couldn't feel good about taking it. Mom's beach was its home. I'll put it down here, right where I found it. There, that feels better. Stay well, little fella.

I keep dragging my feet slowly through gravel to the north end of the beach, re-absorbing a setting I had too long neglected—sounds of gulls, waves, woodpeckers, crows; warming sun, saltwater smells.

Even well before widowhood, one of Mom's biggest fears was that somebody—some valued friend or family member, worst of all a child, perhaps a grandchild—would drown or be seriously injured on her beautiful beach. It would never be beautiful again. She would have to move.

When I reach the property line, I turn around and head back toward the bulkhead. At the spot where I placed the mud baby, I stop for one last look. Mmmm, where is "it"? Ah, here you are. It has absorbed heat from the spring sun, heat I feel against my thigh after I drop it in my pocket and prepare to carry it home to Hawai'i with me.

It's still Monday when I get back to Pālolo Valley. I take the mud baby out of the vitamin bottle I'd packed it in for safe travel. Perfect. No breaks, no cracks or scratches.

Seems to me the perfect home for it would be the shoji-paneled window I added to the bathroom of our Joe Pao house. Framed in unfinished western red cedar, it seems a perfect match for Pacific Northwest beach mud. It looks great notched in grainy cedar near my toothbrush. I don't even try to divine its expression. If it isn't happy now, it soon will be when it realizes what a gift I've laid on him. Was it not an "it" but a "he"? A "they"? Does it have a name? How about "Hotei," the laughing monk? We'll see. Wouldn't that make it a "he"?

I go about the business of re-integrating into daily life. Hotei seems to have accommodated comfortably enough, neither laughing nor raging but still emoting . . . something. Really? Isn't it (I almost said "he") really just a random bit of an inferior class of stone—not only not a true sculpture but barely a true rock at all?

On Thursday morning as I reach for my toothbrush, I feel rather than see a gap, an omission, an erasure. Hotei is missing! Oh, of course, here he is on the shelf below the window where he has fallen.

But fallen how? There's no fan or window opening, no air current to blow him off his secure perch. Was there an earthquake? I finally settle on the idea of a hyper-territorial gecko as the culprit. What else could it be?

We get the call that afternoon. Dirk Potter's grand experiment had failed. One could not live on Marlboros and screwdrivers alone. At least he couldn't. He didn't make seventy. How was Maureen doing? She and Mom will no doubt bond tighter, and she must feel some sense of relief. She could not have thought he would last much longer.

On Saturday Hotei went missing again, and again I found him sideways on the shelf below. This time the call did not come until evening. Maureen, this time. In her sleep. Widely held and quietly spoken opinion was intentional OD. Dirk's lifestyle had not been good for her either. Mom had just lost her two closest friends.

On Tuesday, we get the news that a colleague's son, away at school in St. Louis, had suffered serious complications from a previously undiagnosed heart condition. He might not survive. By coincidence, our son is also going to school in St. Louis. He does not know our colleague's son and feels well himself, but it's a bit spooky all the same. Like a warning.

Like something to take seriously, especially after what happens on Saturday. We're trying to call Daughter One, attending school in Providence. We get no answer by phone or e-mail, most unusual for our hyper-connected communicator. Was it time to worry? What does Hotei say? He stays mute these days, held in place by two-sided tape after his second fall.

Early Sunday morning, we get the call. Daughter One is fine, but she spent the night in the hospital to be near a college friend who collapsed during a pick-up basketball game from . . . is it really a myocardial infarction? That's what I think I hear. What I know I hear is, "He might die."

Never having gone to war and rarely courting real danger, I am not a man well acquainted with death. Recent events are trending worse than worrisome. Two down and two in the breech. Who knows what's to come? Daughter Two in Bellingham. Should we alert her? To what? Watch out! Your friend could have a heart attack? Which friend? Any of them. Sure, Dad.

And Hotei. Do I really think he is the bearer of mysterious powers that he exercises to scare me into sending him back to Hood

Canal? Maybe so. Certainly I'm trending that way. Bad news from Bellingham could win him free passage home.

Our colleague's son and Daughter One's friend hang on and seem to be recovering as we wait and see. Will Bellingham call? For a full week Bellingham does not call, and we begin to relax.

But on the following Monday, Honolulu calls. A former student, an honors graduate and all-around good guy, well-liked by everybody for all the right reasons, has died in a bizarre accident at Ala Moana Center over the weekend. Talk about a gut punch. Prime of life, full of promise. Why him?

Then, on Tuesday, Hood Canal calls. Mom. The beach. Not her beach, but the beach next door, the tall bulkhead where the kids play unsupervised, a toddler girl falls into the water at high tide. She can't swim, nobody sees her, and she drowns. It's not Mom's beach and not her friends or family. Not this time.

It feels not so much counter-intuitive as counter-intelligent. There's no way that I can say logically how a small piece of mineral coagulate like Hotei could actually have caused so much apparently unconnected personal tragedy, but it does not stop me from thinking that from a certain perspective it makes perfect intuitive sense. And who's to say intuition is inferior to rational intelligence as a way of knowing?

When I carefully packed and Special Delivery mailed Hotei back to Mom's, I knew I was putting an end to a quiet reign of terror caused by me, myself, and I. And Hotei, of course. Mom said he was so pretty she had a hard time not keeping him in the house. But she didn't want trouble, so back to the beach he went.

That was it, the end of what you might call the troubles. I'm not as fast on the uptake as my Hawaiian sister-in-law Maya, but set an example and give me a little time and this clueless haole can learn to do better. Patience. I wish Maya were still here to show me the way. True story. Fake names.

ALDEN M. HAYASHI

A Belated Reparation

"Can you believe this?" Mom asked as she shook a piece of paper at me, her voice infused with ire. I looked at her with a sympathetic yet confused expression that should have invited explanation, but instead she simply plopped herself next to me on the living room sofa and handed me the letter. Written on official stationery from the U.S. Department of Justice, it was in reference to the reparations being given to those of Japanese descent who, like my mother, had been incarcerated in a "relocation" camp during World War II. Apparently, she had been ruled ineligible for any redress even though she and her family had been uprooted from Honolulu and shipped to Arkansas, where they were forced to live on snake-infested swampland in hastily constructed barracks.

I was trying to think of how to respond, what words might help bring comfort to my mother's agitated state. Did she want gentle sympathy, or would she prefer my being similarly outraged? But before I could say anything, she added, "They actually rejected me," her face scrunched in anger. "Tell me, what kind of government gives something then snatches it away? Who does something like that? The *nerve*!"

In all my life, I had never heard my mother swear or even utter slightly off-color words. She rarely raised her voice in public, and considered smoking or drinking too unladylike for her tastes. Whenever her patience was tested, she'd subconsciously switch to Japanese, but even then her choice of words were G-rated: *yakamashii* (too noisy) or *jama ni naru* (pest). At worst, she might label someone as *baka* (fool) and exclaim *dame* (hopeless), but that was about it. In English, the worst I ever heard her refer to anyone was "stupid." She'd never even say "shut up" or "damn," and using the f-word was well beyond her limits of decorum. But the way she just spat out "The *nerve*," I knew what she really meant: The *fucking nerve*!

Ironically, at first Mom had no interest in applying for the $20,000 reparation that had been provided for by The Civil Liberties Act of 1988. At the time, I was incredulous, because the money was a mere drop in the bucket of everything her family had lost. But when I repeatedly urged her to apply, her response was always, "It's all in the past," or "That was such a long time ago." And this unforgettable gem: "I don't really need the money." My mother actually said that, even as she relentlessly clipped coupons, re-used Ziploc plastic storage bags, and darned Dad's socks—all so she could eventually save enough money for a trip to visit her older brother, my Uncle Yuki, whom she hadn't seen in more than forty years. Since the war's end, the Matsumotos had been fractured across an ocean, with Mom, Dad, and me living in Honolulu and her older brother and his family in Tokyo.

Yet anytime I would argue with Mom to apply for the reparation, she would always end the discussion with some variation of *shikata ga nai*, loosely translated "it can't be helped," as if the wartime racial hysteria was a natural event, like an earthquake or hurricane. Eventually, I stopped nagging her about it, resigning myself to the realization that those wartime memories were too painful for my mother, and that what she wanted most was to forget about that turbulent time in her life.

One day, though, after I had picked her up in Chinatown, where she had been shopping for some fish and vegetables, she asked me to head toward an area near Aʻala Park. As we drove around that neighborhood, near the edge of downtown Honolulu, she asked me to make a turn here and there while she kept looking out the window, searching for something. "I can't figure it out," she finally said.

"Figure what out?"

"Where our home was. It was a beautiful plantation-style house with three bedrooms and a long lanai that wrapped around the front."

We circled around several times but Mom was utterly lost because the streets had all been changed since the war. The only thing familiar to her now was Nuʻuanu Stream, flowing at the edge of Chinatown. "Yuki and I used to catch tadpoles and ʻōpae there when we were kids, and we'd walk over to the Toyo Theatre for Saturday matinees. We really had such a carefree childhood. Now, though, I really don't recognize anything here, but our house must have been somewhere there," she said, pointing toward one row of Kukui Garden's three-story apartment buildings. With a wry smile, she added, "Well, somebody must have been really happy."

"What do you mean?"

Mom explained that, after Japan had bombed Pearl Harbor and Grandpa had been rounded up by the FBI, Grandma thought it best to convert all the family's wealth into tangible goods. So she and Mom went on a shopping spree at the jewelry stores in downtown, buying pearl necklaces, jade pendants, and gold bracelets. They then wrapped the jewelry in *habotai* scarves, packed the items into tin cans, and buried them deep in the backyard.

"Maybe the cans are still there," I said.

"We didn't bury them *that* deep," she laughed, half-heartedly. "I just hope some poor construction workers found the jewelry, instead of some rich haole developers."

That drive months ago around Mom's old neighborhood might have triggered more than just feelings of nostalgia; it may have also stirred up past bitterness as my mother thought about what her family had endured during World War II. Not only was Grandpa shipped to a federal prison in Santa Fe while the rest of the family was sent to Arkansas, but the government had resisted any pleas to reunite the family unless they agreed to be sent to Japan in an exchange of civilians. This was in 1943, during the height of the war. At that time, the federal government was desperate for the return of U.S. citizens who had been stranded in Japan and other parts of Asia when the war broke out, and my grandparents, my mother, and her older brother, my Uncle Yuki, were swept up in the one-for-one exchange. Adding insult to injury, the federal government referred to this barter of human bodies as a "repatriation," which was an outrageous misnomer. My mother and Uncle Yuki were both born and raised in Hawai'i; they had never even set foot in Japan before.

That day, holding Mom's rejection letter while sitting with her on the living room sofa of my parents' home, I didn't yet fully appreciate her outrage. Unfortunately, I tried to lighten her mood by playfully teasing her, "Well, you didn't even want the reparation in the first place, anyway," but this was the exact wrong thing to do. Mom snatched the letter from my hand and exited the room without saying a word.

***

In the ensuing months, I never once brought up the subject of the reparations, figuring it was best to let Mom initiate any discussion of that painful topic, should she choose to. Eventually, over time, I had even forgotten about her rejection, but all that changed on Election Day 1994.

Ever since I could remember, my parents always took voting very seriously. On every Election Day, they would dress up, with my father in one of his finest aloha shirts, a nice pair of slacks, and polished dress shoes, and my mother usually in either a beautiful mu'umu'u or an elegant blouse and skirt. They would look like they were going out for a fancy dinner at an expensive restaurant in Waikīkī, rather than heading up the street to their polling location. As a kid, I thought that everyone had to dress up to vote, like going to a formal church service. Only later did I realize that it was my parents' way of showing full respect to the tenets of democracy. They never took for granted their right to vote, perhaps because their citizenship had been so egregiously challenged during World War II.

Unfortunately, on Election Day 1994, when our country was deciding between a second term for George H.W. Bush or an abrupt change of course with Bill Clinton, I was running late because of unusually cumbersome traffic on the H-1 freeway. When I arrived at my parents' home to pick them up to vote, Mom was more than annoyed. And that irritation mushroomed into anger when she saw how I was dressed: T-shirt, shorts, and rubber slippers She could barely contain herself as she asked, her voice saturated in equal parts reproach and sarcasm, "Are we going to the polling site or to the beach?"

"Geesh, Mom, give me a break. Traffic on the freeway was horrendous."

"I don't care. We are voting for our next president. This happens only once every four years. Show some respect next time!"

I was taken aback by the pure intensity of her voice, which had quickly reduced me to a young boy in elementary school. The truth was that I had taken the day off from work and had promised Dad that I'd help him with yardwork afterward so I hadn't thought to dress up. But I wasn't going to argue with Mom, especially when she was in such a foul mood.

Later that day, after Dad and I had finished pruning some bushes, he brought a couple of beers for us to enjoy while we relaxed on the patio. It was a sunny, splendidly warm day, and we were both soaked in perspiration. We sat in silence for a while, looking at the backyard, admiring the results of several hours of our hard labor. Then, as Dad returned from the kitchen with some pupus to munch on, he said, "Don't mind your mother. She just got some bad news yesterday."

"Oh no, from the doctor? Is she okay?"

"Sorry, nothing like that. She's as healthy as ever, but she got another letter from the U.S. Department of Justice. Her appeal for the reparation was denied."

"What? I didn't even know that she had appealed the rejection."

"Yeah, she even hired a lawyer to help her, and she had to submit all kinds of paperwork, this document and that file. It was so humbug, but she was really hopeful and then, after several years of bureaucratic bullshit, she was denied again."

"What was the reasoning?"

"Something about her being ineligible because she went to Japan during the war."

I stopped eating the *tako poke*. "But she didn't just go there. She was sent there."

"I know, but that was the excuse. Your mother was furious when she read the letter. I've never seen her quite like that."

"I don't blame her. To be slapped in the face once was bad enough, but then to be slapped twice?"

My father took a big gulp of beer. "I know you meant well, but now I really wish you hadn't encouraged her to apply for the reparation."

I couldn't believe what I was hearing. "Dad, you know that Mom has the right to every single penny of that $20,000. I mean, really, after all that her family lost during the war, and I'm not talking only about their possessions and property."

"I know, I know, but I'm just afraid that she won't be able to let this go."

"Well, maybe that wouldn't be such a bad thing."

Dad laughed, "You have no idea how hardheaded your mother can be." Then, after grabbing two more beers for us from the kitchen, he began telling me something I had never heard before—the story of how he and Mom met in Japan after the war, when he was working for the U.S. occupation forces as an interpreter. After months of courtship they were married, and the plan was for Dad to return to Hawai'i first, to find a home for them to live in, with Mom following several months later. But when Mom arrived in Honolulu, where she had been born and raised, she was abruptly detained by the immigration officials. Much to her horror, she learned she had somehow been stripped of her U.S. citizenship. In stunned silence, she listened as an immigration official explained that she had unwittingly renounced her citizenship by moving to an enemy country

(Japan) during the War. To make matters worse, the Japanese government had declared her a non-citizen as well, even though she was the child of Japanese nationals. The bottom line: Mom had become a stateless person—literally a woman with no country to call her home.

For more than a week, Mom was held at a detention center on Sand Island in Honolulu Harbor while the authorities tried to sort out what to do with her. During that time, Dad visited her every day, pleading with her to register as a resident alien. Then, later, she could apply for U.S. citizenship using their marriage to bolster her case. But Mom was resolute. She would reclaim her citizenship based on the merits of her case, and that was that.

While Mom was in bureaucratic limbo, Dad's brothers and sisters took turns accompanying him on his visits to Sand Island, trying to convince her to give up her seemingly quixotic battle. They were all worried because Mom was so young, only in her early twenties, and appeared so delicate. Also, they were afraid for her after hearing that many of the Sand Island detainees had lice, tuberculosis, and other communicable diseases. Eventually, even Dad's mother went to visit Mom in hopes of convincing her to change her mind. I had to wonder what my paternal grandmother thought. In all likelihood, she expected her future daughter-in-law from Japan to be a dutiful, docile young lady. And yet there was Mom, defiantly fighting the U.S. government over her citizenship.

Eventually, the immigration officials conceded that, because she was a minor when she was sent to Japan, she had not actually renounced her citizenship. After all, what was she to do, remain in Arkansas by herself while her parents were shipped to Japan? She had to go where her parents went, and she shouldn't be penalized for that. It was a sweet victory, and from that day on Mom never took her citizenship lightly.

I sat there on that cloudless day, soaking in everything Dad just told me. "So that's why Mom was so mad this morning."

Dad nodded, "You know she's never, ever missed voting. I remember once, this was before you were born, she was so sick with the flu and our house was almost flooded from a violent tropical storm. She still insisted that we vote, even though the election that day was only a local runoff for a city council member."

"Whew, I guess that's why she really didn't appreciate me showing up late this morning the way I was dressed."

Dad chuckled, "No, I don't think she appreciated that at all."

***

The next four years were a blur. I should have suspected that something was wrong with Dad when he abruptly stopped volunteering at our neighborhood church, the Kotohira Jinsha. He told me that he just wanted to take a break from helping out, but one day when I was shopping at Marukai, I ran into Mrs. Watanabe, a longtime friend of my father's who also was a member of that church. She asked how Dad was doing, and the deep concern in her eyes unsettled me. As we continued talking, I became increasingly dismayed thinking about my father's mental health. She told me that, at first he was having trouble remembering people's names but then he'd completely forget about certain commitments he had made. "The last time I saw him," Mrs. Watanabe recalled, "I could tell he didn't recognize me and was embarrassed having to pretend to know me. But please tell him that we all get old and he shouldn't be ashamed to come to church."

Of course Mom and I had noticed that Dad's memory had been slipping but we had assumed it was all part of normal aging, not anything more pernicious. But after talking with Mrs. Watanabe, every odd thing that Dad had done, like leaving a screwdriver in the refrigerator, accrued such ominous import. An appointment with a neurologist confirmed our suspicions of Alzheimer's, which in my father's case progressed with frightening speed. Within a year he couldn't be outdoors by himself, and within three years his body had forgotten even how to perform rudimentary actions, like swallowing food.

Now, almost a year after Dad's passing, I was still worried about Mom, whether she would eventually rally from the loss of her longtime partner in life, or whether she would wither. She had yet to touch any of his clothes or other belongings in their bedroom, although I had offered a few times to help clear and donate his things to his church and Goodwill. More worrisome, she had let many of her friendships lapse and would leave the house only to shop for groceries.

So I was pleasantly surprised when she called one day to invite me out for dinner. Her voice was light and cheerful, something I hadn't heard in a while, and I was elated at her choice of restaurant: Ideta, our neighborhood favorite for Japanese cuisine. Ideta was where our family had celebrated many important events—my acceptance into college, Dad's retirement, my parents sending in their last mortgage payment.

After we were seated, Mom handed me a small, rectangular piece of thick paper, smiling in anticipation of my reaction. It was a check from the federal government made out to her for the sum of $20,000. I couldn't believe my eyes. "What is this, your reparation?"

"Yes, finally," she beamed.

I sat there in awed silence. Actually, I hadn't really thought about her redress application for quite some time. After her appeal was denied, I had assumed it was a closed matter and had pushed thoughts of it well outside my mind, less I become aggravated about the painful injustice. "Did they just send you the check out of the blue?"

Mom reached for a piece of paper from her purse. It was a letter from the Department of Justice, stating that people had been reviewing an earlier interpretation of the Civil Liberties Act of 1988. Mom explained that, after she had appealed the initial rejection, she learned that she'd been declared ineligible because she had "relocated" to an enemy country (that is, Japan) during the war. She was incensed. "I did not just relocate," her voice indignant. "I was deported."

Before I could say anything, we were interrupted by our waitress, who described the daily specials, with each dish sounding more delectable than the previous. Mom went with her usual shrimp tempura and I ordered one of the specials: *buri nitsuke*, yellowtail fish simmered in shoyu, sake, and mirin. After the waitress left, I said, "I know the federal government isn't known for its speed, but I'm still surprised it took four years for them to admit its error."

"You don't know the half of it!"

Over dinner, Mom recounted her long battle, a crusade that would turn on pivotal information from her past. After several unsuccessful legal maneuvers, Mom's attorney figured out that he had been attacking the problem from the wrong direction. From his research on Mom and her family, he had learned about her earlier immigration difficulties, that she was initially denied her U.S. citizenship when she returned to Hawai'i after the war. He then seized on that information to make his case. He shrewdly argued that, when Mom was detained at Sand Island decades ago, the U.S. government had eventually admitted its error in denying her the right to her citizenship because, as was ruled at the time, she was just a minor when her family was shipped to Japan. So how could she now be held accountable for the decisions that her parents may, or may not, have made?

I stopped eating. "That's amazing, the connection between the two cases."

"There's something more," Mom added. She explained that, according to her attorney, the Department of Justice had recently ruled on key language in the Civil Liberties Act of 1988—text that had expressly ruled ineligible any person who had relocated to an enemy country during the war. The ruling was that the exclusion applied only to those individuals who had *voluntarily* relocated. This then exempted minors like my mother.

As I sat there, trying to absorb everything that Mom had just told me, she handed me a second letter, this one signed by President Bill Clinton. In it, the President apologized on behalf of the country for "the actions that unfairly denied Japanese Americans and their families' fundamental liberties during World War II."

Mom lowered her chopsticks onto her rice bowl, and looked straight into my eyes. "You don't know how much that letter means to me, much more than the $20,000."

"I can't imagine."

Then, her lips curling into a warm smile, she announced, "And this is what we're gonna do with the $20,000. You and I are taking a trip to Japan, where you can finally meet your Uncle Yuki."

"Wow, that would be awesome!"

"We're going to have so much fun. I only wish Dad were still here to join us."

We ate in silence for a few minutes, both of us deep in thought. Then, as Mom finished the last of her tempura, she said, "You know he would often call me 'hardheaded.'"

"Well, you kinda are," I smiled.

"It was a big problem when we first got married and we'd clash even over little things, whether we could afford a color TV, what color to paint the bedroom, which kind of fruit tree to plant, mango or lychee. Thankfully over the years I learned to control my stubbornness, but fighting for the reparation was different. I had to be hardheaded. I just did."

I was suddenly overcome with such emotion. "Mom, I'm so proud of you, your courage to fight for what was right, your not giving up against the federal government."

"What, me?" she chuckled, as she sipped her tea. "Come on, I'm just a simple housewife who didn't even finish high school."

Now it was my turn to laugh. "Yeah, right, as if . . ."

"Wait till you taste the food in Japan," Mom interrupted me. "The dishes here are good, but you're gonna love everything in Japan."

Something told me that the food wasn't the only thing I'd be enjoying about our upcoming trip. It would be the first time I'd be visiting the land of my ancestors and, for Mom, the trip would complete the journey she had long been on. She had once told me that she felt guilty that it had fallen on Uncle Yuki to care for Grandpa and Grandma in their elderly years before they passed. Mom had sent him money on several occasions to help with the costs incurred with that care, but now she could express her gratitude in person for all that her older brother had done.

After we had finished our dinner and the waitress had brought the check, Mom quickly seized it, her fast, nimble reflexes startling me. "This meal is on me," she declared. "Or, actually, this meal is on the U.S. government, as it should be." With that, she smiled, her face quickly softening, with years of bitterness melting into a moment of blissful triumph.

thomas iannucci

boy
a love letter

the boy had been so careful. it was hard to be careful, when you was stoned, not to mention a little tipsy, too. more than tipsy. not quite drunk, per se, but buzzing, definitely buzzing. okay maybe a little drunk but not all buss kine, like the way his dad and his uncles would get buss on the weekends, definitely not lidat. well kinda, it was hard to say, being the one in question who might or might not have been all buss, but still, he had been careful. he had his braddahs drop him off up the road, far enough from his hale that his parents wouldn't hear the grumbling of jayven's beat up tacoma, but near enough that he wouldn't work up a sweat. the boy's dad worked early, and so did his wife—his dad's wife, not the boy's—well, not his dad's wife either, cuz they wasn't really married, but they said they was—it was complicated—she wasn't his mom—well, she wasn't either of their moms, obviously, but she wasn't the boy's mom cuz his mada was dead, but no one really liked to talk about any of that, so yeah, definitely complicated—and anyway the point was that the boy was careful because he knew he wouldn't be able to shower till after they left the next morning, right before school, and so he had to be careful and he had to be quiet.

and he was.

he was so careful and so quiet, he even made sure to spray some wd-40 on the door's creakysqueaky hinges before he left for the party that night, because he didn't want to make a sound when he came back. the boy had been particularly proud of that idea, because he wasn't considered to be particularly smart, and he'd come up with that idea all by himself. so not only was the boy so careful and so quiet, he was also, in his estimation, so pretty damned clever, too, even if he was also little lotta bit buss.

buss, and clever, and careful, and quiet.

and then he opened the door and it all went to hell cuz his old man was sitting right there on his favorite leather chair, grinning like they was best friends, which scared the crap outta the boy because the old man never smiled and they was most certainly not friends at all.

"ehhhhhh boy!" said the man, slapping the arm of his recliner so hard it shook the tiny lamp on the stand next to him. "i was starting to worry you forgot wea you lived! wat, late night study sesh?"

"o, yeah," said the boy, his heart pounding in his chest. his faddah knew, guarantee. he felt sick, from more than just the beer and weed. though being real that wasn't helping either. "lost track of time. sorry."

"'a'ole pilikia my braddah, studying is important. mo bettah you study den you off partying and da kine, right?" the man waved him away.

"right, yeah," said the boy, and for a brief moment his cloudy mind allowed him to hope that maybe, just maybe, his dad was just very, very drunk. wouldn't be the first time. "eh well, i goin go sleep now, i pretty tired—"

the boy's faddah was off the chair and across the room in an instant. it seemed a blur to the boy, stoned and buss—definitely buss, there was no denying it, his head was spinning—as he was. he blinked and the man was in front of him, opened his mouth to gasp but couldn't on account of his faddah's giant hand grabbing him by the throat—and his lower jaw too, he really did have big hands—and pinning him against the wall.

"o wat, you tired, ah?" the man wasn't smiling anymore. his face was hard to see in the dim yellow lamplight that was the only disruption of the darkness in the house, but the boy had enough previous experience to guess what it looked like. barely concealed fury, was his guess. "well guess what, youngblood, i ste tired too. tired of your crap! in fact, i'm exhausted." the hand squeezed tighter and tighter, and the boy was distracted by the fact that he was being choked only by the pain he felt in his jaw as the man's bear paw of a hand dug into it.

"hoi babe, what da hell you doin? its tree a.m." the voice of the boy's stepmother—well, not legally, but what else was he supposed to call his father's girlfriend—aunty maybe but it hurt her feelings, she never said anything but the boy knew so he never called her aunty anymore but even though she was nice he just couldn't bring himself to call her mom so really he just tried his best not to call her anything at all—so anyway her voice coincided with the flipping of a switch, and the dark room burst into light. the man let go, and the boy slumped back against the wall, coughing and sputtering. "we both gotta work in da morning."

"sorry ah babe," said the man. "but i finally bin bust this buggah. try look his eyes. look!" he reached over and yanked the boy back up. "how's dis guy! buggah is all bline. i no even believe! and he had try fo tell me he was just sleepy from too much studying. ha!"

"it's true," said the boy, and then the man shook him violently.

"no eva lie to me, boy! who you tink you ah? lying to yo own faddah lidat. i should broke yo ass right now." the boy's head banged against the wall and he winced but stayed silent. because he knew better.

"babe, nuff already." his wife/girlfriend/whatever pulled the man away, and the boy once again deflated against the wall. "c'mon, just stop it."

"i not da one who gotta stop," said the man, shaking her off him, not violently, no, but definitely firmly. "braddahman here is on a bad path. he know i no like him out late to begin wit, let alone partying."

"you dunno for sure if he had—" the woman began, but the man cut her off.

"brah come on! i can smell da crip from here! and try look his eyes, i'm telling you dis faka is all buss and all bline and even if he neva go party it's da same damn ting!"

the boy, who was in fact all buss and all bline and now in pain and therefore angry and therefore brave because he was as previously mentioned all buss and all bline, stood up and looked his faddah in da eyes.

"brah get off my back already damn! it wasn't like i was out vandalizing stuff we was jus cruzin, we wasn't half as bad as you guys at my age! why you always gotta be dis way?"

"wat?" his old man stiffened. and his voice got quiet, very quiet, and he took a step towards the boy. "who you tink you talkin to boy?"

"i talkin to you!" the boy's voice was shrill with anger and also to be honest more than a little fear too, a lot more than a little. "why you tink i like go out and smoke and drink in da first place anyway, ha? you made me lidat! i ste so stressed all da time and scared too, at least dis gets my mind off everyting!"

"braddah, who you tink you talking to, ha? i look like one of yo friends?" his faddah lunged at the boy, but his girlfriend got between them.

"babe no!" the woman was not small by any means, but it still took all her strength to slow the man down. he barely even registered her, his eyes locked squarely on the boy.

"eh wat, you like puff out your chest ah?" the man said. only he didn't just say it, he was screaming. guarantee he was waking up the neighbors again, which meant the police would be there soon enough. the boy would've been irritated if he wasn't so angry and afraid. they needed a word for this feeling, angryandafraid, cuz he felt it all the time and it was different than just being angry, or just being afraid. it gave him cold sweats and a burning in his stomach and made him want to punch a wall but also to throw up first. definitely it needed a name. angfraid maybe. no that was dumb. but then again the boy always thought about dumb stuff when his dad got like this, it was a good distraction. so maybe it was clever after all. meanwhile his faddah was still going off. "dis boy tink he one hammah now! come you like come den. i like sampo fast kine! wassup youngblood, come i like see!"

"brah why you gotta be dat way?" the boy shifted himself into a non threatening position, but he couldn't keep the frustration out of his voice. "everyting wit you is jus fo scrap. not everyting gotta be lidat, why you always gotta get so nuts?"

"you da one to talk, boy," said his dad. "i heard about you and da braddahs jumping dat haole boy up da road last week. i bet you tink you one killah now ah? we go den, cuz i like see!"

"eh you know what, we go den!" the boy was at his limit. he was so scared he felt sick, he felt angfraidsickdone. done because he was tired and enough was enough and he was just drunk enough that his ang won over his fraid. "i ste so sick of you dad i—" whatever else he was going say next was cut off by the man's fist slamming into his mouth.

"babe! i told you no you faka!" the boys stepmom slapped his faddah and pulled at him. the slap didn't seem to hurt him physically, but he looked at her in genuine shock.

"what da hell was dat fo?" his surprise gave the boy enough time to stop himself from falling over. his old man never hit him in the mouth before, it was usually bodyshots, or maybe a slap to the head. but this was different. he swallowed the blood in his mouth because he knew spitting it on the floor would just make things worse. it was salty. the blood not the floor. though that was prolly salty too.

"you went way too far!" his stepmom was a tough woman. tougher than the boy felt. "apologize!"

"hell no!" said his dad. "if anything i should broke his—"

"no!" his stepmom slapped the boy's dad again. "he's fourteen years old dumbass! you like go jail o wat?"

"brah babe, you always take his side!" the man shook off her slap and ground his teeth. but he didn't raise a hand to strike her. the boy had always been a little jealous over that. "no wonder he so spoiled! dis boy is heading fo trouble i telling you, but i guess nobody can see it but me." he shook his head, and the boy was amazed by the balls the man had. he actually looked disappointed.

"somebody gotta take his side! cuz you always just step on him." the woman put her finger in the man's face and he shoved it away. "he not even my blood but i no can just sit here and watch you treat him lidat. it ain't right."

"nobody ever takes my side," said the man. "nobody ever did take my side, not once. it's just life, you no can baby him or he going be crippled!"

"i not one baby and i not crippled," said the boy but the man ignored him. as usual.

"my mada neva did take my side once!" the man went on. "when my faddah would get all buss and start giving us lickins, she neva got involved. she knew her place!"

"and wat den, you tink i dunno my place?" the woman put her hands on her hips.

"no!" the man shook his head. "no, that's not wat i trying fo . . . my mada knew her place cuz my old man would've buss her up too. instead my braddahs and i learned our lessons and we stayed outta trouble. and i trying fo teach him, but you not letting me!"

"teach me?" the boy really did spit on the floor this time. "wat kine sick lesson is dis ha? teaching me fo be afraid of my faddah? cuz if so, well done!"

"teach you some respect fo one ting, boy!" the man shoved the boy, but this time, he was ready. the boy stepped back and turned away, causing his old man to lose his balance. and then he crashed into the wall. and the boy laughed. the man swore and punched a hole in the wall. and the boy stopped laughing.

"eh dummeh, no laugh, you jus making tings worse," his dad's girlfriend snapped. but the boy was way ahead of her. dat coulda been his face. she turned to da man. "but not as bad as you. you better fix dis."

"i will. tomorrow," said the man, but the woman shook her head.

"i not talkin about da wall," she said.

"i been trying fo fix dis! you dunno wat is correction, ha? i trying fo correct him. i neva had one mommy fo hide behind, so i listened and i learned from my faddah. but you not letting me teach him."

"da only ting you teaching him is fo be exactly like you," she replied.

"and wat?" the man asked. "is dat so bad? i turned out okay!"

"you turned out jus like grandpa!" said the boy. he never did meet the old man's old man. but from what little he knew, it was bad. he was. the grandpa, his grandpa, not his dad's. which was why his dad was such a prick.

"i nothing like my faddah!" the man was roaring now. his eyes was bulging. and so was the veins around his neck. his whole body was taut with anger, and he kept opening and closing his hands, making them into fists. then opening them again. and repeat. "i provide fo dis family! i had buss my ass to provide, right? i kep a job all my life, right? neva get fired, neva go jail, neva cheat or fool around on you, right babe?" he went on before the woman could respond. he didn't look mad anymore to the boy, just desperate— desperate for . . . something. the boy didn't know what, but it was a weird look for his faddah. he never did see him lidat.

"every day, i went down to da plantation and worked, since i was young. and den wen da plantation had close i wen get one job construction. neva did complain! when his maddah died, i paid fo everyting, neva took one handout. kept da boy in school. neva got one tank you. and das okay cuz dats my job." the man looked back and forth between the boy and his girlfriendwife. "and yet you tellin me i like my old man? dat faka neva did care at all wat i was doing, neva did check in wit me and my braddahs, let us get into anykine trouble lidat!"

"i tot you said he kept you outta trouble by teaching you good lessons?' said the boy.

"eh boy, no get smart wit me," said the man. "i learned, whether he meant fo teach me or not. and i da only one of my friends neva go jail. all da boys you ste cruzing wit now, i knew all their faddahs, and all dem guys is trouble. their faddahs was trouble, their unkos was trouble, and they goin be trouble too! das why i been telling you, no go out! especially not wit dem! they goin take you down one bad path!" he clutched and pulled at his own hair. "you like go jail like dem o wat? yo braddah already been in juvie! and da odda one get one court case next week—you tink i dunno but you no can fool me boy, i get eyes everywea. and if you would just listen, you would know i not being mean, if anything i rather give you a little pain now and save you a lotta pain later! i rather hurt and save you than let you ruin your life!"

the boy was trying to listen. honestly. he was. but his mouth was bloody and his head hurt and his stomach was sick and he was drunkandstoned and angfraiddone and just so confused—how did his faddah know alladat? and why didn't he say nothing earlier? and what was he trying fo say right now? all of it was bouncing around in his head and his heart and it was painful and confusing and overwhelming yeah definitely overwhelming honestly it was just a lot—and he just wanted to go home, but this was his home, but it wasn't home, not really, because home wasn't supposed to feel like this, home was supposed to be the place you could relax, the place you felt safest, and this place wasn't that, and the boy figured he never felt anything like that at all since his mom died so maybe she was home and maybe home died when she did and it was all just so much that the boy started crying.

"you serious?" asked the man. "you really ste crying? no be one panty boy, i neva raise one mahu."

"enough," said the woman. "fix dis. look what you did. was it worth it?"

"i neva did anyting, i just—"

"fix it." the woman stared at him until he shifted, uncomfortable under her gaze.

"look, i sorry boy, but i just . . . i neva mean to . . ." he shook his head. "i . . ." his voice hitched, and he cleared his throat. the boy fought for control long enough to look back at his dad. it was hard. but he did it anyway. "da ting is . . . well, you know ah, i . . . uh, i . . ." the man's voice was shaky. and he kept blinking and looking back at her. her being his girlfriendwife. he looked at her and she looked at the boy and the boy looked at him. and the man looked back at the boy and said, "i . . . i no mo da words. i dunno how fo . . . i . . ."

the man looked at the boy and the boy looked at the man and the man didn't have the words and the boy didn't care because at this point he didn't think he could understand his faddah even if he did have them, even if he had all da words in the world, and he said all of dem, even den, da boy wouldn't be able fo understand, he was sure, so instead he said "it's okay dad" and he patted him on da shoulder and went to bed and they neva talk about any of that ever again, even though they both thought about it almost every night for the rest of their lives until one day many years later when da boy was grown up and he had his own boy and den i understood but by then it was too late cuz my faddah is dead and he ain't neva coming back so instead i wrote dis story cuz my therapist said might help, but it neva, and dat is dat is dat. ps sorry ah fo da pidgin but writing normal kine english was to hard so i gave up. da end.

ANN INOSHITA

Get Chance (January 4, 2021)

I was cancer free fo couple years
til my oncologist told me dat my blood tests neva look right,
so I had one ultrasound on my neck.

He noticed dat one of my lymph nodes was swollen,
so he recommended dat I get one biopsy
and arranged one phone appointment wit me
fo go ova da biopsy results.

Usually, I see my oncologist in one medical building,
but dis time I get one video phone conference
cuz of COVID.

Wen he call me on my iPhone,
I can hear him but I no can see him.
No matter to me. I just like hear my biopsy results.

He tell me dat I have cancer.
Den my call get disconnected
cuz da medical assistant wen call me
fo ask if I got in contact wit my docta.

I told her dat I got disconnected,
and I wanna talk to my docta.
She tell me my docta is wit one nodda patient.

I tell her, "I want to talk to *my* doctor about *my* cancer!"
Den she tell me dat he going call me as soon as possible.
Sheesh, so I waiting fo my docta fo fucking call me back.

Wen he call me, I tell him,
"I just found out I have *cancer,*
and I need to *know* what the next steps are."

He wen apologize to me
and said dat he going consult

wit one nodda docta fo next steps.
Dey want to check if da cancer spread
to any odda part of my body.
Dey looking at surgery, scans, and treatment.

I teach and school going start next week,
so I ask him if can teach online dis semester.
He said can. I just going be out wen recovering from surgery.

Afta da call, I try get myself together.
Breathe.
Good ting dey wen find um early.
Going be okay.
Get chance.

ANN INOSHITA

Da Diet dat Make Grown Men Cry

My docta tell me dat I gotta take one body scan
fo see if my cancer wen spread before dey start treatment.
Tree weeks befo my scan, I gotta go on one low iodine diet—
da diet dat make grown men cry.

No can eat iodized salt.
No can eat prepared food.
No can drink tap wata.
Gotta make everyting from scratch.
Gotta cook everyting wit distilled wata.

No can eat seafood.
No can eat soy.
No can eat seaweed.
Eh, I Japanese. How I going do dis?

No can eat dairy.
No can eat pre-made bread.
No can eat egg yolks.
No can eat pretty much wateva you like eat.
I can eat all da fruits and vegetables I like,
but I gotta make my own salad dressing.

Rice take too much wata fo make
and I no like waste all my distilled wata.
I no can be Japanese,
so I try be Italian.
I make minestrone soup.
I make marinara sauce.
I eat pasta.

Now get
no salt ketchup
no salt peanut butter.
Good ting
cuz neva have dis kine befo.

I tired cook,
but wat else I going do?
No mo choice.

I stay lying down on my bed
and turn on da news.
Dey talking about Texas.
Get below freezing temperatures.
Wata pipes wen bust.
Da electric grid went off.
No mo powa.
No mo wata.
No mo food.
Damn.

I stand up,
go to da kitchen,
and boil some distilled wata
fo one cup of coffee
with non-dairy creamer.
Wat I complaining about?
Everyting going be okay.

ANN INOSHITA

Buy da Book

Wen I told my bachan I wanted fo be one writer,
she look at me long time like she neva know wat fo say.

Den she knew wat fo say. She ask me,
"How you going make money?
How you going eat?
How you going pay bills?
You like write? Not enough.
How you going live?"

Den she tell me slowly like I still no undastand,
"People. Gotta. Buy. Da book."

Den my madda gave me one *see I told you* kinda look and told me,
"You no can only write. Gotta get one job.
You can write on da side. How many people stay working."

I knew dey was right.
Even if da book was good,
no guarantee it was going be one bestseller.
Da kine dat going make you rich,
and you can buy everybody one house each.

I kept my job, but I wrote while waiting fo da bus, on da bus,
and wen eva I had extra time.
I wanted fo be one real writer, but I knew dey was right.
People gotta buy da book.

ANN INOSHITA

Wea Pidgin Stay

Da teacha stay writing on da chalkboard,
so she neva notice one Pidgin fly in da classroom.

I neva seen one Pidgin in class befo.

Da teacha heard um and turned around.
She told da class dat Pidgin no belong hea.

She try shoo um out but da Pidgin flew
by da desks, da windows, da walls.

Was hard fo catch um cuz da Pidgin move fast
and neva like go away.

Da window stay open.
How come da Pidgin no leave?

Da bugga neva like go away.
Da Pidgin made big noise, and she got mo mad.

I asked da teacha why da Pidgin no can be in da classroom.
Den she got mad at me and told me I no undastand.

I was going talk some mo but she neva like listen.

Took long time but she finally cornered da Pidgin
and wen grab um. She wen throw um out da door.

Pidgin no stay in da classroom,
but I can still hear um inside.

DARLENE M. JAVAR

Mom's Rules

Over the months, each day
we took a breath,
postured our hearts
before turning into Room 222,
always in compliance
with her rules:
Be strong. Don't cry.

The decisive procedure
wasn't just another
can't-see-she's-going-to-make-it,
call-the-family surgery.
Nurses wheeled that body
back from surgery, its blood
draining into plastic bags and cylinders
at each side of its jet black head,
at each side of its swollen torso,
at each motionless foot,
between its grotesque legs—
spatter on white sheets.
Then she had the nerve
to open her knowing eyes
so we couldn't cry.

LISA LINN KANAE

Excerpt from *Mākālei,* a novel in progress

Chapter 4 Three Birds

Sterling would not stop singing that damn song. The Bob Marley one. You know. About those three little birds. When the four of us—me, Jude, Gleason, and Sterling—walked clear across the shopping center to the big bird cage outside Shirokiya's, Sterling sang that song. He sang that song as we watched the tiny birds hop from branch to branch as fat white clouds hung in a bright, blue sky over that giant cage. Sterling sang when Jude complained about his mother's new boyfriend. He sang when I bitched about how the night shift assistant to the assistant manager stuck me in Dining Room for my whole shift.

I said to Sterling, my whole shift! I had to hot mop every hour, clear tables, and empty garbage bins. Cold french fries and dried up ketchup all over the trays. McDonald's wrappers on the floor.

Sterling started singing about those birds again.

I couldn't help it. I had to know. What is that damn song about, I finally asked Sterling. Does it have a hidden meaning? A hidden agenda like the assistant to the assistant manager has a hidden agenda whenever she calls me ka piñata and I have to tell her for the one-hundredth goddamn time my name is Ka'upena, which is Hawaiian, not Mexican.

Sterling shook his head, rolled his eyes, and sang.

The birds are a symbol, right, I said. We are the birds, right? But what exactly is the message us birds stay singing? What does it all mean, Sterling?

Chill pill, Sterling said. This isn't *Lord of the Flies.* No need broke your brain looking for a thesis. Just listen to the lyrics. Get three birds. They small. They are born to open their beaks and break into song. Birds sing to attract mates, signal rivals, claim territories. It's a form of power.

Bird #1 Everybody Knows

One time, last Christmas, while eating lunch in the cafeteria, I asked Sterling who he thought was more cute—Shawn Cassidy or David Cassidy, but he was staring off into space like I wasn't even sitting across from him. I picked up a Tater Tot from my lunch tray and aimed for his head, and the son-of-a-gun opened his mouth and snapped it up.

He chewed and chewed, and then said, I need to get off this rock. There's gotta be more to life than canned chili con carne and avoiding Junior Bothelo. I'm finally taking Performing Arts, and Junior and his gorillas cruise at the end of the hall picking lice off each other waiting for me to pass by. I no more time for them. I have to rehearse for the Christmas Variety Show.

As long as I've known Sterling Celestino Silva, he was never one to wallow in self-pity, but this time, he was up against Garland Bothelo, Jr. Everybody knew that when Junior had failed to make the varsity football team, he came to school the next day wearing a pair of mirrored aviator sunglasses. In class, Mrs. Hanohano had insisted he take off those sunglasses, and when he did, it was like the air was sucked out of the room. Junior's left eye was swollen shut and dark, dark, purple, and everybody knew Junior's father, Garland Bothelo, Sr., was responsible. Mrs. Hanohano told Junior he could wear the sunglasses, but then they took a walk to the counselor's office. If that wasn't bad enough, Junior's chick, Nalani Mitchell, lead songleader and Tahiti Imports swimsuit model, had just broken up with Junior. She said she had to focus on her studies, but everybody knew he punched her after he found out that she had been offered a modeling job in Japan.

Sterling popped another Tater Tot into his mouth and chewed.

How's rehearsal? he asked me. I saw the gray onesies. With ears and a tail?

And knitted mittens, I added.

Mittens, Sterling said. Frickin mittens?

Madison had pulled together fifteen of us junior girls to perform a disco version of the *Dance of the Sugar Plum Fairy*—in mouse costumes. She asked Sterling to be our Mouse King, but Sterling said no. He told Madison, you don't have to watch PBS to know that the mice no dance during the *Dance of the Sugar Plum Fairy,* and besides, he had other plans. He had a solo performance, and it was top secret. He refused to tell any of us what he was up to even if everybody knew he asked Miss Parsons, the drama teacher, to coach him. He did tell me, however, that the Nutcracker Prince actually kills the Mouse King in Act I but no tell Madison because he had told her she would make the perfect Mouse King.

On the evening of the KHS Christmas Variety Show, the student body gathered into the auditorium along with friends and families of the performers. We were outside the auditorium, fidgeting with our felt ears and safety pinning our tails. We held hands while Madison, who was proudly wearing the Mouse King crown, led us in a prayer. Poor Madison. She got all emotional and started to cry, so we gathered around her—a circle of girls sweating in gray fleece and white mittens—thanking her for all her hard work and leadership until we heard Miss Parsons. Are all the mice present, Miss Parsons yelled. Very good. Follow me, and move swiftly and silently, my friends.

We walked single file behind Miss Parsons, who told everyone to stand in line in order of appearance. We passed the Hawaiian Club girls wearing pink satin holokū and a skinny boy holding a guitar; the Japanese Club boys wearing happi coats and tabis; the Pinoy Club boys and girls fidgeting with their scarves and tinikling sticks; and the Chinese Club girls holding sticks wrapped with wide red silk ribbon. Miss Parsons directed us to stand in line between three boys dressed like Michael Jackson and the pep squad. The pep squad wore cut-off denim overalls and straw hats. Behind the pep squad were the song leaders, dressed in square dance skirts with fluffy petticoats. I searched the line for Sterling, but Miss Parsons got up in my face shouting orders.

People! People! Listen up, Parsons yelled. Enter the auditorium single file, just like we rehearsed. Sit on the lowest bleachers around the basketball court. I will cue you when it is your turn. Watch me. I will be to the left of the stage under the American flag. The campus security officer will be right next to me, so no funny business. May the force be with you.

The first half of the show was traditional cultural dances that we saw at every May Day pageant since we could walk, so everybody knew those groups were practically pros. I really liked the boys who could dance like Michael Jackson, but that skinny, senior boy named Ernie, who accompanied the girls in the holokū, could really sing. They dedicated their song to George Helm, who Ernie called a true Hawaiian. When I overheard one of the parents say that boy was going be famous one day, I wanted to turn in my mouse costume and bail. Ernie was special. When he was pau, the auditorium was filled with cheehoo and hana hou. A few of the adults were even wiping tears from their faces.

Us mice didn't make anyone cry, and I wouldn't call our performance flawless, but we were disco dancing mice. We could do no wrong. After the last shimmy forward, shimmy back, bump to the left, bump to the right, we were bathed with applause and our mouse asses—tails and all—were safely back on the bleachers. I waited for the pep squad and song leaders to take the floor since I thought they were next, but Miss Parsons was motioning for them to stay put. And then, without warning, the auditorium was jolted by the sound of an electric guitar riff and a stomping drum beat. Madison asked, what song is this? I pulled off my mouse ears and said, well your Highness, this song is fucking "Rebel, Rebel" by the alien rock god, David Fucking Bowie. My Auntie Sam has his albums. And I knew. I just knew.

With arms stretched-out wide and long-stemmed roses in both hands, Sterling, all one-hundred pounds of pure drama, entered the auditorium and strutted onto the stage.

Everyone—students, parents, grannies, and grandpas—laughed and screamed and clapped and stomped to the beat of that song. Sterling was a sight to behold. Glittery platform shoes. Black spandex tights. Purple scarf. Bare chest. White, floor-length, open satin kimono decorated with turquoise peacocks. Spiked red wig, and that famous orange and blue lightning bolt painted on half his face. He lip-synced to the lyrics as he strutted back and forth across the stage. He strutted to the bleachers and threw roses to the audience and then he leaped up and down and pumped his fist with every guitar lick. After the last line fist pump, the music faded and Sterling Silva received a standing ovation. He stood there as if he couldn't believe how much the audience had loved him. He took a quick bow and ran to the bleachers into the open arms of us giggling mice. He squeezed his skinny Bowie ass between me and Madison and practically hid behind us. It was as if the laughter and chatter of the audience would not stop, so Principal AhKam had to take the microphone to ask everyone to calm down.

How was I? Sterling asked me. Was I convincing enough?

They loved you, I screamed.

Miss Parsons is crying, Madison said.

I felt so alive, Sterling said. So fucking alive.

With my mitten, I dabbed the tears from Sterling's eyes so his lightning bolt wouldn't get ruined. We laughed and laughed until we saw Miss Parsons give Sterling a quick shaka. She motioned for the pep squad and the song leaders to take the stage.

The cheerleaders and song leaders didn't look very happy about having to follow David Bowie, but the second the sound of an acoustic guitar filled the auditorium, they kicked into autopilot. Their smiles lit up, and they bounced their hips in time to the song "Afternoon Delight" by Starland Vocal Band. Their routine was a slick western-style, hands on hips, heel, toe, heel, toe, slide, slide, slide, giddy up, giddy up, giddy up, cartwheel. Behind the cheerleaders, the song leaders gracefully twirled imaginary lassos with their white-gloved hands. When they tipped their straw hats, winked, and then twirled, everyone cheered and clapped in time with the music. Everyone except Sterling, who was staring at Junior Bothelo with so much hatred, I thought Junior's football jersey would go up in flames. Junior was staring at Nalani Mitchell, who was so beautiful, she didn't have to do anything to be loved by that crowd.

I'll never understand why Sterling did what he did, but he started laughing really loud. Like he was overacting.

Do they even know what this song is about, Sterling shouted. This song is about having sex. In the middle of the day.

Grief washed over Madison's face. But I love this song, she said.

My God, Sterling shouted. Sticks and stones rubbing together? Rockets taking flight? Look at them. Up there under the American flag making all hoedown action as if that song is about the Fourth of July. They not singing about skyrockets. They singing about orgasm.

And then, Sterling started singing over the chorus, oooooffing, oooooooffing, oof-fing for lunch. The other mice raised their mittens to hide their faces. Pretty soon the pep squad and song leaders shifted their eyes towards us. Their faces went from confused to annoyed, but they kept on dancing. Miss Parsons marched towards the audio system and turned up the music to hide the sound of Sterling's singing, and then she headed straight for us. I covered Sterling's mouth with my hand, but the song ended. Sterling grabbed my hand and shoved it away from his mouth. He gave me the most painful stink eye, and then took off his platform shoes and threw them at me.

As the audience applauded for the cheerleaders, Sterling ran to the exit of the auditorium and left the building. The show's last act was Mr. Schultz, the accounting teacher, dressed as Santa Claus with a coconut leaf hat. Screw that, I thought, and I grabbed Sterling's platforms and ran outside. He was gone, so I ran to the mauka side of the auditorium and heard shouting coming from the parked cars near the track. That's when I saw Junior Bothelo's back, and he was standing on Sterling's white kimono. And I knew. I just knew.

I ran towards Junior and saw Sterling, bare chested with his fists up ready for throw.

Fucka, why you make fun of my chick's number, Junior yelled. You faggot. Everybody knows you nothing but a fucking faggot.

You stupid moke, Sterling shouted.

Who you calling one moke? Fucking fag, Junior yelled. Go suck one dick.

Sterling ripped off his wig and threw it on the ground. Why you no throw already, Sterling shouted. Come on. Hit me. Hit the fag.

Junior made like he was going walk away, and then, he swung around and false cracked Sterling in the face. I screamed, Beeeeef!

Sterling wavered and gained his balance. I ran straight for Junior. Right before he pulled back his fist for another jab, I pounced, mouse costume and all, and landed on his back, but Junior, he don't know when for shut up.

Get your fucking fag hag off me, Junior yelled.

Fuck you, I screamed, and I wrapped my legs around Junior's waist piggyback style, grabbed his ears, and yelled, Come on Sterling, throw already!

Sterling Silva, Junior yelled. What a faggot name.

And I knew. I just knew.

Sterling jabbed with his right fist. Boom. Connect. Straight to the side of Junior's head. Junior whipped his body around, and I went flying and landed flat on my back in the dirt. I saw Junior's feet coming towards my face, but then all of sudden his entire body jerked to the right. In the sky above me, I saw the campus security officer's face and then his muscled arm yank Junior to the side. I rubbed the dirt from my eyes and my mouth. Above me, blurry mice, happi coats, and Michael Jacksons were staring down at me. Madison pushed them aside, held out her paw, and pulled me up. As she dusted the dirt off my back, I saw Sterling leaning against a car. The campus security officer yelled at everybody to go home or he would call the cops, and then he handed Sterling the red wig. Nalani Mitchell already had her arm around Junior, like he was some wounded warrior who had come to her rescue. They were about to walk away, but Nalani threw a long-stemmed rose at Sterling's head and said, They're plastic, you punk.

I stepped towards Sterling, but he turned away, picked up the kimono and then slipped his skinny arms into the sleeves. You can yell at me, Sterling said, tell me to shut up, but don't ever cover my mouth. Don't ever silence me with your hand.

He stepped up to me until we were face to face. His curly brown shag matted with sweat and dirt. All that was left of the lightning bolt were smears of red and blue streaked across his forehead and those high cheekbones he was so proud of. His upper lip was cut, swollen and bloody. His wet eyelashes clumped into curled peaks above his large, brown downturned eyes lined in black. For some reason, he seemed so beautiful to me. So brave.

Everybody knows now, he said.

I nodded and pulled him into my arms, and we held each other and wept.

JEDDIE NARUMI KAWAHATSU

At the Back of Kalihi Valley

Will you meditate with me?
Beneath cedar beams and gentle light,
Where the two sides of shadow meet.
It will be in silence, you say,
But I hear the crackle of morning glories
Opening in profile to the moon
And my arms move
(As if on their own) to celebrate the dawn.

I will dance instead, I say.
Silence hurts the bones of my thoughts,
They rustle, restless,
When I am motionless for too many breaths.

Be still, you beg, barely a whisper.

And I see your fear,
Blind pigeons donning the feathers of golden plovers
Migration mapped in your heart,
The impulsive compass of your feelings
Rusted and dark.

I slow the articulation of my foot,
Pause with my palms cast upward,
Scatter the heavens with fistfuls of prayer.
You catch up and I suggest a walk.
A hum halfway between
Silence and song.
Not the dance of a condor or the marble stillness of an owl,
But a form we both can assume.

JEDDIE NARUMI KAWAHATSU

For 31 Years I Refused to Have a Spiritual Awakening

In my household it was a common occurrence
For my father to speak of his astral projection,
Jetted toward the stars,
All spirit, no bones,
Universal freeway.

The beginning and end of humanity was casual breakfast
conversation.

But what if your bones betray you?
Your spirit has never danced under
The spell of cathedrals:
Spires, buttresses, gargoyles, frescoes.
But
A marble lotus commands surrender,
Your eyes sting at its brilliance.

The stone vibrates with the life passed through these walls,
And your spirit passes through them,
And other lives pass through you,
And you are all of them and none.

And a voice is not a voice, but a song,
Not a song, but a prayer
In a language you do not speak
But understand,
And your body calls home to her,
Welcomes the pulsing verse into your veins,
To bursting,
Undoing your skin with her poetry.

Let the tears come,
The shaking,
No need for breath,
You are all water, fire, earth,
Falling, landing, aflight.

When I return home,
I keep this secret because
How could it ever be breakfast table conversation?
This exchange leaves me naked,
I have departed from myself,
Molting one essence for another.
It is like trying on a new soul,

No,
Like having yours scrubbed clean,
No, like—

And I do not want to speak about any of it,
So today
Breakfast is just cereal.

JEDDIE NARUMI KAWAHATSU

Secondhand Personality

I try on the heavy mink of acquiescence.
It keeps off the sun and rain,
But it cannot protect me from myself.

So I disrobe,
Shed the silk lining,
Exit the soundbooth.

I say no,
This is not my coat,
I did not come with instructions.

I arrived naked in the summer heat,
Pebbles underfoot,
Dancing with pain and pleasure,
In my proper skin,
All scales,
Sunlight,
Shimmering like gasoline.

Mixed Aloha

"You're not Polynesian, are you?"

He asks me, only me, as I stand between my coworkers welcoming guests to the lūʻau before we get ready to dance. We wear the same costume but he doesn't ask the others. I smile and put a lei around his neck.

There are a hundred things to say but I only have seconds before he is ushered away to his seat.

Do I explain to him that my green eyes are a gift, smuggled to me through my brown-eyed parents from an Irish woman who defied tradition, culture, and family to marry the Māori man she loved? Would he understand the way she had to sneak out of her house to see him or their secret wedding at the courthouse? Or what about the time he was thrown into jail, accused of murder because of the colour of his skin? This man wouldn't understand the way their children were treated, scorned for using their native tongue, and conditioned by the Pākehā until their heritage was all but forgotten.

Or do I tell him that my skin is fair because of the pālagi man who travelled back to Sāmoa to build a house for his wife's family? The man who embraced a culture and mastered a language that was not his own and earned the matai title Numia ma Aliʻi Pule, or "Mingles with Chiefs." This man wouldn't understand the struggles the young Sāmoan mother had moving to New Zealand and raising her children in a language she was just starting to comprehend herself. He wouldn't understand the night she ate dinner alone because her broken English had started an argument she didn't even fully understand.

"Enjoy your night," I say to him as he walks past, eyes already fixed on the next part of the experience he paid good money for.

There is no time to explain my heritage to him, and if there was, I doubt he would remember it. He doesn't have time for whakapapa or tradition. He doesn't have time to learn about colonization and Polynesia. He doesn't have time for the mixed girl at the entrance who spent years coming to terms with her woven histories.

He'll remember the food though. He'll remember the shiny dresses and pretty flowers at the lūʻau he can't even pronounce. He'll remember the "aloha spirit" he felt as he drove past run-down houses and homeless kānaka maoli to his beach-side resort.

"Aloha," I wave goodbye as he takes a seat in the front row, adjusts his floral shirt, and complains about the heat.

SCOTT KIKKAWA

Excerpt from *Sporting Girl*

I was there when it started. Two days before I found myself out in Waialua chasing down the loveable grifter, I was at Wally Yoshida's house.

Wally Yoshida and I had known each other since McKinley, since we both made the varsity as sophomores. We were best friends, though we were as opposite as two best friends could be. Wally stood about five feet four inches tall and weighed just over 120 pounds; I was almost six feet and about 180 in high school. Wally was our class valedictorian; I turned in half of my assignments late. Wally listened to his mother; I begged forgiveness instead of asking for permission. Wally was quick, nimble, and had good hands. He played shortstop. I was big, strong, and could smash the ball over the fence. I played first base.

Pearl Harbor was bombed near the end of the first semester of our senior year. Wally and I both saw our fathers taken away to Sand Island. His old man was a fisherman with his own sampan and radio and therefore a potential spy; mine taught calligraphy at a Japanese language school in Moiliili and was therefore a potential propagandist. Wally's dad was shipped off to the mainland and spent some months at the "relocation camp" at Jerome, Arkansas. Mine caught pneumonia waiting for the boat and died in a wet tent.

Wally and I both enlisted as soon as we got the chance and ended up together in the 442nd. Wally enlisted to serve his country; I enlisted so my country would leave my family the hell alone.

When we were in Europe, a German grenade took Wally's leg off. I made a tourniquet and saved his life. Wally was shipped back stateside and never had to experience the carnage in the Vosges Woods where we rescued some boxed-in haoles from Texas. I took a bullet to the shoulder—a graze, really—and got shipped back, too. We both used the G.I. Bill to go to Ivy League schools. Wally went to Harvard; I went to Columbia. Wally studied history and stuck around at Harvard for law school. I got my degree in Medieval and Renaissance Literature and came home and became a cop.

I was at Wally's to celebrate his new house and his new wife. He went away to New York City for a meeting with National Democratic Party leadership as one of the party's up-and coming young candidates out in the T.H. and came home with campaign funds for the coming elections and a bride.

Her name was Lydia French, and she was an actress who had seen a couple of minor roles on Broadway and had something of a claim-to-fame as a one-time understudy to Joan Roberts in the role of Laurey in *Oklahoma!*, though she never took the stage in that capacity. Lydia was an ardent supporter of the Democratic Party and an "ardent admirer of FDR" in her own words. She met Wally at a cocktail party given by the Democratic National Committee at the Waldorf Astoria. After striking up a conversation with him about his wooden leg, they fell for each other and married before a Manhattan justice of the peace after a forty-eight-hour whirlwind courtship. I was extremely jealous: she took him to a game at Yankee Stadium.

Wally had not bothered contacting anyone in his family or any of his friends. If he had talked to me, I would've advised him against it. But in a way, I could understand his impulse to take the plunge into sudden matrimony. Up to that point, Wally's love life had been fraught with bad luck. His steady from McKinley, Polly Yamanaka, had not waited for him while he was overseas getting shot at with me. Polly started seeing Ted Kawamoto secretly, got pregnant, and married him. Wally found out the day he got home with his brand-new fake leg. Ever the saint, he congratulated them and even made a wedding gift of the gold ring he had picked up in Italy which he was going to present to Polly when he proposed to her. Jesus, what a sap. I would've punched Ted in the mouth for a wedding gift and hocked the ring and got drunk. Wally always was too nice for his own good.

Then came his hard luck at Harvard. He dated a Radcliffe coed from a family of Massachusetts fishermen named Marie Gouveia and wrote to me often about her. On the day he was accepted to the law school, he was going to propose to her at dinner, but the cab she was in got broadsided by a bus in a busy Boston intersection. Both Marie and the driver were killed. So, when Wally came home a married man from his political vacation, I was not surprised. He told me over lunch in town that Lydia had received a polite but cool reception from his folks, who were none too pleased that he had brought home some mystery haole girl and had married her without telling anyone, but he was convinced that they would warm to her in time because she was such a wonderful person. I told Wally that the world was full of wonderful people and that his folks didn't care for most of them. Lydia was different, he told me. Special. I would find out for myself just how much, he said. That's when he invited me over for dinner. Wally and Lydia had just moved into a nice, new home up on Maunalani Heights. I was only a few minutes away down in Palolo Valley, and the irony was not lost on me that I lived at Kaimuki's lowest elevation and Wally lived at its highest. He had finally gotten taller than me. When I told my wife, Ellen, she became excited at the prospect of visiting the new Yoshida home and meeting the new Mrs. Yoshida.

"It looks like good things come to those who wait," she said.

"How's that?" I asked. "It didn't look to me like he waited at all."

"Poor Wally," she said. "After all that's happened to him. And he was such a good sport about everything. Someone like that deserves all the happiness in the world. And she's a Broadway actress!"

"I've never heard of her."

"Frankie Yoshikawa! The sun doesn't rise and set based on your personal knowledge. There are plenty of important things that happen every day with or without you knowing about them. Just because you've never heard about Lydia doesn't mean that millions of others don't know and adore her."

The former Miss Ellen Aeran Park became Mrs. Ellen Yoshikawa about a year before. When I met her a few months before that, she had been a part-time reporter for the *Honolulu Record*, Koji Ariyoshi's progressive—some would say "revolutionary," and not in a nice way—weekly newspaper. She had been covering a case of mine. We fell for each other and started dating. When the House Un-American Activities Committee, or HUAC, had sent an investigator to snoop after all of the associates of the so-called Hawaii Seven, I feared that Ellen would be a target of the witch hunt. So, I asked her to quit working at the *Record* and marry me to throw the HUAC off her scent. Well, that, and we found out that she was pregnant, too.

It all worked out for us in the end. I was planning to ask her to marry me anyway, and she was planning to say yes. I bought a house in Palolo Valley with a mango tree in the front and big, heavy note payments. For a time, I took stand-in bagman work to make up some of the shortfall, but that heinous arrangement fortunately came to an end when all of that scheme's Department perpetrators came to an end. In the aftermath, Gideon Hanohano, my lieutenant, was promoted to captain, I was promoted to take his place and the bump in salary gave me enough breathing room on my note payments so that I no longer had to resort to strong-arming Chinatown vice lords to raise additional cash.

A couple of months after I was promoted, our daughter was born. Everyone in the family, including Ellen, thought that she was going to be a boy. So much for old wives' tales about how she was shaped or how she moved. We named her Elizabeth Hideko Mi Ok Yoshikawa. Ellen felt that Elizabeth had a regal sound to it, as if anyone with that name was destined to appear on television in white gloves and a hat with a veil, waving daintily from the back seat of a Rolls-Royce in a sea of stiff haoles holding little Union Jacks.

My sisters called her Lizzie and the nickname stuck. She was a plump and beautiful baby with a mostly sweet temperament, except when she got hungry or wet in the dead of night when her wailing would set off all the dogs in the valley barking. Thanks to Lizzie, my evenings were suddenly filled with something besides scotch and Ed Sullivan.

Though Ellen very much enjoyed motherhood, I got the sense that without reporting, a significant void was left in her life, and that manifested itself in her use of me as her outlet for stating her opinions. Her hobby these days was putting me in my place, which she had always been good at, but now the act seemed somehow essential to her. When I got home from work, a litany of personal editorial awaited me along with dinner.

Still, I can't complain. From the moment I met her, I knew that Ellen was a verbal fencer who never backed down when the gauntlet was thrown. And I pursued her anyway. It was really my fault, too, for always throwing the gauntlet. I have yet to learn that I'll never win.

Just before we went to Wally's, Ellen slipped into the role of the drill sergeant she had recently become since Lizzie was born.

"Frankie Yoshikawa," she said. "What are you wearing?"

"It's called a shirt." I had just come out of the shower and was pulling on a short-sleeved madras plaid shirt.

"Don't you think that's a little casual?" she asked.

"It isn't Buckingham Palace we're going to. It's Wally's house."

"We're meeting his wife for the first time," she said. "We couldn't attend their wedding, so this is like we're attending it belatedly."

"Attending belatedly? Where do you come up with stuff like that?"

"Change your shirt. I picked out a tie for you. It's on the bed. I need you to make a good first impression. Besides, she's not from here. She's from Broadway."

"Nobody's really from Broadway. They're from a bus or a train that brought them to Broadway. But she's here now. She'll have to learn to relax a little."

"But not tonight. I already told you. We're belatedly . . ."

". . . attending their wedding. Yeah, you said."

I looked up at Ellen. She was holding out a white, long-sleeved shirt that had been pressed and starched. She was wearing a black cocktail dress and looking up at me, even in heels. Her hair had been done professionally, up in a shiny black regal coif like Audrey Hepburn. She was wearing her big glasses but I knew that she'd remove them once we were in the car. She was stunning and she made me feel like a stock boy in my plaid shirt. I blew out a sigh and changed my shirt.

When I was dressed, I helped Ellen with her pearls, and she went to check on the baby while I poured myself a quick drink from the crystal decanter next to the television.

Ellen emerged as I finished my drink. She was carrying Lizzie who had been dressed in a little pink dress with a matching bonnet. The baby was probably adorable as hell but I couldn't tell because Ellen had also wrapped her in what looked like five blankets.

"Would you put the top up on the car?" Ellen asked. "We'll wait here in the parlor until you're done."

"Put the top up? We're just going up the hill. This is a visit to Wally's house, not a polar expedition." I looked pointedly at my poor daughter bundled up beyond recognition.

"I don't want her to catch a cold," said Ellen. "This is why I told you that the Cadillac has to go. We have a family now, Frankie. Your Eldorado with the top down is not a family car." I'd heard this tune from Ellen before. Chevrolet was coming out soon with something they called the Nomad, which looked like a candy-colored hearse. It was just terrible. Ellen had cut the advertisement out of a *Life* magazine and stuck it up on the icebox door with a magnet.

"Soon," I said, "I'll trade it in for one of those." I pointed at the ad. I didn't mean it. I relented and acquiesced to my wife's wishes and put the top up on the Eldorado. We had originally planned to call my sister Daisy to come over and watch the baby while we went over to Wally's, but Wally insisted that we bring her, even if it meant having to leave early. He said that Lydia loved babies and really wanted to meet Lizzie.

We arrived at Wally's to find a number of cars parked around the new house. The house itself was modern in design, with a lanai that wrapped all the way around the structure to take advantage of the breathtaking view of Honolulu and the deep blue Pacific, with Diamond Head as the centerpiece. All of the house's wood parts were redwood stained with a red-brown varnish, and there was precious little of it because most of it was glass. Out front there were hibiscus bushes and a Japanese-style rock garden complete with a genuine koi pond filled with genuine koi and a single tall coconut palm whose fronds moved languidly in the breeze. It was a nice place.

As it turned out, Wally's new wife was just as nice as his new house.

I knocked on the door and it opened a few seconds later. Standing in the doorway was a stunning little blonde with clear blue eyes. Her golden hair was coiffed in a fashionable short cut. She wore a knee-length silk dress printed with large pink roses. She had the erect carriage of a ballerina and the dazzling smile of a toothpaste ad. She looked like Broadway.

"You must be Frankie!" she exclaimed. Before I could so much as nod, she threw her arms around me and tiptoed to plant a kiss on my cheek. I simply leaned in to her, unable to return the hug as my arms were filled with the two gifts that Ellen insisted we bring: one for the wedding and one for the house. I didn't really see much of a difference as both gifts were really for the house, but I always deferred to my wife on matters of social protocol as most of the house visits I made at work had nothing to do with celebrations.

Lydia was short—about the same height as Wally—and she wasn't wearing any shoes. She had already taken to our custom of removing footwear while indoors.

"You must be Ellen! You're so beautiful! I love your dress and your pearls! And this must be little Miss Lizzie! How adorable!" Lydia embraced Ellen and fawned over Lizzie, stroking her multiple blankets gently. Then she took the gifts off my hands after thanking us profusely. I thought I even caught her bowing, like my mother did when expressing gratitude. Lydia was a quick study.

"E komo mai," she said. "I've been practicing that all day."

"It's perfect," said Ellen. "It's like you've been here for a long time!"

"Come in and have a drink!"

Lydia left us momentarily to put the gifts down near the kitchen. I looked across the parlor to the lanai on the opposite side, where I saw Wally waving at us. He was having a highball with a couple of guys I recognized from our high school baseball team. They looked up and waved, too. We moved into the foyer, where we removed our shoes. The parlor was full of people, eating, drinking, laughing. Most looked familiar or vaguely familiar. "She's really nice," said Ellen.

"Looks like Wally found someone his own size," I said. That earned me an elbow in the ribs.

I took a quick glance around. Everything in sight looked modern or futuristic, or at least like it had come from a place some designer envisioned the future would be. And that place wasn't Maunalani Heights. Stepping into Wally's parlor was like stepping into Buck Rogers, except for the view. The lampshades were in shapes I had only seen under a microscope and even the koa furniture looked like it had been made on Mars. On the boomerang-shaped coffee table was a large floral arrangement of red torch ginger, bird of paradise, lobster-claw heliconia, fern, and ti leaves. The walls were hung with paintings that looked like they were done by blindfolded monkeys given paint to sling instead of their turds.

Overall, the parlor had the feeling of a high-priced law firm's waiting room. I'd say that Wally hired the same guy who did his office if his office didn't look like a dentist's office. I took notice of the fact that none of Wally's family was there. All I saw were old friends from McKinley, a couple of 442nd guys, and a slew of people I didn't know who probably knew Wally through work or his campaign and their families.

Lydia monopolized Ellen and Lizzie while I made myself a drink at Wally's well-stocked bar cart. I took a couple of ice cubes out of a bucket that would be more at home as the component of a jet engine with tongs that were probably the talons of Picasso's pet parrot and dropped them into a tumbler with little gold triangles all over it. I covered them with scotch and headed for the lanai.

I was greeted enthusiastically by my old high school teammates and we spent some time catching up and reminiscing before they moved off to join their wives in getting food, leaving me alone with Wally.

"Well, what do you think?" Wally asked.

"Nice, if you like living in a modern art gallery but without the free white wine," I said, knowing that Wally probably could have had all the free white wine he wanted.

"I mean about Lydia. What do you think?"

"I think she's swell," I said. "So does Ellen." Relief crossed over Wally's face like a cool wave. He swirled the melting ice in his drink and took a sip.

"That's good," he said. "The folks are still a little bit guarded about her, but I know they'll come around. She's just the most genuine person. When I told her about my leg, she said she didn't care. Didn't hesitate at all."

"You're a lucky guy."

"I know it. Almost everything is perfect."

"Almost?"

"See that lady in the corner next to the bookcase? The tall haole lady with the dark hair?"

I looked at the woman Wally referred to. She was about forty and attractive in a patrician way, with alabaster skin and large, dark eyes. Her aquiline nose was perpetually up in the air and she held her drink with a natural, sophisticated ease. She wore a deep green dress and, on her right wrist, a couple of large gold bangles that didn't look cheap. She was about five feet and six inches of cold, hard class.

"What about her?" I asked.

"That's Aunt Meg. She's one of Lydia's aunts from the mainland. She turned up a couple of days ago out of the blue, and Lydia asked if it would be okay if she stayed with us for a week or so. I told her of course she's welcome; she's family and we have plenty of room. She could stay as long as she likes."

"So, what's the problem?"

Wally took a sip of his highball and looked out at Diamond Head and the ocean beyond. The sun was beginning to sink and tinted the sky and sea with fire. "I can't put my finger on exactly why, Frankie," he said, "but Lydia's been a wreck ever since Aunt Meg turned up."

"She seems fine to me."

"That's how she usually is, and she's putting up a pretty good front for all the guests tonight. But when it's just me and her, it's tense and quiet. I caught her sobbing earlier today when she thought I wasn't paying attention. I asked her what was wrong, and she just smiled and said it was nothing I'd understand. New bride nerves, or something like that. But I heard her and Aunt Meg arguing in the guest room last night, and though I couldn't make out what they were saying, I did catch all the nasty names Aunt Meg called her. I asked Lydia about it this morning, and she told me not to worry about it, that Aunt Meg is just a 'little old-fashioned,' which I took to mean that Aunt Meg doesn't approve of Lydia's marriage to a Japanese man. But do you know what's strange? Aunt Meg has been nothing but nice to me."

"Strange," I said, agreeing absently. Admittedly, I had only partially been paying attention to Wally, watching instead his bubbly Broadway wife dote on my baby girl. Ellen seemed to be completely captivated by Lydia. I found her interesting. She had suddenly shown up in Wally's life, and almost as suddenly, this Aunt Meg had also shown up.

"Look, Wally," I said, "maybe you're overthinking this. After all, you're still getting to know each other, you and Lydia. Maybe this is normal for her."

"Well, maybe," he said.

It was a strange little exchange, but largely unmemorable outside the context of what was to follow. The new Mrs. Lydia Yoshida seemed for all the world to be full of charisma and verve and even I could believe that she could've been an understudy to Joan Roberts. I'd never even seen *Oklahoma!* but I thought she might be able to pull off the lead even in a production that big with flying colors.

I made my rounds with all the folks there I knew, and Wally introduced me to a few people I didn't know, including the enigmatic Aunt Meg. I found her charming, cultured, and sincere and didn't get the impression at all that she was revolted by my being Japanese or from Hawaii. I asked her how she was enjoying her visit, and she told me that she loved it here.

We ate meatballs with teriyaki sauce and pineapple. Wally told me that Lydia made all the food herself. It was good, and I was beginning to believe all of the good press he had given her.

After being there for a couple of hours, Ellen told me that it was time to go; she needed to feed Lizzie and put her down for the night. We said our goodbyes to everyone and were getting into our shoes near the front door when there was a knock. Wally ran up, drink in hand, and opened the door.

The voice outside the door said, "How's things, Shortstop? Long time no see."

***

Happy Tokuda. The voice was jarring the same way the odor of something rotten in the back of the icebox is when it finally hits your nose after weeks of resting undiscovered behind the fresh stuff. It was too damn late for me to run away and hide. I was trapped in Wally's fancy foyer in a pair of wingtips with untied laces.

I tried my best to disappear right where I was, kneeling on one knee and bowing my head with my hat on, concentrating intensely on tying my shoes. I heard Wally greet him enthusiastically, saying something to the effect of what a pleasant surprise it was to see him and come inside, come inside, come inside.

Shit. I bit the bullet after finishing with my shoes and looked up to find that familiar wide face and its idiot smile a few inches away from mine.

"Eh! First Base! You're looking good!"

"And you're looking guilty of something."

Happy laughed like a demented chimp.

"Same old First Base," he said.

"Who the hell invited you?" I asked.

"Right Field told me about it," he said. "He didn't think Shortstop would mind if I stopped by. I told him not to say I was coming. I wanted to surprise everybody."

"Caught me off guard," I said.

"Yeah, just like old times," said Happy.

Ellen was suddenly behind us, holding Lizzie in one arm and using the other to brace herself against my back while she stepped into her pumps.

"Who's this pretty girl?" Happy asked. "Don't tell me you married this one, First Base!"

"Yeah, he did," said Ellen. "He knocked me over the head with his club and dragged me by the hair into his cave. I'm Ellen."

"They call me Happy, but my real name is Harry. Harry Tokuda. But you can call me Happy. Everybody else does."

"Happy Tokuda? I've heard a lot about you," said Ellen.

"Really? I'm touched. I didn't think you liked me, First Base."

"I don't," I said.

"Who's this?" asked Happy, ignoring me and leaning over the bundled-up Lizzie.

"This is Elizabeth, our baby girl," said Ellen. She did so with the same joyful, shiny pride she always did when introducing our baby to anyone, including, it seemed, to perpetrators of every misdemeanor on the books with an occasional grand theft thrown in.

"She can't be yours, First Base! She's too cute." Happy reached into his hip pocket and pulled out a crisp twenty-dollar bill. He held it out between two fingers toward Ellen. "Here," he said. "For the baby's college."

I snatched the bill from between them and held it up in front of Happy's face. "Which old coot's pension did you steal this from?" I asked. I flipped the bill at his face. It hit him squarely between the eyes and fluttered to the floor.

"Frankie!" Ellen scolded. "Be nice!"

Unfazed, Happy squatted down, picked up the bill, straightened back up, and tucked it into Lizzie's blankets then gave her a gentle pat. He grinned broadly at Ellen. "Just like before," he said. "Same old First Base."

Wally ambled over in an attempt to smooth things between me and Happy. I noticed how well he moved; one would be hard-pressed to guess that one of his legs was artificial. "Hey, come on, Frankie," he said. "You and Happy go way back. We all do. He just dropped in to wish us all well, didn't you, Happy?"

"Of course," said Happy. "Shortstop with his new house and new wife, and First Base, too. What a cute little baby!"

Happy beamed. Ellen beamed back at the compliment to Lizzie. I felt like a heel. Happy stood in the foyer holding his black beret in front of his chest, vaguely reminding me of a dog begging for table scraps.

"Thanks, Happy," I said. I said it through clenched teeth, but I said it. I even stuck my hand out in a gesture of conciliation, to make up for the uptight jerk I was being. Happy grasped my hand and shook it heartily.

"You're a lucky guy, First Base," he said, fairly oozing goodwill and ease of character. I managed a grin and nodded.

"How about we go inside and have a drink together?" Happy suggested. "We can catch up."

"Thank you, he'd love to, but we have to get going," said Ellen. "It's our little girl's bedtime."

"Yeah," I said. "It's my bedtime, too."

"Okay, then," said Happy. "Stay in a good mood, First Base. I'll see you next time."

"Stay out of trouble, Happy," I said. "Or next time I'll arrest you. Again."

Happy laughed heartily. "Same old First Base," he said.

The purring engine of my Cadillac Eldorado lulled the baby into a quiet doze. The car was almost two years old and still sounded as good as it did the day I drove it off the Schuman Carriage lot. Ellen sang quietly to Lizzie, swaying slightly in the back seat. I stole a furtive glance at them through the rearview mirror as I drove down Waialae Avenue. This was my contentment. I had taken my time winding downhill along Sierra Drive to give Lizzie time to enjoy the soft hum of the car. She was the picture of peace.

We were home in just over ten minutes. Ellen put Lizzie down in her crib while I took my jacket and tie off. I let my eyes roam over the parlor and dining room that were my domain, my great hall. The hard-won castle had come at a price. A lot of note payments had been made in blood money, my take as a part-time bagman until I found a way out of the arrangement and received a fortuitous promotion. In that sense, I was no better than Happy Tokuda. What the hell gave me the right to judge him?

I told myself that what I did, I did for my family. For Ellen. For Lizzie. Our koa-framed sofa in the parlor, once a symbol of our transcendence above our plantation origins, was now a resting place for folded pink blankets, fresh diapers, and a brown teddy bear damp with drool. Happy never pulled any of his scams to fund anything like it.

Who the hell was I kidding? None of it made me better than him. I became annoyed at the fact that I had left Happy behind up on Maunalani Heights and yet I had carried him all the way back into Palolo Valley into the sanctity of my castle in my head.

As was becoming nearly always the case, Ellen had read my mind. I met her in our bedroom after she put the baby down to help her remove her pearls and unzip her dress. "So that was Happy Tokuda," she said. "What is it about him that bothers you so much? He seems jolly and harmless."

"He's a criminal," I said. "Happy has separated not just stupid bad people from their money, but stupid good people, too. He does it with a smile, but he still does it."

"Frankie, you've put plenty of worse ones away, and some of them more than once. But they never got under your skin the way this one does. I've told you this before: I think Happy bothers you because you've never beaten him."

"So?"

"So, you're something of a sore loser, Frankie Yoshikawa. Why can't you just let it go? Wally doesn't seem to have a problem with him, and neither do the rest of your friends, for that matter. You're a homicide detective, now, not just a bunco squad dick. You caught the ones who matter. This Happy is a small fish. Let it go. Nobody thinks any less of you just because he's never been convicted."

Ellen slipped out of her black dress and opened a drawer to select a nightgown. I stood and admired her from behind. One of my great pleasures was watching her get dressed and undressed. It was comforting as well as arousing; that she would perform these simple but private tasks in my presence told me that to her, I was home. It made me feel content and ashamed that I had let someone as insignificant as Happy Tokuda annoy me with all I had going for me.

Ellen was right. I was slowly but surely learning to just shut up and listen to her. Life was easier that way.

Ellen slipped into something pink chiffon that she had pulled from her fragrant drawer of sheer things. She sat down at the vanity to brush her shiny black hair. I threw my shirt into the wicker hamper in the bathroom and brushed my teeth.

MILTON KIMURA

Whither, Aloha?

In early 2020, Nick Rolovich left his job as head coach of the University of Hawai'i Warrior football team to become head coach of the Washington State Cougars. In the welcome ceremony in Pullman, WA, Rolovich remembered UH: "You will always be a part of my heart, and I'm very grateful for the time and the aloha spirit they gave me" (*Honolulu Star-Advertiser*, 17 January 2020).

But he left. He took the new position, probably for a number of reasons among which Rolovich acknowledged "the Cougar climate . . . the passion that I have seen since I set foot in this city, on this campus . . . There is a togetherness here that was real attractive for me to be able to be a part of . . . What attracted me here is not the weather; it is the climate—the Cougar climate." If something quacks and waddles and lays eggs, then it's a duck; if you describe an emotion as a passion, a togetherness, and an encompassing climate, then it's aloha. Right? As someone who left Hawai'i for Pittsburgh, PA, in 2012, I understand Rolovich. No, he's not a hypocrite; he wasn't putting on an act all those years when he was first the quarterback and then the head coach for the Warriors. However crucial a role the university and the state played in his life, it was time to move on. And what he describes as the attraction that Pullman had for him sounds decidedly like aloha. So can aloha be found outside Hawai'i? Can it characterize a town that isn't Waipahu, a city that isn't Honolulu, a state that isn't Hawai'i? Hmmm.

The Magic of "Hawai'i"

All of you know what happens nine times out of ten when you respond to "Where are you from?" with "Hawai'i." You hear about grandfathers who were stationed there, parents who honeymooned there, cousins who attended summer session there, all related with smiles and excited voices. My most memorable such experience occurred in 1967 in the Polish village of Zakopane, located in the Tatra mountain range separating Poland from then-Czechoslovakia. A member of the Gorals of that region dropped the reins of his horse-drawn cart and stopped to speak to us ten American college students and asked, in Polish-English-Russian, where we were from. One student's "Chicago" triggered the response that he had relatives there while another's "California" got a smile of recognition and the response "Disneyland!" But my "Hawai'i" elicited a smile whose glow lit up our group. Getting down from his cart, he bent his knees, raised both arms to his right, and twisted his hips in his version of a hula. He asked if I knew any Hawaiian songs so I sang the first verse of "Beautiful Kahana" that I learned in Mrs. Achi's music class at Waipahu Elementary. He applauded and beamed as he got back up, retrieved the reins, and urged his horse forward. I don't know if he learned about Hawai'i in school or saw a Crosby-Hope movie, but he knew the place and was ready to love anyone from there.

You're from Where?

You don't get that when you reply "Pittsburgh." You might get an "Oh, Pittsburgh" or a "My college roommate was from there" or occasionally an enthusiastic "Hey, Steeler Nation!" Although my partner Donald and I weren't surprised at these tepid responses, it took a while to adjust to the change. We no longer live in a city that figures in people's dreams of an ideal honeymoon, an enviable vacation, or a hard-earned retirement. But it's okay because there is compensation. People come to Pittsburgh to attend Pitt or Carnegie Mellon, to receive high quality medical care, to take a job in a field like technology or energy, or some other reason not related to honeymoons, vacations, or retirements. They will be pleased if they get their degree, are cured or healed, or receive a promotion to a better position. If Pittsburgh delivers on these, there's no need to elicit echoes to your "Aloooooha" or curl into ever-lower postures of ingratiation before visitors. Pittsburgh's visitors will return if we live up to our reputation for quality, not for hospitality.

By the way, we have received one exuberant reaction to our reply of "Pittsburgh." It came from the driver who chauffeured us from the airport to our hotel in Prague, Czech Republic. He smiled extravagantly in the rearview mirror and shouted, "Pittsburgh Penguins!" It turns out that the two big sports in Prague are soccer and hockey and that he coached his son's hockey team. His smile slipped a bit when we had to admit that we didn't know Jaromír Jágr, the Czech player who helped the Penguins to consecutive Stanley Cups in the 1990s. Thank goodness, we knew what the Stanley Cup signified. I have to get to a game before I return to Prague.

It's Not Called "Aloha" But It's Here

Hawai'i doesn't have dibs on aloha. Like Pullmanites, Pittsburghers may not call it the aloha spirit, but they practice it, both on the level of the bureaucracy in government and on a day-to-day basis. Starting from the top, Pennsylvania has a law that assigns every dollar of profit from the state lottery to services for older Pennsylvanians; it is the only state lottery to assign all profits to seniors. And since its inception in 1971, it has provided a total of nearly $22 billion. The funds are allocated according to need, so all we've received personally is free rides on the bus, light rail, and inclines, but some of our peers receive help with utility bills, property taxes, renovations that allow them to remain in their homes, long-term health care, and other benefits. It made me wonder why Hawai'i doesn't put some money where its mouth is when it talks endlessly about the value of kūpuna.

This largesse extends to those not yet eligible for AARP membership. The death in 2017 of Pittsburgh billionaire Henry Hillman reminded many of how much the Hillman family has given to the city with funds for multimillion dollar projects like the Hillman Library at the University of Pittsburgh, UPMC Hillman Cancer Center, and the Hillman Center for Future-Generation Technologies at Carnegie Mellon University as well as smaller amounts that focus more tightly: a venture at Goodwill of Southwestern Pennsylvania that allows cash-strapped nonprofits and small businesses to use Goodwill SWPA's fleet of trucks at reduced rates, assistance for at-risk youth with entrepreneurship, and seed money for the Three Rivers Mothers' Milk Bank. Hillman's obituary in the May 11, 2017 edition of the *Pittsburgh Post-Gazette* calculated the Hillman Foundations'—yes, there are several—worth at $1.2 billion, with most of it targeted at initiatives in southwestern Pennsylvania. But the article also listed other family funds, some even larger, that have the same aim: the Richard King Mellon Foundation with assets with a fair market value of $2.3 billion, the Heinz Endowments valued at $1.5 billion, and the Pittsburgh Foundation at $1 billion. According to a telecast of "Chronicle: Only in Pittsburgh" on WTAE, the local ABC affiliate, these Pittsburgh-based foundations have a total value of approximately $10 billion. All these dollars trickle down. While these foundations support the arts, build medical facilities, and open opportunities for communities, they also work on a neighborhood level to improve daily life. An example is ONE Northside, funded by the Buhl Foundation and aimed at my neighborhood, the North Side. One of its projects takes the form of Neighbor-to-Neighbor grants of $1,000 each. The ONE Northside website suggests the following possibilities: "host block parties, build community gardens, fix up city steps, teach kids to play music, help people start small businesses, help families access support services, and advocate for a better Northside for all." In my 65 years in Hawai'i, I never encountered anything similar. I grew up when the Big Five had replaced the monarchy and were the rulers of the Territory of Hawai'i. What happened to their profits? In what neighborhood is A&B funding neighborhood gardens? In which hospital is AmFac building a cancer institute? Which University of Hawai'i departments are adding professorships endowed by Castle & Cooke? In Pittsburgh, there's no need to demand that the economic giants of a century ago show me the money. But in Hawai'i? Whither, Aloha?

Small Kine Aloha

But aloha is not only a function of money. More often and more meaningfully, it emerges in our daily connections, if we're lucky. This won't be new to any of you who've traveled and received kindness from another passenger on a flight, a front desk clerk in a San Francisco hotel, or a stranger on the street in Manhattan—well, maybe scratch this last one. And why limit it to America? I recall the Czech variety of aloha we experienced in a Prague antiques store. The owner, actually an immigrant from Serbia, invited us to sit and chat over freshly brewed tea and biscuits from Spain—and we hadn't even bought anything yet. For my purposes here, "aloha" means a kindness extended from one person to another that, had it not been extended, would have shone no negative reflection on the giver.

Aloha from the Start

So aloha in Pittsburgh began with the realtor we contacted prior to our first visit, something we'd done in each of the other five cities we visited as we evaluated possible alternatives to continuing to live in Hawai'i. Of these realtors, Chris, a lifelong Pittsburgher, was the most accommodating. On our first visit in 2011, he set aside two half-days for us, twice the time given by any of the realtors in the other cities. He spent the first day driving us through various neighborhoods, pointing out features and describing characteristics. He wanted to give us a context in which to place the properties he would show us the next day, which were specific listings in those neighborhoods. He patiently answered all our questions with a straightforwardness that we found reassuring. And remember, he did all this with no promise of an eventual sale; we had informed him in pre-visit emails that we hadn't yet even picked a city. On our second visit, he gave us a full day, knowing that Pittsburgh had made the cut but that Chicago was still in the running. I can't say for sure that his aloha isn't a possible, perhaps subliminal, reason for our final decision.

Aloha from a Builder

Aloha continued with the builder in charge of the crew constructing our townhouse complex. Tom was an impressive man, from his 6′ 8″ height to his knowledge about construction—his replies to me were peppered with paraphrases from the local building code—to his gracious willingness to give us extras: replacing the light fixture in the dining area with one more to my liking, bolting our recently purchased mailbox to the wall next to the front door, wiring motion-sensitive lights in the back courtyard, and agreeing to take on a freelance job, for which he stayed on after a full day of work to connect speakers in the first-floor bedroom to the stereo system in the second-floor living area; this job required drilling through the living room floor into the garage and then through the wall and closet into the bedroom without compromising the insulation and then threading the speaker wire through those holes. When Donald asked how much this would cost, he quoted an absurdly low price, which Donald, in order to remain on speaking terms with his conscience, doubled.

Expert Advice, Gratis

Let me cite one more example of Pittsburgh aloha from our home-buying days. When we moved into our home, we were concerned about the steep hill whose base begins at our back property line. Our developer had agreed to have a retaining wall constructed, but we wanted to know if that would take care of future problems with runoff and erosion. We contacted a landscape architect to survey the situation and make recommendations. He came out and spent more than a half-hour walking the property, climbing the hill, assessing the makeup of the ground cover, and noting the swale that had been carved into the hillside to steer runoff away from our house. He agreed that a retaining wall would be all that we needed and specified how it should be built and what materials should be used. The price for his services: nothing. He said he was happy to welcome us to the city. We thoroughly enjoyed putting together a mahalo basket of wine and goodies for him.

Tiny Pittsburgh Alohas

Of course, aloha can be found in smaller day-to-day experiences. I regretted the day when Rayney, the front desk clerk at the Allegheny YMCA where I exercise, retired. She was unfailingly friendly to everyone, but she extended herself with me. I remember the day in November when it was unseasonably warm, in the high 70s with a gentle breeze and bright sunlight. I walked into the Y in a short-sleeved polo shirt and light trousers. Rayney's reaction: "Where's your coat? I don't care if it's warm. It's November!" All this before she flashed me a smile and handed me some towels. Aloha can come from strangers too. One morning as I was backing my car out of the garage and waiting for an opening in the street traffic, a woman stopped her car, honked, and waved at me. When I opened my door and looked back at her, she pointed to the roof of my car and yelled that I had something up there. Sure enough, I had forgotten to transfer the recyclable shopping bags from the roof to the trunk. No, not a major problem, but she certainly saved me the inconvenience of pulling over on the street to retrieve the bags later.

Common Histories

While writing the section above, I realized that, while it's not called "aloha," there may be a historical-cultural explanation for its presence here. Pittsburgh prides itself on being a blue-collar town. For every Carnegie and Mellon and Heinz, there were thousands of men and women who actually mined the coal and forged the steel and bottled the ketchup. People who work hard to earn their living seldom have much sympathy for those who inherited their wealth or for those who act as though they inherited their wealth. Pittsburghers don't refer to them as high muckamucka, but they feel the same about them as Hawai'i residents do. It's not cool to put on airs. Perhaps that is why they avoid behavior that smells of privilege or entitlement. Instead, they are considerate of and even kind to others. That gentle attitude may not be as exuberant as the aloha expressed in Hawai'i, but it's genuine, that is, it's not prompted by any need to cajole the recipient to return for another visit in order to ensure that next year's count surpasses this year's 10 million visitors. When I landed in Honolulu on one of my annual winter visits, I was among the first 20 or so passengers to exit the plane. A quick walker, I got to baggage claim before anyone else. There, lined up behind the sliding glass doors, were the professional greeters in their aloha wear, armed with lei and iPads displaying names. They looked tired and bored. I bent over long enough to stuff my scarf and down jacket into my backpack and tie my doffed long-sleeved shirt to the straps. When I looked up again, several of the greeters had spotted their assigned passengers. Now they were smiling and mouthing exuberant alohas, but a careful look revealed that some eyes were still tired and bored. Depending on visitors for much of a state's income and needing to ensure their return can affect its residents more deeply than we know. Whither, Aloha?

CLIFFORD KŌTARO KOBAYASHI
under the pseudonym Mirabile Dictu

In Humble Guise

April 14, 1940, University of Hawai'i
WARNING. Any person, dead or dying, living or to be born, should
not be associated with any character in this story.
— M.D.

Fukuda had waited four years for this day, his son's
homecoming—his only son's homecoming—and now that that day
was tomorrow, he did not know exactly how he should feel. Happy?
Sad? Cold? Angry? Proud? Ashamed? Two months ago, when he had
received that shocking letter from Masami, he had known, but now?
No!

Fukuda knew Kula from one end to the other, for he had been
born in Kula. There in the cabbage, corn, and potato field he had run
and played with his two sisters, who now were gone. There in that
community of scattered truck farms owned by Japanese he had
walked to and from school with Japanese boys and girls. The
Watanabes lived about five hundred yards away from his home; the
Higas farther over the hill, the Maedas, Kubos, and Kawachis farther
on; the Tanakas a mile down the road; and scattered farther down, the
Higuchis, Goyas, Konos, and Tomitas. Indeed, except for the
grammar school, Kula was a transplantation of a farming community
from Japan (minus the rice fields, of course) to Hawaiian soil. Such a
community had molded Fukuda into just another Japanese farmer
with Japanese ideals and Japanese ways. But he was just one step
ahead of the Japan-born farmers, for he could speak both the English
and Japanese languages fluently. After finishing grammar school, he
had wanted to go to high school in Lāhainā; but the pressure of work
in the fields had held him back. Forced by his parents, at the age of
twenty, he had to marry Haruko, who bore three daughters, all of
whom were now married, and only one son, Masami.

Fukuda was now in the orchard. He gripped his trimming shears
and snipped off in rapid succession several twigs from the persimmon
tree. He stopped, looked around to see how his two helpers were
progressing with their pruning, looked at his watch, and resumed his
pruning. Evidently, to his two helpers, Fukuda seemed engrossed in
his pruning; but actually his mind was not on the subject most of the

time, and his skillful pruning was merely automatically done. Yes, the same thoughts which had come to him yesterday, and the day before, and the day before that—thoughts which recurred to him continually and mercilessly—thoughts which nearly ran him mad—turned in his graying head.

Damn these neighbors! They had too much to say about his family. They gossiped about his wife's new dress, his daughters' affairs, his eighty-year-old father; they criticized him too, though not straightforwardly. Moreover, they even prophesized Masami's future.

At the Maui Farmers' Exchange: "Fukuda and his son are too ambitious. What farmer in Kula ever sent his son to the mainland to become a lawyer? A lawyer? Of all things! Masami should be a farmer like his father. Once a farmer, always a farmer. Anyway, who needs a lawyer in this place?"

At the post office: "Fukuda's hired another man. He must be making money. Have you seen his new Plymouth? Some car!"

At the temple: "Fukuda certainly trusts his son. Don't you think he might come back with a haole wife? Sure, who knows?"

Fukuda dropped his shears on the ground, and gritted his teeth, "What the hell!" He picked up the shears, put it in his pocket, and turned toward home.

"Why, Kazuo, lunch isn't ready yet. It's only eleven now," his wife said, as he shuffled into the kitchen.

He paused, looked at her, remained silent, headed for the table, and slumped into the chair.

"Just make some coffee," he muttered, propping his hands under his chin. He stared into space.

"Tanaka told me that he's going to take his family down to the boat tomorrow morning," said his wife, just as the coffee began to boil.

In Puʻunēnē, a growing plantation community about twenty miles away from Kula, she had been born and reared by parents who were Japanese to the core in color, ideals, and practices. However, living among Chinese, Filipinos, Koreans, Spanish, Portuguese, other Caucasians, and Hawaiians, going through grammar school with them, and learning American ways and ideals, had made her into a unique, conglomerate personality, though predominantly Japanese. Like the Filipino and Spanish, she had a flair for finery; like the Hawaiian, she cherished the land and sea; like the Portuguese, she had that peculiar inflection in her speech; and like the Oriental, she did not show her sentiments readily. As a matter of fact, when she was only seventeen, she had been forced by her parents—who had arranged the marriage in strict Japanese fashion—to marry Fukuda. And she had accepted him as a matter of obedience and loyalty to her parents. However, surprisingly but happily, she and Fukuda had come to love and understand each other almost ideally. She had once been beautiful, but the hard work in the fields alongside her husband made her coarse and robust.

Fukuda looked at her. "Haruko, did Ojiisan talk about Masami?"

"No," she replied, pouring her coffee into a cup.

Ojiisan had come to Hawai'i in 1892 as a plantation laborer under a three-year contract to the Maui Sugar Company. After three difficult years on the plantation, he had moved to Kula with his wife as a truck farmer on the then cheap but fertile land. Due to the laxity of the agricultural laws at that time, he had managed to secure a few persimmon plants from Japan, from which the profitable orchard was developed. Fukuda and two daughters had been born to them, one daughter dying in their plantation home, and the other dying during the lean year of 1900, when his crops failed miserably because of a severe drought. When he was thirty-five, his wife died, leaving him with his son to carry on the farming. Ojiisan had become as hard as the life he had lived.

Fukuda remembered how Ojiisan had taken the news about two months ago when he had told him that Masami was asking permission to marry a haole woman in Nebraska: "If he marries her, I'll have him disinherited!" he had fumed. "He will not bring disgrace to our name! Understand? What will the neighbors say? What will our ancestors say? A Japanese should marry a Japanese!"

But now Ojiisan seemed to have cooled down, for he never mentioned Masami, and he seemed to have assumed an air of aloofness from what went on outside by remaining in his room most of the time. His silence troubled Fukuda. Will it mean that tomorrow he would burst out in a fit of anger?

He sipped his coffee slowly. Hell! How bitter it tasted! He grabbed his hat, stumbled out of the door, and headed straight for the orchard. Haruko stood at the door and watched him, shook her head, but understood. She had long forgiven Masami.

Fukuda worked almost madly, trying to dash out—to smother—the burning thoughts from his dizzy head. Neighbors, gossip.

Persimmons, worms, pruning, rain. Cabbage, disease, storm. Masami, law, haole wife. Ojiisan, ancestors. Good God!

The hot afternoon sun beat upon his body, and the effect was good, for toward evening he was unvexed by those burning thoughts. The last rays of the sun pierced the clouds over the west Maui hills, and the oranges, reds, and purples against the clouds and in the valleys agreed with his mood. At this moment of tranquility, a truck pulled up to his orchard.

"Hey, Fukuda!" yelled the driver, pulling up close to him. Fukuda stopped his pruning, squinted a little, and recognized the driver. It was Higa.

"Hello, Higa."

"I heard Masami's coming home tomorrow."

"That's right."

"I bet you're happy?"

Fukuda did not answer, looked worried for a second, and then put on a smile. Higa chuckled and drove off. A mawkish feeling came over Fukuda. Tomorrow was coming. He was afraid of tomorrow.

Surprising to him and Haruko, he had a ravenous appetite at supper. Hard work, no lunch, and the hot sun had made him very hungry. Haruko thought that now—after the meal—was a good time to talk about Masami, for he looked so content.

Smiling, she asked, "Are you going down to the boat?"

He smiled too—a little—but that smile faded as he stammered, "I—don't—I don't—know."

He didn't care to talk about him. He pushed his chair back, walked off into the comfortable, neat living room, fell back in his favorite rocking chair, and lit a cigarette. Was he going down to Kahului to greet Masami and his wife? To be laughed at by his neighbors? To be face to face with that moment he was afraid of? He puffed deeply on his cigarette. Should he forgive Masami? Hell, no! But he loved him—loved him dearly. Fukuda reminisced the same things which he had reminisced countless times before. They had been so close to each other, he and Masami. Masami used to tell him everything of his likes and dislikes, of his wild boyhood dreams, of his school life, and of his ambitions. He remembered that momentous night Masami left for the mainland. For the first time since his mother's death, he could not hold back tears. "Be good," had been his last words to lei-bedecked Masami, and he had answered, "Don't worry, Father. I'll write often." And now what? Should he forgive his son, his only son? No! But he loved him dearly. To forsake him now would mean to break his own already breaking heart.

Having lit another cigarette, he got up from the chair, walked slowly into his room, and threw himself on his bed. On the wall he saw the framed picture of his grandfather, a picture which was very dear to him because it was done in oil by a great Japanese artist in Japan. From as far back as he could remember, he had been taught to worship that picture of an ancestor whom he had never seen. Furthermore, year after year, he had been trained to observe the day of that man's death, and even to go to the temple to pray for him. What that ancestor meant to him, how other ancestors controlled his life, he did not exactly know. But how often he had done certain things—acted a certain way—just to please that ancestor.

The cigarette burned a hole in the bed cover. The hole burned deeper and deeper. He was in profound contemplation . . . He got it! He was going to send one of his farmhands to Kahului!

"Haruko! Haruko!" he yelled. He pulled open the door and continued: "Haruko, we're not going to the boat tomorrow morning."

"But—"

"Haruko, it's the best way," he said.

"But—"

"I'm sending Minoru. He knows Masami well."

And unsentimental Haruko understood.

Fukuda glanced at the old clock on the wall. What? It was already eleven o'clock. "Too late to ask him now. I'll have to see him early tomorrow," he murmured to himself.

Just how he fell asleep, he did not know; nevertheless, he had slept. What a sleep! Strange dreams. Tossing in bed. Kicking the wall. And now it was morning. Hastily he washed and jumped into his overalls, greeted Haruko, who had been up before him to prepare breakfast, and raced for Minoru's quarters.

When he came back into the kitchen, he found Haruko dressed in her best. She looked at him and said seriously:

"I'm going."

He lit a cigarette and did not look at her.

"Is Ojiisan up?" he asked.

"No, not yet."

"I hope he doesn't make a scene."

"Kazuo, how about you?"

"I don't know. I'm not going." He inhaled the smoke deeply.

"Please, Kazuo, it's too late now. You can't do anything else. Forgive him!" she said a little emotionally.

Mulishly, he said nothing. They ate breakfast in silence.

Half an hour later Minoru appeared, and before he and Haruko left in the Plymouth, Fukuda said, "Take your time down. The boat is landing at seven. If any of the neighbors are there, keep your mouth closed."

"Okay," Minoru replied curtly.

Haruko looked at Fukuda; her eyes did not meet his, for he had turned away.

Fukuda watched the shining car disappear over the hill and sighed a sigh of great relief. He lit another cigarette, walked slowly into the living room, and sat in his rocking chair. He sat for some time, as if in a daze. Was he dazed? Dazed? Hardly. He was more detached than that. He was dreaming! Dreaming of Masami. When he came to, he looked at the clock; it was only six-thirty. He stood up and glanced at Ojiisan's room. The door was closed.

He decided that he should go out for a walk; therefore, he went. Down the zigzag path, through the cabbage fields, between the tall corn, through the potato fields, and back under his precious persimmons, he walked in a dawdling manner. In that part of the orchard nearest to the road, he stopped, and then sat on a large empty can. One after another he smoked his cigarettes. Troubled again with his bewildering predicament, he fell into a state of despondency again. One by one the entire cycle of his past thoughts and experiences flashed through his mind and harassed him.

"I'm a coward," he branded himself. He stamped the cigarette stubs into the dew-covered soil. For a long time he was lost in his thoughts, and he didn't notice how time ticked away.

Suddenly the soft, familiar purr of the Plymouth brought him to his senses. He bounced up from the can, which toppled over and rolled on its side. The moment had come at last! Brushing away a few branches which obstructed his view, he watched the car come down the hill, turn into the road leading to his house, and pass in front of him. He caught only a glimpse of them, Masami and his haole wife. She was a dark brunette; he was in a light-brown suit. He saw nothing else. His heart pounding madly, his head in a whirl, he turned around, and aimlessly walked away. Even while he lumbered through the orchard, even at this very moment with his son and daughter-in-law only a short distance over there in his house, he did not know how to act. Coldly? Warmly? He did not know.

"Father!"

Fukuda was startled beyond words. He gulped, swung around, and their eyes met—father's and son's. With arms outstretched, Masami was smiling.

"Father," he repeated.

Fukuda's eyes wanted to smile, but not his mouth; his heart longed to forgive, but not his head. His coldness almost froze Masami's heart. His arms dropped weakly.

"Father, don't you—don't—aren't you—"

"You're looking well," interrupted Fukuda frigidly.

"Why are you like this, Father?" cried Masami. "I thought you understood. You told me in your letter that—" he faltered.

"You're looking well," he repeated.

"This is more than I expected. One thing I ask of you, Father. Please see Jane once. Just once."

"I've seen her already."

"No, you haven't."

"Yes."

"Then just speak to her. Just once. Say something. Anything."

"I don't care to." Fukuda's heart burned.

"Just once," he pleaded, "and we'll leave. Please!"

Fukuda bit his lower lip, said nothing, and followed Masami homeward.

Father and son entered the living room; Haruko and Jane stopped talking. Fukuda saw that Jane was beautiful, and was moved; he saw that she was young, and was sorry; he saw that her skin was white, and was disgusted.

"Father, this is Jane," said Masami.

Jane extended her hand, and as if forced by an unseen power, he extended his hand too.

"Father," said Jane with a deep, sweet, emotional tone, which penetrated his weather-beaten body, causing every nerve in him to tingle.

At first hesitantly, then warmly, then almost too tenderly, Fukuda grabbed Masami's hand, "Forgive me, Masami, forgive me."

"Father, thank you, Father."

Jane kissed Fukuda, and he blushed.

With tear-filled eyes, Haruko the unsentimental smiled. "Now we must tell Ojiisan."

"Let me do it." It was Masami. "Ojiisan, I'm home. Ojiisan!"

There was no answer.

"Never mind," said Fukuda.

And they understood.

Note

This story was the first and last short story written by my grandpa, Clifford Kōtaro Kobayashi. It's dated April 14, 1940—he was a student at University of Hawai'i at Mānoa. The following year, my grandpa started medical school at the University of Iowa, where he was arrested as an enemy alien after Pearl Harbor was bombed on December 7, 1941.

My grandpa was born in Pā'ia, Maui in 1919. He was the grandson of contract laborers from Yamaguchi-ken and the son of a picture bride. He graduated from Maui High, and after earning his medical degree returned to Honolulu where he was the first Japanese American pediatrician in Hawai'i. At the time—according to my grandpa—Queen's Hospital didn't hire Japanese, so he hung his shingle at King and Kalākaua.

The oldest son of an oldest son, he carried the weight of the family name. My grandpa fell in love and married a Korean-Puerto Rican woman from Lāhainā, and family members returned the wedding invitations unopened. He never spoke to some of his relatives again.

When I was a Creative Writing student at University of Washington, my grandpa always wanted me to read a short story he had written back in school, but he could never find it. After he died in 2014 at age 94, my grandma handed me a browning brittle envelope, typed termite-damaged pages stuffed inside, the upper left corner brown from a rusted staple: "In Humble Guise." Despite his "warning" that no "person, dead or dying, living or to be born" should "be associated with any character in this story," the character Masami is clearly my grandpa.

I only knew my grandpa to be stoic and gruff, the corners of his mouth creased sharply and permanently downward. My mom always described him as "Taisho." But he would wink and tell me, "Don't look to the past. Look to the future." This story reveals my grandpa's heart in a way I regret I never saw while he was alive.

—Cathy Malia Lowenberg,
for my grandpa Clifford Kōtaro Kobayashi

JULIET S. KONO

Leaving Haibun

I pull up the thin summer futon to my cheek and feel and smell its lingering summer warmth's weight. Nostalgic, I reluctantly fold the futon and roll up the *shikibuton* I had slept on for the many months of my stay in Tokyo. I had already packed and left my luggage in one of Tokyo Eki's lockers. Soon, the young men of the bedding *kaisha* will come to whisk the futon away, wash and sterilize them for yet another visiting academic's use. Later, the young men will come back to clean my tiny *apaato*. My term up, it's time to leave.

I have a few more days before my husband flies in after working in Guam, and we leave for home. Like a mendicant monk who had been cosseted most of her life, I leave the comfort of my home in Japan to learn more about the Buddha's Teachings by going out into the countryside. But I am setting out not really knowing my path. *Confronted by water on one side and fire on the other, take the middle way*, Murakami Sensei had counseled me, earlier. Leaves it at that. I decide to walk some soft, easy hiking trails close to urban areas in Tohoku and sleep in small inns along the way. Decide to hike up to just the beginning of Basho's trail, a person like me having no companions, vulnerable. While many people had assured me that it would be safe to go further, I had to see for myself. I'm not a timid person, but I didn't want to get hurt before I left.

The next day, I feel more comfortable and walk to the trailhead, talk and walk with others into an early change of colors among the trees. I sleep well at the next inn, most of my trepidation gone. The next morning, the owners, a young couple, Mr. and Mrs. Otani, serve a wonderful meal of musubi, salad, and miso soup topped with an egg. Before I leave, I pay a nominal fee to the shy young couple who run an immaculate inn. Shy, they bow and don't meet my eyes, as if I had already left. As I leave, I look out at the view, surprised at the elevation I had climbed, having looked down at my footing or the trees most of the way.

I watch morning rise
above the brim of blue-green sea
a bird lifts sleeves of wind

JULIET S. KONO

Behind the Mask Breath

More people are using cloth face masks to prevent the spread of COVID-19. The Centers for Disease Control and Prevention (CDC) recommends wearing cloth face coverings in public settings. In addition, it is critical to emphasize that maintaining 6-feet social distancing remains important to slowing the spread of the virus.
    — Hawaii COVID-19 Daily News Digest April 5, 2020,
    Hawai'i State Department of Health

When I eat kim chee,
the mask covers my garlic breath,
such that I can eat the fermented
red chili peppered won bok
with impunity.

The mask hides other things.
I no longer need to use makeup.
Beige foundation for the face dirties
and red lipstick stains
the face side of the mask.

My mouth can be foul under the
cover of my mask. I use words
that I wouldn't dare otherwise
where once "sugars," "holy baloney,"
"fudge" were *de rigueur,* polite.

We learn to talk with our eyes.
Smile, show disapproval—
give um the stink eye—
in our interaction with
the passerby with no mask:
We will bleach you!
Bleach you!

I am envious of any woman
who wears a beautiful mask
of Hawaiian motif.
I am also super-envious of Nancy Pelosi
with her beautifully color-coordinated
masks that go with her outfits.

I have learned to speak loudly,
my voice soft, lacking vibrato.
I now shout my requests at the supermarket,
or an order at Starbucks—*the Venti
not the Grande*—and use my hands
and eyes to gesture and illustrate
different sizes of things S M L.

I've grown to love my masks.
They hide wrinkles and lip lines,
and save my face from the sun,
makeup not needed for the vain.
It's fun to try to guess what the other
person looks like and if you see
someone you don't necessarily
wish to talk to, you can further your
social distancing or you can turn your
face and remain, unrecognizable.

JULIET S. KONO

This Is War

*COVID-19 recommendations are changing the rules on how much
physical distance individuals should keep from each other. Canceling
events that do not allow attendees to be at least six feet apart—the
equivalent of two arms-length—and avoiding unnecessary physical
meetings with others are proven strategies to mitigate the spread of the
virus.*
— Hawaii COVID-19 Daily Update March 18, 2020,
Hawai'i State Department of Health

Above the frontlines—
the hospitals below us in Punchbowl—
we emerge from our fortified trenches
of home and sleep,
outfitted for battle, donned
with masks, gloves, wipes,
and armed with small bottles of Purell
clipped to our belt loops like grenades—
and walk out into the still
tenebrous—a word too lofty
for this time and morning—air
of the lethal enemy territory
for the ungodly six o'clock
opening of our neighborhood supermarket
for kūpuna sixty years or older,
ID requested for those looking younger.
(My husband and I, never asked.)

We are diligent about following
the rules of distance in the aisles
of stocked shelves, treacherous territory,
as we buy a week's list of food:
avocados, strawberries, oranges—
a quick buy of perishables an act of faith,
not considered if sweet or sour, or rotten within—
and other essentials—flour, TP, hand towels—
all still in short supply.

Our walk throughs are mindful, purposeful,
our strategy—find the pickles, before the chips,
the milk before the meat—
as in an earlier reconnaissance.
We have learned to pivot,
from anyone who we deem potential
carriers of the unseen enemy,
different people, having differing
cultural or personal spaces,
all of this, like having to negotiate
a treaty in a foxhole.

MARI KUBO

Hermit Crab

I try to feel good about
the clothes I wear,
the hair I wear,
the cares I wear.

I try not to part with
the memories,
the family tree,
the essential me.

I don't know why
I love myself,
hate myself,
feel the need to
change myself.

MARI KUBO

Reflection

to L.

I realized I was alone
when I was three
and had to look after myself
and my brother who was two.
Those were funny days,
though no one was laughing.

Other children looked at me
as if I were an alien,
because I wasn't a child
though I appeared to be.

Ask what it takes to survive
and I will tell you—
ignore the bad things that no one
likes to hear about.
Keep one step ahead of loneliness.
Wake up each day fearing the worst
but hoping for the best.
Pray that the one person who has been
looking for you will say,
"No matter how hard your life has been,
you're mine now and I'll never let you go."

LANNING C. LEE

High Noon, Happy Hour #1, Happy Hour #2, Midnight, and Dawn

Day one, my very first day in Madison, Wisconsin. I have pre-registration with my English department advisor.

I wait for the signal to change so I can cross University Avenue. Four fresh-faced farm lads pull up in their jalopy in front of me.

The front passenger side kid rolls down his window, shouts, "Remember Pearl Harbor!" Bursting into raucous laughter, they roar off.

***

My parents met in the UW's Memorial Union's popular eating spot, Der Rathskellar.

One day my Korean dad marched to the table where my haole mom sat with her sorority sisters. "Stand up," he said, "and if you're not taller than I am, I'll take you to a movie."

My mom stood. She was a bit taller.

After they'd dated awhile, my mom was asked to leave her sorority.

***

Manual typewriters = all-nighters. I'm writing a paper entitled "God sI Love: Reversals in E.M. Forster's *A Passage to India*."

I reach for cigarettes, find I'm down to my last one. Gotta buy more.

Out in the snow trudging to Stop & Shop, I light up. A haole guy bumps into me, drunk, wants to bum a cigarette.

"Sorry. This is my last one."

"You slant-eyed son-of-a-bitch!" I hear his "Fuck you, gook!" fade away behind me.

***

I sit reading at the bar of my favorite haunt, The Wooden Bottle, on University Avenue. I'm part of the "usual crowd" by now but always am alone at the far end. The rest of the usual crowd, all White local males, including a 60-something professor in the English department, constantly roll dice on the bar to see who buys the next round.

On the TV, *Tora! Tora! Tora!* blazes large in living color. As the movie progresses, the usual crowd begins cheering and yelling, louder and louder.

"Kill those fucking Japs!" becomes a chorus of theirs.

I finish my beer and leave by the back door.

***

I need a job. The ad reads, "Record and tape sales."

At 8:00 a.m. a tall, dark man walks in and to the back, grabbing my application off the secretary's desk on the way.

Minutes later he buzzes me back. Not looking at me, he asks, reading, as if he'd never heard of my hometown before, "Honolulu, huh?"

"Yes," I say lamely, "that's in Hawai'i."

He stands up beaming, extends his hand. "Al Souza, Kamehameha School, Class of '62."

End of interview.

I know nothing about retail work; he hires me on the spot to manage Galaxy of Sound–West Towne.

Al Souza, mahalo. I mua Kamehameha.

JEFFREY THOMAS LEONG

Revolutionary Love

On a cool damp morning the second Thursday of January, I boarded a United Airlines Boeing 747 with Emil De Guzman and flew from San Francisco to Honolulu. Emil was a Strike comrade, a second-generation Filipino American who grew up in San Francisco's Richmond district and a leader in the I-Hotel's fight for low-income housing. We were scheduled to speak on a couple of panels for the Ethnic Studies Interim Conference 1971 at the University of Hawai'i at Mānoa, to talk about the UC Berkeley TWLF Strike and how young people were committing themselves to community organizing in Chinatown and Manilatown.

"Have you been to the Islands?" Emil asked.

"Yeah, just once, in the summer of '69 right after the Strike. I worked at Dole Pineapple."

"Cool. Sue was there then too, wasn't she?"

"Right, but that was a long time ago, bro'." Exactly seventeen months and nine days.

And it was Sue who met us at the airport and drove us over to the Kaimukī house on 10th Avenue where we'd stay. It felt strange to see her again after almost four months. The house was an older Honolulu wooden bungalow, set back from the street with a small palm out front, red dirt and clumps of grass for a yard. On its wide verandah, the lanai, was a tattered sofa, some chairs, and a ceramic Primo Beer ashtray filled with cigarette butts. After passing through a rusty screen door, we entered a small living room with slat wood walls and a built-in sideboard on the far side. The only thing missing was a beat-up Chevy in the driveway to make it real Island-style, like for a Waimānalo 'ohana.

"Aloha! I'm Wayne Hayashi and work with Ethnic Studies. You kine guys can stay here while visiting. Tomorrow we go up campus for da conference panels, but you might relax to get used to da heat. Too hot for you brahs, eh?" as Wayne watched us sweat even in February.

We proffered "no problemo," and peered around the empty house. All of its occupants were up at UH preparing for the conference, and Sue had vamoosed too after dropping us off.

Ethnic Studies like back home had just been established at UH and was already suspect as an academic upstart. The two-weekend conference was meant to interrogate and celebrate its mission by inviting key speakers from political movements all across the mainland, including Juan González of the Young Lords Party, Carmen Chow from I Wor Kuen, and Herb Takahashi, a local organizer. My compadre from UC Berkeley Ysidro Macias spoke the first weekend about the Chicano movement but there were no African American speakers that I recall. Ethnic Studies in Hawai'i focused generally more on local history and communities, that of Asians and Pacific Islanders. I was sorry to have missed Ysidro, but it would turn out that Island-style suited him and his wife Veronica; along with their kids they'd later go into business and morph into the Tortilla King family of greater Hawai'i.

The speaker lineup reflected an ethnic radical contingent, people of color struggles led by vanguard cadre with Marxist ideology. At this stage, Emil and I didn't exactly fit that model, though we'd have a go at it later; we then were small potato middle-class college graduates working in the community.

For session one, they placed Emil and me at a table on a raised dais before the large auditorium. We found the University of Hawai'i at Mānoa campus to be lush and beautiful, sitting at the entrance to one of O'ahu's rainiest valleys, hence their mascot's name: the Rainbow Warriors. The thick and humid air beguiled us with the scents of plumeria, pīkake, and other tropical flora. How could the local Hawaiians fight for revolution in such gorgeous surroundings? we wondered. Sue sat at the next table over. She and I needed to talk but it'd have to wait. We gazed out to an audience of aloha-shirted brothers and sisters staring back at us with curiosity.

Emil started by describing the I-Hotel and the history of Filipino farmworkers on the West Coast, how after their years of work, they were left on the trash heap of history. What we young organizers were dealing with in improving housing and health care for the community. I spoke about San Francisco Chinatown and the stereotype of how mainland Chinese had made it financially; not true, I said, Chinatown is an ethnic ghetto and poor. New immigrants from Hong Kong arrive every day to live in its dirty and crowded rooms and to be exploited in sweatshops and cheap restaurants.

This last point was important to make because the social structure in Hawai'i was so different from the mainland. Using the "internal colonialism" model favored at the time, we saw that haoles had married into the Hawaiian monarchy to gain control of the land (in the same way that gringos had married into landed Californio families to gain control of the ranchos). In 1893 the Hawaiian monarchy under Queen Lili'uokalani was overthrown and fealty established to the U.S., and the haole landowners continued to import succeeding waves of Asians to work the sugar plantations in agribusiness. These waves—first Chinese, then Japanese and Korean, and later Filipino—were ethnically distinct and kept separate in an age-old strategy of divide and conquer.

At the bottom were indigenous Hawaiians, the vanquished natives who were subject to the happy-simple-people stereotype but actually suffered from poverty, a lack of health care, alcoholism, and drug abuse, and made up a disproportionate share of the prison population. So I had to argue against the myth of Chinn Ho, Hiram Fong, and other wealthy Chinese of the Hawaiian business class in explaining how Asian Americans were a part of the Third World movement back home. It was an important distinction because Asians in Hawai'i, though originally subjected to racism and discrimination, had found a niche in a system based on settler colonialism.

That evening, after the last panel we had a big blowout back at the house, everyone relaxing Island-style after work, with Primo beers all around, ahi sashimi, maki sushi, teriyaki chicken, pork tonkatsu, lomi lomi salmon, char siu chow mein, and guava mochi. A drift of pakalolo filled the air too! Emil and I were feeling right at home.

I noticed Susan walking towards me, and asked, "Is there a place we can talk?"

"If you want some privacy, probably have to be in the shed in the backyard."

"Okay," I agreed, and she told everyone she and I had a "meeting" in the shed, so don't bother us.

The so-called "shed" was used for all kinds of nefarious activities that you didn't want in the main house. After slamming shut the flimsy door, I sat on the mattress and said awkwardly, "It's good to see you." And she said likewise.

"Things are a little different now," I began. "I don't know how to put this, but remember Michelle, we worked together in Asian

Studies? Well, we started seeing each other recently." Sue raised her eyes in surprise, but didn't seem upset.

"You okay about this?" I asked.

"We're not really together anymore, but I still feel close to you. It's been crazy. Since I started working with the collective, I'm feeling mixed about relationships. I've seen some other guys too."

"You have?" I expressed with some degree of disquiet at this revelation of would-be mutual unfaithfulness.

"It's different with them. It's not like Harvey, Steve, Shannon, and Jean down at ACC. These people are more intense and committed. They don't see relationships the same way," Sue said.

It was true that the youth of the '60s were experimental, yet I wasn't sure if this was going to be my scene. Political collectives everywhere were bending interpersonal rules along with political ones.

"So what are we while I'm here visiting?" I asked her. "My friendship with Michelle is important to me."

"I don't know. Old boyfriend and girlfriend, maybe? I'm glad to see you and that you came to Hawai'i. Let's be friends." And with that we embraced and kissed for a brief moment, but not quite like just months before. Then it was time to go back in and join the party.

***

I'd told myself that I was here in Hawai'i to see if I could live and contribute to the Movement in a new environment. But what did I really know of Hawai'i having not grown up here? Life in the collective was fairly serious amongst the mostly young descendants of Japanese plantation workers and a few Chinese too. There were some native Hawaiians affiliated with the house but they lived outside. Inside the rooms we were paired same gender, though the house itself was coed. They'd study ideological theory from Chairman Mao's *Little Red Book* during morning, afternoon, and evening sessions. As a house guest I did not participate in these study sessions and was on a kind of trial run for membership depending upon my long-term plans for staying in Hawai'i.

To their credit, they welcomed me as a fellow movement activist, and I understood the importance of security from my ACC experience, though I did feel a little left out. There was the basic contradiction that I carried with me from the Bay Area: Was I committed to be in Hawai'i or would I return to SF Chinatown? From their point of view, if Sue had recruited a committed activist from the Bay Area to work in Hawai'i, that would be a plus for their movement. However, the risk was that I wouldn't pan out and would take Sue with me, and they'd lose a valuable organizer. They had to be careful how they played their cards.

But for me, after just graduating from college, deeper questions began to occupy my thoughts. What would I do with my life? Did I want to marry and start a family? Go back to school and learn a skill or profession to serve the people? The good news was that all paths were open, but that was also the bad news; I'd have to make choices.

My house roommate George was a student at the East-West Center and co-leader with Sue and Charlene Young of the Chinese American history class at UH Ethnic Studies. Like me, he was from the mainland and seemed to like living in Hawai'i, but he also had a school connection. I was a floater without an institutional or work tie, a recent grad searching for direction, exactly the kind of individual the collective wanted to recruit.

"Eh brah, you like go KG's?" Wayne offered.

"What's sat?" I said, my accent attuning to the local pidgin, and soon to be subsumed in its melodious tones.

"You'll like it. It's da kine grinds," he said. We jumped into his car, drove down the main drag Wai'alae Avenue up toward the University, and into the Kuhio Grill's cool air-conditioning. A couple of beefy looking officers of the Honolulu P.D. were sitting at the bar. The café restaurant was a favorite of students looking for cheap eats. Sandra, our waitress, knew Wayne and motioned us to a corner table in the back.

"Da usual?" she asked Wayne, and then brought out five bottles of Primo and a plate of tender beef stir-fried with pineapple chunks and green pepper.

Great, I thought, but there was something missing. "Where's the rice?" I wondered out loud.

There was an eruption of laughter around the table. "Eh no rice, brah. Dis is da 'pupus' come wit da beer!" said Koji with a big fat smile. I'd discovered free food given by bars to encourage longer stays and bigger tabs. I think I'm going to like it here, I thought. Especially after the delicious miso butterfish came, the ahi sashimi, yakitori, nigiri sushi, and tako poke too, primed of course with more Primos, and topped with one big tip.

As part of my visit I had to prepare for a series of talks on organizing to Ethnic Studies at UH–Mānoa and with high school students in the community. It was a wet February and one afternoon between their study groups, a bunch of us went across the street to Kaimukī Community Park for a game of football in the rain. Football, rather than baseball or basketball, was the most popular participatory sport in the Islands and everyone joined in, young or old, boys or girls. We sloshed around, skidding in the pooling water in the low spots of the grass, yelling and passing the ball. I had a pretty good arm for quarterback but decided to just lay low and play nickelback on defense.

Once, I went with the gang out to Waimānalo County Park on the Windward side, just south of Kāne'ohe, and we swam, picnicked, and played football on the wide white sandy beach. The pull of the current is stronger on that side of the island, and as a mediocre swimmer I had to be careful. The surf was the out-of-bounds line, but the trick was to time your passes when the water was receding then curl back around towards the end zone. It was a kind of cheating, but when the wave changed its mind and you got hammered by a crest of falling whitewater, everyone laughed and piled in on top of you. It seemed that the object of the game was not to win with the highest score, but simply to get wet, loud, and loose. It was pretty cool.

My pale Chinese skin darkened after a month in the sun, and my pidgin was almost da kine. Shopkeepers kept asking what high school I'd attended and everyone spoke to me in the local dialect. As an Asian American it was very easy to slip into local culture, so much of it derived from the earlier Asian agricultural workers but mixed in with Hawaiian, Portuguese, and other influences. And with all the intermarrying, the hapa haoles, the part Pakes, Mrs. Chings who were also of ancient Hawaiian heritage, it felt like my San Jose multicultural roots except with more interracial blending. I couldn't help but like it.

But what separated me from my welcoming hosts were little things. They knew which rock upon which you should cast out into the surf at 'Ewa Beach to catch the biggest ocean perch, the mountain lane on Tantalus where you could smoke pakalolo and dance naked in a tropical downpour, which high school bad boy cousin Jason went to that threw him out after his father died. Hawai'i was their present and their future, their home.

So what was home for me? I wondered. Home was bigger than physical every day, and its roots ran backwards and deep. It was not only where you kissed your first lover, but where your parents embraced the first time, or your grandparents had gotten married. It was where they slaved in the fields or canneries so that their children could get an education. Where they were disappointed when that troubled oldest took to drugs, or was lazy and dropped out, all the things that can happen to children.

And on a different level, it was where your Queen Lili'uokalani was held in house arrest and wrote "Aloha 'Oe," one of the sweetest love songs ever, to the 'āina and her beloved King Kamehameha, who threw his enemies off the Pali, and in turn, the enemies who so loved the land, that at great odds they would fly in the air to their deaths for a chance to claim it.

This was a real sense of place, of home, I'd not encountered before. The Islands. How the Beamer Brothers could write their iconic "Honolulu City Lights," or Olomana, their "Ku'u Home 'O Kahalu'u." You didn't even need the lyrics; you felt it.

And now that I'd witnessed it for others, where could that be for me? As a San Jose boy adopted by Berkeley and San Francisco, son of Chinatown and Locke, third and fourth generation from the cities and fields of California, my ancestors had built the West, had loved, lost, and died upon its fertile soil. Could I love my home ground as much as the Hawaiian locals did theirs, never taking for granted its blessings of light, air, and sea? I wasn't sure, but I began to feel that I had to find out.

***

One of the quarterbacks in our pickup football games impressed me, a large gentle giant of a Hawaiian guy, Kalani Ohelo, who had been a featured speaker at the Ethnic Studies conference. His self-deprecating talk was filled with comments about losing his notes, but his passion about saving Kalama Valley from destruction was inspiring, allowing pig farmers like George Santos to stay on his land and prevent urban development, the building of homes for the rich. Da braddah was da kine, local and full of fire. He didn't live at the house (I don't think it could contain him), and I took an instant liking to him. In his mellow down-to-earth nature, he reminded me of Ben Rodriguez, my Chicano high school friend and college roommate. But Kalani in his true Hawaiian warm way was also one of the early founders of the Hawaiian Sovereignty movement, and I was pleased to see years later Save Kalama Valley mentioned as an early Sovereignty inspiration in a Hawaiian history display at the Bishop Museum.

I was worried about my upcoming high school presentation and that afternoon decided to ask Kalani for advice.

"Eh bruddah, wot you tink I talk story about wid da high school students at Farrington?" I asked outside on the lanai. He was smoking a cigarette watching the two Central American guys practice marksmanship by firing a BB gun at a soda can in the driveway.

"Good shot, brah!" then turning to me, "Wot you mean wot you talk story about? You know da kine already!"

"I Pake boy from da mainland. Wot dey want to know?"

"Eh brah, you cool. Jes be yourself. You know da kine teacher dirty looks. Da kine no way outta here, got nuttin' to lose."

Yeah, he was right. I had made it to UC Berkeley on my Chinese heritage but I had plenty kine friends who never made that journey and went to Vietnam instead.

"Tanks, brah! You geeve me some ideas. I tink it be okay," I mustered in my poorest pidgin.

"No problem, brah. You like a Primo? I could use one, eh."

***

I now felt fully prepared for my talk at Farrington High School in the Kalihi neighborhood of Honolulu but still a little nervous too. Kalihi was in an industrial area, near the Dole Pineapple cannery where I'd briefly worked as a lid machine operator two summers before. Demographically, it was working class, Filipinos and Hawaiians, local kids who didn't necessarily have the UH–Mānoa East-West Center in their sights. And this is the place I felt most at home. Together with the blahlahs and titas of my own San Jose childhood.

"Okay, how many of you have been to San Francisco Chinatown?" I asked the group of thirty or so brown faces before me. The late morning sun beat hard through the half-closed venetian blinds. No one raised their hands. Was this some kind of trick question from this long-haired, bespectacled skinny guy from San Francisco?

"But what do you think of Chinatown? You've got one here near downtown. Is it rich, poor, fancy, or dirty?

"Mr. Jeff," a young girl in a orchid-print smock said, "If it's lak heah, it's kinda dirty wit pool halls and lotsa old tatas sitting around talk story."

"Kind of like Aʻala Park, I'd say," I offered in response. With that a lot of aha's around the room.

I went on to dispel the myth of the rich Chinese, and that in San Francisco, they were working class and struggling just like most of them. They were bundled into ghettos like Chinatown. "Can you imagine not being able to live outside your neighborhood, or where white people live because they won't sell you a house?" Lots of nods, this they could easily imagine from their Kalihi vantage point.

If these students were like my San Jose High classmates, they hadn't really wanted to be in American History that morning. They came in as the hardscrabble, mixed children of the Hawaiian melting pot, with futures as busboys, hotel workers, shuttle drivers, etc. in the exploding tourist industry, where a college education meant little. And they'd been put down by the Punahous, the ʻIolanis, the Mid-Pacifics, private schools for the Island's elite. With their pasts erased, what future could they have? So I would reflect their truth, if only for part of one morning.

I ended with an exhortation on the importance of knowing who your people were and where you came from, on the significance of ethnic studies. I said that you students have to demand this from the administration just like we had in the Third World Strike. I was rabble-rousing as much as ever except in Kalihi, 3,000 miles away from Berkeley.

The students really dug what I had to say, and even though my pidgin was half-baked, my message was cooked. The social studies teacher beamed. Not only did she not have to prepare a lesson plan for the day, the guest speaker had her students stoked. And maybe they would get an ethnic studies course sooner rather than later.

***

In February one late afternoon after about a month in Honolulu, Sue and I took a ride in her parents' huge American car up from Kaimukī to the mountainside of Pālolo Valley, past the housing projects on to the nicer middle-class neighborhoods. We parked to talk; she was taking a break from her endless study groups. Daylight was longer as the end of winter approached, and it'd been threatening rain all day, which in Hawai'i might come in intermittent torrents then give way to brilliant sunshine.

Up to then Sue and I'd shared but a few days, mainly presenting about Chinatown organizing at the Chinese Historical Society or before UH–Mānoa students, but rare one-on-one time, with her living at home. I'd observed in her work with the 10th Avenue collective and UH's new Ethnic Studies, how she'd blossomed into being a local leader, steady and hardworking as she'd been in Berkeley, but now more assertive and outspoken. I realized she was in her element, her growing-up place with the weather and landscape she knew, collaborating with new friends our own age for a collective cause. And with her TWLF Strike and ACC experience, the others looked up to her as a movement veteran. It was less important that the material conditions in Hawai'i were not the same as on the mainland; a successful community organizer would analyze the local conditions and work with that. This she was doing, and I saw it as a good thing.

"What do you think of the house?" she asked as we sat close together in the front seat.

"The collective?" my mind wandered. "They're pretty serious and dedicated. A little different from ACC back home, but I think we're getting there."

"Yeah, I think so too," she said and before I could interrupt, added, "I don't know how I fit in here long term. I'm just not sure."

"Really?" I said surprised. "Why so?"

"Some of the guys in leadership can be a little cold, a little cutthroat. I love Kalani and a bunch of others. But using people bothers me, even for the movement." It seemed she felt safe confiding in me.

"That's something ACC won't do. I trust everyone to have my back. We're comrades, but also friends," I replied.

"I know," she said. Then changing the topic, "So what are your plans?"

But I wanted to pursue this line and asked bluntly, "Do you think Hawai'i is where you want to be? You seem to fit right in."

"I like it, it's true. There're certain good people here I can see getting to know better. But I don't know. It's only been a few months."

"I've learned so much from everyone already," I shared with Sue. "Everyone's so attached to the 'āina, the land. It's all about place and what it means to be 'local.' That's pretty cool, and I'd like to feel that way too."

"You don't think that it might be here?" she asked.

In the past few weeks I had given it some thought lying in my dorm-like bed at the 10th Avenue house. As much as I was enchanted with the local Hawaiian culture, even down to my Zhongshan Chinese American bones, the fact was I grew up somewhere else.

"I'm not sure, but it'd be a stretch. I'm afraid I might get rock fever. My family's back in the Bay Area," I said. And in articulating my thoughts out loud, they seemed more real and had greater heft, as if a path were emerging out of fog. I had to decide where to spend my energies.

"I can see that," Sue said in comradeship and sisterly love, but not without a wisp of disappointment. If I returned to California, I'd miss confiding in her, hers was advice I trusted. I'd have to find it elsewhere, and perhaps this would be the greatest loss.

Rain began pelting the front windshield, and we wondered at its timing. In the intimacy created by the crying skies, we held onto the reality of the other for a few more moments and kissed. Sheets of water slammed slick glass as if the Hawaiian gods were watching. It reminded me of that night over two years earlier at the Berkeley Marina, also sitting in a car, but a yellow Rambler American, at the beginning.

***

The leader of the collective gave me the Talk. Though not much older than myself, he was very convincing. He'd said that the best candidates to recruit for the movement were new college graduates (like Sue and myself) because they were looking for something meaningful to do. They were susceptible and vulnerable and ripe material for indoctrination, he said. They were the dissatisfied intellectuals seen in every revolution where the old order has lost its legitimacy and the young want to replace it with something better and more congruent. But each had to decide whether to follow that path. Had I any clue?

He was right of course, and in that lonely state of Hawai'i without my Chinatown friends and former girlfriend, I nearly swallowed his logic whole. There was a part of me that was wordy and nerdy. I enjoyed almost to a fault the nuances of intellectual stargazing, its near-perfect mathematical structures and conjecture, but I've learned to balance this with a more practical plan of action. That is the only path for those of Piscean nature to achieve their goals.

If I returned to the mainland, I would first work with my Chinatown colleagues to investigate long-term commitments to political struggle, form a Marxist-based ideological construct, sink roots in a variety of hot topics to heighten contradictions and expose the capitalist machine. But this was only one side of me. The serious intellectual part.

Balancing these heady impulses was a stupid faith in love. Not the sloppy, slathering type, wandering the earth after lost hope, a dream, but instead finding passion in what you believed, then making it happen against forces who'd just as well stop you in your tracks. Fighting for your community like a Kalani Ohelo, not this manipulative leader of the pack. I intuitively knew what I needed to do if I'd just trust my judgment.

So I told him it wouldn't be in Hawai'i. I hadn't demonstrated a long-term commitment to organizing in the Islands to the leader because I had none. I realized that despite my own best intellectual protestations, my professed fantasies with Michelle, that it was old girlfriend Susan and all the political and personal memories of growth in love and life at UC Berkeley that drew me for a last look and try. I'd wanted to find out. And I had.

***

Near the end of my six-week sojourn to Honolulu I moved into the bedroom of a radical local Korean-American guy from Makiki Heights, attending school on the mainland. Sue had made the connection for me. It got me out of the house on 10th Avenue though with good wishes from all my new Hawai'i acquaintances. The local family with whom I stayed that short while was politically savvy and welcoming.

The night before my departure Sue stopped by to say goodbye; we kissed and she brushed her fingers through my hair wondering out loud who would do that for me again. We'd become friends and been through a lot. But the distance between us, miles of Pacific Ocean, meant the odds of sharing in letters or visits the life we would lead, were small.

Sue drove me to HNL the next day at around noon. I'd already written my mother that I was returning, and the plan was for Emil De Guzman who'd returned earlier right after the conference to pick me up at SFO and drop me off at ACC where Harvey would bring me home to Keith Avenue. My brothers always had my back. As I walked up the gangway to board the 747, I saw Sue wave a strong but gentle hand, as if bidding me the best the future could hold. And I returned the gesture.

After the aluminum-foiled macadamia nuts and cans of guava nectar, I relaxed in my window seat looking down upon a white-capped Pacific, 35,000 feet below. From this vantage point, huge freighters were like tiny toy boats in a bathtub. A wash of cumulus and airy wads of white shadowed the ocean's surface as if great gray whales were swimming just below. On the sea was reflected a whole changing world, much wider than I'd ever known, and now I was crossing it, going from there to here, here to there.

In the distant future, I'd cross more oceans, ones I couldn't then possibly imagine: to Maui on a honeymoon with my wife, over to Hong Kong then up to Nanjing to adopt our daughter. I'd do other things and meet other people in finding love in my life. But I'd something more immediate coming, Chinatown and what's after. Having grasped these particular pale clouds, that certain bluish sky, I looked forward to a fast-upcoming tarmac, then taking first steps on familiar new ground.

R. ZAMORA LINMARK
(Writing as Jericho Salvacion, Senior Class of '86, Campbell High)

Ode To My Old Self

I permit you the lifespan of a turtle

To grow old like Grandpa Tomo
who comes to life every Tuesday
inside Daiei Waipahu
where everything is 10% off
so he can stuff his face
with shrimp tempura
SPAM musubi, namasu,
chicken katsu, S&S Saimin, mochi
then hibernate 'til next Tuesday

I permit you a closetful of elastic waistband pants

Like Grandma Gladys
who survives by dyeing
her hair purple
penciling in two eyebrows
and dressing up
just in case her suitors
march back from the war
to propose a good time
elsewhere

I permit you to fart as you please
silent but violent
or loud and proud,
like Uncle Gary
who suntans
on a chaise lounge
in black extra-tight Speedos
on the driveway
for the Peeping Toms
and nosy-rosy neighbors

I permit you arthritis, liver spots,
wrinkles, skin tags galore,
hair loss or receding hairline
all the way back to Okinawa
like Uncle Milton's

I permit you to star in your own Bufferin ad
or pain-reliever-of-your-choice commercial

I permit you a cane or a walker
to your next chess match at Chinatown

I permit you an elevator to get you
to the next stage of the day

I permit you unlimited daily dose of nostalgia
with your mahjong pals
still breathing or in spirit

I permit you endless Pleasant Holidays to Las Vegas
like Uncle Ray who calls Caesars Palace
the eighth wonder of the world
and shoots for the jackpot
from his electric wheelchair
with an oxygen tank
and a plastic urinal
when it's not a urinary
drainage bag hooked
onto his arm rest

I permit you to deposit all
of your Social Security checks
into the slot machines
then cry out your losses

I permit you bi-monthly
nervous breakdowns
like Auntie Francine
who has never been the same
after Uncle Herbert dumped her
for a woman half her age

But I won't permit you to act stupid
like Uncle Jimmy
who acts like sixty-six is the new twenty
and to prove it
bought a secondhand motorcycle
and broke all the bones in his right leg
and almost lost the power of his left testicle

Or for you to end up like Uncle Rudy,
openly gay since he came out screaming
from between his mother's legs
but forever single at fifty-five
and a raging bitch
I permit you all the C words you can be:
Cantankerous,
Crabby,
Cranky,
Curmudgeon,
Crusty . . .

I permit you weekly blind dates
and even Neanderthal sex
so long as it's with a Trojan

I permit you to get up in the middle of a dream
and pee endlessly like an ageless stud

I permit you an unlimited supply of Pepto Bismol;
Alka-Seltzer; fish oil;
cranberry, apple, and prune juice;
and ginseng pills to stretch your memory

I permit you to repeat what you just said five
four, three, two minutes ago

I permit you to space out
blank out
blame the ghost
of your deceased husband
for hiding your dentures

Senior Bus Pass,
pearl necklace, gold-plated locket
double-A batteries for your hearing aids
and transistor radios

Most of all, I permit you to age gracefully
or with rage
slam the door
or keep it slightly ajar
for small surprises
still to come
and with God's help
I permit you
endless train of memories
to last you past the last station.

CHRISTIAN HANZ LOZADA

Maybe Life Is Better When

For years, we selfishly worried about our elders,
the ones who kept their Hawaiian tongues secret
when the state dictated them cut.

There were so few in the family, we fretted
none would be there to pluck a child's name
from the world like picking flowers for lei—

a gift at a greeting—no matter
that Queen Lili'uokalani's birth name
was picked for the sore eyes her elder suffered.

As time passed, our elders did, too,
and we joked about blindly stroking
alphabetical lists of Hawaiian baby names

or going *pull Pilipino* and selecting one
based upon joyful pops across taste buds,
words without context and removed

from meaning other than being unique
and just foreign enough for future butcherings.
Maybe our child won't have a Hawaiian name,

we consoled ourselves, *Papa didn't, and he was*
the doorway to culture by blood and knowledge.
Maybe Hawaiianess isn't in a name but in the blood

and the heart, and maybe we don't have enough
of either to have a child, and maybe we could have
named him Kawika because that sounds so much better

than simply David, and I never talk
to my cousin David anyway because
he's an asshole. And maybe life is better

when you cut out the parts of you
you think are important, and maybe
life is better childless.

Home Feels Like

The buffet booth across the walkway
filled with dark brown skin, curly hair,
and far more tattoos than vinyl seat.

Three Polynesian cousins bicker about me
between mouthfuls of overly-sweet Chinese.
"I seen him at Uncle's last week."
"Which uncle?" "Junior's."
"Which Junior?" They all laugh.
"You right, I seen him there, too."
"Stupid, you don't know which Uncle."
"But I seen him."

The three of them get up for more buffet.
Come back, two plates each: one a mix
of bland grease and meat, one a mountain
of crab legs. Three mountains make a range.
We make eye contact. I flick my head up,
a straight out the '90s nonverbal, "what up?"
One of the cousins returns it. "He seen us."
"Yeah, just now." "Stupid."

I smile, never feeling comfortable in my skin,
too big to be Filipino, too brown to be White,
always a shock to my own groups,
always having to chant my lineage as a greeting,
never that dude from an uncle's party.
But here, at a Chinese buffet with Samoan cousins
I've never seen before I have a place to belong.
I don't need to prove it, except to me.

CHRISTIAN HANZ LOZADA

Boiling on the Fire

Papa would let me help him into a sitting position,
saying in his version of breathy-age: "Sometimes
during cremation, the muscles contract and the body
sits up." But I could feel a concert of sinew
pull together to stand. But I could feel ghost weight
push me away when he walked.

When I stripped him naked to clean and cool bronze skin,
he felt no shame, had no struggle, gasping out: "We took care
of the elderly in Kamehameha School. We spent hours washing,
walking, hearing their stories." But when I dressed him,
he'd say, "Whoever said these were the golden years
was full of shit."

When I took soiled sheets and clothes to wash, his voice
filled out his body, thick and whole. He was a young man again,
tiger-striped from belt beatings but always mending the broken.
"Boil them," he'd boom. "Leave the sheets boiling on the fire
when your cousin Kamaka goes home
to Moloka'i with the other lepers."

Boy and Uncle: No Can Remembah

—Uncle, why you walking back and forth to da kitchen?

—*Huh? What. I donno. I no can remembah.*

—Dey say retrace your steps and den you going remembah.

—*Das what I doing. Why you tink I going back and fort? Not easy.*

—Okay, okay. Get your exercise anyways.

—*Retrace your steps? No work! What if you no can remembah where you was before? Tsah! Old age, eh.*

—I can help you, Uncle.

—*You no can help if I cannot tell you what I like remembah. If I could remembah den I wouldn't need your help. And if I no can remembah, you no can help. Sorry, eh. Not easy getting old.*

—Das awright, Uncle. Sometimes no can help. Bumbye going come back to you.

—*You mean like one boomerang you trow um out dere and going come back and slap you in da back of da head. Going have stars and exclamation points and birds tweeting like in da cartoons.*

—Yeah, den da light bulb going on!

—*Ah foget it, my light bulb burn out awready. When da ting burn out, no can replace. Funny ting, most times, light bulb no give warning, no get dim, dimmer, den finally kaput! Most times work perfeck until you go turn um on one day and no work. I tink my brain like light bulb. On. Off. Work. No work. Das da origin of "da kine" or "whachamacallit." When da light off, you gotta say, "Ah, whachucall . . . ah boy . . . ah try bring me da . . . da . . . you know . . . da . . . da . . . whachucall. Da da kine. You know which one eh?"*

—Ah, no. What?

—*Yeah, da light bulb in da ice box no work. Long time now. But I no can find da one dat fit. Regular light bulb no fit.*

—Take da bulb with you to da store, Uncle.

—*Sometimes I open da icebox door and no can remembah what I was going get. So I close um and open um again. Dark inside. Da smell of kim chee, rotten orange, meatloaf, teriyaki sauce come out but I no can remembah. Auntie tell, "Why you standing in front da refrigerator letting all da cold air out? Close da door!" So I close um. And stand in front da closed door. She tell, "Why you standing in front da refrigerator door? Get outa my kitchen." So I go by da TV and look at da refrigerator from dere. Still no can remembah. Ah, nevah mind.*

—Das awright, Uncle. Jes tell me what you need and I get um fo you.

—*You good boy. But I in trouble if I no can remembah what I like going from da couch to da kitchen. Maybe I get Alls-hammer.*

—Alzheimer's. I no tink so, Uncle. You jes fogetful.

—*No, what if I get Alls-hammah? What if I drive someplace and no can remembah how to get home? What if I foget my wallet, no mo ID and I no can remembah my name . . .*

—Whoa, Uncle. Take it easy.

—*What if somebody tell me dey like my ring and I give um to dem? I heard dat went happen to somebody in Chinatown, you know. What if . . .*

—Uncle, get all kine tings to help people.

—*No can help me. I no like you put me someplace where dey lock da door from da outside.*

—Das fo safety, Uncle.

—No. You call dat jail! Boy, no put me in jail!

—Uncle, you not going be put in jail.

—You donno. Maybe dat could happen. You donno.

—Ah, what you wanted from da icebox anyways? I get um fo you.

—I told you! I no can remembah. If I could remembah, I would get um myself. You hear!

—Uncle, no worry. No worry. Take a rest little while.

—I go store. Auntie tell me no foget take da list. I foget da list. I stay in da store trying to remembah what on da list. I go up and down erry aisle maybe if I see um I going remembah. Nutting. No see nutting das on da list. I buy bread, milk, and eggs. No can go wrong wit bread, milk, and eggs, eh?

—Smart. Good move, Uncle.

—Only ting when I get home I get scolding cause we get plenny bread, milk, and eggs from da las time I went store and forget da list.

—No can win, eh?

—Mo worse, I get my bread, milk, and eggs in my bag and I push da cart outside. Where I went park da car?

—Ai-ya!

—I no can remembah. So I figgah I gotta go methodical. How I usually drive in da parking lot. Go up da first row, down da second one, la dat.

—Good plan.

—I telling myself, white SUV wit roof racks. Easy. You know how many white SUV wit roof racks get? Millions? Get one in erry row!

—You jes gotta try remember before you go in da store.

—*Somebody said good to do puzzles. Good exercise fo da brain. So I try do crossword puzzle but Auntie already went do um halfway, in ink. And I tink she get some words wrong because she cheat and try put two letters in one box. I try tell her das not da correck way to do crossword puzzle. Gotta match da clue. Gotta match da space. And gotta connect to da uddah words. But she say I can do crossword my way and she can do crossword her way. No can argue wit her, so I get Wite-Out and erase all da ink but kill fight awready 'cause maybe some words correck. Make you wondah, eh? I used to like da kine in da Weekly Reader elementary school time. Get all da words listed undahneat. And one long one already filled in. I not good at puzzles.*

—Try park da same place, Uncle. Or maybe way far in da parking lot where nobody go. Only going get one car, your car, ovah dere.

—*I try park da same place errytime but sometimes busy so I gotta park in one new place. Das why I tink always get cars waiting blinking da blinker because dey like park da same place allatime. Try look. All senior citizens waiting fo one spot open up in dere favorite row. One time was raining and I had my cart, full of frozen stuff. I go da place I usually park. No mo. I go da second place no mo my car. I go back to da first place, maybe I miss um. Raining harder. Eggs and bread getting wet. I figgah I going back to da store and ask dem to watch my cart and den I going walk up and down erry row. I no like say I went foget where I park. From now on I going be one of dose blinker guys. Wait fo da spot to open up in da same row. All. Da. Time.*

—Uncle, maybe try take pickcha wit your phone. Help you remembah.

—*Good idea but pretty soon I going get all dese parking lot pickchas on my phone and I gotta figgah which one is which. Ah, next time I going go my same old spot and put my blinkers on.*

—Uncle, jes remember which way da arrows going: away from da store or going toward da store.

—Yeah, I do dat. I tell myself, "Up, up, up." Or "Down, down, down."

—Smart. Cut da number of rows you gotta look in half.

—Except den get da rows dat go two ways, up and down. Ho, I in trouble again. Used to be easy find my car. My old car I had one orange ball "76" decoration dey stick on da antenna when you go buy gas. Easy to find eh. Even if get plenny orange balls in da parking lot, you cut down da possibility, eh.

—Ah, Uncle, no mo da old-fashion antenna nowadays. No place to put your ball.

—Da last resort is you gotta ask da security guard drive you around da parking lot. Ho, I see plenny old futs riding around in da cart looking worried. Dey almost stand up to see if dey can spot dere car. Da guard only smile and drive slow. J'like he in da Kam Day parade. He wave at people. Da guy who went lose his car no wave. He stay all shame, anuddah stupid senior citizen who no can remembah where he went park. I not dat old. I can remembah tings . . . from fifty years ago. Parking space from twenty minutes ago? Not so good.

—No worry Uncle. Remembah how you used to take me buy ice cream? And you wait and wait and wait until I decide which one I like. You no even buy one fo yourself. We jes sit in da car. You watch me eat until I suck da stick clean and you laugh laugh laugh at me. Even if I spill or get da seat dirty.

—No even wait to go home. Park undah da big tree. Eat ice cream. Yeah, I remembah. Nowdays I get all futless because I no can remembah. My mind jes go blank. Fuzzy, like da TV connection went out. Only snow on da screen. No mattah what channel you change um to. Sometimes I feel lost, Boy. I donno where I going. Where I stay. Where I was. Scary sometimes, Boy. Scary.

—You know what, Uncle, when you feel la dat come pick me up and we go park under da big tree, eat ice cream.

DARRELL H.Y. LUM

Shopping Day

Saturday was shopping day. A full half-day circuit: Piggly Wiggly, Foodland, Chun Hoon, Chinatown, and usually ended with lunch at a chop suey house or sometimes at the Kress lunch counter downtown.

My father drove. My mother shopped for specific things at specific stores. At the Oahu Market full of meat, fish, and vegetable stalls she did her rounds: cabbage and watercress from one place, bean sprouts from another, sometimes she got a bunch of green onions tucked into her bag for free. Fresh water chestnuts, wet black nuggets that she picked from a wooden crate. *Harm gnee*, salted fish, pressed flat and coated with a thin layer of salt and packed in a wooden crate full of sawdust. She pawed through the pile and sniffed each one. I don't know what she was looking or smelling for. My father took me by the hand and we wandered through the stalls. We looked at the fish lined up on ice. He looked longingly at the colorful ones: kūmū, uhu, onaga. The fish seller held up a kūmū, red and glistening, so we could see its clear eye. My father looked at the price tag stabbed into the ice and muttered, "J'like gold," before we turned and walked away. We circled around to the roast pork stalls where the butchers would run their cleavers over the crispy skin, *ting, ting, ting* if we looked interested. The sides of golden roast pork, char siu red and shiny with honey glaze, and roast ducks dripping juice were all hung on hooks under a string of lightbulbs like they were onstage. The cleaver was usually parked upright, stabbed into the chopping block, a huge hunk of tree trunk. We watched the show as the butcher took an order and sliced one pound of meat off the slab, chopped it into pieces, picked it up with his cleaver, and dropped it perfectly lined up onto the waxed paper, weighed it, and wrapped it in pink butcher paper. I liked watching the tape machine that, in one crank of the lever, dispensed three inches of gummed paper tape and "licked" it on a wet sponge. The meat was sealed and safe.

We walked through the roast pork vendors, looking for the best one. As we approached, the *ting, ting, ting* was like a bell calling to us. If we stopped, the butcher chopped a bit of meat and offered us a sample. I loved the greasy fat and the crunch of the skin. "Very good," my father said. And we moved on. We sampled the next stall, then stopped at one who didn't offer a sample, although we still looked closely at the roasted meat to judge the layers of meat and fat and the crispiness of the skin. We went back to the first one and Father ordered, "Ah Sook, *yut bong siu gee yuk,* one pound roast pork, no chop. And half-pound char siu, no chop." Father liked to chop it at home so that it didn't get dried out. I carried the pink package like it was gold. I could smell the smoky, salty aroma through the wrapper.

Once in the car, if the pork was still warm, Father opened the package to let it cool off to keep the skin crispy. The smell wafted through the car and mixed with the sticky sweet of the char siu. I rode in the back seat and guarded the meat.

When we got home, Father wrapped the meats back up but snapped a piece of skin off the chunk of roast pork and handed it to me. I carried the pink package into the kitchen where my mother was already washing the vegetables. I put it next to the chopping board, still chewing the piece of skin, like a piece of gum. My job was done.

DARRELL H. Y. LUM

Finally, Peace and Quiet

for Russ

Small kid time, summer time nevah have nutting fo do. Was hot inside da house. Was hot outside da house. My older bruddah Russo no like play wit me. He go next door to Brynie's house fo play. When I follow him up da driveway, he turn around and tell, "You no can come. Go home!" I follow him two mo steps and he turn around again, "Go home! Go play wit somebody else!" But no mo anybody else. So I go home and sit on da steps outside da back door where can see Brynie's house and hear Russo and Brynie making noise and shooting cap pistols and making dying sounds. Somebody, I donno who, try sound like Pancho, "Si, seen-yore." He da funny guy to da Cisco Kid. Den dey playing da Long Rain-jah cuz somebody yelling, "Hi-ho Silvah, awaay!"

I like play too, so I make da horse sound like Silvah, "Neighhh, neighhh . . ." Russo stick his face by da window and yell, "Go home, I said. You no can play wit us!" I neigh again because I already stay home and I can neigh as much as I like. So dey play cowboy fight. Fight da bad guys. Can hear da cap pistols going off: *pak, pak, pak.* Come quiet. I donno if errybody went die or dey ran out of ammo or if dey playing something else.

Russo get everyting. Me, I get nutting: only what Russo no like or went use up awready. I always get his leftovahs. I gotta wear all hand-me-down stuff from him. I nevah have nutting new. Shoes, shirt, pants. All too big but Daddy said I going grow into um. Mama jes sew um smaller and say, "Good enough." Daddy only buy me new Bustah Brown shoes cuz Russo's shoes look like clown shoes on me and give me blistahs. And by da time was my turn fo join Cub Scout, Daddy too tired fo take me. He wasn't too tired fo take Russo. So I nevah have one Roy Rogers cowboy suit wit double holster six-shooter cap guns. Russo sometimes let me use one but he only gimme da one wit da ammo roll almost use up, so when we play, I run out of shots quick. No matter how many times you shoot, nutting. No sound. No spark. No nutting. Das why I lose to him all da time. He hog da ammo. Das why I no can win.

Bumbye, when he went Kawananakoa Intermediate, he wanted to join da band. All da boys only like play da trumpet. All da girls only like play da flute. But da teacha, Mrs. Harris, went look at Russo's lips and tell, "You going play trombone." At first he nevah like 'cause da trombone big and da case heavy and he gotta carry um on da bus plus his Pan Am bag.

When he come home, almost every day he set up da music stand and one chair and start to practice da scales: *da da da da duh, da da da da da duh, da da da da dee.* Ovah and ovah. And when he rest he blow all his galagalas out into one plastic cup thru da spit valve at da end of da slide. When he pau he wipe erryting down with one soft soft chamois. Da school trombone look like one juckalucka car: all dented and dull, smell old and stink. I wondah how many trombone players went blow thru um? I wondah what kine sounds came out? Maybe da same hold-yo-ears kine sound like Russo. Hee, hee.

Russo grumbo dat da school trombone junk. Dat da school case too big and heavy. Grumbo, grumbo, grumbo until Daddy say okay. We went Harry's Music Store and da man bring out one shiny new trombone. He look at Russo, "You brought your moutpiece?" Russo blow da scales, jes like at home, *da da da da duh, da da da da duh, da da da da dee.* Da man smile. Russo smile. Daddy no smile but he reach fo his wallet. Jes like dat, Russo get one new trombone.

Came wit one case wit soft red velvet inside fo hold da new trombone like one jewelry box. Russo shine um up until can see your face wit one big nose in da bell. When he snap all da latches close, you know da trombone safe inside. You can shake um but no mo noise. Nutting move. Stay safe inside. Shiny.

I wondah if later on I gotta play trombone so Daddy no need buy one diffrent instrument. Russo said Mrs. Harris said gotta practice all da time. Gotta carry your moutpiece wit you and when you wait fo da bus, practice buzz your lips. When you pau eat lunch, practice buzz. Russo even take um in da shower and can hear him buzzing after da water stop. Da witch lady, Miss Victoria Lee, live in da big house next door. We call her dat cause she always scolding us: no play in my yard, no steal flowers, no trow rubbish, you gotta ask first if you like get your ball. I donno how we supposed to ask first if we no can go in her yard. She mean. Her house dark. Front door closed. Curtains closed. Except when she yell at us. Russo tell, "Maybe she one witch. Dey like da dark. You seen her skin? All white. And red red lipstick.

Long nose. Long white fingahs wit red red fingahnails. She must be one witch."

She catch bus and when she come home from work she walk down da long driveway past our house right when Russo practicing. She tell real loud so da we can hear, "Toot, toot, toot. Every day. Toot. Toot. So much noise." Must be she can hear in her house too cause aftah her front door slam, you can hear da windows slam: bang, bang, bang. One two tree.

One time, da phone ring and Russo answer. "Hello?" Nobody there. "Hello?" No mo sound. Click hang up. Couple mo times dat happen. And we can hear from next door, "Finally, peace and quiet." Das how we know das Vicky calling. So next time when da phone ring, "Hello?" Silent. Russo blast um wit his trombone. I tink he said was one B flat. Hee, hee.

Upon Learning That the Digital Version of My Book *Expounding the Doubtful Points* Has Over 600 Unique Hits on the Open Access Edition Repository Site at Kapiʻolani Community College

(Remarks delivered at A Program for Exploring and Using the Bamboo Ridge Archives for Pleasure or the Classroom, March 26, 2022, at 10:30 a.m.)

To Li Po

I liked that poem
—the one about getting drunk,
three hundred gold cups of wine,
to drown away the sorrows
of generations.
                In those days
for every poem you wrote
a million Chinamen suffered to die.

   pen from bone
   brush from hair
   ink from blood

They were illiterate, you knew.
Better than words,
the liquor was solace enough for them.

This poem was written in 1972 in New York City, as an attempt to articulate what I had gleaned from some of my early readings of Li Po (also known as Li Bai) and other ancient Chinese poets. The next year I moved to Hong Kong to study Cantonese, and one day serendipitously discovered in an English language bookstore a collection entitled *The Poetry of T'ao Ch'ien*. It was a translation, with annotations, by James Robert Hightower of this poet's extant work, totaling about 60 poems. The poet, also known as Tao Yuan Ming, lived around 400 AD, and is regarded as one of the early Chinese masters.

Tao has been viewed as a recluse because early on he retired from government service out of principle to live as a farmer. In his pastoral setting, he wrote about the natural world around him, and is considered part of the "field and garden" school of poets. He has a whole series of poems entitled "Drinking Wine," and so many lump him with drunken immortals like Li Bai. Tao's famous poem "Peach Blossom Spring" may be one source for James Hilton's utopian society Shangri-La.

Yet, for me, what has been the most inspirational are two things. First, Tao wrote in a direct, down-to-earth style, without a lot of ornate allusions. Second, and most importantly, he maintained a vision of life which has grounded me for these nearly 50 years.

Life, Tao maintained, is short. In one of my favorite lines, he wrote:
　　The ancients grudged even an inch of time—
　　When I think of this I am afraid. (191)
(Hightower points out that the first line above is literally "an inch of shadow," measured on a sundial.)

Tao went further in another poem:
　　Human life is seldom long,
　　And worst of all, is wrapped in suffering. (89)

To me, it seemed like Tao did not subscribe to any afterlife. Neither the traditional reincarnation of Buddhism, nor the spirit world of China's folk religion (e.g., where at Ching Ming families offer food and facsimile gifts at the graves of their ancestors). But if there is no such solace after the hardships in this life, how are we to survive, how are we to now endure?

Tao was very clear-eyed about this:
　　Die old or die young, the death is the same,
　　Wise or stupid, there is no difference.
　　Drunk every day you may forget,
　　But won't it shorten your life span?

Doing good is always a joyous thing
But no one has to praise you for it.
Too much thinking harms my life;
Just surrender to the cycle of things,
Give yourself to the waves of the Great Change
Neither happy nor yet afraid.
And when it is time to go, then simply go
Without any unnecessary fuss. (43–44)

In several other poems he succinctly tells us "I clung to firmness in adversity" (147), using a term from Confucius. (To me it is the equivalent of the slang expression: "suck it up.")

Only in a few instances does Tao offer a modest hope beyond such perseverance:
Life is short but our desires many;
And all mankind finds joy in living long.
. . . .
But what is the thatched-hut gentleman to do
Who helpless views time's revolutions?
The dusty cup shames the empty wine cask,
The cold flower blooms uncelebrated.
Drawing tight my robe, I sing to myself,
In my revery deepest feelings stir.
There are many joys in living here,
And just to see it through is something gained. (47–48)

Tao was acutely aware of his physical self as mortal—a short and hard life, which he faced squarely with fortitude notwithstanding his knowledge that ultimately he would succumb. The alchemy he sought was not to prolong the quantity of life, but to enhance its quality. Amidst sorrow and dread, he focused on celebrating whatever joys he could manage.

And Tao's greatest joy was literature, the reading and the writing of poetry:
A good poem excites our admiration
Together we expound the doubtful points. (74)

It is not clear to me what Tao thought of his poetry, his spiritual self, facing the same existential limitations. His writings were not much recognized during his lifetime, and that seems to have been a source of disappointment for him. At one point he declared: "it matters not at all what eulogies are sung after my death" (6). Elsewhere, though, Tao looked to the past for guidance and esteemed what Hightower called certain "historical models of self-denying rectitude" (176). Of one such old master, Tao commented:

Alive, his name was known to all the world
And after death is handed down forever. (171)

So maybe leaving one's good name or perhaps a core body of poetry for posterity indeed would have mattered to Tao.

In any event, enough of his poems were copied and shared and then passed down to succeeding generations. This was employing the technology of the times—scribes with brush and ink and rice paper rolled up in scrolls. Fortunately, he was rediscovered by Tang poets like Du Fu and Sung poets like Su Shi, both of whom acknowledged Tao as a major influence. It was then that he achieved a longevity (though not immortality) that was probably beyond his wildest comprehension.

And, as luck would have it, after some 16 centuries—transcending both space and time, and also language—I too was able to find his work on a dusty shelf in a not well-patronized bookstore in a city far away. It helped me to articulate my own formative intimations of mortality and suffering, which I have tried to incorporate into my writings throughout the years.

My first collection of poems, *Expounding the Doubtful Points*, was published by Bamboo Ridge Press in 1987, as its issue #34/35. Tao was one of its two dedicatees, as much of its tenor was due to his long-standing impact on me. It went through four printings, totaling 3,744 copies. Ten years ago, there were fewer than 100 copies left. Then in 2020 the last copies were sold and the press declared it out of print.

At the same time though, Bamboo Ridge embarked on its preservation project in cooperation with Kapiʻolani Community

College and with the support of the Hawai'i Council for the Humanities. One of the last hardcopies of my book was sent to India, its binding removed and its pages scanned one by one, to be converted into a digital file. This version was then posted on KCC's repository site for viewing free of charge. Since its inception about two years ago, there have been over 600 unique hits, with downloads from even Romania, the United Kingdom, and Sweden. This kind of reception, in my mind, is nothing short of flabbergasting.

It is a mini-resurrection, though nothing compared to Tao's. Still what I had thought had been forever buried has now sprung back to life. It has in fact generated more interest in these old poems than there has been for decades. Obviously, having free and immediate access at a click of a few buttons is the reason. I will take whatever I can get.

I will end with a poem I wrote in 1974 in Hong Kong. I was renting out a room from a church in Quarry Bay. Two others, an old lady and a young girl (who was a freedom swimmer from China), had interior rooms. Mine came with the window, which was great because I could dry my newly washed clothes by placing them on hangers hooked onto the cast iron gratings of my window.

To the Old Masters

> "They may have left behind an honored name
> But it cost a lifetime of deprivation." — T'ao Ch'ien

I have no wife,
much less a son, to lament over
when he has died
in his infancy. I have never
seen a peach
blossom in the bud,
nor stood beneath
the Red Cliffs awed by
their towering history. Alcohol
tastes bitter
to me; I have always shunned
such classic delights.
Few friends

of mine write
poems—even letters are hard to
compose: how can we
swap our sentiments? Poring
over your lyrics,
the translations at my
side, I worry about how
muddle-headed my past innocence
has made me. This
is my only
claim to sorrow. Whatever
glimpses I have
caught of the vision within
your words must be due to
your daring: as
the moon on this night
illumines to the far reaches
of my room,
beaming through a window
cluttered now with
clothes, drying in the breeze.

Quarry Bay, 1974

Works Cited

Hightower, James Robert. *The Poetry of T'ao Chi'en*. Oxford: Clarendon Press, 1970.

Lum, Wing Tek. *Expounding the Doubtful Points*. Honolulu: Bamboo Ridge Press, 1987. UH System Repository for the University of Hawaii. http://hdl.handle.net/10790/5201.

WING TEK LUM

The Laundryman

Inspired by Paul C. P. Siu, *The Chinese Laundryman*

You would think
our work would be fresh and clean,
bathed as we are in soap and water.

But I can only see in front of me
the day's crumpled shirts,
full of sweat and grime,
the urine-stained underwear
and mud-splattered pants,
napkins smeared with food and drink,
sometimes bedsheets with menstrual blood
or handkerchiefs caked in snot
—all gathering in the humid air
in small spent piles in the back room.

They will need to be steeped in hot water
and scrubbed over the washboard,
then cranked through stiff rollers
to be wrung out to dry
and pressed down flat
by a sadiron straight from the stove.

Only later, as eyes adjust to night,
can they be fluffed and folded,
wrapped in rice paper,
neatly tied into separate bundles
and placed on a shelf behind the counter.

Only then will they be ready,
waiting for you to pick up at your leisure.

The Banquet

Before

You cut off the bottom of the stem
and then lengthwise
slice the white cabbage into quarters.
With the leaves facing down
you shake their tips
in a bowl of water
to remove any bugs.

In another bowl of water
you mix in some salt
and then lay in the clams.
Throughout the day
you change the water and the salt.
As they settle in
the clams express
the grit inside their shells.

You try to pick out bits of feathers
stuck to the bird's nest
made from swallow's saliva.
It takes good eyes and nimble fingers.
If it is too dry,
you moisten the jelly
to loosen it up.

After peeling the shrimp
—their heads and legs,
their shells, segment by segment—
you make shallow incisions
along the curve of their backs
to pluck out any veins
blackened by waste,
washing them off your fingers
into a cup of lukewarm tea.

You cut the coil of pig intestines
into tubes the length of your thumb.
Then you push a clove of garlic
which you had steeped in oil
through one open end
working it all the way to the other
to scour out the crap.

After

There are leftovers—
sometimes braised shark's fin
or fish maw or snow ear fungus.
But you also see
the cigarette ash in the soup
and the half-eaten drumstick
and instead throw them all
into the trash.

You soak the plates and bowls
in hot, soapy water.
After a while you rinse everything off
and wipe them dry,
stacking each in its place
on the back shelves
ready for use the next time.

Some of the still-hot tea
you pour over the chopping block
to help break down any grease
when you scrape it
with your cleaver.
You whisk the wok too
—a few quick swishes—
with a stiff bamboo brush.

You sweep the floor
making sure to get into the corners.
The dirt and grime
you collect in your pan

you dump out the door.
It is the same when you mop,
wringing out the dark water
onto the street.

You set out a tin of water
for the neighborhood cat
and shut the windows
and then turn down the lamps.
Everyone else has gone,
and when you leave
you carry out the garbage.

MARION LYMAN-MERSEREAU

Excerpt from *Kanani and Kainalu*

Prologue

She stops at the beginning of the trail near a ti-leaf plant and removes one of the large green leaves from the stem with a sharp downward pull. Then she finds a golf ball-sized stone and carefully wraps the ti leaf around it. Her small offering is placed near several other similarly wrapped stones on a boulder beside the trailhead. She starts her hike up the trail as she slowly finds her uphill pace, matching her breath with her steps. This familiar rhythm allows the tension in her mind to slide off her body like soap from her early morning shower. Her mind feels cleansed. There are only the surrounding sounds of birds, the breeze blowing through the trees, her breath synchronized with her evenly spaced steps.

She notices the difference between the lush plant life of the Koʻolau mountain range above Honolulu where she regularly hikes and the dryland forest of the Waiʻanae mountain range. The invasive vines that are strangling the watershed forest on the Koʻolau Range are not found here. She is on a hunt for a particular species that she knows is in this area. When she stops to admire the view of Mokulēʻia, she can see the Dillingham Airfield and the shallow ocean's turquoise stretching into its indigo depths. Just then she notices a medium-sized white dog on the trail several yards behind her. The dog stands still and watches her but keeps its distance. The woman continues hiking, thinking this is just an abandoned pig-hunting dog that couldn't keep up with the pack. While constantly scanning both sides of the trail for the plant she wants, she finally sees a sapling with a few leaves and the identifying flower on the slope below the narrow trail. The woman carefully sideslips down the steep angle of loose dirt to uproot the young plant. With her prize in hand, she struggles up the unstable incline. She looks up and sees the dog on the trail above her growling and baring its teeth. She backs down the hill, hoping the animal will lose interest in her. The dog disappears from her view. She resumes her climb to the trail—step by sliding step and reaches for a shrub to aid her final step to the trail. Just before she reaches the trail, she struggles to gain her balance—a flash of teeth with terrifying speed lunges at her. She recoils in time and quickly backs away from the beast and heads down the mountain.

She picks up her pace of her frantic descent. Her heart beats faster as the growling grows louder behind her.

Chapter 1—Mokulē'ia

I was on duty with my partner, Ricky, when the call came in from the dispatcher who informed us that hikers had found the body of a young woman at the Mākua Lookout above Peacock Flats, mauka of Mokulē'ia. We dumped our half-eaten shave ice cones which meant we didn't get to the treats at the bottom, my sweet, maroon azuki beans and Ricky's ice cream. We pulled out of our parking space at Matsumoto's and headed out of Hale'iwa toward Kaukonahua Road, through Waialua, past the fields of sugar swaying in the trade winds onto Farrington Highway. I wondered how much longer an industry that required a ton of water for a pound of sugar could last. Ricky wondered how much longer an industry that exploited its workers could last. We continued toward Dillingham Ranch which was the easiest way to gain access to the Peacock Flats trail.

Ricky Oshiro had been my partner for three years. What I'd learned so far was that he was sansei, what we call third-generation Japanese in Hawai'i. I knew he was a Kamehameha grad—somehow some Hawaiian blood could be traced back in his ancestry. I'd heard that some of the first Japanese to land in Hawai'i were fishermen who had been blown off course in a storm. His father had been part of the highly decorated "Go for Broke" 100th Battalion. Dr. Oshiro lost his arm in combat, but if it wasn't for the miracle drug, penicillin, that halted the insidious gangrene that was on the move to ambush his unsuspecting heart, he would have been make-die-dead. When he returned from the war Ricky's dad used his G.I. Bill to study and eventually earn a doctorate in agriculture—a fitting course of study for someone who grew up on a sugar plantation in Hāmākua on the Big Island, where Ricky's grandfather had gone to work from Japan. Ricky had big shoes to try and fill with a war hero dad who had a doctorate. Ricky's mind and mine were similar—like manini—small fish that stayed in the shallows, in English, known as Convict Tang. But he had innate skills that made him invaluable as a partner. He was an affable guy who could ho'omalimali with the best of them and since he was short he wasn't as intimidating as I was, his taller, haole wahine counterpart. Actually, I wasn't intimidating—I just surprised most people when they saw a woman in a police uniform.

Ricky was super observant and knew the names of most plants; he was always very keen on informing me of their names even though I couldn't care less. He said that knowing a plant's name meant you were "in relationship" to it. Ricky liked to be in relationship with everything and everybody. I didn't think I needed to be in relationship with plants—it's all I could do to be in relationship with people. I think this plant relationship thing came from his father being a Tropical Ag man at the university.

I remember hiking this mountain trail as a summer counselor at Camp Mokulēʻia. We found a scraggly ti-leaf plant nearby, pulled off one of the lower leaves, wrapped it around a fist-sized lava rock, and placed the ritual plea, asking for our safety on the mountain, on top of a larger rock which had several similar ti-leaf-wrapped stones. Most local hikers knew this Hawaiian ritual of asking permission and protection of the gods when going mauka. About halfway up the trail, we found the hikers who had called and soon after we saw the body of a young woman who looked like she was of Hawaiian descent. I didn't want Ricky's sharp observational skills to completely outshine me as usual so I made a point of noticing all that I could as we cordoned off the area and thanked the hikers for calling and telling us what they could. I noticed the woman had a swelling at the back of her head. There was a small uprooted plant in her hand and a short trail of plants matted down, footsteps climbing and descending as though she had changed her mind. I also noticed some footprints of a medium-sized dog.

"I ka nānā no a ʻike," the ʻōlelo noʻeau goes. *Through observation, one learns.* This reminded me of The Legend. The Legend was known for his observational skills—his kilo. I often thought about The Legend of the department while on duty. He was retired now but I knew he sometimes gave advice to rookies who asked the curmudgeon the right question. I'd learned so much from him, indirectly, from stories that older officers told about him, rather than from him personally. He didn't talk much about himself or his cases. What I learned rang similar to lots of detective stories—you do the work and you solve the case—but I wasn't much of a reader of mysteries so I got it from stories I heard. The Legend was a cynical WWII veteran who had a knack for paying attention to details most people would miss; he listened to his naʻau—literally his gut feelings—he learned to trust these feelings from his Hawaiian boss. This special way of paying attention, of observing evidence surrounding the case as well as his feelings, helped him find a path through problems when the path seemed obscured. He also had a penchant for quoting Dante and Shakespeare and other classic literature. If I wanted to get smart, I decided that The Legend was the one to learn from. There were so many cold cases in Hawai'i and we were such a unique place, isolated as we were in the middle of the Pacific, as Twain said, "the loveliest fleet of islands that lies anchored in any ocean . . ."

Medeiros and his forensic squad arrived, which allowed us to leave the scene. We heard the rescue chopper overhead, which would take the body to the morgue, as we headed down the trail. Ricky was unusually quiet on the hike down and the drive back to the station at Wahiawā. I figured the death of a high school-aged kid was a bit much to take in one morning so I let there be quiet for a while, and then finally I asked if there was a problem. After a long silence he spoke softly.

"I knew that girl—her brother was a classmate of mine at Kamehameha. Her family and my family were friends on the Big Island. He was a boarder, like me, and president of the hiking club— Hui Mālama 'Āina o Uka. I went on a few hikes with the club. He was the one who organized everything. It seems his kid sister also loved going mauka."

"What was her name?"

"Kanani—she lived up to it, didn't she . . ."

I agreed that she was an attractive young woman in keeping with her Hawaiian name. I wondered if she'd been hiking alone.

"If she was like her brother, she was a tough wahine, in which case, it's likely she was alone. Her brother told me she had a boyfriend who was a surfer who she always hoped would go hiking with her but he always wanted her to go to the beach with him."

"Sounds like oil and water."

"I found out about him because I kept checking on her, I had a crush on her when she was only in eighth grade."

"Go easy, brah!"

"Shut up. I was waiting for her to graduate and so I was always asking her brother if she was going out with anyone . . . I'd have gone anywhere with her . . ."

He had clearly been smitten with the girl but we had a job to do. I asked Ricky what he'd noticed at the scene. "I just was so stunned to see her . . ."

I decided to let him be quiet in his grief. It was almost the end of our shift anyway—I figured taking him to L&L for some chicken katsu might cheer him up—I knew if I picked up the check, he'd be upset but I wouldn't let him play the "gentleman always pays" game with me; he needed to get over his chauvinist attitude—we were partners after all.

On my way back to town, satisfied with my choice of seafood combo with chicken, I was looking forward to relaxing in my one-bedroom condo apartment near Maryknoll School. I was definitely a "townie." I liked working in the country, on the North Shore, but I felt more comfortable in Honolulu—it's where I grew up. Living in this condo, however, was like being in a goldfish bowl. I hated curtains, and my apartment was on the bottom floor of a three-story building that housed enough people to qualify as a parade as they marched past my picture window on their way to their mailboxes or the pool every day. My bedroom, thankfully, was not open to the public eye—but the window opened to the parking lot so I could inhale all the fumes of the early morning trying-to-beat-traffic workers. So it was either toxic fumes or a parade, but this parade wasn't nearly as entertaining as the Kamehameha Day or Aloha Week parades that my grandmother always loved to take us to with the marching bands, the floats, the Shriners clowns, the horses and their beautiful pāʻū riders. My brother and I would sit on a curb with my grandmother and watch it all go by. Sometimes I feel like a spectator in life watching an entertaining parade go by—not really participating—just watching, admiring—or not. Like today, I was trying to be as observant as possible, since Ricky had set the standard, but I felt like I was watching a movie—that I was somehow detached from it all and I just kept wondering—how could this happen to a young woman? What kind of karma had she chalked up, past or present, that her life had ended so early and so abruptly in such a beautiful place? I remember what Martin Luther King Jr. had said about the arc of the moral universe bending toward justice but in my experience there were more cold cases than solved ones. So where was the justice? These meandering musings were punctuated by Simon & Garfunkel's "The Sound of Silence," which didn't help my state of mind.

The next morning I met Ricky at the station in Wahiawā. He seemed a little less depressed but said he wanted to go home to the Big Island in a few days to pay his respects to Kanani's family. He heard they had come over when they received the news of her death, but they were going home soon.

"I'd like to tell the family that I was one of the first to see her after we got the call."

"Do you want company?"

"Did you want to come?"

I said I'd like to join him because I had family I hadn't seen in Hilo for a while but it was really just because I wanted to keep an eye on him. He seemed somewhat depressed, and after all, he was my partner and we'd become friends. My dad spent his younger years in Kohala so I always felt a connection with the Big Island. It's where most of the Hawaiian-Chinese side of the family lived, but they looked a lot more Hawaiian than I did. When I cut a pie into eight pieces I always look at one of the pieces and realize that's the Hawaiian-Chinese part of me, and when I cut the eighth in half, I realized that's how much Hawaiian I am. My na'au feels I'm at least half Hawaiian but my skin tells a different story—it's as pale as Waikīkī sand.

DANA R. LYONS

The Soloist

Kawika couldn't quite hit those high notes. The times he practiced at home, alone, no problem. But this was performance. In front of everyone. His hands were shaky as he held the silver of his instrument.

"*Ferrp, Ferrrp, Feerrrpp,*" came the sound. Everyone is watching.

He felt the sweat forming on his brow. He hunched down lower in his chair, attempting the scales from low C again.

Same thing. In the lower registers, he was in tune and on point. Fingers moving deftly pressing the valves. Until he hit the high notes. Then came that sound again,

"*Feeerrrrrrrppp.*"

A bead of sweat ran down the bridge of his nose. He looked up toward the front of class. Mr. Hara peered straight at him, red in the face and his eyebrows pointed inward.

"Straight Outta Compton"

"Ay, aaayy! I'm open, I'm open!" Kawika yelled as he raced down court, hands up in the air to make an easy target.

Boy flung the ball upcourt toward Kawika's outstretched hands. Kawika caught the ball, stopped on a dime as his defender ran past him, fake spun to the right, then swiftly turned left. He took one dribble to create space and leapt vertically, releasing the ball at the apex of his reach. Kawika held his hand aloft, wrist bent at the top. The ball arched upward before falling through the rim, the net snapping in a satisfying, "*thwick.*"

"Oooooh!" was the collective response.

"He tink he Penny Hardaway!" said a boy in a red Bulls jersey.

"Game!" Boy yelled. He ran up to slap Kawika's hand. "Good shot, Kawiks!"

"Good pass, Boy." The two walked to the sideline. They took a seat on the grass surrounding the basketball court, shaded by a monkeypod tree. Their backpacks and instrument cases were piled indiscriminately near the base of the tree. Another kid sat on one of the tree roots, blue L.A. Dodgers cap turned backwards, nodding his head as he listened to the music from his headphones.

"Eh, Booda," said Boy. "Whatchoo listening to?"

"Hea," said Booda, handing Boy the cassette case. Boy took the case and looked at the cover.

"Aahh, yeah. My braddah dem was telling me about dis one," Boy glanced down at the cassette case, passing it to Kawika.

Kawika wiped sweat off his brow as he looked at the front cover, examined the scowling faces, heads adorned with baseball caps and appearing to look down at him, as if he, the viewer, were lying on the ground. The owner of one of those faces held a gun. Kawika's eyes scanned the cover and fell upon the black and white, block lettering that read: PARENTAL ADVISORY EXPLICIT CONTENT.

"I like try listen," said Kawika, nodding his chin upward toward Booda.

"Hea." Booda untangled the headphones and passed his yellow and black Walkman over. "Try check 'um out, brah. Buggah is mean, cuz."

Kawika put the headphones on and pressed play.

"8 Ball (Remix)"

"C'mon! You guys are in the eighth grade already!" said Mr. Hara to the trumpet section. "I have kids in the seventh-grade class that can play this piece better than what I'm hearing right now." He tapped his baton on the podium four times quickly to reset.

Kawika and Boy, in the third-chair section, held their trumpets aloft, waiting. The piece that Mr. Hara alluded to was "Merry Christmas, Darling." Kawika knew the song from the Carpenters' Christmas album he remembered his mother playing leading up to the holidays.

"Now, we're just four days from the Christmas concert," said Mr. Hara. "Think of your families in the audience. They'll want to hear how much you've improved since last year." Mr. Hara counted down and began keeping time with his baton. He motioned lightly to the flute section, evoking the opening melody. He lifted an open hand toward the percussion, encouraging a crescendo. He asked the bass instruments to bring their volume down by a slow downturn of his wrists. At the point Karen Carpenter's voice would enter, he gestured to the clarinets to move the song forward.

Kawika counted rest measures in his head, waiting for the trumpet part to begin. "One, two, three, four. Two, two, three, four." The third chairs had a simple part, providing some background support—"fullness" was Mr. Hara's term—to the first-chair trumpets, who were supposed to stand for a solo during the bridge. "Three, two, three, four. Four, two—"

Boy tapped Kawika on the leg. When Kawika looked, Boy jutted his chin in the direction of the flutists. Kawika's attention was immediately drawn to the clear view they had of Jenn Oishi, one of the first-chair flutists. Boy knew of Kawika's affection for Jenn, and he again tapped Kawika's leg, nodded, and grinned.

Just then the first-chair trumpets stood and on cue began playing their solo. "No, no, no!" said Mr. Hara, waving his baton in frustration and bringing the song to a halt. He glared at Boy and Kawika. "Late coming in again!"

Kawika slouched in his chair, trying to hide behind the stand holding his and Boy's sheet music of "Merry Christmas, Darling."

Mr. Hara continued staring in Kawika and Boy's direction. A muscle in Hara's cheek twitched and he blinked once, slowly.

"I can tell you guys aren't practicing," Mr. Hara put down the baton and folded his arms. "I see Gary Takata in here every day after school, practicing his scales. Sharon Lin, she's in here. Courtney Teruya. Every day. She cares about improving. That's why she's first chair, playing the solo. They're not out there, playing basketball every day after school," Hara pointed toward the exit doors. "They're not walking to Jack in the Box and Gibson Department Store, going to buy cigarettes. Listening to anykine music. They're practicing."

Kawika and Boy remained silent, stone-faced. The rest of the class was either looking in their direction or down at the floor. The fluorescent lights overhead seemed unusually bright. Mr. Hara tapped his baton on the podium again, indicating a restart.

After school, Boy and Kawika found themselves on the basketball court again. Kawika hit baseline jumpers as Boy fed him the ball on each make. Booda, in his baggy jeans and oversize T-shirt, stood leaning against one of the poles holding up the backboard.

"Eh, how come Hara know we stay buying cigarettes from Gibson's?" said Kawika after another swish.

Boy silently rebounded the ball and bounced it back to Kawika. He hadn't said much since band class ended earlier that afternoon. A mauka breeze carried light rain over the court, granting a respite from the warm sun.

"Brah, I betchu was fricken' Courtney," said Booda, pulling his headphones down around his neck. "Membah dat time she wen' ask us fo' walk her home 'cuz she was skeaad fo' walk Undah da Bridge by herself. Fricken' teachah's pet!"

That's right, thought Kawika. Like several of the students at their school, the boys frequently walked home to their apartments by crossing a shallow stream beneath the freeway overpass. It was a much shorter route than taking the sidewalks along the main road and they could stop on the other side of the freeway for burgers, soda, and junk food. The local department store, Gibson's, had a large, brown vending machine that sold cigarettes. When the clerk wasn't paying attention, the boys would pool their lunch money to buy a pack for $2.30. Outside the jurisdiction of the school, "Undah da Bridge," as it was called, was the place young couples would go to make out or rival middle school students (usually boys but sometimes girls too) would show up to fight. Kawika sometimes noticed discarded needles on the high side of the stream bank.

"Eh, Kawiks," Boy finally spoke up. He nodded in the direction of the band room. Kawika turned to see Jenn and Courtney walking toward the basketball courts. He immediately felt his heartbeat quicken and couldn't help but notice how much he was sweating.

"Eh, Courts, you da one wen' tell Hara we stay buying cigarettes at Gibson's?" said Boy.

"Not even!" said Courtney. Then, with a nod and gleam in her eye, "Ho, you guys wen' get chewed out today, ah."

"Psshhh," said Boy. "Das nattin'. But we know was you anyways. No need lie." Booda let out a chuckle and shook his head as Courtney and Boy continued their banter.

"Sup, Kawika."

Kawika was already looking directly at Jenn but somehow couldn't fathom that she was greeting him. "Ay . . . Jenn," he was suddenly aware that he had visibly sweated through his shirt. He casually tugged at the back, trying to let some air in to cool him down. He ran his hand over his wavy, sun-kissed hair. "Wea you guys going?"

"Ah, we're jus' going to the vending machine at the girl's locker room to get Cool Ranch Doritos and soda. We gotta go back and practice some more."

"Oh," said Kawika. "We—"

"Ah, us guys jus' as good as da firs' chairs," said Boy. "No need practice. Watch, you gon' see."

"Okaayyy," the girls said together, as they walked off smiling at each other.

"Ch-check you out latah," said Kawika, although he wasn't sure Jenn heard him.

Boy waved a dismissive hand toward the girls, picked up the basketball, gave Courtney another look before turning back to Kawika, shaking his head, and muttering, "Fricken' teachah's pet."

Boy whipped a pass that Kawika barely managed to catch in front of his chest. He took one sidestep dribble and pulled up at the same baseline spot. As the ball released off the tip of his fingers, Kawika felt that familiar, momentary satisfaction.

"*Thwick.*"

Booda put his headphones back on and pressed play.

"Gangsta Gangsta"

Tap, tap, tap, tap. "OK, gang. Here we go. Imagine your family in the cafeteria audience. They got dressed up to hear you play. Your parents work hard every day for you. So you can have a place to live, clothing, food. Game Boys, Super Nintendo, Sega Genesis." Some of the students chuckled at the mention of their video game consoles. "This is one way for you to show them appreciation for their sacrifices. Some of your grandparents may be there. Siblings, aunties and uncles, your cousins. Remember, Christmas is a time for family. Let's give them a good show."

Mr. Hara's dark mustache twitched as he raised the baton. He took a deep breath, then brought the baton downward.

The band started "Merry Christmas, Darling." Hara made his usual conductor gestures, raising his hands toward the saxophone section here, turning one palm down toward the French horns there, while maintaining the steady rhythm. Mr. Hara allowed himself the slightest smile and lifted his eyebrows at the cohesiveness of the eighth-grade band.

"Six, two, three, four. Seven, two, three, four," Kawika kept the count. He couldn't help glancing every now and then toward Jenn in the flute section, who was concentrating on playing her part. Ever since she had greeted him on the basketball court after school the other day, he kept reliving the moment, wondering if he could have said something to keep the conversation going a bit longer. "Eight, two, three, four."

A few chairs to Kawika's left, Courtney readied her trumpet, preparing for the first chairs' solo. "Nine, two, three, four." Courtney and the other first chairs stood up and Kawika readied his trumpet.

As Kawika played the third chairs' supporting measures, he could hear Boy, sitting to his right, playing a different part. He directed his eyes toward Boy's fingers on his trumpet. Boy was playing the first chairs' part! Kawika was certain of it.

The band suddenly stopped. Kawika immediately looked in Mr. Hara's direction. The lightness of his face was gone, replaced with redness, a downturned mouth, and inward tilting eyebrows.

"Leonard Kealoha!" said Mr. Hara.

Boy nearly flinched at the sound of his given and family name. He returned Mr. Hara's stare.

"You have not earned the honor of playing the solo part! Who do you think you are, taking their hard-earned work from them?" Mr. Hara gestured toward Courtney and the other first-chair trumpet players.

"Nah, Mistah, was only playin' aroun' an' den," said Boy.

"Insubordination!" Hara stepped down from the conductor's podium. The class was silent. Mr. Hara walked to his office, opened a drawer, and picked up a notepad and pen. He scribbled on the pad, tore off the top sheet, and walked back out to the classroom.

"Get out of my class." Mr. Hara held the slip out toward Boy.

Boy twisted the mouthpiece out of the trumpet, opened its case, and placed the trumpet and mouthpiece inside. He closed the case and turned down the clasps. Then he slipped the case under his chair. "K den, Kawiks," he whispered as he stood.

He walked toward Mr. Hara and took the slip from his hand. Boy looked at the slip and headed for the exit. Mr. Hara made it back to the podium. The silence of the class broke when Boy slammed the door so hard Kawika felt the noise-proof walls of the band room shudder. Mr. Hara stopped mid-step, turned, and glared at the exit doors. But Boy was gone.

As Hara turned to walk back to the podium, his eyes met Kawika's briefly. Kawika blinked and looked down.

After school, Kawika met Booda under the monkeypod tree. He wasn't in the mood for hooping that day. "We go," said Kawika.

The boys didn't say much as they crossed the school baseball field, exited through the far gate, and walked down the trail toward the stream. They hopped from rock to rock until they reached the other side, tilapia sucking for air beneath their feet, then walked up the other bank running parallel to the freeway guardrail. When they got to Undah da Bridge, Booda took his headphones off and placed them around his neck.

"Brah, wat you tink gon' happen to Boy?"

"He probaly jus' gonna get small kine detenshen again," said Kawika. "Scooping rice on top lunch plates fo' cafeteria duty."

"I dunno. I heard his faddah wen come home las' night."

"Waat?" said Kawika. He knew that meant trouble. Boy's dad was often in and out of his and Boy's brother's lives. Boy didn't talk about it much, but from what Kawika gathered, Boy's parents got into awful fights, sometimes resulting in violence. Booda and Boy were second cousins and lived in the same apartment complex. There were many nights that Boy spent at Booda's place. "Frick."

"Yeah," said Booda. "I no mean wat you tink gon' happen regarding da detenshen. I mean, wat you tink gon' happen wen Boy get home?"

Kawika didn't have an answer. The boys crossed Undah da Bridge, but they did not stop at Jack in the Box or Gibson's. They walked straight to Booda's place. Kawika waited a few hours outside for Boy to come by, but he never showed. "K den," said Booda, as Kawika put on his backpack, picked up his instrument case, and headed home.

At dusk, Kawika pulled his house key from the front pocket of his Levi's. Just before placing his key in the lock, Kawika paused to put his ear to the door. Silence, but he wasn't expecting anything more.

The apartment was already dark. Kawika dropped his instrument case and backpack next to the shoe rack, took off his Nike high-tops, and walked to the kitchen in his socks. He opened the fridge and found a cling-wrapped tray on the top shelf, with a note stuck to the top. Kawika pulled the tray out of the fridge and read the note, "Make rice." He pulled the cling wrap off the tray and sniffed. Tuna casserole.

Kawika went about the routine of washing rice, measuring the amount of water to add by placing his index finger on the top level of the rice, then bringing the water level up to the first crease of his finger. He covered the rice cooker and pressed the on button. He took his backpack and instrument case to his room and sat on his unmade bed.

He opened the case, pulled out his trumpet, and fixed the mouthpiece into the slot. Kawika wiped down the instrument with a cloth. He pulled a folder from his backpack, opened the folder, and took out the "Merry Christmas, Darling" sheet music, placing it on the bed next to him.

Kawika brought the trumpet to his lips. His fingers pressed lightly on each valve. He opened the spit valve and drained any saliva contents in the cloth rag. He then pursed his lips and inhaled through his nose, eyes closed.

The phone rang down the hallway. Kawika placed his trumpet on the bed and walked down the hall. He picked up after the third ring.

"Hello?"

"Oh, hi," said a girl's voice on the other end of the line. "Um, is Kawika Reyes available?"

"Das me." He was pretty sure he knew who was calling, but not wanting to jinx it, Kawika asked, "Who dis?"

"It's Jenn," followed by a brief silence, then, "I got your number from Booda. Hope it's OK I called? Are you busy right now?"

"Nah. It's all good." Kawika suddenly became aware of his heartbeat. "Watchoo up to?"

"Nothing really . . . that was kinda crazy what happened to Boy today, yah?"

"Nah, gonna be minahs. He no skeaad Hara. He no skeaad da principal too. He jus' going do couple days detenshen probaly."

"I see," said Jenn. "Are you nervous about the Christmas show tomorrow? I'm so nervous! My grandparents are flying in from Maui to come to the concert."

"Ho, fo' reals?" said Kawika. "You stay nervous?"

"Yah! I've been practicing a lot. Is your family coming?"

Kawika remembered the tuna casserole he left on the kitchen counter. He sat down, leaning against the wall of the hallway, and brought the phone base onto the floor. "Nah," he said. "Dey no can. Jus' gonna be me."

The sound of children laughing came from a neighbor's apartment. Another neighbor was watching *Wheel of Fortune*. Kawika and Jenn kept talking as other households went about their Thursday evening.

In the kitchen, the button of the rice cooker popped up. The rice was done.

"Express Yourself"

Standing outside the back entrance of the school cafeteria, Kawika pulled at the collar of his aloha shirt. It was a blue-gray shirt from Liberty House with reverse-print hibiscus flowers. It took him forty-five minutes to iron after he and Jenn got off the phone last night. Another student, glasses sliding down his nose, handed him a kukui nut lei.

"No forget fo' put 'um on," said the kid. He walked to each male student in the band class, stopping to take a lei off his arm and hand it over, giving the same instruction to each.

Kawika put the lei on with his right hand. He gripped his trumpet in his left. He looked up and saw faint clouds drifting past the cafeteria, then over the basketball court. He turned his head left and right, but there was no sign of Boy.

"Kawiks!" came a voice from the crowd of students.

Kawika turned to see Jenn emerge, flute in hand. She waved with her other hand as she approached him. He gave a half-wave in return then gave a slight tug to the collar of his shirt.

Jenn was wearing a white and blue muʻumuʻu, in hibiscus print to match the boys' aloha shirts. She had her black hair in a braid. Kawika thought she might be wearing a bit of makeup.

"It's almost time!" said Jenn. The students around them shuffled about. A group of five boys and girls near Jenn and Kawika let out a collective laugh, then quickly dispersed. A half-moon shown through the clouds above, emitting a glow on the grassy area where they were all waiting.

"No be nervous," said Kawika. "'Memba how much you wen practice? No worries, you gettum." He again looked left and right, then stretched his neck to look over the crowd.

"I'm sure he'll be okay," said Jenn. She placed a hand on Kawika's forearm. "Boy is Boy. He'll be alright."

Kawika turned toward her and nodded.

"Let's go, gang!" said Mr. Hara "Everybody get in place."

"Ok, gotta go!" said Jenn. "Good luck."

"K . . . you too."

Kawika entered the cafeteria and was struck by the hum of voices and laughter from the parents and family inside. Some parents called out the name of their child. Others pointed their child out to a younger brother or sister. Several held bags containing lei for after the performance. A few students waved after catching sight of their family members. Kawika took his seat with the other trumpet players. To his right a chair sat empty.

Once the band was settled, Mr. Hara strode to the front podium and addressed the audience.

"Merry Christmas, everyone! Your children have been working very hard and it has been my pleasure teaching them this semester." A wide smile formed under Hara's mustache. He closed his eyes for a moment, then resumed. "Whenever we come together like this, it's a special time. We should cherish these moments. Your kids are growing up every day and the time goes by so fast. But, of course, Christmas is a time for family, for loved ones to gather. And here we all are. So let's begin."

Mr. Hara turned to face the band. His eyes panned across the students sitting in a U-shaped curve around the podium. He mouthed "Merry Christmas, Darling" as he held one hand in the air. Then he brought the baton up, started counting, "A one, a two, a one, two, three, four . . ."

The band flowed into the Carpenters' song, each student playing in harmony with the others. Each keeping count, directing their eyes to the sheet music, then to Mr. Hara's conducting, and back again. Kawika began his rest count.

"One, two, three, four. Two, two, three, four . . ."

He sensed the emptiness in Boy's chair even without turning to look. He watched Jenn play the opening flute part. She didn't look at all nervous.

"Four, two, three, four. Five, two, three, four . . ."

Kawika looked at Mr. Hara. He had never seen Mr. Hara so light. The smile remained. Occasionally, Mr. Hara would close his eyes and lip sync the song's lyrics, keeping the rhythm with his baton. That never happened in class.

"Seven, two, three, four . . ."

He searched the faces in the crowd. The mothers had brought their jewelry out. Gold Hawaiian bands, pearl earrings. Some wore muʻumuʻu, others Christmas dresses. The dads, with their aloha shirts untucked, clean-shaven, and hair gelled, often with a younger child sitting on their knee, stretched their necks to get a better look. A gray-haired Japanese man clapped to the beat. A frail grandma, hand still on her cane, swayed in her seat. These were all strangers.

"Eight, two, three, four . . ."

Kawika looked to his left. Courtney waved her bangs off her forehead. She took a deep breath and readied her trumpet, the silver gleaming like the moonlight through the clouds just a little while ago. The time goes by so fast.

"Nine, two, three, four."

Courtney stood up, pressed the trumpet to her lips. Kawika stood up with her and the other first chairs. He looked directly at Hara, raised his trumpet over the French horn players sitting in front of him, closed his eyes, and began playing the solo.

Kawika was lost in that same momentary feeling he got when releasing the basketball off his fingers, following the parabolic rise and fall, swishing through the net. The fleeting thought that none of it truly mattered. The only thing real was the sound, *"thwick."*

The soloists sat down. Their part was just four bars that seemed in the moment to last far longer, yet it had all moved by in a flash. The rest of the band continued.

Sweat gathered on his forehead as Kawika felt his heartbeat slowing to normal. Eventually, the song came to its conclusion.

Kawika glanced over to Jenn. She briefly returned his look with a slight smile, then turned to the crowd. The parents, grandparents, uncles, aunties, brothers, sisters, and cousins were all standing, clapping, cheering. Someone in the back let out a loud whistle. A few parents with cameras moved to the front to get a better shot. Mr. Hara turned toward the crowd with his arms outstretched, bowed, then directed the crowd's attention to the band. As he began clapping, Mr. Hara looked directly at Kawika. Red-faced, mouth downturned, eyebrows drawn inward.

Kawika returned Hara's look, narrowed his eyes without blinking. He held his trumpet in his left hand. His right hand was on Boy's empty seat.

As the families kept clapping, Kawika turned away from Mr. Hara and looked to the right of the crowd. There, in the walkway, leaning against the cafeteria wall, was Booda with his headphones around his neck and his cap turned backward. He smiled at Kawika and clapped. And kept clapping even after the crowd's ovation went silent.

ALAN D. McNARIE

At Halemaʻumaʻu

I'm sorry. I'm not here to worship you.
I'm a stupid haole, and don't know how, and wouldn't presume.
I'm too small to negotiate with goddesses.
I've heard you like gin,
but with my family history,
that would be like a rat offering warfarin.
So I'm here just to show my respect,
and let you know
what we're doing here.

We're living in a white house
in the rainforest
that will someday burn again
in your excrement of fire,
and will grow again from the cooled stone
when you let it,
without the house.
Someone else built the house there.
I wouldn't have dared.
But since it already stands there,
and there are still trees around it, we've moved there.
The forest will live around us
and we'll bother it as little as possible;
will take from it the calls of ʻapapane and ʻamakihi in the air,
the cold thin breaths of altitude,
a little sulfur sometimes burning in the lungs to remember your
        nearness,
certain weeds that don't belong there.
We'll take the Himalayan raspberries freely and then cut back the
        bushes;
we'll take the ʻōhelo berries and sow your half in the cracks
to grow new ʻōhelo.
We'll take, I hope,
inspiration.

We'll be quiet and respectful neighbors
and the forest will be there
when you want it back.

ALAN D. McNARIE

Dreaming I Cried for My Father

1.
last night I drove an hour to feed a friend's pets
because that's what I should do
she'd flown to Indiana to see her father
in a beige room after open heart surgery
though he told her not to come
because that's what she should do

and she is not a really close friend
though perhaps she will be
but to help her to love someone even more than her three cats
and her little black half-wiener dog
who mourns so much when she's gone   he won't eat
is worth an hour's drive nightly

last night I drove home and dreamed I cried for my father
ascended to the attic of the farmhouse we'd lost
the place I never went when we owned it
whose only memories are from the viewpoint of a head peeking
         through a trapdoor
at spiderweb citadels
of rats at night
thundering across the ceiling like a horizontal avalanche

but in my dream I ascended without fear
sat cross-legged on a crossbeam   blocking the rats' highway
no spider webs   plenty of light
I bawled great sobs worthy of a bear's mourning
howled my grief without shame
and though I was a man   the attic was child-huge
the roof beams soaring like a cathedral
so high a pro basketball team came up and played
dribbling the ball expertly crossbeam to crossbeam
shooting great soaring shots gable to gable
even though I was mourning
even though I've always hated sports

even though this was the most private spot of our house
in *my* dream
so I ignored them
meditated in the deep calm after a good cry
somehow descended cross-legged to a green field
where a second-string quarterback covered me with warm turves
and said   leave him alone
as he should have done
eventually he'd need the turves back to kick away   divot by divot
he played special teams too
but for now the turves were safe and warm though heavy
and I curled up
to be there

2.
Midwestern farm men don't cry at funerals
they talk about crops and weather
just like at church   the feed store   everywhere else
and though my father was no ordinary farmer
was the first McNarie to hold a college degree,
owned a wall of *National Geographic*s,
channeled blue-ribbon science fair projects through his son
was a demigod to his children
and always a demigod to himself
or at least a minor prophet
never cried until he was drunk
and he never touched a drop
until he was 45   his children were leaving
and the town gossips turned against him

then vodka snuck up on him
because demigods couldn't become alcoholics
and for two decades the whole family politely ignored him
without knowing how desperately each of us   alone
pounded on that great bronze shell of alcohol
trying to wake our father our husband our son

he had to fall off a tractor
get run over with a wheeled disc
and dry out in the hospital so violently

Mom told us he was dying
before we began talking to each other
and it was years more
and his legs were so wasted
from a demigod's diet of potato nectar
that he couldn't walk
before we finally convinced him
he was not a demigod
just a failed Midwestern farmer

he never touched a drink after that
he never forgave us
never cried again

3.
the old demigods always cried
Odysseus bawled and howled at every opportunity
wailing great gobbets of noise
to match his great griefs
Cú Chulainn my lost ancestor
mourned himself into a bear
Odin shook the timbers of Asgard with his sobbing for Balder
Israel tore its garments   gnashed its teeth
and even in the least of verses
Jesus wept

Who gave us this commandment of ice?

I didn't go to my father's deathbed
until the last hours
and had no words to make up for the morphine underdose
prescribed by the Fed-fearful doctor
as Dad felt the cancer liquefy his own lungs
and struggled to force the words past his disease-slurred tongue
to crack one last joke
and no one dared laugh

and at the funeral only grandmother sobbed softly
no men cried
least of all me

having mourned him years ago
and this being the Midwest

4.
In the dream the quarterback was about to kick off
the last layer of turf
so I emerged
went into an auction tent
full of Greek vases
and staring at a freeze frieze?
of tall stiff warriors
awoke

so this evening I drove an hour to scritch the ears
of Keiko the half-wiener dog   grieving by her untouched food
while her mistress did what she could
back in the Midwest
where you only cry
in your dreams

JONATHON MEDEIROS

Living Near St. Catherine School
(Ghosts from the Past in the Faces of the Present)

I don't recall the question or the response I gave, but I remember the frustration rising in the nun's face, creeping up her neck before turning her mottled brown cheeks dark purple. She asked again, her words clipped, her lips tight, her long black habit shivering with her consternation, as the class nervously giggled. And another response from me, possibly the same response. I don't remember saying the wrong thing on purpose. I wasn't trying to be smart or funny. There was clearly a gap between Sister Scholastica's query and my understanding of her desires, a gap that distressed me as I watched it yawn open—

She grabbed one of those overlarge chalkboard erasers from behind her and threw it at me.

"Tssst! Jonathon!"

I ducked and the eraser clattered across the floor. The class was silent for a moment before a loud guffaw snapped the air.

She grunted, reached back behind her again, maybe embarrassed that she missed or maybe angry at Kama's laughter. Her searching hand found the teacher's edition of the social studies book. This she hurled with two hands and an audible, guttural effort. Kama ducked and the book hit someone else squarely in the face.

I can't imagine this did not break that student's nose but I can't recall the immediate aftermath. I don't remember blood or crying or Sister Scholastica being in trouble or even being embarrassed by her anger at children.

Later, some other day, maybe during the uncomfortable week when the nuns taught us about where children come from, I remember listening to Sara cry from the broom closet, its door locked tight inches behind my head. I wonder what Sister Scholastica would say now that Sara is out of that closet and all the others.

I live just a few tenths of a mile from the school now, up on a hill over town. Every Sunday I hear the bells ring and it is a pleasant sound. But as the chimes roll over the treetops like the church itself breathing out a sigh and a prayer, if I think of anything, I think of that book flying across the room, I think of the sound of Sara crying, I think of Alma telling me I had nice shoes and how Sandra always talked to me at lunch and how strange it is to miss a friend you haven't seen in 30 years because you will never see her again.

I remember the volcano we built, the way I broke my front tooth on the monkey bars or the time I had no money for lunch, so I sat in the classroom with one of the nuns. I sometimes remember the line of cacti behind the cafeteria, the time the invisible spines irritated my hands for days, or the hard ice we bought from Mother Superior's office at the end of the day on Fridays.

I remember the time an 8th grader told me to stand against the wall in the bathroom and so I did, my corduroy pants hot on my legs. The way the tile felt cool against my back even through my undershirt and button up. The sound of his feet as he ran across the room and kneed me full speed in my crotch. The way I bent over in pain but didn't make a sound and how his laughter turned to some kind of an apology about how he thought I might move. I remember also the time I wasn't allowed to go to the bathroom or maybe I didn't ask to go out of worry and so I sat in my own urine-soaked seat, hoping no one would notice, hoping it would dry while everyone else had recess. The nun did not speak to me as I sat there alone. She must have known, right?

The school is still basically the same as it was: two long buildings, parallel, with a courtyard in between. I remember needing to look for Maile every morning, after the all-school prayer in the yard. She was in 7th and 8th grades when I was in 1st and 2nd, I think. She was tall and her hair was thick and black, like a crashing wave of ink roaring off of her head, framing her long nose and dark eyes, her smile, a flower always right there behind her ear. Always. I loved to look for her and watch her walk away, to see her impossible hair almost touching the ground as she strode, barefoot, back to her class, around the corner in the other building.

Sometimes when I go to the bank in Kapaʻa I think I see Alma, from that day in kindergarten. I see flashes of these people, 5-year-olds, 4th graders, former teachers, first crushes, youthful tormentors, briefly dancing behind the eyes and smiles of the people who walk by me in my present life.

Isn't that you, Ms. Kaye? I think as I drop my daughter off at daycare and wonder about time folding over on itself, the past touching other moments across our timelines.

I don't ask or confirm when I see these ghosts in the faces of the present. I just let the memories visit, passing me like the sounds of the bells on Sunday, like the scent of plumeria on the breeze, like the crunch of ice between my teeth as I walk up a hill under the sun, like a woman walking on the path, her long hair trailing down, like the smell of urine in a hot restroom, like the sound of a book hitting the floor.

JONATHON MEDEIROS

Looking for a Pink Falango

The words the kids invented
The way language bubbles out of them
And carves at the corners of our lives
Turning unspeakable observations
Into the syllables that we find in the OED.

And some are mere switches of sounds
"Hand tanisizer." "Mazageen." "Falango."
And some are somewhere between actual and onomatopoeia
"A-top-a-top" as the helicopter chops the air above our heads.
And some are pure creation, searching for connection
"Dibbee" when we should do that again.

The words that kids invent
The way language orders a deliriously messy world
The way we separate ourselves from our surroundings,
Our existence,
As we name it,
But also the way we see something suddenly
And we can share it,
Build community between each other,
With a word, invented as they all were,
Out of gibberish,
Sewn together out of sound and a need to touch each other's
Experiences, hearts, minds.

JONATHON MEDEIROS

The Other Importances of a Forest

Standing under the twisting branches,
The crescent moon sickles,
The delicate, firework pops,
The twisting dark green creeping,
The sweeping, dripping, hanging and reaching,
The lace and tendrils,
The dried blood reds and white gray blues—
Standing under the broken light,
The sun just flickering in but reaching everything,
The cool touch of the wind and the not-rain,
The licorice and fern and dirt,
The smell of growing and decomposing and recomposing
(and now the music and the language of composition)—
Standing off the trail, just a few steps away from
Kalua Puhi or Halemanu or Pu'u ka ohelo,
And the other importances of a forest
Are all around you:
 Being under a tree
 Being under another tree
 Being a person being under a tree with another person
 Being in a place that is home to all the worms and mushrooms
  and beetles Being in a place that is home to the sounds that
  birds make,
 A home to the sounds that birds stop making when another sound
 announces itself
 Being in time,
 In nothingness,
 Being in the air that is so rich, so thick, it smells different, and
 what is that for? Being under all the trees under the taller trees
 covered in the vines and crawling with life under the sky that is
 sometimes blue and sometimes a different blue and some times—

JONATHON MEDEIROS

To the People on the Cruise Ships

Smoke Meat.
Pickle Mango.
Shave Ice.
Crack Seed.

These are not imperative sentences
But it is imperative that you know
That these phrases are missing no letters.
They miss nothing, want nothing,
Least of all your grammar.

These are fragrant, folded, complicated nouns
That carry the weight of the childhoods of specific humans
Who grew up on actual humid streets, back jungle drives,
Who ran with glee out to the road at the rumble of the busted truck
And the man yelling "Akule, akule, A-KU-LE!!" *Beep beep.*

These words, hand painted on crude plywood
Roadside signs, carry the weight of the ghosts
Of the plantations, the cane roads, the spiders
And the mongoose, the pig and the goat,
The manong, the unko, the tita, dat guy who bumbye gon bus yo lip.

These words are food for actual people
Who live in an actual place,
Who are trying to grow and heal from an actual past.
$2 dollah, 1 bag, Honest System.
Resist the temptation to fix these signs you can't read.

TYLER MIRANDA

Another Portagee Histrionic Minute

Welcome to yet another episode
of *Portagee Histrionic Minute*,
brought to you by Know Education Werx,
painstakingly helping Portagees learn da three *R*'s,
reading, 'riting, and 'rithmaticking,
for over three weeks now.
I your host Aunty Agnes Texeira.
And, *ai koresh*, I so excited!
I get one very special show fo' you today.
All you guyses out there
already know all da invasive stuffs us Pochos wen' enhance da
islands wit', ah?
Linguiça, cane field *lunas*, Nativity competitions.
Some of you buggahs might even know dat da motor mouth,
da kine dat only go faster and faster,
like you gassing your car in neutral: 'ass ours.
But not many braddas and sistas know da *shaka* came from us
Portagees.
'Ass right.
It all started wit' Portagees on da plantations.

Now, most braddas and sistas out there
tink da *shaka* wen' invention around May 17, 1912,
from dis buggah by da name Hamana Kalili,
one ranch-hand-turned-security-guard at Kahuku Sugar Plantation.
So sad, Hamana wen' lose his middle three fingers
in one hotly-contested dominoes tournament.
It's thought his unique salutation
of just da thumb and pinkie
was da origination of da *shaka*.
But Aunty know different:
da *shaka* actually one concoction of two Portagees.
'Ass right.
Was 1901,
and Elvis Camacho,
one day laborer at Oahu Sugar Plantation in Waipahu,

wen' forget his face panty on da crucial slash-and-burn day.
Anybody who ever live by one cane field know,
wen da black snow falling,
only natural, da whole face come itchy, ah?
Get hard time breathe 'cause all da sooty particulate.
So wit' one hand,
Elvis cover his mouth.
But wit' da other hand,
him start cranking his nostril wit' da pinkie finger,
trying fo' open up one air passage.
Wen his crewmate by da name Francis "Chickie" Furtado
wen' ask if he all right,
Elvis just made da "thumbs up" signal
'cause he no could talk,
but at da same time, kept right on torquing his nose hole.
In one display of playful brotherhood,
Chickie wen' emulation da curious thumb-and-pinkie gesture
and called out,
"Shuck 'em, brother! Shuck 'em!"
'Cause, to him, look like
Elvis was going fo' broke,
trying fo' dislodge one nose goblin
da same way we twist Kahuku corn cob from da skin.
But what Elvis heard
was Chickie teasing in broken Portuguese and English:
"*Chocar*, brother! Chocar!"
Ho, wow, shocking, bradda! Shocking!
Elvis thought Chickie was giving him da gas,
as if Elvis was making da kine scandals
by wringing out his nostril in da middle of one cane field.
So Elvis did da only sensible ting he could.
He wen' exaggerate da motion,
digging his nose at Chickie so vigorously,
he no could help dat day wit' da slash-and-burn
'cause he had fo' go infirmary.
But 'ass another story.
Thus, "shuck 'em, brother" and *chocar*
became *shaka, bradda*
as both da gesture and da name wen' catch on
like one gaslit fire

wit' da other workers commemorating da spirit of da event.
So much so dat by 1907,
da *shaka* had come to be understood across all Hawai'i Nei
as one expression of good-natured fellowship and group unity,
all thanks to da relentless ingenuity of two Portagees.
And, of course, Elvis's broken nose, ah?

Well, dat time has come,
but join me again next week
fo' another installment of *Portagee Histrionic Minute*.
We going continue fo' explore all da true stories
of just how da Portagees wen' whip
not only da islands but da entire world into shape.
Next week, we going conclusively prove
was da Portagees, in fact,
wen' first discover all da rings around Uranus.
Dis is been Aunty Agnes Texeira,
and from me to you,
from da thumbprint of Ka'ena Point
to da pinkie of Makapu'u,
I like send all my braddas and sistas out there
one warm, heartfelt Portagee *shaka*.

TYLER MIRANDA

Why Dis Still One Problem?

Da coronavirus wen' give us someting
precious

someting
sacred even

one chance
fo' improve
fo' evolve
fo' embrace what da buggah trying fo' teach us

Da coronavirus no care if you
Native Hawaiian
Pōpolo
or one Haole

Da coronavirus no care if you
Pākē
PI
or one Pocho

Da coronavirus no care if you
GOP
Indie
or one Dem

Da coronavirus no care if you live
Wai'alae Iki
Pearl City
or KPT

Da coronavirus no care if you
Bus Driver
Big Shot
or one Beach Bum

Da coronavirus no care if you
Catholic
Buddhist
or one Scientologist

Da coronavirus no care if you
Hetero
Māhū
or one bigot

Da coronavirus no care if you
Tūtū
Hāpai
or one keiki

Da coronavirus no care if you
believe in 'em

Da coronavirus no care if you
believe da vaccine work

Da coronavirus no care if you
understand
wearing one face panty is fo' ev'rybody
but you

Da coronavirus no care
'cause da buggah got 'em figured out:
us all same/same

So

if one simple organism can tell
maybe one day
us can too

Nā ʻAumakua

"He haki nuʻa nuʻa nei kai"
I had practiced this chant for months, standing in my yard under the ironwood trees.
"ʻO ʻawa ana i uka"
And here we are, seven of us on a heaving boat, squinting in the noontime sun, asking permission to land.
"Pēhea e hiki aku ai ʻo ka leo"
The island, hovering close now, had lived in my dreams for so long.
"Mai paʻa i ka leo"
The wind snatches my words before they could make a sound. But our collective voice sings out. The two men in the Zodiac inflatable boat alongside our larger boat chant in reply, welcoming us on behalf of Kahoʻolawe[1], the revered island also called Kanaloa.

We step from our boat to the Zodiac for the short ride closer to shore. From the Zodiac we slip overboard like clumsy boulders into the chest deep water of Hakioawa Bay. We find our footing in the surf and help pass garbage-bagged luggage to shore. We are the last boatload, joining the others to make a group of forty-four: volunteers, kua (helpers), and members of PKO (Protect Kahoʻolawe ʻOhana), the island's caretaker group.

The fatigue of our 3 a.m. wake-up call creeps over my excitement at landing. But before food or rest, ceremony. We circle up to count off and receive instructions. Pule, a blessing, then into the water again to give individual thanks to our ancestors for bringing us here, for keeping the island and ourselves in health. Rocked by waves, I face Haleakalā across the water and give silent thanks to everyone I can think of—grandparents, aunts, uncles, siblings, generations back whose names my mother's genealogy work unearthed. I thank my Norwegian-from-Minnesota father for marrying my mom, adding me to this family web.

We return to the beach in our own time, dripping and quiet. The shadows of earlier times move around us.

***

The next morning it is still dark when we hear the sound of the pū. I dress, zip the tent, walk toward the beach, then up the short cliff. Bobbing head lamps show where others make their way in the dark. At the top I join a dozen others all facing the ʻAlalākeiki Channel to the east, some standing, others sitting, some near the cliff edge, some farther back.

I scan the sky—gray now—looking for hōʻailona, signs from the natural world. The silence contains the sea, the wind, our thoughts kept closely to ourselves.

Waiting for sunrise is a gentle test of patience. It almost always takes longer than I expect, especially if the waiting and watching begins in full darkness. As soon as the gray lightens, I take out my sketchbook to draw the looming outline of Haleakalā across the water.

I draw the mountain twice, both times thinking I will capture all of Maui on my paper—the sweep from the West Maui uplands to the shores at the east—but both times Haleakalā fills the page. There's a largeness I can't diminish. With my hands busy, doing something no one else is doing, I somehow feel more a part of the group. This is my self-designated role all weekend, recording secretary, so I draw the scratchy, stunted trees, I draw the open thatched hale, I draw the cook house and folks singing and playing guitars and ʻukulele. I take notes, the only one I see writing.

As the edge of the clouds catch on fire, we chant the sun up.
"E ala ē
Ka lā i kahikina"
Voices together accompanied by hand claps. Although I learned the chant years ago, the claps are a new addition for me. I catch the rhythm tentatively at first. The words come not once or three times but over and over until the sun is fully revealed. Day is here.

***

Our service is trail work. We are widening, leveling, and lining the path that will be used for Makahiki ceremonies later in the year. Up ahead the young guys hack back thick growth with weed wackers. I and several others clip back sharp branches of kiawe and koa haole. Gray skies keep us cool until 10 a.m., when clouds wisp away and we bake. I help in the line moving stones. Hand to hand they go from the scrubby hillside to the rock necklace lining the trail. This must be how the menehune did it, by dint of numbers in the absence of technology. Hand to hand, hand to hand. I stumble under the weight of a large stone and am ever more passed over by the stronger and younger in the line. If I wasn't already, I am now in the "aunty" category.

Most of our group are in their twenties or thirties, students at UH-Hilo or recent graduates. I'm an add-on from Oʻahu, folded in by my friend Drew who is our coordinating faculty member. Our group of volunteers are joined by the Waimānalo Limu Hui—fewer and older men and women, but more boisterous by a power of ten. As we work the trail, they're the ones telling jokes, working like demons, and singing Hawaiian songs spontaneously full throttle across the hillside.

Work. Eat. Bathe. Rest. There's a simplicity to the schedule here. Everything but sleep is together. Work together. Cook together. Eat together. Bathe in the ocean together. Explore the coast together. It is for safety, on this island still riddled with unexploded ordnance, surrounded by an untamed sea. But it is Hawaiian too.

I have never had so much togetherness throughout the day. My Oʻahu home life includes oceans of daily solitude. Do I like all this togetherness? I do.

***

Day Three, our last full day on the island, we wake and eat quickly in the dark then gather to begin hiking before sunrise. Our goal is the top of the island where we will perform ceremonial protocol. On the trail we'd worked the day before, we climb stair-step-steep hardpan, the red earth naked and worn. The grade lessens and our group spreads out, small clumps and pairs continue to walk together. I walk along between groups, often grateful for the arrows someone earlier thought to scrape with their shoe to mark the main route among ribboning paths.

Finally at a junction of dirt roads our whole group stops to rest, the stragglers catching up. Circle and count up, all here. I stand with and apart, both. It is 10 a.m.; we've been hiking for hours.

Refreshed, we walk the road to Puʻu Moaʻulaiki, our first spot for ceremony. All in silence we put on kīkepa, take off shoes, and form three lines in front of the ahu. On this dry, hot island our ceremony is draped in mist and wind, a true blessing. Pū to the four directions. Offering of ʻawa, then our individual offerings of wai collected and carried from our home places. My part is small—but as big as everyone's: placing my water and stating, "'O Leiokanoe ko'u inoa, mai Kailua, Ko'olaupoko, O'ahu." Then oli, hula, gifts of poetry and movement. I stand a long while silent and watching, barefoot on the rough and stony earth without feeling cold, without impatience.

Ceremony pau, we descend again, back to boots and socks, leaving our silence and heading to lunch. Staff from KIRC—the Kaho'olawe Island Reserve Commission—who operate restoration programs at the opposite end of the island, share water barrels they'd brought on their electric trucks. Then they disappear, joining us again after we have eaten and rested. We head then together down a long side road to Pu'u o Moa'ulanui, a taller pu'u and highest point on the island. We gather in grassy shade at the base of the knobby hill, the KIRC folks hanging back yet conspicuous in their light-colored work clothes and white skins. They look as awkward and unsure as I'd felt landing on the beach at Hakioawa.

Our second ceremony begins with climbing the steep rocky trail in barefoot silence. The mist had lifted long ago but the wind remains. At the top we find our places, not in lines but scattered over rocks and the path. A large bell stone—silent today—overlooks the coastline far below. It's a stunning, expansive view. More oli and hula, performed by just a few this time. The KIRC folks still hang back, respectful, wondering, looking uncomfortable. Our group welcomes them but leaves them apart. With our ceremony finished, we all explore the pu'u top and the Navigator's Chair slightly below, the stone seat where voyagers of old viewed the Kealaikahiki Channel, the ocean path pointing southwest to Tahiti.

I stand in the wind, looking and looking. The lei of islands sits so close across the water: Lāna'i, Moloka'i, Maui, Hawai'i, truly a family in this vast sea. Kealaikahiki leads to the past, taking my imagination to those voyages that crisscrossed time and currents. Navigators had stood here, where I was, to study the ocean and the heavens. Sailors who were my ancestors had traveled those seas back and back and back in time, a long and sinuous chain that linked to me here now. Here now and long ago all at once. For the first time I feel deep in my na'au the reality of that ancient and alive history. I stand silent in the wind, drinking in the sight of islands.

Our hike down follows a different route. Our UH group stops to take photos with Mauna Kea clearly visible across the water. Today similar ceremonies are taking place on all the island chain's main mauna in solidarity with the kia'i protesting the telescope project on

Mauna Kea. Photo ops taken, we descend at a trot, eager to leave the sun and bare, eroded uplands. I hike alone, lost in the images of the day. One foot in front of the other, down, down, down. Finally Hakioawa comes into view, the trail dropping into the back side of camp, near my tent. Hot, tired, dusty we all head straight to the beach. Where to find Hawaiians? In the water.

***

We rise in the dark one last time. We have slept in the open on the beach or nearby to save the time and trouble of packing tents in the dark. Headlamps flit past, catching me as I brush my teeth in the lee of a brush pile or crouching to double bag my gear for our ocean passage.

At last we all gather by the boathouse to wait for Uncle and his motorboat that will gather us from the Zodiac. We count off. We review our instructions. We pule.

Then Uncle's lights wink at the mouth of the bay and we load the Zodiac. My group waited longest on Maui for the journey over so we are the first to leave. Out in chest-deep water, I heave myself onto the inflated boat gunwale, hoisted by others to flop over the side and onto the boat floor. Inelegant but successful. Transferred to the fiberglass *Pualele*, we chant our farewell, requesting release from Kanaloa. The island now looks, in the earliest light of day, like something magical, as delicate as a flower, as enduring as the heavens.

We cross on calm seas. Less than halfway to Kīhei we can clearly see both Mauna Kea and Mauna Loa to the southeast. Later they are obscured. The nine of us are largely silent, our cheeks salty with both tears and salt spray. For an hour we are together and each alone with our own thoughts.

At Kīhei boat landing there is the business of unloading, washing out coolers, and bathing ourselves in the outdoor public shower. But first our group's helper, Kasha, pulls us aside to contemplate where we have been. Our group forms a circle, instinctively erecting an energetic shield against the dozens of tourists who troop past just yards away to board snorkel excursion boats. They seem as foreign as Martians.

"Remember you have the island in you now," Kasha says. "You've been changed, all of us have changed, but not everyone will understand. Even your family may not understand."

We each acknowledge out loud one thing that has shifted in us. We all have something. We hold that together in silence and clasp each other's hands tight. I stand anchored to the sand, my roots reaching deep down into this place, into these islands and their part of the sea, this planet. It all feels whole. It all lives at once both inside and outside of me.

We ask in chant one more time:

"E mālama 'oukou iā mākou
   Safeguard us
E ulu i ka lani
   That we may flourish in the heavens
E ulu i ka honua
   That we may flourish on earth
E ulu i ka pae'āina o Hawai'i"
   That we may flourish in the Hawaiian Islands

Note

1. Kahoʻolawe, the smallest of the eight main Hawaiian Islands, was commandeered by the U.S. military during World War II. It was used then and for decades after as a live fire training ground and bombing range. In 1976, the Protect Kahoʻolawe ʻOhana (PKO) formed to protest the continued bombing. In 1990, President George H.W. Bush ordered the bombing stopped. In 1994, the island was transferred to the state and the Kahoʻolawe Island Reserve was established. The Kahoʻolawe Island Reserve Commission (KIRC) currently stewards the island until such time as jurisdiction can be handed to a sovereign Native Hawaiian entity.

L. NISHIOKA

Return to the Garden I

I
Is that the Last Emperor
wielding a battered watering can
over the graying chives,
stalks dull and splayed
like the thinning hair
of an aging peasant?

Now, as he
approaches The End,
is he to be pitied,
stripped of all things
save the tending
of a vegetable garden
planted in wooden crates
lining a bustling alley
in dusty Beijing—
one of the masses?

II
Who is that young man
peeping like a fugitive
through the perforated screen
of the giant monstera leaves?
Great Grandpa at 18
a gardener's helper
—ashamed—
hiding from his classmates,
guests of the Moana.

Is he the same Gramps
55 years later leaning on his hoe
retired at last to the beloved garden
of his suburban estate?

Who, at 93,
legs and back brittle as
the avocado twigs littering his garden,
still dreams of working spade and sickle.

III
Is that her
crouched close to the earth
retired to the garden like those before,
thinning the wayward chives
shedding seeds like raindrops?

She reminisces, *"Versailles, Giverny, Kew—*
Kōraku-en, Ginkaku-ji, Kenroku-en . . ."

A light drizzle begins.
Crystal beads off the ti,
bursts into blossoms
struck open by the morning sun.
A white eye blinks against the flash.

The iridescent petals shimmer over her.
All things fall away, save for a sensation
—fleeting as the mejiro's flight—
of *Tranquility*, her Buddhist name conferred
before The End in Kyoto
where those who came before her
lived in the light of their gardens.

Paradise Cafe

The song would be a gift. Bestowed on Grace with a kind of, well, grace. But before receiving it, she'd have to kill time after her father's funeral, wander around downtown with her suitcase, and get caught in a downpour that swept in off the bay.

Rain was soon slanting beneath the overhang where she'd taken refuge and running in rivulets along the sidewalk. She remembered the drugstore near her father's old office. She could dry off there, she thought, have a cup of coffee, then take a taxi to the airport. Grasping the handle of her suitcase, she ran to the end of the block and pushed open the door.

"We don't serve till 5:00," someone said. Grace suddenly noticed the young woman behind the cash register, folding napkins and scowling at the water Grace had tracked inside.

"Sorry about that," she said. "I wasn't expecting—" she looked around with a sense of dislocation. Dining tables set for dinner had replaced the shelves of liniment and cold remedies, racks of comic books, and the glass case where she used to admire the pocketknives. A neon sign on the wall where the pharmacy window used to be blinked on and off. "Paradise Cafe," it said.

—*a restaurant*, Grace thought. "Can I get some coffee?" she asked, "and the restroom?"

The hostess waved her toward the back. "Bar's open."

Grace crossed the room and lugged her case up the several steps. The old soda fountain was now a full-service bar. Liquor bottles glittered against the mirrored wall. Behind the tiled counter, a woman with purple hair, nose piercings, and a towel slung over her shoulder was washing glasses. The only customer in the bar hunkered down in one of the booths.

Grace parked the suitcase next to a bar stool, ordered coffee, then ducked into the restroom. In the fluorescent light, she looked like a drowned rat, her face a roadmap of the past week. She ran a comb through her hair, peeled off her jacket and draped it over her arm. She hoped it would dry. If not, she'd have to change at the airport in Honolulu. The thought suddenly depressed her. Get a grip, she thought, and snapped shut her purse.

As she sat down, she noticed that the customer in the booth was beckoning her over. He looked like someone frozen in the late 1950s, aviator glasses, gray hair slicked back into wings, big gut straining the buttons of his aloha shirt. A napkin hung from his open collar. He waved again. Grace glanced at the bartender.

"He's harmless," she said.

Grace walked over as the man struggled to remain upright in the confines of the booth. He'd been eating a bowl of chili, or soup, and the table was littered with cracker crumbs, cellophane wrappers, and bits of white paper.

"I'm sorry for your loss," he said, thrusting out his hand. "My name is David Soares. You didn't see me, but I was at the funeral Mass. I had to leave after the service."

"Thank you," Grace said, taking his extended hand. His fingers, she noticed, were callused and his fingernails were long and tapered, like a musician's.

She introduced herself, out of politeness more than any wish to connect. He said, "Won't you join me?" and indicated the seat opposite.

Grace glanced at the mess on the table, hesitated. She had wanted time alone to gather herself, from the rain, from the long day. Coming back for her father's funeral had been more difficult than she could say. She hadn't planned on spending her last hour in Hilo with a stranger.

Yet she laid her jacket over the raised handle of the case and slid into the booth. The table had been varnished over, but the carved names of students had been preserved, like insects in amber.

David rapped his knuckles loudly on the tabletop, bellowed, "Wanda, two coffees!"

"Making a pot," she bellowed back.

They sat in silence for a few moments regarding each other. He had sad, dark eyes, long sideburns that he'd probably cultivated since adolescence. His face, fleshy now, might have been handsome once, but it sagged with the weight of years and probably too much beer, Grace thought uncharitably. Finally, he ventured, "Unbelievable, this rain."

The wind was throwing it in gusts against the windows above the booth. Grace had forgotten rain like that. Thank God it had waited till after the burial.

He suddenly seemed to notice the napkin in his shirt and whipped it off, flashed a nervous smile. "It's good you brought him back. Most people these days, they just cremate them, throw the ashes in the bushes."

Grace winced, said, "It's what he wanted." She didn't add that she would have opted for cremation had it been her choice. But her father had it all arranged, funeral Mass at Saint Joseph's, burial at Homelani Cemetery, lunch at the chop suey restaurant, all of it, even the cost of shipping his body from Honolulu. Her mother, though, that was different. No stone, no epitaph, no reminder that her roots lay here.

"How'd you know my father, Mr. Soares?" she asked.

"David," he said. He tore off a piece of napkin, began rolling it between his fingers. "I knew him from the old days. We sang in the glee club. I was the youngest. A tenor. Like your father."

He paused and glanced over at the bar where Wanda was pouring coffee. "I used to see him here lunchtime. At the fountain. White shirt, bow tie, smoking his pipe. 'Hey David, take a seat,' he would tell me. When your mother came, they sat in this booth." He ran a hand over the table. "There was something about them in those days. I don't know, something. I didn't want to—you know—butt in."

Wanda, holding a tray with two mugs, interrupted them, scolded, "Look at this mess," removed the debris, wiped up the crumbs, and set down the mugs. After she left several paper napkins on the table, David reached for his wallet and showed Grace a photograph.

"My wife's much younger, as you can see," he said of the round-faced woman standing between a boy and a girl who appeared to be in their early teens. "Filipino girl, from Honoka'a. We didn't marry until after my mother passed." He then removed a business card from his wallet and handed it to Grace.

"Aloha Taxi," she read out loud. And wondered, where was this going?

"Keep it."

He said he worked with two other drivers out of a small stand on Kīlauea Street, next to Mamo Theatre.

He began fingering a napkin. "I remember when you guys moved to Honolulu."

The statement had come out of nowhere. "Wow," Grace said, surprised. "That was almost forty years ago."

"Yup. But I remember. I remember because of those years we sang together, your father and me, and then we didn't, and then one day somebody told me he'd sold the business and moved the family."

"It was pretty final," Grace said of the sudden departure that had occurred the summer after her sophomore year.

Honolulu was only an hour's plane ride away, but it might as well have been Australia. The only time they returned was for funerals. Grandparents. Two uncles. An aunt. Her father rarely showed his feelings. He'd wept, though, when they lowered his brother Steve's coffin into the grave. It had struck her at the time that her father had never really wanted to leave. It had been her mother's wish, to pull up roots. Grace and her sisters had adjusted quickly. It had been less easy for their father.

"You still living in Honolulu?" David asked, regarding her closely.

Grace shook her head. "San Francisco."

"Ah, Frisco." He told her he'd stopped there once on his way to Las Vegas. His wife, she was crazy about the slot machines.

The door to the street pushed open, and the sound and smell of rain and asphalt filled the room. A man in a soaked bowling shirt sat at the bar. Grace glanced at her watch.

"What time's your flight?" David asked. She told him, and he said not to worry, he had his taxi parked outside and they had plenty of time. He settled back in his seat. "You know," he said, "I had a chance to leave once."

"It's a long story!" Wanda shouted from the bar.

"Bring us some more coffee!" David shouted back.

The coffee was strong, with a slightly bitter aftertaste. Grace tried to remember who said there were people who took salt in their coffee, that it gave it a savor that was both peculiar and fascinating. That's how it tasted now.

David's eyes lit up conspiratorially, and then he reached for something on the seat beside him.

"I think you know this ukulele," he said.

Grace recognized the long neck and unusually shaped base. The wood was worn near the opening from years of playing.

"A Kamaka," she said.

"A Kamaka Pineapple," he corrected. "There's a difference." He rested a hand on the oval box. "This belonged to my father. I never knew him. He died young. But I know him, thanks to this ukulele. And my mother." He ran his hands over the strings.

Grace listened without interrupting, let his story unfold at its own pace. She gave up trying to figure out where it was going.

In the old days, he explained, the political rallies were the biggest entertainment in town. Everybody went. Not just for the speeches, which could be entertaining, but for the music. The cars lined up for blocks. His father was crossing the street after a rally when a car struck him down. He died a few days later in the hospital.

He paused, reaching for another napkin, which he tore neatly in two and then as the story unfolded, into smaller and smaller pieces.

He'd inherited his father's love of music, took up the ukulele at a young age, inherited his father's love for campaigning. In the sixties, right after statehood, John Burns was running for governor, and the Democrats were campaigning hard because they knew that for the first time in history, they had a chance to seize power.

"Those days I had the dream of singing professionally," David said. "I had a tenor, like my father, and I used to perform with his ukulele on the campaign trail. Just like him."

He strummed a few more bars, hummed in a high, clear tenor, and Grace thought, he does have a beautiful voice. Her father had had dreams, too. He'd sung for years with the Hilo Glee Club and in the thirties had gone on a tour around the islands. When the steamship landed in Honolulu, they sang the "Hilo March" as they disembarked, accompanied by the 'Iolani Palace band. An article about it had been among her father's effects, clipped to the steamer ticket. How Grace had wished he'd told her about that trip. She wished she'd known to ask.

David described how one Saturday he'd been campaigning on the Kona side of the Big Island, driving all over the hills, handing out postcards to the coffee farmers. Afterwards, he decided to drop by the Kona Inn and have a drink. The Kona Inn in those days was a beautiful hotel, no tourists like today, no shopping center in front, just the lava rock building surrounded by a green lawn and coconut trees. He'd walked in with his ukulele and ordered a drink at the bar. Sam, the bandleader, came up and asked if he wanted to sing.

"Sure," David told him and went outside to tune his ukulele.

He never liked preparing himself in front of a crowd. There was a small grass shack next to the main building, and that's where he sat quietly tuning his instrument and deciding what to play. He didn't have a big repertoire, a dozen or so songs that he sang well, but they were good songs, and he told Sam he'd sing old favorites "'Akaka Falls" and "Waipio," and then he went to wait his turn by the stage.

As he stood there, a crowd began to arrive, maybe fifty people, fresh from the political rally in Kailua. They were all dressed up, a gay, happy crowd wanting some good entertainment. Eventually, they filled the room.

"I was beginning to get nervous," David said. He held up his arm and pointed at something beyond the bar where Wanda was setting up for the evening crowd, beyond the door to the kitchen, pointing all the way to Kona. As he talked, Grace pictured the setting, the green lawn lit by lū'au torches, the seawall, and four especially tall coconut trees lined up against the sky. "Just look out over those trees when you sing," he had told himself, and "you'll be all right."

As he positioned himself at the edge of the stage, a man walked into the room. He was dressed all in white and wearing a red carnation lei. A tall man with a presence about him. Hands reached out as he walked among the tables, and he paused like royalty to exchange a few brief words with his adoring fans as he made his way to a front table.

David closed his eyes for a long moment. "Oh, brother, I said to myself. Oh, brother, it's Ray Kinney." When he opened them again he looked intently at Grace. "Do you who he was?"

"A singer, right?"

"Born and raised in Hilo."

The family was mixed, he went on, and they spent a lot of time on the Mainland. Utah, mostly, though they toured other states, performing. Ray was on the light side; you could see the Scottish in him. David Kinney, one of his brothers, was dark. That was often the case in families of mixed blood. All of the Kinneys were good singers. There'd been many great singers in Hawai'i. The Beamer family, for one, Helen Desha Beamer, and Baby Beamer, whose rendition of "Ke Kali Nei Au," the wedding song, could break hearts. Another Hilo boy, George Kainapau, famed for his falsetto, streak of white hair, and the diamond in his front tooth. Charles K.L. Davis, whom David paid two dollars and a half to hear at the Hilo Auditorium, which was a lot of money in those days. And Clyde Sproat, one must not forget him, who once performed at Carnegie Hall.

"My point," David told Grace, "is that there were many great singers, and Ray Kinney was in my opinion the best."

And there he was in the audience, just as David was about to step on stage.

"Sam!" David said to the bandleader. "Sam, can I change my numbers?"

"To what?" Sam was a little huffy because he'd already told his group what David had planned to sing.

"Across the Sea."

"You sure, David?" "Across the Sea" was Ray Kinney's signature song!

What Sam didn't know was that Ray Kinney's signature song had special meaning for David. Kinney had co-written the song in 1926, the year David was born. Kinney had been touring in Utah at the time, and he got a telegram saying that his mother was very sick and to come home. He dropped everything and took the first boat back to the islands. It was on this voyage that the song came to him. When the island steamship made the turn by Pepeʻekeo Point, Kinney completed the last lines.

"I see you know it," David said to Grace.

"It was my father's favorite, too."

"Well, we have something in common."

***

After the car hit his father, David said, the doctors didn't know how seriously he was hurt. They put him in a ward, thinking all he needed was a little rest. After a day of agonizing pain, he asked the nurses to move him to the bed by the window. They moved him there and cranked up the bed so he could look out on the green coast of Hāmākua. "Bring me my ukulele," he told the nurses. And they brought it to him. And then he sang Ray Kinney's song. And when he finished, the nurses asked him to sing it again, and he did. Then he lay back and said, "I'm tired." Two hours later when they went to wake him for lunch, he was dead.

"When my mother told me that story, I was maybe thirteen, fourteen years old," David told Grace.

He'd been raking leaves in the yard while his mother hung clothes under the house, for they were expecting rain. He went to get some burlap bags for the rubbish, and when he saw his mother, he realized she was crying.

"What's the matter, Ma? You got hurt?" he asked.

"No, honey."

The radio was playing upstairs, and his mother said, "You hear that? That's Ray Kinney. And that's the song your father sang to make you go to sleep. And that's the song he sang the day he died."

David's story lingered in the very air of the Paradise Cafe. And then Grace realized that the rain had stopped, and new people were sitting at the bar. Grace glanced at her watch. "David," she said, "I have to get going." She hated interrupting him.

He glanced at his watch. "Okay, let's go."

With a pull at her heartstrings, Grace said goodbye to Wanda and the Paradise Cafe.

David loaded her suitcase into a maroon Buick of uncertain vintage. Hilo's rush hour had begun, so he did a U-turn at the stop sign, crossed the main street, and then headed out along the highway. The bay was the color of slate, and waves hit the breakwater in white puffs.

Grace said, "So you sang 'Across the Sea.'"

He did, and halfway through the song, Kinney stood right up in the crowd, and he stayed like that until the last notes died away. The crowd was silent, waiting for Kinney's reaction.

David suddenly wanted out of there. He ran off the stage. He could barely breathe. He didn't hear the reaction of the audience. All he wanted was a drink to calm his nerves.

Before he reached the bar, a commanding voice called out, "Young man!"

David stopped in his tracks, turned, and thought, oh brother, now I'm going to get it. But somehow, he summoned up his courage. "Mr. Kinney, what can I do for you?" he said brashly, as if he were the famous one and not a kid with ambitions beyond his means.

Ray Kinney drew back dramatically. "What?" he exclaimed. "Do you know me?"

"Well, I know you're Ray Kinney!"

Mr. Kinney threw back his head and laughed.

They sat, they ordered drinks in the bar, and Ray Kinney said he came to Kona many times, looking for talent. And then he lifted his glass and stared straight at David and said, "And I found what I wanted."

***

The highway ended at a stoplight. David paused the story. Grace turned to him, waiting. She didn't know what to think of this wandering story, which seemed to go on and on, even as it held her. He'd told it many times, she was sure. Yet it seemed shaped especially for her. What did it mean?

"What did he want?" she asked.

David replied, "He asked, 'Do you have Hawaiian blood?' And I said, 'No, I'm Portuguese.' He said, 'Never mind, you look Hawaiian.' And then he said he wanted to take me to New York City, to the Lexington Hotel, to sing with his group. He said he would be in touch with me in a few days."

They crossed the Wailoa River and soon were passing through what had once been the village of Waiākea. The buildings wore a temporary look after the last tsunami, as if put up to come down quickly. On the highway, warehouses and shopping malls slipped by. Nothing looked familiar.

Grace tried to remember something her father had said when she asked him why they'd left Hilo. He'd said, "It was important to your mother."

"But you didn't really want to leave, did you, Dad?"

She was trying to draw a story out of him. But all he'd say was, "Some decisions you make out of love."

***

"And did Ray Kinney call?" she finally asked.

"Oh, yes," David said. "A few days later, down at the airport where I was waiting for a fare, this guy—he used to write for the newspaper—he tells me that my name's on the front page, with Ray Kinney. Sure enough, there was this article about me going to New York with the great Ray Kinney.

"I went home as usual after my shift and found my mother lying in the bedroom with a towel over her head. She said she had a headache. Before I could tell her the news, she said she read about me in the newspaper and congratulated me on my good fortune.

"The next day, she couldn't get out of bed. When Ray Kinney called to make the travel arrangements, I had to tell him I couldn't go. He told me, 'David, this is your big chance. Are you sure?' I told him, 'She's my mother.'"

David pulled behind a line of cars dropping off passengers at the departure area. It was busy, people unloading suitcases, plastic coolers, and cardboard boxes and lugging them to the check-in counter. The air smelled of flowers and something else vaguely familiar. Ashes, she thought, recalling the mysterious odor she'd noticed the day she arrived. One would have thought the rain would wash it away.

"Here in plenty of time," David said.

Grace thanked him, then reached out and patted his arm. "Any regrets?"

David shrugged. "My mother was more important. Some people might say that I missed my calling," he said philosophically. "But even today I would do the same thing."

"Thanks for the coffee," Grace said, "and the story."

"Wait, you gotta hear the ending," he said, reaching into the back seat. And then he told Grace how every night at bedtime he'd put Ray Kinney's record on the turntable and switch the machine to automatic. Then he'd get into bed and listen. As soon as "Across the Sea" was finished, he was out. His kids had to turn off the machine.

He strummed the familiar intro and began to sing. Grace listened, feeling the connection an old song can create. Between people. Across space and time. David really had a beautiful voice, a little strained now in the high notes, but so fine in the middle register, almost as fine as her father's.

SUSAN MIHO NUNES

The Old Couple of Takasago

Kiyomi dragged a chair to her husband's bedside and uncovered the embroidery she'd brought to the hospital. She rested the large frame on her lap, tilted it against the mattress, and glanced at Hitari's mole-spattered face.

She said, "Who's the tiger now, old man?"

When he didn't stir, she picked up the needle, took her first stitch. She felt her shoulders relax as the needle pierced the taut silk with a satisfying pop, followed by the hiss of thread as she pulled it through. She stitched with both hands, Japanese style as she'd been taught, right hand to push the needle down, left to pull it through and push up again. The bottom of the rectangular frame still felt awkward on her lap, but she could thread the needle now without crying in frustration.

She had started the piece a lifetime ago, when her hands were steady, her fingers agile, and her eyes sharp and clear. In those days after the war, when they had once again taken up things Japanese, she used to catch the sampan bus once a week to her embroidery teacher Mrs. Endo's house on the other side of town. Those had been happy times, and when they suddenly ended, Kiyomi had vowed she would never touch an embroidery needle again.

She paused to run her fingers along the faint blue lines of the design. The unfinished piece was called "Takasago," and it was a favorite of the older advanced students. Mrs. Endo allowed only the most skilled stitcher to attempt the Takasago. Kiyomi had to admire her old satin stitches. They looked painted, they were so fine. Her new ones were like, well, stitches. She smiled to herself, thinking how her teacher would now admonish, "*Dame, dame. Tokimasho.* No good. Take them out."

Most of the women in Kiyomi's embroidery class had been of the second generation. Born in Hawai'i, they had grown up in the meanness of the sugar plantations, led lives of work and sacrifice, endured the privations of the war, and were rewarded only much later by the successes of their children. When they took up embroidery as adults, their desire was to make something beautiful, something they could turn to and know, "I did this." *Shishū* taught patience and endurance; it taught a way of seeing. The patterns used in class had been created by her teacher's husband, Mr. Endo, who often demonstrated with crayons how shadow and light played on the surface of a feather, petal, or leaf. The type of stitch—and there were many to learn!—and the thread itself were the stitcher's media. Sensei often said that a stitcher transferred to the finished work something of her own character and state of mind. Other designs might be more challenging—the tiger and hawk, for instance, or the pair of cranes—but the uniqueness in the Takasago lay in the expression on the two old faces.

"You are ready," Kiyomi remembered being told. "You have done wisteria, leaping carp, and tiger."

As if on cue, a loud snore emanated from the bed. Hitari was sprawled on his back with a plastic oxygen mask clamped to his face. The rubber strap had chafed raw the skin above his ears, but he no longer felt it. All the effort of his body was focused on breathing, and with every labored exhalation the mask misted over. It reminded Kiyomi of the insides of the flasks they used to breed and grow the orchid seedlings. After the second stroke, two orderlies were needed to turn him—they were moving him every three hours to prevent bed sores—and Hitari's big head, shorn of hair and mottled with age spots, made a profoundly deep dent in the pillow. It seemed to Kiyomi the heaviest part of him now.

She followed the spare landscape of his body to the foot of the bed and the two peaks where his toes thrust up against the thin hospital blanket. She had a fleeting thought of him as he used to be, the long torso and short, powerful legs, the body she'd both feared and desired. Not much of him now, she thought. And, considering her own, blue-veined hands, not much of her either.

The evidence of passing time greeted Kiyomi every morning in the blur of her bedroom. Getting out of bed, joints aching, shuffling to *benjo*. It took all her strength to push out that thin trickle and then, hanging onto the towel rack, pull herself to her feet. She used to be able to heft a bag of tree moss from the truck, dump it into a wheelbarrow with several others, push the load along a gravel path between the rows of orchids to the farthest greenhouse. She, whom men once admired, had shrunk to a bird-boned woman with a hump on her back, her only nod to vanity the monthly visits to the discount beauty salon at the shopping mall. She had stopped dyeing her hair long ago. Her last birthday, her 85th, which occurred while Hitari was recovering from his first stroke, her daughters had insisted on marking with their husbands and children at the chop suey restaurant by the town's bowling alley. They'd eaten quickly then driven Kiyomi back to the rehab center where she sat at Hitari's bedside until visitor hours were over.

He was still relatively lucid then, able to walk with assistance, able to complain about having to turn over the business to their son-in-law. His second stroke had rendered him completely helpless. It was in those difficult times that Kiyomi had found the unfinished Takasago.

She had been looking for an old sheet to cut up for washcloths and came across a small bundle tucked into the folds of a futon. She'd quickly pushed it back, as if it were scorching hot, and stood for several minutes with her back pressed against the closet door. It took several days to work up the courage to unroll the piece on her bed.

The pinprick holes along the edges where she'd once stitched the silk to the frame were still visible. How perfectly spaced they were! The aged trunk and stylized branches of the sacred fir glistened in the lamplight. The two figures were far from complete, yet their garments had the sheen and depth of real cloth. Kiyomi found it hard to believe she'd ever been so good. Her eyes were drawn to the faint blue lines of the unfinished sections, the woman's broom, the motes of dust, and the finely penned features of those two faces.

At the base of the tree trunk was a spray of bamboo leaves. She had been working on those her last day of class. As soon as her fingers touched them, she felt her breath catch. Dare she? She had held the thought, surprised at the wave of emotion.

What was she thinking! The art of *shishū*—painting with thread—could not be abandoned in youth and then suddenly resumed in old age, like collecting stamps. In the old days, mistakes could be corrected. "Barbershop!" the students merrily cried when someone had to snip out offending sections. But attempt a Takasago at this stage in her life? After all this time?

The basement was dark as she descended the stairs. She groped for the ceiling cord. The bare light bulb illuminated a stack of boxes, tools suspended from nails, an old washing machine. Above it was a shelf with some dusty bottles, and next to the shelf a row of hooks where she used to hang her empty frames. Her heart sank when she realized that all of them were gone. Against the wall near the water heater, she searched through sheets of old lumber and plywood that

Hitari was too cheap to throw away. There, at the back of a stack, she found the frame Mr. Endo had made specially to hold her Takasago.

She had wiped off the dust with a damp cloth and, tucking the frame under her arm, returned to her bedroom. After cleaning it carefully, she laid the frame on the bed and placed the Takasago within its confines. The piece would have to be fastened with heavy thread sewn through the holes she'd made years before along the edges of the silk and then looped around the wood. Framing was an art. Mrs. Endo, who had been born and raised in Japan, used to tell her students how she'd spent two years learning how to frame embroidery. Kiyomi touched the silk. Chances were she would tear it and the decision would be made for her. The thought gave her confidence.

She found her old sewing box and retrieved some heavy thread, searched until she found the right-sized needle. She worked till her fingers were raw, wept with the effort, wept for the skills she had lost. When she was done, she held the frame to the light. She would never forget the sense of triumph she felt when the piece was ready to sew.

***

Working on the old piece had kept her going through Hitari's long hospitalization. Allowed her to replay the events of the past, things she had kept buried for so long she thought she'd forgotten them. The recollections did not come easily. Tinged with resentment, they rose to the surface, challenging her like the stenciled lines of the design.

Like the last day of her embroidery class. Pulled from the past stitch by stitch. She had risen that morning with Hitari's actions of the previous day still raw in her mind and heart. Hitari was in a jovial mood at breakfast, bragging how his orchids would ride in the Rose Bowl Parade, and what was the matter with her, moping around over a few pieces of cloth. A few pieces of cloth! She'd picked up the Takasago and taken the bus across town, trying to banish from her mind what Hitari had done.

There were six of them in class that day, seated with their frames propped against the dining table. Kiyomi, her hands shaking, struggled to concentrate on the bamboo leaf.

"That will not do, Kiyomi-san," Mrs. Endo had said, frowning at her work. "What is the matter?"

Kiyomi had burst into tears that would not stop. Finally, unable to speak, unable to explain what had happened, she left with the Takasago, uncovered, under her arm. At home she'd snipped the silk threads that tied it to the frame. She ran outside and threw open the lid of the garbage can. The smell of fish heads and fermented rice made her gag. She hesitated, the metal lid in one hand, the silk in the other.

***

Now she reached over and gently adjusted Hitari's sheet. "If you survive this, old man, they will move you back to the nursing home, and I will have to visit you every day. Why do I do this? Because it is expected of me, because this is what I have done all my life. But for love, Hitari? Has there ever been that between us?"

They had married after he returned from the war, flushed with what he had accomplished, he and the boys of the second generation. His single-mindedness, was that what had attracted her? They had saved and borrowed and scraped together enough to buy three acres of rocky land near the old railroad on which to grow flowers. Orchids and anthuriums, mainly. The business of flowers. The first years were difficult. A typical day meant rising before dawn to prepare breakfast, feeding and dressing the two girls, washing the family laundry by hand, mending clothes, tending the vegetable garden. In between, she worked side-by-side with Hitari, fussing over the baby orchids, fertilizing, cutting, and then in later years packing the boxes to be shipped to Honolulu and, eventually, the mainland. She had wanted to raise and breed the flamboyant cattleyas, but Hitari said there was no money in them, and he needed the greenhouse for the more lucrative dendrobiums. The flower business demanded huge investments in time and effort, hands raw from the chemicals, and then the selling and marketing, the dealing with buyers. As the business grew, Kiyomi began to handle the paperwork, take the orders, pack and mail the flowers. Not once had Hitari acknowledged her contributions. He was of the old school, who believed that words were cheap and effort was everything.

"How come you want to waste time on sewing!" he had scolded when Kiyomi mentioned her desire to sign up for embroidery classes. The children were still young, and she'd almost given in, even scolding herself: Why can't you take pleasure in the raising of such beautiful flowers? But she ached for something truly hers. For Hitari, orchids were just a business. Maybe if he had appreciated their beauty, she would have been content.

"It won't take time from my work," she had promised him. "It's only once a week. You won't even notice I'm gone. You won't have to drive me. I will go on my own."

And once a week she'd taken the sampan bus across town, and for two or three hours she'd sew with a half dozen other women at the big table in Sensei's dining room. How shy she was at first! And how much she admired the way the women talked with such ease about their lives.

Like the other students, Kiyomi had begun with the basic techniques of stitchery and simple designs on linen runners. Her very first was a chrysanthemum, which called for the long-and-short, outline, and satin stitch. Wood roses, partially filled in, came next. Then hibiscus, three red ones surrounded by leaves in varying shades of green. Oh, and there were the red cherries spilling out of an overturned basket. Mr. Endo, who designed the patterns, lamented that he drew the cherries round, but the ladies sewed them square. How they all laughed at that!

The stitches had to be perfect. "*Kitanai, tokinasai*! Not clean, take it out," Sensei would say. Or the usual, "*Dame, dame*, not good, not right."

Poor stitches remained forever, Sensei would tell her students, like the bad choices one made in life. Stitches could be taken out and redone, unlike life, which could not be relived. Kiyomi's Takasago, she'd taken out the stitches of the old man's trousers, a risky business since it would leave holes in the silk. One always removed the stitches from the back of the piece, never the front. The faces of the old couple she had known would be the hardest part. The other students had already warned her that they would have to be stitched with half a strand of silk thread, a task so difficult that some of the students vowed they'd never do again. (Though here she was!) The thread was so fine. And old, too. Sensei had brought silk thread from Japan and parceled it out only for certain pieces. Like the horse. Or the hawk's eye.

Her best work over the years she had framed and hung up in the living room of the house. Her wisteria, the modest flower she identified with. The leaping carp, which she had planned to give to a future son-in-law on his fortieth birthday. The cherry blossoms for her daughters. And those voluptuous peonies—what could she have been feeling when she chose them! Years of work, each piece finer than the last.

"Well done," Sensei had said, commenting on the eye of the tiger she'd sewn for Hitari. "Frame it and hang it in a place of honor." Kiyomi had thought of Hitari as she'd sewn the eyes, so perhaps that explained the tiger's fierce expression. Some of the women, when doing their tiger eyes, stitched them cross-eyed!

After finishing the tiger, she had considered attempting a Takasago, but quickly put the thought aside. Mrs. Hirabara, one of the older students, was just completing hers, and the other women had gathered around, praising her work. "You and your husband must have a good life," Kiyomi had said, admiring the expressions on the couple's faces. Mrs. Hirabara had flushed with pleasure.

All the way home on the sampan bus that day, the tiger embroidery resting on her lap, Kiyomi had thought about what the women had said, both about her tiger piece and Mrs. Hirabara's Takasago. She had seen many tigers—they all worked with the same patterns—and yet each one was unique. In some the skin rippled, in others the skin looked flat and lifeless. She planned to hang her tiger in the parlor near the Shinto altar where she set out rice every day in memory of her parents. Hitari never seemed to notice her other work. But perhaps he would this one since she had had him in mind.

When she finally showed Hitari the piece—already framed, for that much she'd done on her own, paying for it with her grocery money—he had surprised her.

"Not bad," he said. "He looks hungry."

Flushed, she began to explain the difficult parts of the piece, how she had stitched the black stripes first, then the golden, how the whiskers took a white thread as fine as a human hair. She had paused, embarrassed at her own enthusiasm, lest it show she brought too much attention to her own efforts.

"Umm," Hitari had said, already bored. "I need some help with the receipts."

But he didn't refuse her request, and she hung the tiger in its place of honor. Now, every time she thought about it, it was with a stab of pain. Where was the tiger now? Where were all of them?

Here, take them. I insist. She can make more.

***

Why, Hitari?

Sitting at her husband's bedside, that was the question she returned to, even though she knew there were no answers.

The buyers were from Los Angeles, and Hitari was ordering flowers for the Rose Bowl Parade. Thousands of flowers, orchids, anthuriums, their biggest order ever. Hitari had been ecstatic, beside himself with pride. The buyers were coming by the following day to see the nursery and give them a deposit. Hitari brought out his best Scotch from the kitchen and set it on the console in the living room, beneath the framed embroideries. "We will do our business here," he had told her, "Beneath your tiger." He gazed at the beast in its gold frame. "Am I not like a tiger, Kiyo," he said boastfully, and she had agreed he certainly was.

"It was why I made it," Kiyomi said now at his bedside.

Yoku dekimashita. Well done, she remembered.

"That was what you said, Hitari." Kiyomi stared at her husband and the oxygen mask misted over again. "Well done. And I thought, there is goodness in this man, and he deserves to succeed. I was happy for you. For us. I started the Takasago. And when the two buyers came, I brought out the sushi you told me to make, and you poured them a drink and you drank. And then one of them said—the tall one with the blond hair, Mr. Harman, that was his name—he said, who did these paintings, and you said, they are not paintings, nothing so fine, they are my wife's embroideries. Embroideries! Mr. Harman said, and I could see he was impressed. He walked over to the tiger. It looks like paint, it could have fooled me, he said. And then you said—Hitari, and this is what I cannot forget—you said, Take it, it's yours. And he said, Oh no, I couldn't accept something so fine. And then, as if that wasn't enough, you insisted he take them all. I remember his face, the buyer from Los Angeles. I remember. He was embarrassed. When he complimented my work, he was not asking for it. Do you not see that, Hitari? Why was my work so easy to give away? If you could tell me that . . ."

***

A few days later, as Kiyomi stitched, the hospital door opened, and her daughter Elaine dragged in with an armful of student workbooks, which she set on the bedside tray.

"What a day. I'm so tired." A big, stolid girl, already defeated by life.

"Why don't you go home? I can watch him," Kiyomi offered.

"Don't be silly, Mama. Carolyn is coming at midnight." She sat down on the other side of the bed, turned on the television. "They told me at the nursing station that he hasn't been eating."

Kiyomi slipped the needle into its case. "I wrote down miso soup and egg for his supper. Perhaps he'll eat that." Though she knew the soup would just sit there on the tray, getting cold.

She gathered her things and fit the embroidery frame into a cloth sack. "Eddie's waiting in front?"

"Same place," Elaine said, her eyes glued to the television set.

Kiyomi found her son-in-law by the no parking sign, the door on the passenger side of the Camry already open. He didn't say anything as she climbed in. Kiyomi suspected this ferrying of people back and forth to the hospital was beginning to annoy Eddie. He would have to go home and feed the children, put them to bed while Elaine sat with Hitari, and Kiyomi couldn't escape the feeling that Eddie somehow blamed her. He would never complain directly to Kiyomi, but she suspected Elaine was probably getting an earful. She thought of saying that she didn't think it would be long now, that it would end before he knew it, and then his life could go back to normal, and the business was now his. But she didn't.

Instead, she sat staring out the side window as they passed through the homesteads. The orchid farm was about four miles from the hospital. A long driveway passed through the rows of tree fern stumps on which they grew the orchids. Rows and rows of them beneath clouds of purple. Every orchid plant fixed by hand to its medium. Hitari had done very well, plowing every spare dollar back into the business. When he had his first stroke he was dealing with buyers from Seattle to Los Angeles. And Pasadena! Where her embroideries now resided.

"Hey, wake up," she heard Eddie say, and realized she was home.

She ate her supper alone in the kitchen, warmed-over rice, a piece of chicken from the night before, sliced tomatoes with mayonnaise. Then she went into the family room with her embroidery and turned on the television. It was a poor substitute for conversation, but the noise of it in the background was as close as she could get to the old days, with the women laughing and talking and telling tales. She sat at a small table against which she could rest the frame. She threaded purple for the old woman's kimono.

Shortly after midnight, her other daughter Carolyn called, in tears.

"He's gone, Mama."

"Gone where?" As soon as she said it, she realized what Carolyn meant and how ridiculous her question must have sounded.

"When?" she asked.

"A little while ago. I didn't even realize it. The nurses came in to turn him and that's when they told me. Mama, I'm so sorry. But it was his time, wasn't it? I mean, he wouldn't have wanted to go back to the rehab center. It's better this way." There was a pause. "Mama?"

"Where is he now?"

"Still here. They said they'd wait till you came. Ken just arrived. Elaine and Eddie are on the way to pick you up."

Of course, Carolyn would have called them first. Kiyomi felt a stab of regret for the example she had set for her daughters. Just as quickly, she set it aside.

***

The funeral was a simple affair, held at the Soto Mission. The crowd was respectably large, friends of her daughters mostly. Afterwards they drove to the cemetery and interred Hitari's ashes in the columbarium where one day her own ashes would lie, next to his. It had been another decision Hitari had taken on his own, without a word to her of his intentions, and she had accepted it as she had every turn in their married life. But she had said her piece to him, and somehow it was enough.

It took her several weeks to finish the old woman's kimono, the dust, and the last of the bamboo. Now, at last, it was time to consider the faces.

When she had begun the original piece, she had listened to her teacher's lecture on the significance of the old couple. The woman's face was of someone happy with herself and her lot, and the man's face reflected no sense of loss of boyhood dreams. At the time it had been Kiyomi's wish to stitch into the piece her own dreams for the two of them—her and Hitari. Their life had been hard, but one day they would be like the Old Couple of Takasago. Jo and Uba were inseparable symbols of a long and useful union.

Now she had to ask herself, what did the fabled couple possess that she and Hitari had lacked? Was the fault in the myth, the design, or something else?

In her sewing basket was a small skein of silk thread, left over from what Sensei had given her for the whiskers of Hitari's tiger. The strands were finer than a human hair, and Kiyomi had to wind some between her fingers to create a thread that could be pushed through the eye of the needle. It was a while before she could begin on the old man's face.

***

At the first year's observance of Hitari's death, services were held at the temple and then the family gathered at Kiyomi's house for a meal and saw the finished Takasago for the first time. Mounted and framed, it hung on the wall where Hitari's tiger had once glared out at the world.

While Eddie and the grandchildren played outside and Carolyn opened the containers of Chinese food, Elaine and Kiyomi discussed the embroidery.

"That's not bad, Mama," Elaine said, looking over her mother's shoulder.

"My hands aren't what they used to be," Kiyomi demurred. "But I wanted to finish it."

Jo, the old man, wore brown trousers, green vest, and purple undergarment. She'd used the glossilla thread, and there was a satiny sheen to his clothes. Uba, pictured in profile and facing her husband, wore a jacket the same color as Jo's vest over her purple kimono. She was holding a broom in her left hand, reluctantly, it seemed to Kiyomi, dragging it behind her and leaving a trail of dirt and leaves.

"Sensei told us they were taking care of the sacred fir," Kiyomi explained. "On the shores of Takasago, in Hyōgo Prefecture."

"With their brooms," Elaine said.

"Sensei said they're supposed to represent a long and successful union. The woman Uba is supposed to be happy with herself. Fulfilled. That's what Sensei said, anyway."

"Is that why you chose it?" Elaine asked.

Kiyomi paused. "Yes."

"I thought so. Did Papa ever see it?"

"Not the finished work."

"Too bad. He would have liked it. I remember he liked the tiger. He used to tell us you made it especially for him, but he had to sell it to help the business. He said it fetched a pretty penny."

Kiyomi let the comment pass.

Carolyn joined them. Kiyomi showed her daughters where her old work ended and the new work began.

"I remember it from the hospital," Carolyn said. "Honestly, I can't tell the difference. Those stitches! I could never have the patience."

Elaine looked closer at the embroidery. "I don't know, Mama, but to me Uba looks a little cranky."

"You think so?" Kiyomi had a moment's concern that her daughter would see what she had stitched into this piece.

"Yes, look at her face."

Carolyn followed suit. "You're right. But look at him. Really pleased with himself. Just like a man, huh?"

Elaine put her arm around her mother. "Well, it's good you finished it. Eddie and me, we were worried about you, if you would have enough to occupy yourself. You know, after Papa."

"It's my last piece. But don't worry, I'll have plenty to do. I was thinking, maybe I'll go to Los Angeles."

"Los Angeles?" both girls exclaimed. Their mother might as well have expressed the wish to travel to Timbuktu.

"Pasadena, actually," Kiyomi said. "We should all go, bring the children. I was thinking, I would like to see the Rose Bowl Parade. That is where our flowers end up, you know. Your father had a lot of connections up there, and they were always telling him, come any time and we'll show you around. Of course, we never went." Her voice faltered. "We were too busy."

"You surprise me, Mama," Elaine said. "Los Angeles!"

"Why not?" Carolyn said.

"Yes, why not?" Kiyomi replied, as the idea took hold. If her family couldn't come, she could join a tour. They must have tours to the Rose Bowl Parade.

She gazed at the Takasago. No, Uba wasn't cranky. She was simply annoyed that she couldn't retrace her steps, do things a little differently. But perhaps after all, she had no regrets.

DEREK N. OTSUJI

Ode to Grandma T

Grandmother of the ready proverb
and quick reproof, who preached life's
sermon with her hands, with which she turned
the dirt, made onion bulbs grow big as boulders,
and knowing weeds to be opportunists,
worked in the yard six days of the week,
pulling, planting, pruning, mowing, trimming, raking
—taking only Sundays off for church.

Trailing blue ribbons of glory
from the county fair, all recipe cards
written on her taste buds and fingertips,
as she measured out flour by fistful and hand feel.
Frugal to a fault but generous in equal
and opposite measure, deploying her daughters
on seasonal deliveries of sweet rolls wafting
heavenly smells through the neighborhood.

Lover of groves who squeezed sunlight
from lemons, sugar from sticky tangerines,
popped popsicles from ice trays, and balanced
each fruit jewel on a toothpick. Whose pride shone
in painstakingly clarified red gold jellies,
and richly thickened jams. Believer in all things
butter. Keeper of the diabetic contraband
stashed atop the white fridge, Virginia Slims
in a secret drawer. Devotee of the daily soap opera
and afternoon nap. Early riser who daily
swept the community park clean of Coke bottles
and beer cans, which singlehanded industry
kept the local scrap yard in business ten years.

Friend to JW and Mormon missionary.
Guardian of the address book, the punctual longhand letter.
Globe-trotter, travel magnet collector,
zealot of the balanced register, the strict account,
who hummed while she worked hymns of Christian grace.

CHRISTY PASSION

Birthday Lū'au

Another Kāne'ohe night cool and crisp—
at the end of Adams Lane past Punini's house with the big pua
        kenikeni tree,
the open field with green canvas tarps atop weathered silver poles
and the imu still steaming through the burlap bags
is backyard party perfection. Cars are triple parked from two streets
        over
and even the young braddahs are putting in some effort with Axe
        cologne
and throwback Jordans; Auntie Dot's 80th promises to be lit.
The entertainment stage fronting the chain link fence is decked out
in green ti, red ginger and two big Bose speakers facing outward
like navigators scanning the ocean. Keiki are welcomed
first, plumeria kūpe'e and purple pā'ū brighten
in response 'Ae to kumu's Mākaukau and slap
of the ipu heke, start little feet sliding. Mommies in black leggings
dart across the lawn crouching low to capture the perfect insta pic
#Hawaiianstyle #culture #misskeikihula
The men in their aloha shirts stay seated at cafeteria-style
tables covered with brown paper and ringed by green bottles
cackling smaller bravados with friends not seen in too long.
Kalua pig, squid lū'au, and fried menpachi tempting in silver pans
with Sterno flames beneath and teenage girls above doling out
precise ladlefuls into each compartment of the lū'au tray.
The hunk of haupia made with real coconut (not that package stuff)
served at the end of the line, glistens like the treasure it is.
Auntie Dot and her sisters are seated separately, served specialty
        items
which are the envy of all: 'opihi pulled off the rocky Ka'ū reef, Big
        Island,
and hand-carried in a blue Igloo on this morning's flight by Uncle
        John.
Auntie Dot can only take a few bites before another cousin brings her
        lei
and kisses which she receives with the half-smile of a burdened
        monarch.

Jolene comes by every so often to remove a few layers of pīkake and
      tuberose
so Auntie can keep eating. The glow of the lanterns fastened overhead
      mimic the glow
of everyone here laughing and chee-hooing so by the time the boys
      take the stage with
their ukulele belting out their best Kapena, everybody is ready to
      dance.
Auntie jumps up when she hears her favorite song, shaking it at the
      table
and even Momi—her lazy chihuahua is running in circles, delirious.
We pause when her son Derek makes his way to the microphone
for the birthday toast; Auntie doesn't hesitate as she throws back a
      shot of Hennessy
her eyes sparkling, *Put the music back on—I'm getting old.* We roar
      back fearless
knowing some things cannot be taken from us.

CHRISTY PASSION

Signs

COVID Week 23:
On the medical unit waiting for an ICU bed

85% on a non-rebreather mask and he's barely responsive.
The MICU charge asks if I can hold onto him a few more minutes,
housekeeping is still cleaning the room. *I'll try . . .*
look over to the frail Filipino man in bed who
looks like a worn teddy bear tattered and flattened
He doesn't look good
No one does

The automatic BP cuff starts to cycle but Tata doesn't flinch
a bad sign to go along with all the other bad signs:
his eyes are sundowning and lips are purple, he's guppy breathing
fast and open-mouthed while the rib cage expands and falls like
the sound of a police siren at night. The high-pitched hiss of oxygen
pushes over each
jagged breath

80/40. I yell through my N95 through the glass door
to Kelly standing on the other side, her face turned
with her ear to the glass to better hear
Get me a liter of NS, have someone call the elevator
and hold it, we're gonna move soon. She gives
me the thumbs-up. I switch the oxygen tubing
to the transport tank and check the gauge, the arrow's closer
to red than green. Kelly cracks the door just enough to pass
through the saline. Quick—
to keep the virus in.

He starts to slump so I grab his shoulders and straighten him
Tata! Tata! His eyelids flicker, then thankfully, black eyes
look back at me—*Stay with me Tata, I got you.* There is a guttural
        noise
from the back of his throat *Don't talk Tata, save your breath*
He keeps his eyes on me, brows furrowed, slack jaw gnawing

as I connect the IV tubing and push the roller clamp wide open
scan the waveforms on his monitor, readjust the mask, recycle
the cuff. I avoid looking at his face but keep touching
his shoulder grounding me,
I hope us.

Our plastic gowns make a crinkling sound rubbing against the side
     rails
as we move the bed to the elevator bay, I look to the monitor then
     Tata again
his eyes straight ahead, glazed. Kelly calls to him; no response
I squeeze Tata's left calf sharply—he startles—eyes blink, shoulders
     pull up
I'm sorry Tata, almost there reflexively I tap my pockets feeling for
the epi syringe *almost there almost there* my breath matching his
I dig my fingers into his calf again
as the elevator
descends

The room doors are wide open so we slide in;
housekeeping is just pulling out the UV light, a silver cylinder
on wheels like a tricked-out radio flier. *You didn't call,*
the charge nurse accuses from outside the door
I step to the side so he can take in Tata, his head folded down
chin to chest, the small shallow breaths, rag doll arms *Didn't have*
     time
He yells for Dr. Guo who appears with the glide scope
and Ray from RT is not far behind with the vent. *Hang on Tata*
On three we move him over to the ICU bed this time
a cry sharp and loud, he tries to push us away
a good sign

CHRISTY PASSION

Soft Opening

COVID Week 18

So this is how you remind us—
hidden for two months, waiting for the mourners

to congregate, for the pastor to offer up
the old familiars: *mercy, time, comfort*

where you moved over white lilies and plastic chairs
settling into palms, pressed from lips to cheek to cheek

Such easy targets: the aunts who brought boiled breadfruit
in aluminum trays for fellowship after the service

the youngest nephew, broad as his older brothers
strong enough to help lift the coffin

the elder men in long-sleeved white shirts and women
in simple flowered dresses, all with their bibles

have been brought to us. Seventeen over five days
three directly into the ICU today. The unit weighted

with Chuukese and Filipino bodies, the gravity of their
aloneness pulls us down, without family to carry them

is its own death. So it is we who line the rim of their eyes
with Lacri-Lube so their corneas don't scratch, put foam around

ears, nose, heels to protect the skin, we swab their parched
tongues, rotate their ankles so they don't lock up, lift their limp

bodies to change the urine-soaked sheets. We write our names on
our face shields so if they open their eyes, might know who we are

Calling Home

On my newsfeed
storefronts being shattered, glass falling
to the ground with armfuls of Nikes and iPhones
escaping into the night. Fires in the background
and broken business owners at the fore crying as their life
burns, the smoke like an offering to a god who demands
more than we can bear. You are there in the middle
of that madness, Seattle PD, one of many Hawaiians
who set sail on a Pacific Northwest star.
OneBravoSix—your callsign dispatch uses
as you are suited up in 75 pounds of gear:
ballistic helmet, gas mask, face shield, molded vest,
blended into the line, unable to identify individually
easier to look at as a group—the police—and all that
loaded word is. To put a stop to my incessant texting
you finally call, proof of life, but something's different
about you, there's a change in your voice that's more
than just fatigue. I can't seem to ask the right question
and in my fumbling over *where, how long, when*
you cut right to the heart of it and tell me the story.
The nights are violent; there's chatter that the police station
will get hit, possible bomb, your team is assigned to stand guard.
A skinny white kid, maybe eighteen, comes up to you
several inches from your face shield and begins quietly at first
I'm a Jew, you're a Nazi, I'm a Jew, you're a Nazi
and with each passing repetition he gets louder,
more animated *I'm a Jew, you're a Nazi* making sure to
capture it on his cell phone, spitting and screaming
though careful to not make physical contact.
You see in his eyes that each utterance brings belief
I'm a Jew, you're a Nazi, you're a fucking Nazi, fucking Nazi
and you want to explode. You want to pull down your
mask and let him see your brown skin and dark eyes
you want to scream *I'm not white you asshole*
I'm Hawaiian. This isn't my world, you don't know me you stupid
fuck

but you keep your mask on, you keep it together and eventually
the current of protest pulls him away. You go quiet and I feel you
drifting so I drop anchors: Kahi's new job, your old Corolla,
the homestead in Waimānalo. Your tone changes
but I still can't tell where you are. You promise you'll text
so I won't worry, but I will.

NORMIE SALVADOR

Secondhand Aloha II: Kukui Nut Leis

My secret
thrift store. No, I not
gon tell you wich one,
fine yo' own.

I was shock firs' time
I spock all da kalakoa
leis kapakahi:

ribbon, yarn,
kukui nut, shell,
an' feathers, but

no mo' flower, leaf,
origami, candy,
an' no cash money lei
das fo' sure.

My firs' thought was,
"Who gon buy dis?"
My second thought was,
"Score! Mo' cheap dan da lei
stands come graduation time."

I neva like
get da ribbon ones
'cause fo' real I no rememba
all my nieces' an' nephews'
skools' skool colors.
Same deal wit' da feathers.

An' I not gon buy yarn.
'Cause can buy my own
an' make 'em on one hand
or one French knitter

if I like be all fancy-kine. Yeah,
I know how knit. You no know?

I seen shell leis couple-chree
times in couple-chree years.
Hard fo' tell if real, if plaster,
an no get enuff fo' give regular.

I was like I just gon get
kukui nut. Polish 'em an' pau.
Good fo' go give hana hou.

Of course, I spock em firs'.
I count 'em too. Tirdy-two stay
da magic number.
Shame if no can go ovah yo' head.

But if manini?
I still buy 'em.

One nut broke? Missing?
Still buy 'em.

Stay plastic?
No buy 'em, no wert.

Waste money?
J'like poho if I leave 'em
'cause can fix easy.
Jus' untie da bow,
hemo da nut, untie da knot,
hana hou, hana hou . . .

Afta I hemo da broke nut,
I go look fo' one match.
I get plenny loose nuts.
Eh, no make.

Slide 'em on top
one wire threader—

make 'em from one hanger—
pull da ribbon, pull da nut,
tie one knot, an' pau.

Upcycle? Dis stay recycle, no?
Das why I no shame give.
Wat? Why shame?
How come one lei
only can aloha one time?
Who said can give 'em jus' once?
Das poho, ah?
                    Not like
wen run out. J'like
dis aloha 'renewable,' ah?
No say you no get
aloha fo' give.
Stay 'sustainable' dat kine.

NORMIE SALVADOR

Secondhand Aloha III: Wood Bowls

I neva wen plan for dis pandemic
hobby: woodworking, but
stay da ting I neva wen know
I wen need until now.

Was in Goodwill one Tuesday
in da aisle wit' all da glass
an' wood. Was looking fo'
one brand name shot glass.
No can jrink no mo', but
gon look nice on da shelf, ah?

I wen turn fo' slide pass
somebody an' das wen I wen
spock one wood bowl. I no
see plenny 'cause sell out fas'.
Was natural, no mo' varnish.
One manini chip on da lip.
Small kine scratches all ovah.
Two-ninety-nine. Shoots. Deal.

Was impulse buy, ah? Goodwill
stay da kine place dat not gon have 'em
nex' time you like buy 'em. If you
put 'em back, you lettin' 'em go fo'eva.

But wat I was gon do wit' one bowl?
Had plenny change cause scared fo' touch
hands, mo' betta wave dat microchip
debit card. Good enuff reason, ah?

Now how fo' make 'em look good?
I rememba li'l bit from high skool
shop class wen we wen make one
wooden puzzle cube

an li'l bit from watchin' my dad . . .
Brah, I neva know wat I stay doin'.

I wen surf da web. Read stuff hea, dea.
Watch YouTube tutorials. I wen make
myself one informed amateur. Wat?
You thought I was gon say,
I one expert now? You was, ah?

Lowe's fo' real one one-stop shop.
Sandpapah, wet an' dry.
Mineral oil. Beeswax.

I neva wear mask firs' time I sand.
No good cough wen get pandemic.
No can say, I fo'got fo' wear one mask.
Not akamai dat.
              But I wen learn:
fo' sand from splintah to powdah,
'til no can feel da grain, 'til smood;
wood dat dry thirsty fo' mineral oil;
dat real beeswax attract bees, an' dat,
afta dat one time, I know I stay allergic.

Dat firs' bowl was acacia. Afta dat,
monkeypod, kamani, even couple teak.

Scars

At night my mother would cry into the phone, hopeless tears that left briny rings on the receiver. Tūtū listened helplessly four thousand miles away saying she had no more folk remedies left for us to try. No more prayers or rituals to make a difference after sending us packages of ti leaf and Hawaiian salt, consecrated oils and holy water, amulets and charms.

Tūtū said she would ask her Podagee friend for advice. Her friend was the daughter of a feiticeira, a witch, who would tell us what to do. Desperately we listened and placed a scissors underneath my mattress to sever me . . . from whatever lingered at my bed. But in the morning the scratches still appeared. Longer, deeper, and angrier than they had ever been before.

I was twelve when my father got orders to Fort Bliss, Texas. It was our fourth move in two years. The quarters we were assigned to were built during WWII. One in an identical row of concrete boxes, it was an unbreathable home with tiny windows, sun-faded paint, and a dead lawn full of kukus. The exact same across the street because if the ARMY wanted you to have a personality then they'd issue you one.

The house was small and run-down, patched up over decades with plaster to cover wounds left festering in dust. But we'd only be there for nine months before we'd have to leave. It wasn't the worst house we'd lived in. We'd make the best of it.

There was a long crack in the ceiling, bisecting the room I shared with my sister. It was just above my bed and I would stare at it. Every day I'd wake up with aggravated scratches on my legs and arms, my chest and belly, and even down the very center of my back. Three long lines descending all thirty-three of my vertebrae.

My mother filed down my nails, made me sleep with gloves, long sleeves, and soft pants. We saw a doctor who covered me in prescribed lotions. We bought a new mattress and new bedding. We exhausted all of Tūtū's folk knowledge and still, every morning, there would be new scratches.

I was scared to fall asleep. Even on the couch in the living room I was restless. In my dreams I'd still be laying in that bed, with the crack above me getting wider and bigger as if the house were being pulled apart from the outside . . . or *pushed* apart from the inside. And just before the house would crumble around me I'd suddenly wake, weary with unknown grief.

One day, I told Tūtū about the dreams. How the crack in the ceiling cut my bed in half and the dark would spill out to swallow me. In an ah-ha moment she said, "Mebe you in da way. Move your bed, no sleep underneath. Could be one walking path. You in da way!"

There weren't many configurations to work with in the meager space, but we moved my bed. The scratches stopped. The scars remained.

I didn't know the native history of Fort Bliss—what the ground beneath my feet had been before it became a military base. Only later did I learn about the displaced Pueblo peoples of the El Paso plains whose history and trauma were so similar to the peoples of my own history. Looking back, I shouldn't have been surprised at my experiences there, the feelings of enmity and strife.

Every duty station left a mark, an impression on us. Every house we inhabited had a story. We would reside in reverb, living among the echoes of the soldiers and their families who had been there before us. And of the people who populated those stolen lands even before them. They would all leave something behind.

Out of the five of us in my family I was most sensitive to these remnants, susceptible to the forgotten fragments. In Arizona, singing songs I'd never heard and telling my mom about nearby places I'd never been. In Germany it was voices in languages I didn't understand because the ARMY built our elementary school next to a mass grave of refugees from a Nazi internment camp.

In California, it was the overwhelming feeling of sadness every day at noon when the side door of our house would open on its own, even when it was locked and bolted. The spot where, just three years before us, a soldier had hung himself and. . . "Stop, Daddy! You shouldn't slam the door when he opens it. He's only coming home for lunch." A strong craving for tuna sandwiches with pickles, even though I hated pickles.

In Nevada, it was a soft, childlike giggle and shapes that moved across the walls like fleeting shadow puppets. But Texas . . . Texas was the first time I was ever scared of these encounters. Afraid because the experiences I had grown up having had manifested themselves so violently there.

When my father finally had an opportunity to bring us back home to Hawai'i, he took it. Grasping the so-called privilege of being assigned back to his H.O.R., "home of record." Not his native birthplace, nor his ancestral land, but his "home of record." We lived in AMR for a time, Āliamanu Military Reservation, before they updated the sixties-era buildings into what you see now.

We were home but it was the worst house we'd lived in, crumbling at the top of the crater, the railing of our lanai spotted with rot and mold as it hung precariously over a steep decline.

We played at the park on dilapidated equipment, braving tetanus and potential dismemberment, the rusted metal redder than the red dirt streaking our hands.

In what was once open and sacred, we existed out of time and place, separated from the larger local community by a guard shack and a steel fence. Looking out behind "No Trespassing. Government Property" signs with neighbors who couldn't pronounce our names and scolded us for picking plumeria from the common areas. As if we didn't plant cuttings to replace what we had taken. As if we didn't leave something behind.

Living in the crater I was a ghost too, watching the spectral forms of native men and immigrant workers pass through the rock face of the hillside. Back and forth from the caved-in lava tube tunnels they died in while building ammunition bunkers. I wasn't frightened and yet, I felt terror there.

Now, when I see the scars on my legs and arms, I remember every place I've lived that has marked me. But the scars that I've gotten in the occupied spaces of Hawai'i are not as visible. They are etched onto my bones, genealogical, inherited, and persistent. They are not scars. They are scratches, raw and open. Longer, deeper, and angrier than they have ever been before.

ERIC PAUL SHAFFER

Ceremony, In the American Twilight

In college, I lived in a house with too many roommates.
    We were the bane of the neighbors with our loud,
late nights of rock, our unmown yard of grass long gone

    to seedy stalks, our primered cars of blown mufflers
and blue exhaust. One afternoon, one of us half-baked
rebels tacked an American flag the size of a loose-leaf sheet

    to the wall above a ragged couch, cinder block
bookshelves, and cable-spool tables. From another life,
I knew when to raise and lower the colors, how to hang,

    fold, and drape the flag, all the regulations
    governing the cloth we live and die for. That night,
after the rest passed out or crawled to bed, I couldn't sleep.

    I snuck into the living room and reversed the colors,
placing the blue properly on the left. Through the long days
    of the semester, the flag hung, pinned and rippling

in the occasional breeze from the front door, open, forgotten.
    The holidays came. The roommates dispersed.
Some were gone for good, and more were coming. The flag

    was in tatters, and whoever left last tore
the colors from the wall. I found the flag in the kitchen trash
    and fished the cloth from egg shells and orange peels.

    As light faded, I found an empty coffee can,
and three short, broken laths; a wad of newspaper; a book
of matches. Outside, the sun was gone. Clouds blackened

the horizon, and the blue was tempered with twilight.
In the backyard, I constructed my pyre, dropped a match
    into the can, and watched flames wave at the sky.

In one hand, I held the tired flag, and I gazed into the fire.
    "What you doin'?" said a small voice from beyond
the chain-link fence. The old woman next door was barely

visible, seated in a rocker on her back porch. Caught,
I blew all my breath into the rising shadows, and said,
    "Burning the flag," adding apologetically, "It's old."

A vague shape in the gloom, she paused long, then spoke
a single word, "Glory." She surprised a laugh from me,
    but I had no more words. The fire in the coffee can

was snapping and glad. In the dusk, I squatted over oily earth
    and gray cinders, the glitter of shattered beer bottles,
and fed the cloth into the flames. The light within showed

broad bars of red and white brilliant again when the fire
    caught. Night was coming. From the faded blue field,
orange sparks rose into the darkening sky and became stars.

MIRA CHIEKO SHIMABUKURO

Boxing on the Primo Line

Small kid time, Dad
was one warehouseman.
Work Hawai'i Cold Storage.
Plenny ice dere. Plenny ice
fo store da food from da ships.
Got to put on one big coat
fo go inside. Ey! We say,
dis jes like winter
if we was on da Mainland.

Dad wen join da Teamsters
at da plant. Said if only get one
chopstick, can break em (*Snap*)
Get plenny chopstick,
no can break. Strong.

Laytahs, da plant wen shut down
cause ass when da big chains
came. Dey got deir own warehouse,
got deir own ice. No need Dad.

So now Dad work
fo Primo Beer. Assembly line.
Cardboard come down,
dey fold em, put cans,
bottles, whatevahs. But
dey get Teamsters too.

Before, we useta put
"Warehouseman" for Dad's job
on any kine application
but now he say
he no do dat awready.
So we wen ask,
well, what write den?

An he say, well, I make boxes.
Try put down "Boxer."

An know what? We try
do dat. Like tell people,
daddy's one boxer,
dat wen he go work,
he go fight.

From the "Manoa-Eye Muse"

MIRA CHIEKO SHIMABUKURO

Dey say I wen fall

outta da window at Lusitania Street
when I was one baby.

All dese stories, dey tell me. Tom s'posed
be watchin me, Toki s'posed be watchin me,
Dad s'posed be watchin me

an I wen fall out   hit da si'walk   mash
my rib   ass why da breath stay
trapped in da body sometimes

All dese things,
I tink about. Baby fall outta da window, cry
an cry an cry. Ass what Ma said,
but I don know.

Dey say Dad wen hit Tom fo my time. I no
remember Dad hittin us. I tink he wen stop
by Manoa house time. But dis one day, Sam
                    wen make Dad so mad,
              he wen tie em up ou'side
                 wit one rope. He no hit,
              jes tie em—to da tree an I
              wen sit right in fronta him,
            "So why you do stuff lidat? See
          what happen when get so bad?"
     Sam no remember I wen say dat
but he member
      he no can move   member rope
        mashin his body   holdin him
            back from da yard where Ann,
              Ned an me stay play Bus
                on da ground   Back den
                  we like push two-by-fours
                    through Kalihi and Lusitania
                      da routes we like make in da dirt

one giant fingapaint a da city
we could make move
wit our own   two hands.

From the "Manoa-Eye Muse"

JOHN E. SIMONDS

Medicine Shoulders the Burden

Smooth-soled shoes and wet concrete
put my left arm in a sling.

Landing on grass was the good news,
hydroplaned feet losing it all
but missing the backyard walkway,

head clear but left shoulder broken
and bent, barely able to move—

proximal separations at work here,
the bone from its glenohumeral joint
and me from the house—

Inching 15 feet to sliding screen door,
shouts to neighbors unanswered,

back-crawled into house through
open door, unable to lift or move
forward on parquet floor.

More shouts to neighbors,
most at work or beyond earshot.

Neighbor's daughter drove in early
at noon, heard my shouts for help.
Her 9-1-1 call brought ambulance rescue.

Up on a gurney and into a truck,
sirens sounding to lead the way
through Wednesday noon freeway traffic
to an overcrowded medical center.

busy with routine pandemic pandemonium.
Emergency room beehive stirred to high frenzy

with radio calls arriving from ambulance drivers
orders and signals from rooms everywhere.

Hospital beds were scarce long before COVID
added its land rush for room space.

Aide viewing screen reads off meds I don't take
until we discover another patient, nearly same-named,
is not me, so time to start over with input of data.

Blood thinner reading is high, so cut the Warfarin.
Fentanyl's holding off pain, Oxycodone's warming
in the bullpen in case we need more.
Order CPAP mask, not sure staff can find one.

Time to move, a nurse advises, pushing my gurney
out of the curtained room and into a gurney-packed
double parked route of zig-zagged table-strewn hallways,
arriving in quiet, side alcove of curtained-off spaces.

Papers exchanged among new and old handlers.
"Sorry, we have to move you back,"
the last handler returns with a crazy laugh;
this room can't take CPAP plug-ins.

Return trip angling bumper-car style through gurneys,
racks, and tables on wheels, back to Room 22 where we started,
blue-suited aide laughing all the way.

Other trips for X-rays and CAT scan, plastic bottle
in tow to soothe my busy bladder,
and back to the room for overnight rest.

CPAP showed up to link sleep with oxygen dreams.

Mealtime surprise has its place on the menu,
kitchen schedules preempting the others;

breakfast wheels in unannounced as we're
easing away from a freshly-filled bed pan.

A bell somewhere sounded *ding-ding-ding* like an alarm stuck for
     minutes.
Nurses and techs continued to work as though no one heard it.

No one sees my waving arms, bell button not reconnected after recent
     visit.
With cellphone I dialed the ER switchboard to ask what's going on.

"What room are you in?" a voice asked.
"Twenty-two," I answered, minutes before a nurse showed up.
"Sorry, I was busy elsewhere," she said, finding a switch
to turn off the dinging, which no one but I had heard for an hour.

Late Thursday a room opened up on a tower top floor eight stories
     above,
many corridor turns and two elevator rides away.
Far from the chaos of intake, troubled patients crying,
"Nurse!," "Help me!," "Is anyone here?," and "Where am I?"

"Where is your sling?" was a question I often was asked.
On Friday a sling showed up, a blue off-the-shelf garment,
one-size-fits-none, a therapist taught me to arm, adjust, and remove.

"No, thanks," I said to the Oxycodone—I'd been there before
and survived toilet pains only polyethylene glycol could ease,
but Tylenol allowed me to sleep, until awakened at night
by a sweet-whispered voice of a nurse taking blood pressure.

In the dark she cuffed the upper arm of my broken humerus,
squeezing air tightly around the green-purple bruise,
then slipped away in the night. The pressure read 181.

A new nurse turned up a few minutes later,
cuffing the uninjured right arm and logged a 171.

"Pain can affect your readings," she said,
leaving me and my startled BP to recover.
Hospital care was hectic but good,
not a place to look for perfection,

with all hands on deck and nurses
from elsewhere pressed into duty,
shock troops deployed at the ready,

it's a wonder the health help survives,
let alone patients.

The bill for it all cost me $10,
a bargain, no doubt, for a three-day co-pay.

A hospital doc deemed surgery unneeded.
My own MD said the break would self-heal.

The orthopod showed me X-rays of bones still apart.
Keep surgery on the table, he said. I might need it.
Odds of self-healing are 80 per cent, he agreed.
But this might need knives and pins to restore full use.

His X-rays showed space between the humerus top
and neighboring bones near the socket.
Decision mine, the ortho doc says, but keep options open.

At 86, I ponder the trade-off—full use of left shoulder
and more hospital hours, more days in a sling
and back to One Recovery Square,
an address I'm hoping to miss, or—

The healing question's still open,
like the space between bones
and the doctors' separate opinions.

Bawal: Forbidden Philippines

The Philippines: Land of a thousand islands, Pearl of the Orient![1] It's more fun in the Philippines! Why not visit today?

- Bask in the tropical glow of one or more of our thousand islands. Enjoy tropical sunrises and sunsets with a drink in hand.

- Snorkel tens of thousands of beaches, inhabited and uninhabited. Perhaps you'll find a pearl![2] You will enjoy an abundance of sea life.

- Partake of food at the crossroads of Asia: Chinese-style noodles and spring rolls! Coconut dishes reminiscent of Thai food! Pastries in the European style! Our very own sweet rice cakes! And, of course, an abundance of fresh seafood!

- Manila nightlife! We export talent all over the world.[3] Why not experience that talent here first in the many vibrant bars, clubs, and theaters of Manila. Who knows which of those performers will go on to become a star!

- Enjoy the famed Filipino hospitality! Wherever you travel you will find our people gracious and welcoming![4]

- Visit family! Discover your family history and learn about the rich culture and history of the islands![5]

Unfortunately, due to SARS-CoV-2 and resulting global pandemic, the year-long temporary closure of the Philippines continues. As with our war on drugs, we believe extreme measures are the only real option for responding to this threat. During this closure, we will treat the ill and wait for everything to return to normal. Also, we will be able to vaccinate the Filipino populace with Sinovac and Sputnik vaccines.[6] As soon as our vaccination campaign is completed, we will reopen. While those who refuse vaccines will not be shot[7], they will be jailed. We expect rapid and cheerful compliance. Stay tuned!

Travel Advisory: June 2021

Entry is permitted only for those who fall into one of the following categories:

- You are an Overseas Foreign Worker. Welcome home, kababayan! You have contributed to the Philippine economy by working abroad. We appreciate the risks some of you have taken as low-paid workers, occasionally having your passports confiscated, toiling long hours at housekeeping and childcare, being beaten by employers, possibly surviving sexual assault, enduring the ambivalence of some ambassadors meant to advocate for you, and so on. It's a lot! Now that you're home, please avail yourselves of hand sanitizer and health forms in the immigration area. You may complete those forms while waiting in the three-hour line for COVID testing. Also, you will need to quarantine for fourteen days, ten of which must be in one of our designated quarantine hotels. But at least you're home! And we've found only the cleanest hotels for your convenience. Yes, you will need to pay and it may seem like a lot of money. But, think of all the fellow Pinoy workers you are helping to support here at home. They also need jobs. And, yes, you may have lost your employment due to COVID, and your employers deciding to cut costs, and lack of access to vaccines, but, you can still make this final contribution to the Philippine economy. Remember, we appreciate your sacrifice.

- You are a foreigner with money to invest: Welcome! The Philippines is not off limits for you! Presumably you have received an exemption entry document from the Department of Foreign Affairs and possess a valid 9(A) visa. Please be prepared to prepay for your multiple COVID tests upon arrival. We can direct you to money exchange locations and provide other assistance. You will find Filipinos a friendly people and the Philippines an environment in which you may bask in tropical amenities (i.e., household help and entertainment are readily available) (Please refer to endnote 4.). You do have to quarantine in one of our designated hotels, ready to cater to your every whim.[8] We can assure you that Philippine hospitality is alive and well even in these times of

Coronavirus. Consider prolonging your stay indefinitely by applying for a Special Investor's Resident Visa for a mere $75,000 investment.

- Diplomats, members of international organizations, and their family members: To our Chinese compatriots, welcome, unless we are having a spat over the Kalayaan Island Group[9], in which case, we see you. Americans, please remain in your foreign compounds. We will let you know when it is safe to re-enter Philippine society. Also, you all have to quarantine. And fill out health forms

- Special residents and retirees: Yes, the cost of living here is lower. Yes, you can have a lot of household help, so you can focus on your work. Yes, medical care is cheaper. But, there is a Coronavirus. Now that you've left and returned, you must quarantine. So, we advise you stay in place and don't leave again any time soon. Retirees, as you know, wheelchairs are available upon arrival.

- Foreign nationals with 9(A) or 9(C) visas: Welcome! Remember that you must undergo a fourteen-day mandatory quarantine unless you are fully vaccinated and have arrived from a government-designated "Green Country." In that case, your quarantine is only ten days, only seven of which must be spent in a quarantine hotel . You are one of the lucky few (twenty-two today, to be precise) allowed into the country. Considering our daily maximum of 2,000 entrants, it's quite remarkable you're even here. Please enjoy your good fortune.

- Dual Citizens: See the next category.

- Balikbayan: We are surprised you have chosen this time to visit, but welcome, former Filipinos! We welcome you back to the homeland and hope you enjoy your time here. We hope you are vaccinated! Regardless, you must quarantine and get COVID-tested, but we have many hoteliers and friendly medical technicians to assure your visit home is as comfortable as possible. Our Balikbayan from the U.S. will notice they must quarantine for longer than others. This has absolutely nothing to do with U.S.-Philippine relations under the current administration. Uncertain if you are or are not a

Balikbayan? It's more complicated than you think! Please refer to our handy guide below.

Thirteen ways of looking like a former Filipino, a.k.a. a Balikbayan[10]

- You still possess and can produce your old Philippine passport.

- You are a dual citizen. See exceptions under the fourth bullet point below.

- You have a PSA-issued[11] birth certificate indicating both your parents were Filipino at the time of your birth.

- One of your parents was a Filipino citizen at the time of your birth.

  o Exceptions: If you were born before 1973, then your status is described under the 1935 Constitution, which stipulates your father must have been a Filipino citizen at the time of your birth. If only your mother was a Filipino citizen at the time of your birth, then you must have elected Filipino citizenship at the age of 21 in order to qualify as a Balikbayan.[12] If you did not elect Filipino citizenship, you can't have dual citizenship either.

- You were born in the Philippines to foreign parents prior to the adoption of the 1935 Constitution <u>and</u> your parents served as elected officials of the Insular Government of the Philippine Islands, which preceded the Philippine Commonwealth.[13] In this case, welcome! You are a fortunate beneficiary (possibly one of two or three still living) of the Tydings-McDuffie Act![14] And colonialism. Time to relive those "days of the empire"![15] Wheelchairs will be provided upon arrival for our nonagenarian returnees!

- You were born after 1973 and your father <u>or</u> mother was a Filipino citizen at the time of your birth. Lucky you! You have benefited from the Marcos administration, the establishment of martial law, and the resulting Constitutional Convention![16]

- You can recite and/or sing the national anthem in Pilipino.[17]

- You can recite and/or sing the Pilipino alphabet.[18]

- You can define one or more of the following terms: Misa de Gallo, Simbáng Gabi, Santo Niño.[19]

- You can identify one of the following and provide a basic explanation: *John en Marsha, Tawag ng Tanghalan, Kwarta o Kahon, Iskul Bukol, Darna, Student Canteen, Eat Bulaga!, Aawitan Kita, Asiong Aksaya*, María Clara, Juan Tamad.

- You can explain the mystery and majesty that is Taal Volcano.

- Without explanation, you understand how to hail a jeepney and how to pay for said jeepney ride. Also, you do not accidentally board the wrong jeepney.[20]

- You understand what "First Republic" and "Second Republic" refer to.[21]

There may be further exceptions to the above indicators of a Balikbayan, which may preclude your entry to the Philippines during these times of COVID. Please contact your closest Philippine consulate or embassy via email or phone, if such contact information is published on the consulate/embassy website. If you cannot find either on the website, you may need to visit in person. If the consulate is temporarily closed due to COVID, you will need to wait until reopening. Also, please refer to the FAQs that follow. You may find your answer there.

Frequently Asked Questions

- **Question:** My mother/father/grandfather/etc. is ill, and, feeling the pull of filial piety, I believe I must return home to nurse mother/father/grandfather/etc. back to health.

  - ○ **Answer:** Your return now is not necessary. Yes, upon entry, you would be quarantined and tested multiple times. And, yes, you may be vaccinated. And, yes, most COVID cases involve local transmission. But we are busy dealing with those! Surely someone in your family must still live in the Philippines. Call upon that person for assistance. These are family members. They are trustworthy. In lieu of family members, remember that you may gainfully employ a fellow Pinoy to care for your mother/father/grandfather/etc. Send money for care.

- **Question**: My mother/father/grandmother who never left the house is ill with COVID. This has caused me great worry. I do not understand how this has happened. I do not know if I will ever see my family member alive again. I would like to visit my elderly family member.

  - **Answer:** You understand we are dealing with COVID, right? Do you know how much of the Philippines is still unvaccinated? Ninety-eight percent! You may be vaccinated, but we are not. Proof of this is in the fact your secluded elderly relative has contracted COVID. We do not need your visit! We need efficacious vaccines!

  - **Answer continued:** Also, we need storage freezers! We have been forced to use meat and fish freezers for storing the vaccines we do have.

  - **Answer continued:** We have already run out of ICU beds!

  - **Answer continued:** COVID is not a death sentence. People do recover from it. OK, so a lot of Filipinos have died in the Philippines. A lot of Filipinos have died of COVID abroad as well. Many Americans have died. British. Italians. South Koreans. And many have lived. There is a fifty-fifty chance of survival. Also, please consider the use of Facebook video chat to talk with your elderly relative. This is widely available to most Filipinos accessing the internet using cellphone data. Please avoid use of Zoom. Those of us able to work from home need the limited bandwidth to get work done. We need to keep our jobs!

- **Question:** My mother/father/grandparent has died. I would like to return to carry out the cremation, as I understand only cremations are permitted during these times of COVID. My relative's body is still in the hospital morgue as we are having trouble locating family members willing to leave their homes during COVID to accompany the body to the crematory. I also would like to participate in the wake and funeral for my loved one.

- o **Answer:** Wakes are forbidden.

- o **Answer continued:** Please refer to the answers to the previous question.

- o **Answer continued:** We are still not allowing entry. Again, please avail of assistance from family members. May we also direct you to this[22] Catholic resource, and this[23], and this[24]. All provide prayers for occasions such as this one. May you find solace in those prayers. If you are not Catholic, we cannot assist you.

- **Question:** I would like to enter the Philippines because my cousin/aunt/other non-immediate family member is ill/ill with COVID/has died.

  - o **Answer:** We offer our best wishes for a speedy recovery or condolences. You may wish to consult the prayers at the aforementioned websites.

We wholeheartedly apologize for our continued closure. Remember, we are taking extreme measures because the world is black and white. Although we are brown. But you know what we mean.

Although entry is currently challenging, we look forward to welcoming you soon to the Philippines![25] Remember, good things come to those who wait!

How are we doing? We invite you to submit feedback regarding this informational page at this website.[26]

Notes

[1] This, of course, is a reference to the esteemed Dr. Jose Rizal's final poem, "Mi Ultimo Adios," which refers to the Philippines as "Perla del mar de oriente, nuestro perdido Eden!" Don't focus too much on the "lost Eden" part. Instead, consider that this poem, read before the U.S. Congress in 1902, convinced congressmen (no women yet) that perhaps Filipinos were not barbaric. The power of poetry!

[2] This is not meant as a guarantee. Best to think of the experience itself as a metaphorical pearl, to be treasured upon your return home.

[3] The lead singer of Journey, female leads in various iterations of *High School Musical,* performers in *Glee,* and, of course, our very own Lea Salonga.

[4] This does not apply to the southern Philippines where an Islamic insurgency against Philippine central government control, really a struggle against colonialism, continues. This also does not apply to areas controlled by the Communist insurgency, the New People's Army, which arose from the World War II guerrilla movement against the Japanese Army. So, basically, it doesn't apply to areas in which colonialism, past or present, is still a sore point.

[5] Whether you have lived outside the Philippines for eight months or your family emigrated eighty years ago, you may still come home and support the Philippine economy.

[6] Yes, their efficacy is questionable and won't allow us to travel abroad, but we're patiently waiting for people in developed countries to decide whether or not they want vaccines, so Moderna, Pfizer, AstraZeneca, and Johnson & Johnson can be sent on to us.

[7] Per presidential statements on 21 June 2021, those who refuse Sinovac and Sputnik vaccines may face jail time. However, those involved in drugs should be shot, on orders from the President reported here (www.rappler.com/newsbreak /iq/philippines-president-rodrigo-duterte-statements-shoot-to-kill-drug-war) because extreme measures are the only solution to any problem.

[8] Please note the wide range of price points for your budget.

[9] These are also known as the Spratly Islands by Americans and Nansha Qundao by the People's Republic of China, but we know what they're really called. We have filed protests against Chinese-built airfields meant to bolster ownership claims. These protests have been supported by Japan and Malaysia. Oh yes, and Brunei. Taiwan and Vietnam also have claims. Yes, these are islands, reefs, shoals of biogenic carbonate, basically the skeletal remains of marine life, but they are strategic, and they are ours.

[10] The last seven bullet points in this list are not requirements for entry but really should be if you're going to call yourself a Filipino. At least answer one.

[11] The Philippine Statistics Authority has all your documents. Yes, this may sound ominous, but really it is quite safe. The Authority is the clearinghouse for birth, death, and everything in between.

[12] Of course, if you had elected Filipino citizenship, you would not be a _former_ Filipino, so really that last part makes no sense. Think of it as a brain teaser.

[13] This was the American Period. So, basically, this applies to Americans born in the Philippines.

[14] The Tydings-McDuffie Act put us on the road to independence! Written by Senator Tydings and Representative McDuffie, it established the process by which the Philippines was to become independent of the U.S., while simultaneously tightening immigration provisions so only 50 Filipinos could enter the U.S. annually beginning in 1934. Sometimes you have to take the bad with the good. On July 4, 1946, we breathed the free air of our tropical isles! And then we changed our independence day to June 12, to honor our Katipuñeros and because we realized why July 4.

[15] To quote Louis H. Lisk, a former American combatant turned teacher during the period of the Insular Government of the Philippine Islands, a.k.a. the American Period.

[16] Aforementioned convention began meeting in 1971 and completed work in 1973, after President Ferdinand Marcos declared martial law and expelled eleven members of the convention. Well, truthfully, they were arrested. More importantly, the constitution was upheld by a vote of the Filipino people. And, yes, the validity of the vote was challenged in court, but it was upheld by the Philippine Supreme Court. What more do you need?

[17] Special provisions are made for those who attended primary school during the Insular (American) Period and, thus, only know the anthem in English. We will accept your English version. But, upon entry to the country you must provide a PSA-issued birth certificate as proof. If your birth certificate was destroyed by the many fires during World War II, you will need to file a delayed certificate of birth at your local registrar's office. This must be done in person.

[18] Not the English alphabet. Not the Spanish alphabet. The Pilipino alphabet.

[19] For our non-Catholic kababayan: You should know these. You have lived in a primarily Catholic country.

[20] Also, you know what a jeepney is.

[21] These are not *Star Wars* references.

[22] www.usccb.org/prayers/prayers-death-and-dying

[23] https://prayerist.com/prayer/thedeadcatholicphilippines

[24] laycistercians.com/catholic-prayer-for-the-dead

[25] Please note entry requirements are subject to change based on deliberations of the government's Inter-Agency Task Force convened to address COVID. Please check IATF advisories on the webpage of your nearest Philippine consulate and/or embassy. If the advisory on the consulate/embassy webpage has not been updated in months, go to the Philippines Bureau of Immigration page. New advisories may render some or all of the advice on this page invalid. Also, increasing cases of COVID, nursing staff resignations, health care provider deaths, and the collapse of the healthcare system will affect entry policies.

[26] www.padlab.ph/DLS/passengerCIF [Editor's Note: URL redirects to "Page Not Found"]

CATHY SONG

At the Bishop Museum

The school children marvel at the gigantic
whale hoisted above the main gallery,
hanging like a prized catch from the ceiling,
ribs on one side exposed
as if such an imposing creature couldn't be
realized without revealing its bones.
Once I too gazed up in wonder, passing
through these halls on a fourth-grade field trip,
the year we were to learn about our islands,
the Department of Education's inclusion
of Hawaiiana into our curriculum.
We peered inside a typical dwelling,
decided if not for the rope across the entrance,
the hale's cool interior would be a good place to hide.
The thatched grass had the scent
of dried lei left on a grave.
The small-scale model of a heiau
invited the errant placement of a toy
soldier breaching the walls.
We didn't see the irony
but did find it funny.
The fierce gods glared down
as we checked off in our workbooks
stone implements, woven nets, dog teeth lashed
to war clubs, necklaces roped with human hair.
Dutifully, we followed the timeline.
The early navigators mapped the sky into the mind,
read the wind on the water
and, riding the great currents on canoes,
voyaged to these islands.
We underlined *an incredible feat.*
As the first human inhabitants
they found no resistance.
They brought dogs and pigs and chickens, hauled rocks,
built fishponds, managed the rain,
terraced from mountain to sea a kingdom.

When we came to the birds,
hunted to extinction to adorn the aliʻi cloaks,
we turned the page to the appropriate illustrations
and, with red and yellow crayons,
colored in the feathers.
By the time we reached the missionaries,
we grew bored.
Strictly measured as the hymns they taught,
we were told to listen to their legacy with grateful hearts.
They must have appeared stark as crows
stepping on to shore in tall black hats and coats.
Dispatched to make out of the barren rock
an Eden, they brought dishes and utensils,
manners to match each knife and fork,
the rules we adopted,
confining as the windows that frame
the view from our churches, our cramped houses.
The whalers and the mosquitoes that came with them
were barely mentioned,
how they jumped ship—
tubercular, syphilitic and wheezing,
bowels inflamed by dysentery—
and swam ashore.
Finding little resistance to the thirst they brought,
sought what they had had in every other port.
What was brought could not be undone.
Our attention turned back to the whale.
On closer inspection its skeleton resembled a prison.
I know how the lesson ends.
The children are hungry.
They are getting restless.
It's all on display,
the brief sad history.
The businessmen sidled up to royalty.
They married the daughters.
They unfurled plans ambitious
as the sails of that first ship
anchoring in blue waters.
They imported labor from the Azores and Asia
for the cattle they unloaded,

for the long-tasseled crop they brought,
for whatever the world at the moment craved,
fortunes were to be made.
Caught in a portrait of sorrow and dignity,
the last queen, corseted and caged, bids us farewell.
We know her song by heart,
the truth of the travesty done,
a melody of resistance, hummed
under our breath, or sung.

JOSEPH STANTON

A Kitchen Conversation

"There's a barracuda in your bathtub,"
I mention on returning to the table.

"Yea," he acknowledged with a shrug.
"Seko caught him, off the pier."

"What are you going to do with him?"

"We're feeding him tilapia from the canal,
trying to keep him alive for the Super Bowl party."

After a pause, I asked the obvious question,
"Which team is he rooting for?"

EILEEN R. TABIOS

No Guarantees

— Bauang Beach, Philippines, circa 1965

She knew she should know
better

I was barely older than a
toddler

I had played with her only
daughter

during those summer days of
Innocence

by a sapphire sea warmed by a gentle
sun

When vacation ended and it was time to
leave

she lowered her gaze from my
face

as she carefully suggested I
give

her daughter one of my
dresses

"An old one no one would
miss"

My eyes that squinted all
summer

opened wide and saw the
World

ravishing with its poverty and
desires

ravishing with its grief, such
grief

Suddenly, someone cried out in
pain—

her nearby daughter had stumbled to
fall

Alarmed, she rushed to pick her
up

As she comforted her daughter she began
crying

I realized she understood she could not
guarantee

what she was saying: "It's okay. Pain will go
away."

GARY TACHIYAMA

I Tired

Everybody here, no stay okay.
When rain, even small kind,
the roof leak and water
out of nowhere seep
thru the floor.
I drowning I tell you
and I tired of feeling
like one wet rat.
I tired.

How often rain over here?
How often the floor wet?
Das right, just like every day.
And when rain hard,
we not talking damp.
We screaming inches.
No tell me anymore
how never reach
the sofa and beds and stuff.
Never yet, but going soon.
That's why I tired.

No tell me no make waves,
I only thinking of me and
the landlord going raise
the rent to kick us out.
No tell me he no going
Fix nothing and get plenty
looking for one cheap space.
Cuz I tired of thinking that way.

I tired of wait for everybody
be tired of this shit too.
We drowning in all this
and you tell me no be tired.
I tell you what

this the last time
I tell you I tired.
Next time you going see.

O. WINI TERADA

boku no orin

boku no orin.
Hell's bell. Sound i grew up with,
long high chime from our
Buddhist family-altar's small
not too shiny brass bowl bell.

September is still
summer warm but more humid.
i am not going
to see you, Marie, because
i am going someplace else.

Pak-lan has finished
blooming, a few blocks away,
sweet, citrus-like scent.
You always cheered me on to
write, even nuts stuff like this.

When my parents died,
my good friend Antone hung out
with me to keep me
company, and at seaside
at Cromwell's, in between sets,

he told me his mom
died when he was still high school,
and he still misses
her every day, and then we
were surrounded by the sea.

The sound of this bell
makes me think of you, calming,
smiling. When my eyes
roll way back, and the police
are called for the one last time,

i'll be listening
to this bell, feeling its hum
in my bones. Many
things are taken away from
me, my youth, strength, knowledge, pride,

even memory
but no one can take this sound
from me because it's
a part of the vibration
of my body, or maybe

it's just tinnitus
ringing in my ears that i've
come to make peace with.
i take that last leap, into
the ocean of here, to here.

i grit my teeth here.
i bet going have hard liquor
so i going throw up.
i bet going have clean cocaine
so i going have mean seizures.

i bet not going have
pakalolo, beer, and wine
and sake. i bet
going have choke made-up sexy
women so i going catch all

kinds of STDs,
no rubbers in hell, brah, but
plenty porn for get
you going. i bet going have
choke slick gamblers trying hard

to out-cheat me as
if they can. Even in hell
i'll hear it as i'm
breathing like in aikido,
really long and slow and hold,

maybe not so deep
so those superheated fumes
won't burn my lungs much.
In hell, i'm going to be calm,
to not make waves in the sea

of shet up to my
nose i'll be tiptoeing in.
And i'll be smiling,
from way deep inside, except
around fuckahs like you guys.

i'll be listening.
i'll hear it through the roar of
the fires. In hell, going
to have some of my friends here
with me, man, those of us who

did enough bad stuff
to not rate with St. Peter,
disqualified, 'cause
Jesus was recalled giving
out too many free passes.

We're off to meet up
with our enemies, fuckahs.
Love you. Thank you. Still
not enough Four Noble Truths
in me, not enough Eight-Fold

Path traveled, i'll be
reincarnated as a
citizen of hell,
where i'll listen for this bell
chime, long and slowly fading

away, like my hopes
of ever being lifted
high up out of the
eternal endlessness that
my life will surely end as

BILL TETER

At the Fisherman's Grotto

It's a chilly San Francisco afternoon:
Fisherman's Wharf, bright sky, sharp breeze.
He stares into the camera, hands deep
in that battered corduroy coat he gave away
when he moved to Hawai'i.
He leans against the railing
and she snuggles against him,
borrows his warmth.

You haven't seen that coat in years
And you haven't seen that expression
either, not in many years—
that easy confidence, that assured smile,
the look of one who knows he is loved.
He—you—felt her love that afternoon
as a miracle, and his smile—yours—
told the world he barely understood
how he could have been so lucky.

Do you remember what she saw in you?
Do you remember how different the world felt?
Didn't you smile that afternoon
because you believed she would always be there?
If you could look out of that photo
across the years
to the person holding it now and
looking back at you,
wouldn't you have trouble believing
we were the same person?

BILL TETER

Makiki in the Rain

You were standing at the foot of the hill
on the bridge over Makiki Stream.
It was dark, cold, very wet.
The rain had always sounded so gentle from
inside her cottage
but here, outside, away from her,
it was heavy, hostile.

The stream thundered under the bridge.
You could not see it, only hear it
growling beneath you.
You pictured it tumbling massive boulders
down from the mountain.
You felt its thunder.

Up the hill, up the quiet dead-end street,
one pale square of light, dim
against the darkness of the cottage wall,
broken up by a tall stand of ti
just outside her window.

You remembered that room—but not that light.

It was always dark in her room. She kept her place dark.
"I feel safer in the dark," she told you once.
You recalled her body in silhouette
as she stood in the doorway before
she turned off the kitchen light and
returned to her bed—returned to you.
You remembered the dim red numbers of her digital radio—
3:17 a.m. You could not believe
how good your life was.
Standing here in the rain, looking up the hill
to that square of light, you remembered
the glow of the tip of her cigarette in the dark.
And you heard again the catch in her voice

as she said, "It's really hard for me trust anyone"
and later—
"How do I know you won't be like him?"

And you realized that though you knew the answer
you could not answer her.

Her light went out.
She was safe in her darkness.
And you continued standing in the pounding rain.
You knew you should go back to your car.
You knew it did you no damn good
to stand there in
that merciless rain.

You stood there.

DELAINA THOMAS

The Moon Had Not Let Go of You

for LeiHina

the moon had not let go of you
when they cut you out of me
twelve days before the due date
the vernix covering your body pearlescent
they carried you to a tray
under bluish pans of light
and laid you on the white silk from Pauline

hushed voices deft hands
rubbed vigorously from your limbs onto the silk
patches of bloody membrane
trickles of fluid
and the thick shroud of mucus
that saved you from salt of the amniotic
as the silk grew heavier with textures
and colors of what you swam in
the way here

the glow you did not shed of the moon
as your Father's diesel mechanic grip
on the surgical shears took four tries
to cut what bound you to my insides
the thickest cord the doctor said
she'd seen in a long time

in the hesitation of a moment
everything we'd known as one body
your pulse within my pulse
danced outside that rope's gravity
and fell into our voices
separately
as the luminous coils were lowered
into a plastic container and labeled 122478

the glow you did not shed of the moon
was spreading to your Father's face
those moments he first held you
and rearranged his heart
into someone I knew
would appear when you did

as they stitched back together my uterine wall
and my abdomen
for the first nonemergency
of three C-sections
by which my children had been pulled out to life

the moon had not let go of me
when I found my way back to this room
and poured out of the container
onto a linen handkerchief
your umbilical cord to dry on the dresser

odorless it remained clear and hydrated
for days with opal rivers veined
and spotted here and there
with black resembling seeds of lilikoi
or tadpole eggs

half a cycle of the moon later
the colors have turned to grays
and the drying has left a sinewy hardened rope

I have not decided whether to bury it the Maori way
of your Father
near roots of a long-living tree
perhaps the kōpiko

or to burn it as our Filipino neighbor suggested
on some windless day
in gardens your Father bermed around this house
and planted with rare endemics
I could douse it with alcohol and light it
in one of the depressions he kept

face up to pool rain
on boulders he retrieved from canefields
and lowered in place with the excavator
I could spread the ashes across nehe and pāpala

or as your Uchinanchu great-grandmother did with her nine
I could wrap our bond whole in wax paper
and stash it some secret place
I or you could find the way back to
if the need should be
evidence of the first extension
the moon gave you
to me

DELAINA THOMAS

This Time Away

for Napua, age four

there is no one else at Māliko estuary
we walk to see the guppies their black eyes unblinking
their tails aligned with the flow of the warm brackish current

I've taken you for this time away from your father
for months you've watched him thinning to bone
the doctor told him last week he wouldn't survive
removal of the tumors
and now he discerns your presence only sporadically

the onshore breeze rifles through your wispy ehu hair
you climb over the huge slippery boulders glistening in the sun
'opihi clinging like gray stars to the undersides

on one boulder you spot a ladybug
carefully you pinch it off
bending close over it as it crawls slowly across your small palm
there is nothing else going on in the universe

the gossamer wings unfold
suddenly and it jumps between your fingers
the swirling foam obscuring it as soon as it hits the water
oh no it fell I exclaim
the wave rushing out
you don't say anything
you glance at the horizon and turn away to the sandy shoreline

I piggyback you into the water
you cling to me as if I were solid as a mountain
the surf pounding against us
I strain for balance at the impact on my slight body
each cold wave splashing you higher and higher
has you shrieking with delight

you are his only child
he will not see the magnificent lady you will become
no tide will bring him back
these hours will leave us
the sun will lower into the horizon

one day I will remind you how this morning
you grabbed a noni from a stall at the open market
and held the light green translucent fruit up to me in your fist
saying *I'm taking this to my dad to make him better*

for now it is better to forget everything
but the taste of the salt water and the smell of the oil
of kukui nut hulls washed up in swales along the muliwai

KEN TOKUNO

The Fan

The sign on his desk was made by a felt-tipped marker and in his own ragged printing. It read: "Chatsworth Miyamoto, Assistant to the Assistant Sports Information Director." That wasn't his formal title. It wasn't what anyone called him. What they usually called him was "you" as in "Hey You!" He did work for the Assistant Sports Information Director of the University of Hawai'i. It wasn't even his desk, but a classroom armchair. Still, it was his dream job, because he got to know the athletes, all of the athletes, famous or not, male or female, tall, strong or fast.

Chats's main task at his job was walking. He walked to give a memo to the head golf coach or to check on how a linebacker was feeling or to find out where the new reporter from the *Honolulu Star-Bulletin* had gotten lost and escort him to his boss. Yes, he was pretty much a gofer. Still, it was his dream job and it gave him enough income to afford a dumpy studio apartment on Kalo Place, a stone's throw from the athletic fields of the University of Hawai'i. His place was a mess, but that was okay because he was the only one who was ever in it, except for one visit from his parents. His mother, an overly fastidious Chinese woman who had named him after her father, took one step into the apartment, said "Ah-yah" and never returned. His father had merely shrugged and followed his wife back to their car. That was okay with Chats, who saw his parents every weekend anyway. Carless, he rode the bus to 'Aiea to get free meals, do his laundry and crash for one night. Sunday evening saw him back on the bus, his laundry having been cleaned and neatly folded by his mother.

What made his apartment so messy was all of the sports memorabilia he had collected since he was a child: pennants from the great Les Murakami baseball teams of the late 70s; football programs from many years—a special stack of them from the immortal 2007 victory over the University of Washington that had sealed an unbeaten season; bobbleheads of June Jones; baseball cards of Kolten Wong; and all kinds of jerseys, some autographed. His prized possessions, though, were boxes full of autographed footballs, basketballs, tennis balls, volleyballs, and even golf balls, along with a few sweaty T-shirts. Thus, his place was a rather smelly mess. Still, it kept him close to his dream job.

Even in high school, Chatsworth would root more for the University of Hawai'i than for his own 'Aiea Na Ali'i teams, especially in football and basketball. He could see UH games on TV as opposed to having to drag himself out of the house to go to see the Ali'i lose another game to Kahuku or Campbell or whomever. When he got into the University, he finally attended some of the football games in person, as many as he could afford, and was overwhelmed by the spectacle: the enormous players, Aloha Stadium, the band, the cheerleaders, and especially victories over colleges that everyone in the country knew, like Brigham Young and Arizona. The basketball games were almost as good and he discovered volleyball, tennis, and on and on. It was amazing that he found time to study, but he did manage to get his degree in business, largely because he was good at math.

Now, one might suppose that Chatsworth had just gotten out of college and was awaiting some kind of career opportunity, but no, he was thirty-seven and had no intention of doing anything else but this job that let him hang around his old school and bump shoulders with the star women's volleyball players, the all-state guard who had joined the men's basketball team despite being recruited by UCLA, and even the top-rated diver in the conference whom few others had even heard about. It was his privilege to do whatever needed to be done to spread the word to all the news media in Hawai'i, even if he never wrote a line of press release or spoke to any radio commentators. It was his privilege to bring lunch to the media room when national sports journalism figures came to Hawai'i to cover a game although his dream of meeting Al Michaels never came true.

The bad part of his life was on weekday evenings when he went to his place alone. He would get there late because he always had dinner in the Center; on game nights this was always two hot dogs from the vendors upstairs. Otherwise he had to reheat a cold plate lunch he had bought at noon from the lunch wagon. His best friend was his TV set, which he turned on as soon as he got home so he could see what was playing on the all-Hawai'i sports channel. He would watch whatever was on, usually re-broadcasts of old games, then shower and flop on the couch in his underwear under an old blanket. In the morning, he would gobble a bowl of Wheaties, the Breakfast of Champions, using a carton of milk that was practically the only thing in his tiny brown fridge. Then he would either go to work or catch the bus. He had been doing this for fourteen years.

When he graduated from the University of Hawai'i he had tried to find a regular job at the urging of his mentors in the Athletics Department. He had been a solid student assistant and they all thought his reliability and energy would get him a solid position in any of a number of companies in Honolulu. They gave him glowing recommendations and he landed a job in a financial services company where he lasted only four months. You see, he had no interest in anything the company did, so his heart was not in doing the work they assigned to him. When he gave the wrong files to Mr. Cristobal that resulted in his losing the Parker, Jones, and Taniguchi account, he was fired.

What could he do but drag himself back to Stan Sheriff Center and explain to Randy Machiyama how he had screwed up? Randy was then the Assistant to the Sports Information Director and old enough to have known Stan Sheriff before he had become the legendary Athletic Director of the University. Randy, feeling sorry for Chatsworth, hired him into a job that did not exist but was willed into existence out of student help funds. Athletic departments have more leeway in such matters.

His position was supposed to tide him over until he could find a "regular" job, but Chats was captivated by being in the thick of things, getting to collect souvenirs of all the sports and getting to chat with the athletes. It didn't matter to him which athletes either. He was absorbed in all of the sports including golf, sailing, and water polo that the public paid little attention to. Thus, he never even tried to find another job. Between his low salary, his lifestyle, and his total attention to UH sports, he also never tried to find a girlfriend.

Now, despite how all of this sounds, Chatsworth Miyamoto was otherwise what some women would call a "good catch." He was slim, of average height, and not bad looking. He was neat, well dressed (his mother saw to that) with just enough clothes, and polite and kind to a fault, which was why he was so well liked by the athletes. Those same athletes, however, merely saw him as just a cog in the Athletics program so none of the female athletes gave him a second thought. At this point, too, they were over a decade younger than he was. No one gave him a second thought until Persephone showed up.

Persephone Rodrigues, was a part Filipino, part Hawaiian, part Portuguese, part Korean, part German, and, naturally, part Greek woman who had started working for the Sports Information Director shortly after Chats turned thirty-seven. She herself was in her early thirties. The first time she saw Chats, she was drawn to him, but then, she was drawn to almost any single man within twenty years above her age. Besides, all the other men at work were married or old or both. She did like his strong chin, wondered if his thin hair was a sign of balding, and did not trouble herself over his small eyes. She was, of course, unmarried. Her old high school classmates would have been surprised at this since she had been so popular at Kaimukī High for reasons most of the boys could tell you.

Persephone was no beauty, but she was what could be called "pleasantly plump," with a cute face, no figure to speak of, and hair that always looked dry no matter what she did with it. Her job as clerk typist was her third move within the State of Hawai'i system, all intended to gradually place her work closer and closer to her parents' home in Kaimukī, where she still lived. As she saw Chatsworth dabble by her desk eight times a day, she was determined to get closer and closer to him. By her second week, she had wrestled an invitation from Chatsworth to visit his apartment after work, and naturally he escorted her there as any gentleman should.

Now we all know that Chatsworth never got to his place before seven, so even he was surprised at how many strangers he encountered walking up to the third floor, all of them his neighbors coming home from work. They were just as surprised to see him, most of them having no idea who he was, but pleasant in greeting him as Hawai'i folks tend to be. The one neighbor he knew was Mr. Kim, who lived next door and said to him, "Ah, nice to finally get to meet your missus, Chats."

Looking as embarrassed as a 37-year-old virgin could look, Chats said, "Um." It was up to Persephone to say, "I'm just Chatsworth's co-worker. He has been so kind to let me see his apartment. I'm Persephone." Nonplussed, Mr. Kim just said, "Nice to meet you," and ducked into his door, #303. One more door down the hall and there was Chats's place, #304. He fumbled for his key in his right pants' pocket, and just for a second, thought he'd lost it for the third time this year. The landlord said he would have to pay double to replace any more keys, but he found it in the left pocket.

Entering the front room, Persephone smelled the distinct odor of mold and a faint smell of old sweat. One thing she would need to fix when they got married: his cleanliness. She saw the row of bobble-heads along the windowsill, flanking the one struggling houseplant, a wilting sansevieria, in a blue pot with orange polka dots. One more thing to fix, maybe two in the same place. What dominated the room, however, was clutter, at least what she took to be clutter: Chats's priceless collection of University of Hawai'i sports memorabilia. Picking their way through the stacks of programs, boxes full of balls, helmets, and rackets, they made it to what passed for Chats's card table, not what most people would use to eat on, but Chats liked it. It held some of his best autographed programs. There was just about enough clear space on it for a bowl of cereal.

"Can I get you something to eat or drink?" said Chatsworth, forgetting that all he had was Wheaties and milk.

"Do you have any Sprite?" said Persephone.

"Uh, sorry, no. All I have is, um, milk."

"Okay, just give me a glass of ice water, please."

"Is just water okay?"

"You mean you have no ice?" Another item to fix.

"Sorry," said Chatsworth as he filled his one cup, hoping he had washed it recently. Slowly drinking the water as she surveyed the room, noting that there was only one other door leading to the bathroom, Persephone realized that any intimate dinners would not be taking place in his apartment, so she thanked him for the grand tour, told him that she had to be home for dinner, and said goodbye.

It is perhaps some measure of Persephone's persistence, some would call it desperation, that she ignored these not so subtle hints of Chatsworth's failings and spent the next weeks, filing for, flirting with, and fidgeting around him. He was not so naïve to not notice; after all, he had done some dating in his college days, but had never found a girl with enough passion for sports to pursue her. Nor did he realize that he was being reeled in like a canvas tarpaulin on a ball field after a rainstorm. A month after his grand tour, she managed to get an invitation to have dinner with his parents. She said she could drive him to 'Aiea.

Since he had not bothered to tell his parents that he was bringing a guest home for dinner that Saturday, they were a bit hard-pressed to set a table for four, but there was enough nabemono to go around. Japanese stew is easy to stretch and since that was Mr. Miyamoto's favorite, his wife had become proficient at it, forsaking her training in Chinese cooking almost completely. For her part, Persephone did not mind the informality of the occasion, the meager servings of dinner, or the straitlaced manner of Chatsworth's parents. She took note of the nice furniture, the elegant wall hangings, and the size of the house as a whole to see that her Chats stood to gain a good inheritance. It did not hurt that he was an only child.

After that dinner, they started to eat lunch together daily. This ritual began the very next Monday when Persephone bought Chats a plate lunch from the food wagon that was parked near the Center. She told him that it was in return for the fine dinner his parents fed her. He agreed to this one, but (as he had gotten a degree in business management) he knew that neither one of them had a salary high enough to buy two lunches every day and he told her that. She was delighted at his tacit agreement to have lunch together regularly on workdays and that the Dutch treat arrangement was a metaphor (as she had gotten her degree in English) for their forthcoming life together.

Their conversation centered on sports, only UH sports. This was natural enough since they both worked for the Athletics Department, but Persephone wanted to speak of other things.

"You know, Chatty, you're the first person I've ever met who didn't ask me about my name." said Persephone.

"I know your name. It's Persephone," said Chats (who hated that she called him Chatty, but he couldn't say why.)

"I mean why is that my name?"

"I don't know why is that your name?"

"Do you know Greek mythology?" said Persephone, then not waiting for his response, "She had to spend six months a year in Hell and six months with her mother on Earth."

"Whoa, bummer," said Chats in his best imitation of a surfer dude, which he was not and would never be.

Sometimes, thought Persephone to herself, *I feel like this is my time in Hell.* She was gradually realizing that despite his degree, Chats had no depth, unless it was knowing everything about UH sports. She was eager to please him, though, so she would often sit with him as he watched men's basketball, women's basketball, beach volleyball, men's volleyball, and women's track and field as they played on campus, or if there were time conflicts, replays on television. It seemed like he spent half his work time watching sports. She could not afford to spend quite that much time and she did not understand a number of them, although she was amazed at how powerful some of the women who threw the shot put looked. She just didn't understand why they would want to do it.

If Chats had a favorite sport, it was basketball, both men's and women's. He never missed a home game and he saw all of the games they played on the mainland via television when they were on. He did not rate being able to travel with the team. He thought the men's team this year was excellent and they had a chance to go to the NCAA "Big Dance" by winning the Big West Conference, which would all be broadcast on national TV. Knowing how much he wanted the team to win, Persephone agreed to come to his place for the first time since she had visited, to watch all the games the Rainbow Warriors played in. This was a bad idea.

As UH won the first-round game by defeating Cal Poly, Persephone was not surprised by how enthusiastic Chats was with each Hawai'i score nor how badly he swore at the referees with every foul called on the Warriors, even when she could see that the call was correct and she knew almost nothing about the game. What dismayed her was the way he jumped up and down and screamed with the final score as if he were all alone. It seemed like the rantings of a psychotic. He did not notice how scared she was and even as he calmed down he merely asked her why she wasn't excited that their team had won. She left his place wondering what might happen if they lost. She found out the next evening.

The game was in Las Vegas, so it was broadcast at 5:00 in Hawai'i. Persephone brought dinner because she noticed that Chats had gone without eating the day before due to his preoccupation with the game. The game did not go well for Hawai'i as they lost to the University of California Irvine in a close game that ended when an Anteater made a last-second shot. Looking at Chatsworth as the game neared its end, Persephone stopped worrying that he had not eaten the food she brought nor taken a drink of his soda since halftime. She worried if she would leave his apartment alive.

He was sweating profusely and not because it was hot. His face was frozen in a catatonic grimace as he stared at the screen. The score narrowed. The time diminished. Game over. Chatsworth stood, stiffly. His face was so red it was almost purple, and he was panting like a marathoner at the end of the race. Persephone could not begin to describe the expression on his face, but it was somewhere above anger times despair multiplied by frustration and divided by less than zero tolerance for anything near him. Sensing this, she carefully crawled away from the couch where they had been sitting and watched him annihilate a pillow, then the dinner and the tray table it was on. He almost threw part of a dish through the TV, but something economical stopped him before he turned around and saw Persephone. She smiled at him hoping to remind him of who she was. Maybe he was reminded, but what he did was scream so loudly it startled every dog in the neighborhood who all started to howl. "How can you smile at a time like this?" he asked non-rhetorically. "Get out!" She was only too happy to oblige.

The next morning at the Stan Sheriff Center, there was no sign of Persephone Rodrigues except for a letter of resignation, and no one ever saw her within a mile of the Center ever again. Chats came to work and did not ask about her but looked at the remaining baseball schedule. He liked the way the pitching staff was shaping up.

LEE A. TONOUCHI

Imagined 1903 Okinawan Help Wanted Ad

Coming Soon Jinrui Kan*

Wanted

Performance artists for interactive captivity exhibit.

Okinawan Females with primitive tattoos needed.

Excessive facial and body hair preferred.

Must like working with people in close confinement.

Competitive wages.
We will match any pay (if) given to
Korean, Ainu, or Taiwanese aborigine entertainers.

Meals will be provided.
Must be able to catch food that is thrown.

Looking for job security?
Why not live, work, play . . . in a cage!

*I first read about da Jinrui kan (native people exhibition) from scholar Wesley Ueunten. In his essay "Okinawans on Mainland Japan: Discrimination, *Imeeji*, and Identity," published in *Reflections on the Okinawan Experience: Essays commemorating 100 years of Okinawan immigration*, Ueunten tells, "We can link the image of Okinawa being exotic and different to the idea that Okinawans were 'inferior.' One of the most deplorable examples of this was the *Jinrui kan* at the Fifth Osaka Industrial Exposition in 1903. For this exhibition, exhibition organizers put Ainu, Taiwanese aborigine, Korean, and Okinawan women on display for Japanese to gawk at their 'primitiveness'" (49).

JEAN YAMASAKI TOYAMA

Picture Words

Lesson 1
My teacher told me he knew tricks
on how to remember
the intricacies of kanji—漢字.
Remember this one is made of water,
grass and other things.
His hot breath brushed my ear
as he took my hand to show me
the stroke. He was an artist.
You'll need my help to learn.
I'll make it simple.

Lesson 2
Take for example onna, woman—女
Someone sitting at home.
See her there in the chair,
so relaxed? A wonderful picture, that.
Along with child, woman is love 好.
Along with delight, woman is happy 嬉
See how it works? he asked, his hand
brushing my cheek.

Lesson 3
It was only later that he taught me
that *woman* with *dry* 干
is *wickedness* 奸.
Woman 女 with *again*, 又,
makes *slave*—奴.
There's many more I will teach you,
he said, this is only a start.

JEAN YAMASAKI TOYAMA

The Wilted Voice

From the time he was an infant, Shunji (俊士) fulfilled the promise of his name. His head was superbly shaped with perfectly matched ears. Even as a newborn, his eyes focused without wavering. He learned quickly how to talk and walk, rarely stumbling as ordinary babies did. His mother and father acknowledged his gifts and his sisters and brothers, understanding the ways of life, hoped for him a wonderful future without a hint of jealousy.

Growing up, Shunji liked to spend time in the hills behind their farm, foraging for *matsutake*, fern, and other wild plants with his *nēsan*, Bun, the eldest sister.

"Look over there, some *negi*," Shunji said (wishing to share the pleasure of discovery).

"What a sharp eye! Didn't see it."

While Bun moved to pick the onion, Shunji pursed his lips and gently blew. A lovely, crisp melody floated in the air.

"Listen, isn't that a *kurotsugumi*?" Bun said, lifting up her head to listen. "How wonderful."

He hoped to delight his sister with his thrush song.

They explored the woods listening and watching for its living wonders. When they saw a speckled wood butterfly, a creature known to be the bearer of the recent dead, they would imagine whose soul it might be carrying.

"Maybe it's Sasaki-san? He's only been gone a week."

"Perhaps he can see us," Shunji replied. "Smile and wave."

They were fascinated by this butterfly's eggs, which were magically translucent. The multi-convexed shells dazzled them. They would peer through the clear covering and marvel at the red eyes of the growing caterpillar staring back at them.

"Maybe the soul glows in those eyes."

As he grew older Shunji often wandered off by himself, returning with loads of mushrooms or whatever he was able to forage from the woods. None of his family questioned his solitary walks, though he returned with stories that made them wonder about things no one else had ever noticed. The boulder near the waterfall was a fire horse to him. Fire horse? The grasses sang, when the wind blew through them.

Grasses don't sing. Shunji made the familiar strange. The one story they recognized was about the shapeshifter *tanuki*, the rascal raccoon.

"Believe me, I saw it with my own eyes. His *kintama* blew up from down there and turned into an umbrella. It protected him from the rain. I got all wet."

They laughed and shook their heads. Expandable testicles!

But there was one thing Shunji never told them about: the voice. The first time he heard it, he was sitting under a pine tree, eyes closed, listening to the crickets and the frogs, breathing in the spring air. A gentle breeze came up and something like a smudge of sound was embedded in the soft whoosh. He felt it was not only the wind, there was a voice, a wilted voice, floating inside. *Kareta*, like a faded flower not quite dead. It gave a lingering taste to the tongue. He didn't yet understand the words but was confident that one day he would. But he kept all this to himself. No one must know. They wouldn't believe him.

The children grew older, but conditions in Japan didn't get better. Bun agreed to go to Hawai'i to marry the son of a farmer from the neighboring village. Her absence weighed heavy on Shunji. He became reclusive, spending more time in the mountains alone. He started visiting a small cemetery where he examined the oddly shaped stones that graced the ancient graves of ancestors. Perhaps he was looking for his ancestors, but the stones had no names because the people didn't have surnames until the Restoration. Their family name had been concocted from the woods in the mountain, Moriyama 森山.

Shunji would wander to this graveyard more often because this was the place where he would surely hear the voice. Without Bun he had no other close companion. It didn't matter that he didn't understand the words. The sounds enchanted him with hidden meanings, imagined or real. The thrush's song no longer could compete nor the red eyes of the butterfly. Sometimes the voice seemed to settle in his head, somewhere in his inner ear. At other times it was still out there floating on the wind. He became lonelier and sadder, except when he roamed among the gravestones. The priest of the temple would often see him there.

"Shunji-kun, you don't have ancestors here, do you?"

"No, I don't think so, but I have strong feelings. I like to look at these odd stones. They all have different shapes and unclear markings. They attract me."

"Can you tell me why?"

"When I'm here I feel something, you know. I can't put it into words. This temple must make you feel something, no? Peace? Gratitude? For me it seems like time evaporates and space seems to disappear. But I really don't know what I mean by these words."

The priest shook his head, neither agreeing nor disagreeing.

Suddenly, Shunji fell to the ground. Clutching his breast, he whispered. "Do you smell it? Bitter, bitter. Rancid. Wait . . . Do you hear it? It's saying 'Shunji.'" His body shivered and he lost consciousness.

The priest rushed into the temple and returned with a potion. He made Shunji drink. Immediately Shunji felt like a gravestone had been lifted off his breast. When he looked at the priest's face, all he saw was his shimmering smile, an explosion of colors. He opened his mouth to say something, but instead, his body quivered and he fell asleep.

Later the priest accompanied Shunji home. There he recounted these events to the young man's mother. He strongly advised her to have him leave the area.

"This place is not good for him," the priest said. "He sees strange things. He feels strange things."

"We know he's not ordinary," his mother said, "but he's always been that way. He's told us a lot of unbelievable things, but he's all right. He's healthy, strong."

"Is it normal to spend so much time among the dead?" the priest asked.

"The dead?"

"He comes to our cemetery almost every day."

"Cemetery?!"

His family did not know of this new fascination. They had become so inured to his ways that they had not paid much attention. Soon it was decided that Shunji should go to Hawai'i and join his sister, Bun.

Before he left Japan, Shunji visited the priest to thank him. In return the priest gave him a pouch that contained the makings of the potion that had revived him. The priest thought that he might need it someday. He explained that it was made from a special mushroom that turned purple when handled. Shunji was grateful for the gift that had given him much relief. He regretted leaving, but he was troubled by all the feelings that had passed through his body. The pleasure of the voice sometimes brought pain and that troubled him greatly.

When Shunji arrived in Kōloa, it was as if he and Bun had never separated. Even though his shoulders had filled out and he was now taller than she, as soon as he greeted her, it seemed that nothing had changed. Their mother's letters had warned her of his recent obsessions, but this reunion reassured her. She had always accepted that he was a different human being and believed that he would do better in Hawai'i.

After introductions to the doctor, Bun's employer, and his family, Bun took him to the back to meet her husband, Ryoji, and their young daughter, Mieko. The house stood behind the main structure, close enough for service to the family but far enough for a little privacy. Shunji would live in a back room. When he looked out the window, he felt less homesick seeing the jabong tree that Bun had brought with her as a sapling. They soon settled into a calm routine.

"I think that the change here will help you feel better. Mother wrote that everyone was worried about you. You didn't make them laugh anymore. Do you want to tell me anything?"

"No, not right now. Don't worry, I think, I will do better here."

Bun smiled and nodded.

Shunji settled into a routine of taking care of the grounds, cleaning up the doctor's offices, and doing whatever needed to be done. He also explored the mountains beyond the cane fields taking note of familiar edible plants. Bun sent him off to look for some *kikurage* which he had foraged in the woods in Japan. Now she called it pepeiao and pointed to her ear. That's how he learned his first Hawaiian word. He was happy again, surrounded by trees, the sounds of birds and crickets. He smelled the fragrance of yellow blossoms whose name he did not yet know and plucked a flower for Bun to identify. The mountain breeze brushed against his face and sounded in his ear. As he said pepeiao to himself, he wondered whether voices also floated on Hawaiian winds.

He followed his sister's directions and found the place where they were supposed to grow. Looking up on the trunk of a tall tree he saw pepeiao protruding out of its bark and carefully plucked enough from there and the surrounding trees to fill his bag. He made sure he left enough for the next person and for the next harvest. Peering into his bag, he felt a breeze brush past his ear and thought he heard a familiar sound. At first he was pleased, then a little anxious. He listened carefully, turning his head this way and that. Then he swallowed hard. His heart pounded stronger. The sound seemed to come from everywhere and nowhere. Old feelings rushed back. Joy. Curiosity. Excitement. And then anxiety.

He didn't hear any words, but for the first time he knew what the voice was saying. "Go straight, turn right, go beyond those trees." He obeyed. Soon he smelled something woody, strong and pungent, like burnt herbs. He looked around trying to find the source of that odor.

He recognized the smell of sandalwood incense from the temple. He had never seen a sandalwood tree, but he remembered that fragrance. He looked around. There were no trees. He breathed. Feelings swept over him again. He felt dizzy. He heard that voice, now saying, "Breathe more deeply." He obeyed. One. Two. Three. Then pain followed wave of pain. Though the voice seemed familiar, the sense of it was stronger. He tasted the sound in his mouth. Rancid. It went to the pit of his stomach. If suffering had a smell, that's what he smelled. Hunger mixed with fear and sorrow. He looked around, but there were no gravestones. His legs quivered slightly, but he was able to gather the pepeiao that had fallen out of his bag and make his way home.

Bun was pleased to see Shunji through the kitchen window until she noticed him stumbling. She ran out to catch him before he fell and helped him to his room.

"What happened?"

"I just got a little tired. Don't worry. Everything is fine. Here, I got a bag full."

Bun took the bag. Though she furrowed her brow, she said nothing. "I'll get some water."

In the meantime, Shunji got the pouch of mushroom given to him by the priest and placed some of the powder in the hollow of his mouth. When Bun brought the water, he drank it down. Soon he was asleep feeling no anxiety. Later that evening he tried to convince his sister that he was all right.

A few days later he asked the doctor about the area where he smelled sandalwood. Though they had no mutual language, Shunji was made to understand that once long ago the mountains were full of sandalwood, but then it had all been harvested, and sugar cane came. That explanation still didn't bring any understanding of the great sorrow and pain that he had experienced. There was no cemetery there. He needed to learn the history of that place, but for most people it was just part of the landscape. Sometime later he learned about Dan Yone, one of the Gannenmono, the first to arrive from Japan in 1868, who had married a rich Hawaiian woman. Though advanced in years, he might know something. Shunji sought him out.

"So, you smelled something like sandalwood *senko* in those hills?" Yone said.

"Yes, a strong smell." Shunji paused while looking at the old man's wrinkled hands. "Maybe you know why?"

"They grew all over the hills. But they're all gone now, the sandalwood."

"I know, everyone told me they're gone, but I smelled it. I swear I could smell it at that place." He stopped and stole a glance, this time at his white beard.

"They say that wood never loses its fragrance."

"But there were no trees."

"Maybe you smelled the ghosts of the trees," Yone said.

"Please, this is not a joke," Shunji said, looking at the old man's face.

"I'm not joking. There's a lot we don't know about trees and animals, life and death. The universe."

"But trees having ghosts?"

"Why not? They're alive. At least they were, almost a hundred years ago. Trees must suffer when they are cut. Don't you think?"

"But I didn't smell sandalwood everywhere."

"I don't know, something else might have happened, where you smelled the sandalwood. The Hawaiian peasants suffered a lot while harvesting. Sandalwood brought riches to some but pain to the trees and the people."

Shunji looked the old man in the eye. "Please don't tell anyone," he paused, "but I had strange feelings, too. Sadness. Fear. Physical pain and suffering. It almost crushed me."

"Well, that makes sense. The harvesters were starving. They were forced to neglect their own fields and cut the trees. No taro. No vegetables. They hardly had time to fish. They were forced to cut the sandalwood day and night until there was no light. All to pay tribute to the royals. They had to eat wild, bitter herbs, moss, anything they could find in the mountains. Their only clothing against the cold nights was their loincloths. Maybe some people died there too." He looked Shunji in the eye and paused. "If what you say is true, you felt all of that."

Shunji said nothing.

"Buddha tells us that life is suffering," Yone said.

"But do I have to feel it? And from the past?" Shunji finally replied.

"You're right. There's enough suffering in the present. No need to suffer past pain." He paused. "You know about the strike on Oʻahu, don't you. And there's the influenza. Many people are dying today. Families are suffering. Don't you feel like you want to help? Maybe that's what the pain is telling you. Help stop today's suffering."

Shunji leaned back in his chair and turned his face toward the old man. "Please listen, Yone-san, I mean no disrespect and it's not that I'm uncaring. But I believe that sometimes more harm comes when you act."

"Well, that's a very ancient thought. Believers of that idea lived in caves. In any case, if you ask me, that's a sad way to think. You can't do anything about past suffering. You can do something about the present."

"Maybe that's true."

Yone gave a sigh. "You'll never get anywhere. You will always be helpless." He looked intently at Shunji. "Yes, you are indeed a strange young man."

Shunji sat silent. He had disclosed nothing about the voice for fear of being ridiculed. He thought that if he were supposed to do something, the voice would tell him.

Shunji didn't see his sister much during this time. Forced to make extra money, she kept taking sewing orders in addition to her usual work. Fortunately for Shunji the work to be done for the doctor was not hard. He kept the grounds clean, did odd repair jobs to keep things in order, and took care of the vegetable garden. What concerned Shunji were these strange feelings, the uncertainty of hearing that wilted voice. The mushroom given to him by the priest was almost all gone, so he started looking for something similar.

One day while walking through a cow pasture, he saw mushrooms coming up from the dung. When he crushed tl turned purple. That was the sign. He knew of the dangers mushrooms, so he asked around about this strange harvest the working men laughed when he showed them the mushrooms.

"No, they won't kill you, but maybe you might want to die." Then they laughed.

As long as they don't kill me, Shunji thought. So he dried them and kept them in his pouch.

One day Ryoji suggested that they go to the reservoir to explore another part of Kōloa. Shunji agreed because he wanted to find out more about his brother-in-law, who was now his elder brother. Ryoji was proud of being entrusted with the water that irrigated the fields, so he wanted Shunji to see his domain. They walked to the company corral and saddled Ryoji's horse. It was a brown mare, large enough for both of them. Shunji sat behind him and held on to his elder brother trying not to appear afraid. He had never ridden a horse before.

"Don't worry, she is very gentle," Ryoji said, and they trotted to Waita. "Waita is a man-made reservoir, you know. It furnishes the water for all the cane, but it must be controlled with sluices. They tell me it's the largest in Hawai'i." Ryoji paused. Soon Shunji relaxed and turned his attention to the rows of passing cane. There was no wind so the cane stood still in the hot air.

"I hear you talked with Yone-san."

"Yes."

"He's a good old man, but sometimes he has strange ideas."

"I know, he thinks trees suffer."

"What?"

"Never mind."

They stopped talking for a while, then Ryoji, turning his head back toward Shunji, lowered the tone of his voice: "You know, at first Bun didn't want me to take this job."

"Really? Doesn't it pay more? And I bet it's important."

"Right, but there are stories about the waters."

"What kind of stories?"

Ryoji was silent. Waita loomed in the distance, a huge iridescent lake surrounded by lush green mountains. On the far side of the reservoir they could make out some children jumping into the water ιd others picnicking on the shore. Some even had fishing poles. Shunji looked towards the mountains and felt a cool mist from the waters. He started to feel a slight tingle around his ears. Some ducks flew overhead and landed on the water. Shunji pointed to them. "Oh, they're migratory birds. They'll be gone in a month," Ryoji said. "You know, some people say there was a forest here under the marsh before they built the reservoir, way before the Hawaiians. People with imagination got scared, especially . . ." Ryoji stopped talking.

"Scared? Why?"

Ryoji did not answer.

Shunji made a face. "You don't trust me?"

"It's not that. One of the reasons the plantation has me watch the reservoir is because . . ."

Before Ryoji could finish, Shunji interrupted, "Listen, do you hear that?"

"What? The ducks?"

"No. That sound, that wind, it's saying there's a dead woman in the water."

"What? I don't hear a thing, It's your imagination, Shunji."

Shunji insisted and forced Ryoji to gallop to a place where something red was floating about a hundred feet away from the shore. They dismounted and walked to the water's edge. Ryoji was a good swimmer so he removed his clothes and got into the water. He swam towards the red object and dived down. It was a long obi that led to a body. In a few minutes he came up and swam to Shunji. "You're right, it's a woman."

Ryoji had been instructed to report such things to the plantation immediately. So he galloped away leaving Shunji to keep watch.

Shunji couldn't stay on shore. He removed his clothes and dived into the icy water. Keeping his eye on the red sash he swam towards it. He took a few deep breaths and plunged downward. Soon he saw long black hair undulating in the underwater current alongside the red sash. Then he saw her face. It glimmered in the light that shone through the water. Even dead, that face moved him. Shunji was bewitched. A huge stone was tied to her leg keeping her in one place. Shunji almost forgot to breathe. He quickly rose to the surface, filled his lungs, and descended again. He couldn't let her stay there in the deep. He undid the stone and moved to the top holding on to the sash.

Shunji struggled to get her to the shore, pulling on the sash as he dragged her behind him. By this time of day, the sun was out and reflected sharply on the water. He struggled but finally pulled her onto the shore. Exhausted, he lay next to her and felt that he had done something good. She would no longer be alone in the cold. He turned around to see how beautiful she was. He looked, then cried in horror. Her head was barely connected to her body except for a few tendons, most of the flesh of her neck was in shreds. Only one eye remained in its socket and her nose was barely hanging on to whatever face was left. The heat of day had accelerated the putrefaction that had been delayed by the cold of the waters of Waita.

Shunji didn't remember much of what happened afterwards. The truck, the men, Ryoji's angry words. He did remember her story. She had arrived several months before to marry one of the plantation workers. Within a short period of time there were cries and screams coming from their house. At first people thought that her husband had killed her, but he confessed only to having thrown her body into the water. She had hung herself with her red obi. He was ashamed of her suicide and wanted people to believe that she had run away.

Shunji puzzled awhile about the lack of suffering that usually accompanied the voice. Was there no suffering in her death? Or was that a blessing?

Within a year Shunji decided to leave Kōloa in search of a cave somewhere on the other side. He took his pouch with him.

JEAN YAMASAKI TOYAMA

Study Abroad

Marilyn Monroe was found dead on August 5, 1962 but I didn't hear about it because I was on my way to New York via Greyhound bus to catch the *SS France* to Paris. There were no radios on the bus and none on the boat, so I heard nothing. Once in Paris her death was old news and even if they had discussed it on French radio I wouldn't have understood. My French was so bad.

I know that if I hadn't left Hawai'i, my mother would have gone on and on about Marilyn and her early death. When she sang for JFK's birthday celebration a few months before, Mom said under her breath, "Something's going on." If I had been at home, Mom would have said, "See, see, what happens!" She had such a suspicious mind; it's a wonder she let me go to France. For some inexplicable reason she said yes. She didn't even give me any kind of advice except "Just keep your legs together." She expected me to understand. Certain things in our family were left unsaid, mainly about sex and sexuality. When I had my first period, she handed me a pad and the Kotex booklet. "Read this," she said. That was the extent of it.

So I was in France, blissfully ignorant.

Even my roommate didn't know that Marilyn was dead and she was her idol. (We were both too poor to buy *The International Herald Tribune*.) Carol dressed like Marilyn, you know, mostly tight sweaters, because she had these breasts. She wore her hair in soft curls but not platinum, just dirty blond. Aside from that ample gift, which I lacked, she had Marilyn's pout down pat. I once caught her looking at herself in the mirror trying out different lip shapes. Lower-lip-protrude. Upper-lip-curl. Sometimes she'd pout at me and try out her Marilyn rasp, even in French. Of course, she didn't let on that she was imitating, though I did at times almost ask her what she was doing. She was touchy, you know, and I didn't want to make trouble. I acted like it was natural. I'd never had a roommate; in fact, I never had close girlfriends or friends in general, so I had to learn how to communicate. Mostly I just listened and tried to please. So we got along.

The guys in the group may have made the Marilyn connection, maybe not, but they hovered around her vying for her attention. When she ignored them, they would come to me. I'd be carrying messages between Michael and Carol, Drew and Carol, Cary and Carol . . . etc. I became fatigued by this shuttle diplomacy. If I didn't like it, I suppose I could have stopped hanging out with her, but like I said, I didn't make friends easily; I believe in Fate.

When we learned that Marilyn was dead, she stopped the obvious Marilyn mimicry. I guess to continue would have been disrespectful. Even so, she kept wearing tight sweaters. We'd sit on a bench in the Jardin du Luxembourg and some Frenchman would invariably come around trying to start a conversation with her. They'd only turn to me if she didn't answer them, but most of the time she would—answer, I mean. She'd look them over, lift her left eyebrow and then say, "Oui." Sometimes, the pout would appear. It was hard to break the habit.

That's how we ended up at a "surprise partie" with Claude and Jean-Louis. Through the whole night I danced with Jean-Louis—lean and handsome—and Carol with Claude—short and stout. I felt so wonderful. Finally, I thought. It was worth coming to this strange place, to find a new life. A few days later I get a letter from J-L, asking me whether Carol really liked Claude because he, Jean-Louis, was in love with Carol. Wait! He was dancing with me! He didn't even mention me in the letter. He didn't think I would be hurt by his words. I guess he didn't even care. It reminded me of eighth grade. It was the same old story, just like in Longfellow's poem. Even if what's-his-name got the girl in the end, I didn't like only being the go-between.

I accepted my role. But now that Carol was preoccupied with J-L, I was on my own. I had things to think about. My mother always told me to watch out for strangers, from the time I was in second grade when I had to take the bus to school. Look straight ahead. Don't take candy from strangers. Act like they're not there, and you won't get in trouble. I grew up and they were never there. That was the trouble. How was I supposed to learn French? I hadn't really thought about it before I left. I just had to leave. So I went to the other side of the world.

From observing Carol I learned a few lessons, even practiced the pout and added some reinforcement to my bra. I went to class, too. Art, 19th century French Literature, film, phonetics, the usual, with the usual people living in their usual cocoons, just like me, I guess. They all found their own cliques. Mine was only Carol and now she was occupied. I couldn't just stay in the library during free time, after all, I was in Paris, so I thought I'd venture out on my own. I wanted to go to the Petit Palais for a free exhibit, don't remember of what. It was a fairly breezy day and my hair kept getting in my face. I looked around and there were gendarmes all over Place de la Concorde, with their machine guns, huge and black. I started to feel afraid, I had never seen such a sight. What's happening? I was about to cross the street, when I felt a hand pulling me back to the sidewalk.

"Attention! Vous êtes folle? Cette voiture allait vous écraser," a voice said as I felt a car whiz by. Then I saw a very handsome face.

"La voiture, la voiture, vous n'avez pas vu la voiture?" He wagged his finger at me, like I was a naughty child.

He spoke so fast, I sputtered. "What the . . .?" Very impolite in French. When he understood that I didn't really speak French, he said, "The car . . . the car . . . didn't you see?" His voice was hypnotizing.

I said slowly, "The machine guns, the machine guns . . ." while looking into that gorgeous face that matched the voice.

"Aaah!" he said, still holding my arm. We crossed the street together. "N'ayez pas peur. Don't be afraid, it's nothing."

My first Frenchman, I thought, not daring to take a second look. It must be my reinforcements. Then I looked down and saw my coat buttoned up to my neck. I was puzzled. I didn't need my Marilyns.

At that point I didn't much care why or how, I just basked in this new, tingly feeling while listening to a history lesson and loving it. "Today is the anniversary of the Paris massacre," he said. Even now I can hear his voice.

"Massacre? Was there a massacre here? Ici?" I pointed to the ground for emphasis, looking for more machine guns as we continued to walk through the Tuilerie Gardens.

"Last year there was a demonstration. Many Algerians died. Mais c'est trop tragique; you don't want to hear about this, do you? I hope you don't think me too . . . how do you say, you know, for taking your arm that way. I didn't know what else to do. You were going to walk into that car."

I did something I never usually do. I looked straight into his eyes . . . into those eyes. He hadn't removed his arm from my waist. "Et vous vous appelez?" I gave him a blank stare.

"And your name?"

"Oh, oh, Charlotte, Charlotte, je m'appelle Charlotte."

"Moi, Alain. Bonjour." Realizing he still had his arm around my waist, he said, "Oh, pardon," and let me go. Then we shook hands and continued walking in silence, no longer attached. After a while he asked, "Japonaise, tu es japonaise?" switching to the informal form of the verb.

I felt a little dizzy and I wished he still had his arm around my waist.

"Non . . . non. Américaine, américaine," I said.

"Non, non, non japonaise, japonaise," he responded.

Alain was a Frenchman who didn't much like Americans so he preferred to think of me as Japanese, which was fine with me. I no longer felt like a go-between. This was direct learning. I heard my mother's faint echo in my head. "Eyes straight ahead!" "Legs together!" My heart was racing, before we had even walked past the Louvre, her voice got lost in the traffic. Instead, I heard that irresistible accent. I imagined that I, too, would soon make those r's and u's. Before we knew it, we were crossing the Seine near his apartment, so he suggested some tea. He was born in Roussillon, a little village in the Vaucluse, where he would have to return for a week. We exchanged telephone numbers and addresses with a promise to see each other on his return. Things were going a little too fast for me. I couldn't stop thinking of what had happened and couldn't wait to talk to Carol.

It was one of those rare nights when she was home. I hadn't gone out bench-sitting with her for quite awhile so I felt the need to ease into a conversation. I asked her whether she had met any interesting Frenchmen lately. She looked at me with a sly smile, "I already have one and he's quite a handful. Jean-Louis, you remember him, don't you?" I knew she thought I had a crush on J-L.

"Oh, sure, I'm glad you're still together."

"Really? You never talk about him."

I wondered what that meant. Did she want to talk about him? I looked at my book and gnawed the tip of my pencil.

"In fact, Charlotte, you don't say much. You're just like a clam, especially when the subject is personal. You don't talk about yourself, do you?" I wasn't looking at her; I was watching the snowflakes float past the windowsill. I knew she was looking at me. "You hoard your moments, you know. You're stingy with yourself, Charlotte. Is that because you're Japanese?"

I turned to her and looked at her lips. Her barrage of words startled me, her tone of voice, her staccato rhythm saying the same thing in different words. Finally, I said, "Hoard my moments? Stingy with myself? What does that mean? And what has that got to do with being Japanese?" For some reason I stomped out of the room. I must have felt insulted, but by what? I returned a while later, realizing I still needed information from her.

"Ok, Carol, explain what you mean by my parsimony." I thought the word change would soften the meaning.

Shaking her head, she sniggered then said, "I'm not talking about money. I'm talking about words, feelings, stuff you just don't give."

I felt my heart beat a little faster.

"For example, when I talked about my father . . . I even told you that he beat me sometimes. That's very personal. You didn't say anything."

"I said I was sorry."

"But that's all. I expected you to say more, ask questions, wonder why. I was telling you something very personal. That's what friends do." She paused. "At least you could have told me something about your father."

I took a deep breath. "My father never beat me." I took another breath and blurted out, "I don't even know what it feels like to have one, I never had one."

She stopped a beat as if changing direction but plowed ahead, "So why couldn't you have told me that?"

I looked out the window and saw flakes gently falling. "I don't know," I said and went out for a walk in the snow.

It's not that I had secrets, I just never learned to talk about myself. Not like Carol. I was shocked by all the things she told me, so matter-of-factly. I kept what was going on in my head in my head. I barely even commented on what was going on around me. That didn't mean I wasn't thinking about stuff. But most of my stuff stayed inside me, because it was my stuff. And I didn't want to offend. We never talked about things like this at home. I didn't understand this need for what do they call it? Intimacy? I thought that would come later, when I would find the right person. I just didn't know how or with whom.

After a few days I tried again because there were still things I didn't know. We were taking a film class together and had just seen the New Wave film, *Jules et Jim*. (I learned to stop saying "movie.") It was about a love triangle with one woman and two men. We speculated about the suicide-murder at the end, but both of us thought the double cremation bizarre. We had discussed the whys and the wherefores of these relationships in class but not sex. I still needed that essential from Carol.

Finally, I asked, "How did she get pregnant?"

She looked at me in disbelief and was about to say something, thought better about it, and said, "What kind of question is that? We were talking about their complex relationships. Are we talking about love or sex?"

"Isn't that the same thing?"

She shook her head and muttered something like oh, boy. Then she said, "You don't want to get pregnant, do you."

"No! But if I know how it happens, I can avoid it."

"You must be kidding. How old are you?" Turning from her notebook, she peered into my eyes. "You've never done it, right?" I didn't look at her. But I knew that she was giving me that nasty smile.

"It, it, what's the it?" I asked.

"I knew it. I told Frank you were a virgin."

Frank was her fiancé, a lawyer from NYC. I didn't know what kind of arrangement they had, but apparently Carol wasn't hampered by it. She received a letter every other week, sometimes a phone call. After gloating about having guessed my status, she gave me the lesson I had asked for without any snide remarks. I was grateful. Blushing doesn't show on my face, but I felt hot. Her final words had to do with her judgment of Catherine. "You know why those two men wanted her, right?"

"I guess she was fascinating. She certainly was beautiful."

"Frank would say she was a country road not a super highway."

I must have given her a blank look. I could make nothing of the comment.

Carol gave me a wink and went to her room.

I waited and waited and waited. I looked at the calendar, peeked at my watch. Had he forgotten? Was he really going to call me back? Maybe he was lying. I was full of doubts, wondering who I was trying to fool. What was I trying to prove? I kept thinking about Carol's description and my mother's last words at the airport. "Keep your legs together." Mom said something else, but I couldn't remember.

Finally, he telephoned. As soon as I heard his voice, I felt a huge sense of relief. I hadn't been deceived. After welcomed apologies he invited me to see an opera, *Madame Butterfly*. I had never attended any opera, let alone this one, though I had heard parts of it on the radio, Cio-Cio-San's solo. I loved it. The music went straight to my bones, I felt it. An opera would be quite different from what happened that first afternoon at his apartment.

It had been so funny and strange. After arriving there and having a pleasant conversation about my studies and his work—he was a lawyer—he gently put his arm around my waist. I felt a tingle all over. It was just as I had imagined. "At last!" I sighed, "Baise-moi." To my surprise he let me go and said, "Pardon? What did you just say? Do you know what you said?"

"Kiss me. That's what I said, because I've never been kissed."

His face softened as he leaned back on the sofa and laughed. "Your French is dangerous."

My eyes grew wide. "Pourquoi?"

"Un baiser, noun, a kiss. Baiser, verb, to do the dirty. Is that what you want?"

"Non, non, noun not verb . . . I didn't know."

We laughed at my mistake. He said, "So you've never been kissed, eh bien, now you'll never be able to say that again." And he gave me a light peck on the lips. "We shall proceed slowly, Charlotte." Then we went out for some French fries, nice and crisp, just like I like them.

Alain told me he had made a mistake on the schedule and *Madame Butterfly* was not being performed in Paris, so we ended up listening to it on his stereo. I was so disappointed and, with this change, worried. After a few uncomfortable moments getting reacquainted and some sips of wine, he asked if I had seen *Madame Butterfly* performed or read about it. I didn't want to seem like a complete ninny, so I said something vague about a tragic love story and magnificent music. "The music itself is enough, non? Magnifique! Magnifique!" I explained that I thought the music was enough to convey the meaning: they love each other, he has to leave, and she dies in the end. Magnificent. I kept on wondering why, why this opera. It was going to be a strange date. After the last encounter, I was expecting something different.

We didn't listen to the whole opera, just special parts. He would carefully lower the needle on the record at the spot he had chosen for our lesson. Sometimes there'd be an awful scratch when he missed the mark, but mostly he was quite skilled. Sometimes I would yawn when he wasn't looking, wondering where we were heading. He explained the story about this American naval officer looking for adventure in exotic Japan. The wedding, the parting, the baby, the hara-kiri.

As Cio-Cio-San's voice soared, so did my feelings. In the end I was in tears. Such a love story! I was carried away by emotion.

"Why are you crying, Charlotte?"

"It's so tragic, so beautiful." Then I needed to know. "Why are we listening to this opera? Why opera? Is it because she's Japanese, is that why you had me listen to this opera?"

"Non, non, non. It's Pinkerton."

"What about him? He has a great voice. His songs are soaring."

"But what kind of person is he?" Alain insisted.

His question stymied me. I hadn't thought about him. I didn't understand the words. I listened to the music.

"Don't you see what a cad, un vrai salaud séducteur Pinkerton is? He's there with his wife to take away their son! He cannot even face Butterfly. Sends his wife! Beautiful words, beautiful music, but what a salaud!"

"Salaud?"

"Bastard."

"That's the essence of seduction, Charlotte, all that beautiful music and you are lost."

"So you don't want me to feel?"

"Feel, yes, but think, too."

I was amazed by his words. I thought he wanted to seduce me, but when he didn't, I knew it was because I was no Marilyn. He just didn't want to hurt my feelings. But I was wrong. He explained that his sister, the one he went to visit in Roussillon, was recovering from a misadventure. An American had seduced Emma, his virginal sister. "You can imagine what she went through after he disappeared. Terrible bouts of depression. That was a year ago."

"Did she have a baby?"

"Fortunately, no, but that didn't mean she didn't suffer. He had told her that he loved her and they would marry. What he didn't tell her was that he already had a wife back home."

"What a piece of shit!"

"Oui! Charlotte, do you know how easy it would be to seduce you? I knew it that first afternoon: you are no challenge. I don't like easy. For me the greatest challenge is to educate you, to help you make good decisions instead of being carried away by the music." He took my hands in his and looked into my eyes. "You know, Charlotte, before you can give yourself to someone, you have to know what you are giving."

I didn't know exactly what he meant, but it sounded profound. He was right. I knew nothing. Just like Gretel, I would have followed every crumb some appealing guy might have thrown in front of me. The music would have swept me off somewhere I didn't know. But I wanted to go.

When I told him how Carol's fiancé had described women as either country roads or super highways, he was horrified. "That is the crassest thing I've ever heard, and not very imaginative. He shows no respect for women." I didn't understand until later.

I never saw Alain after that; he had other challenges to find, but he gave me a lot to think about. It was years after that I understood why my mother let me go to France. She knew that I'd make it there or I wouldn't make it anywhere. After that I didn't wear my Marilyns again.

CHERYL TREIBER-KAWAOKA

Don't tell my husband that this is a love poem

a sonnet, compact and contemporary, unrhymed and relaxed,
just like Gerry, a man without a dress shirt, only aloha prints
and silk-screened memories of National Parks, family trips preserved
in folded precise origami squares. He's my CPAP companion,
       sleeping
in the exhaust of our machine-expelled breath. He's an engineer-cook
       creating
complex tables, alternate routes to firm vegetables in a slow-cooked
       stew.
His Japanese body, low to the ground, balanced, keeps us steady.
He wears a tool belt slung around his hips and swaggers like a paniolo
       ready
to rope and fix all that's broken. His aura alone can raise a dead
       remote
and confound the digital demons spinning on my screen. Slow of
       word, warm
of heart, his sleepy-eyed morning hug can coax our daughter from her
       hoodie
cave. When he is washing dishes, a sudsy display of white on blue, I
       kiss
the single mole below his silver-streaked hair but first, my one finger
       lands
softly, locating this small brown oasis, unseen by him but loved by
       me.

Inspired by Diane Seuss's unrhymed sonnets

Hānai

Lydia smelled the morning sun through the window before she felt it. It was strange, knowing the sun was up without feeling its driving power. She understood the scorching downtown Lahaina heat and didn't quite know what to make of the substantially gentler Kahana mornings. Kahana and Lahaina are only ten minutes apart, so it shouldn't have made that much of a difference, but because of the shape of the mountains, or some secret atmospheric mystery, it was at least ten degrees cooler in the Parks' spare room than in her room. Lydia tried to go back to sleep and only succeeded in freezing in place. She didn't want to move. She didn't want to stay. She wanted to be somewhere else but there was nowhere she could imagine sending herself that would be safer than where she was. It was weird to be safe where she was, weird enough to push her upright and out of bed.

Two weeks ago, a few days before the beginning of their freshman year of high school, Lydia called Tori in the middle of the night to tell her she'd run away from home, and immediately Tori and Aunty Bethany, Tori's mom, picked her up from the horrible McDonald's near the meth wall. Now, she was trying to force herself out of their guest room on the second Saturday of the school year, three weeks after her first period and almost six months after her thirteenth birthday.

Once she stood, she was out of the room almost immediately, but paused in front of Tori's closed door. Almost every night, when the two of them brushed their teeth side by side in the upstairs bathroom, Tori would wipe her face on her towel and then tell Lydia to come in if she needed anything. Lydia couldn't need more if she tried, and she wanted to save her days of draining Tori's energy for the days that were a few degrees past too hard, the days that she not only wanted to die but found it inevitable. Tori wouldn't ever say if anyone— especially not Lydia—was invading her space, but Lydia couldn't help but believe she was. Beyond that, everything bad happened at night (or usually happened at night), and mornings were easy— usually—so Lydia moved on and went downstairs. Of course, Uncle

Aaron was already awake; Lydia nervously snapped to attention, back ramrod straight.

Uncle Aaron didn't notice. He just stirred some powdered Coffee Mate into a mug of the ultra-dark-roast coffee he liked. Years ago, the first time she slept over, she didn't understand why Aaron and Bethany drank different coffee roasts, why they didn't just use one that they could both live with, but now she liked the familiarity of how different they were and how absolutely oblivious they were to the little concessions they made to each other. Aunty Bethany almost always bought groceries at Foodland; Uncle Aaron stopped at Times at the end of his shifts.

Of course, Aaron and Bethany weren't related to Lydia, but because this was Hawai'i, Lydia couldn't remember a time before she called Uncle Aaron and Aunty Bethany "uncle" and "aunty"; when she realized her parents' brothers and sisters were actually her uncles and aunts, it was a shock to her system. Several times over the last few weeks, Lydia wondered if she should try to contact her mom's siblings. They'd be surprised to hear from her, surprised enough to wonder why she was reaching out. Lydia wasn't sure if it would be worth it to tell them why, since none of them—not a one of the five of them—had ever tried to contact her. Her mom disappeared from her life when she was four. Her life was punctuated by fours, in a weird way: her dad remarried when she was eight, bringing in the stepmom she could barely consider and Jack, her stepbrother who—almost from the beginning—took her as his possession.

"Sleep okay?" Uncle Aaron asked.

"Yeah, pretty good," Lydia lied.

"You're up early. It's Saturday."

"I'm sorry, I can go back upstairs if . . ."

Uncle Aaron sat down on the recliner and grinned. "Nope. I'm glad to have the company, as long as you don't mind watching Saturday morning cartoons. Tori usually comes down by eight or so. And I picked up some more cereal when you're ready for breakfast."

Lydia settled onto the sofa half-reluctantly. She liked Uncle Aaron, and liked that he watched cartoons on Saturday by himself. He was letting her stay in his house for an indefinite amount of time and with no promise that doing so wouldn't backfire. Aaron was a firefighter and Lydia's life had been on fire for a long time, and there were lots of ways it could get worse—but for the life of her, she just couldn't figure out why he was kind and so willing to entertain his daughter's request that she be allowed to stay.

Somewhere between *Kirby* and *Teenage Mutant Ninja Turtles*, Lydia fell asleep on the couch, curled around an ancient, formerly decorative pillow. The landline rang but it didn't matter until the phone robotically recited Lydia's home number. Aaron answered the phone before Lydia could open her eyes.

"I understand. She's also asleep right now. I can tell her you called. There's no need . . . sir, there's no need to get mad. She's just sleeping." Lydia hadn't heard Uncle Aaron's voice so tight before. His voice sounded like a sharp knife still in its sheath. There was a pause.

"Okay, I will let her know. Yes, Lydia's fine. Bethany also wanted to let you know she really appreciated the pizza you guys sent last night. No one was in the mood to cook."

Her breath hitched. There were only two people who would call her, only one who would call her here and not on her phone. She squeezed her eyes shut then jumped up and off the couch. Out of the corner of her eye, she saw Tom and Jerry go through their motions in silence. Aaron must have muted the TV when the phone rang. Lydia held out her hand and Aaron sighed.

"Yes, she actually just woke up. Here you go."

"Hey, kiddo."

The air was sucked out of her ribcage and through her belly button into the kitchen. She wasn't sure if anyone else could feel the temperature drop. The thought of hanging up didn't occur to her. Options were for people who had chances and hope and all kinds of other things that didn't belong to her. "Hi, Dad."

Ever since she'd left home, talking to her dad was more like trying to win a chess match than talking to a human. When he brought a bag of her clothes—a duffle bag with random clothes grabbed out of her dresser in handfuls—she told him why she ran away and that she'd cut Jack. He argued that she misread why he came into her room, or was blowing things out of proportion, especially given how sweet Jack was in general: his deference, his warm, freckled politeness. They were at a stalemate. Lydia didn't want to believe that her dad didn't care about her—he was the one calling, after all, and the one who kept her when her mom chose her friends down by the meth wall over her—but in the end he didn't care enough to keep her safe. He didn't believe her because he couldn't. He couldn't have chosen the wrong woman twice—he had to have gotten it right the second time.

His calm tenor reverberated through the line. "I want you to come home. We miss you. Heck, even Jack misses you."

"I'm sure he said that." Lydia's voice hardened. She'd never been away from Jack for two weeks at a time before. Even though there were often stretches when he wouldn't force himself on her, he'd never lost the ability to do so for more than a couple days.

"Not in so many words, but he's willing to forgive you for the cut you gave him. He says it was all a misunderstanding. I know he would never hurt you, not on purpose, and whatever's happened is in the past."

The air that had been cold was suddenly liquid, as though Lydia were holding the phone underwater, swimming through the vastness of the ocean, or chained to the tile floor of a friend's house. She tried to stab him and for the first time, when she was trying for the violence, their bodies hadn't connected.

Lydia used the last of her breath to say, "I'm never living with him again. Ever. And if you try to make me, I'll be gone. I won't tell you where I went. I won't tell anyone." Aaron and Bethany's eyes were on her, but she didn't care.

Four years and a few months. That's how long she'd let him believe the family was fine. It was no wonder he couldn't see that she'd lied by silence, that now she was telling the truth.

"You sound like your mom." He sounded tired, but not surprised, like he'd given up on understanding the situation and was only trying to get through it.

"Dad . . . no. Don't say that. I'm okay. I'm safe, I just can't come back. I can't live there. Please, just don't make me go back."

"Fine. We'll talk more soon. Goodbye. Love you. Despite what you think, I love you."

"Love you too." Lydia said it out of instinct and the words left the aftertaste of bile. She handed the phone to Aaron and went back upstairs, to the room that wasn't hers, and prayed that she wouldn't be forced to leave.

The first time Lydia prayed was the same night her stepbrother Jack first came into her room, the first time he'd begun the process of laying claim to her body. The prayer had gone something like: God, please, no, please, no. It hadn't worked, but somehow she kept praying it, and the idea of praying, the idea of a maybe-Jesus, kept her afloat. She came around to Jesus because of the sensation of floating, as though she were Rose on a broken door and Jesus was in the freezing ocean, dying for her. It all sounded very good in her head, except it never seemed to do anything to stop Jack, not until Tori and Ikaika had given her a knife and she'd stabbed him in the stomach—not very deep—he'd not even gotten stitches, just taped up his stomach and showed his friends his "cool new psycho bitch scar"—but enough that she ran away. And now she was curled in a ball praying again that she could stay where she was, now that she'd said out loud that she wanted to. That was always the mistake she made: saying aloud what she wanted, as though it helped. But now she hoped against hope that it would be okay.

Hope wasn't enough. Lydia threw on some real clothes—a bra, a belt, deodorant, all bought at Ross with Bethany's money, money that Lydia couldn't pay back—and went for a walk. She wasn't going anywhere in particular, but she was going somewhere because there had to be a somewhere.

The night after she talked to her dad, Lydia woke to the sound of her own screaming and the taste of blood in her mouth and a burning pain in her tongue. Footsteps pounded in the hallway and she heard the soft whump of a body colliding with another.

"What's wrong?!" Aaron barked.

"No! Not you!" Bethany said, followed by a muffled, "Not unless she says you can come in," and then she burst through the spare room door. "What happened?"

"I don't know. A dream. I don't know." Lydia knew exactly what happened in the dream because, until recently, it was a part of the normal cycle of her life: the quiet click of the doorknob lock popping open, the smell of boy-skin, the somewhere-else in her mind that Lydia would run to even while she tried to fight the body away from her. That's what she called him in her head: the body. No living person could do what Jack did to her, what he did again and again, but more than that, she would have to look him in the eye at breakfast and know there would be no escape. She swallowed a mouthful of blood.

"Can I come over?" Tori asked, standing behind her mother in the dark.

Tori's fists were clenched the way she always clenched them when she was running, that something told Tori not to rush to hold Lydia until she was awake. Tori was a hugger, draped over one or another of her friends like they were the bases in a game of tag, but she was standing in the middle of the guest room like it wasn't the guest room of her damn house. Lydia nodded and Tori sat on the edge of the bed, placed a hand on Lydia's back. She flinched, and Tori drew her hand away, then crawled around her so that she could be beside her against the headboard.

"Lydia. Can I come in?" Uncle Aaron asked. Lydia tried to answer but felt her throat close up, the feeling coming more from the outside than the inside, like a hand wrapped around her neck. She worked her lips and no sound would come. Her tongue swelled on its bite. Aaron's frame, broader and less practiced than Jack's, filled the doorway. He didn't move forward. Instead, he sat down, feet propped against the doorway, outlined by the hall night-light.

"You're safe here. Go to sleep," Bethany said, patting the pillow. "Aaron and I will double-check all the locks downstairs and make sure the alarm is on."

Lydia tried to lie down, finally succeeded, and let the soft nothingness of Tori's breath beside her bring her down to earth, back into her body, and when her throat reopened, she fell asleep. When she woke again, Bethany and Aaron were gone, but Tori was beside her, curled toward the wall. Tori would be fourteen in November, and when they were awake, Tori felt older than Lydia, but sleeping, Tori looked young. Small. When Lydia slipped up and away out of bed, Tori slept on. On Lydia's pillow, there was a crescent moon of blood where her mouth opened in her sleep. No one was downstairs to greet her, and she ate cereal alone, poured the two-percent milk that she and Bethany both preferred. Tori and Aaron both liked the red-cap milk.

Even when everyone woke up and there was the get-ready-for-church rush (punctuated by Tori's grunts of annoyance at her own wardrobe), no one said anything about her nightmare. Even so, sitting one seat away from the family at their small church, the broadly-speaking-evangelical one in the strip mall, Lydia was sure that it wasn't okay to wake up the house in the middle of the night and prayed it wouldn't happen. Once was enough—she'd leapt through her own window and into the darkness, only to be found barefoot outside the golden light of a McDonald's—the gross one with needles in the grass, not the nice one near Tori's house—but a second time was unacceptable. It could not, would not, happen again; she made a plan during the sermon of how she would keep herself small and allowed to stay; she finalized her thoughts and froze them in place while Aaron clapped a little behind the beat and Bethany sang a soft harmony to the final worship song.

From then on, she slept lightly, pressed her face into her pillow when she first realized she was awake to be sure there would be no scream. When it was impossible to go back to sleep, she would carefully lift the screen out of her window and climb onto the porch roof. To the east, the West Maui mountains blocked the warmth and light of the sunrise so that it didn't have the subtle fading and garish majesty of sunset; sunrise was a sudden affair that changed from dewy blue morning into almost-instant day. The west was more Lydia's speed: she could see Moloka'i and Lāna'i across the ocean, the islands hemming in the Pacific until it looked like it could be a very large lake instead of an ocean that separated her from the rest of the world. Some nights, especially on the nights that Uncle Aaron was working a 24-hour shift at the fire station, Tori would climb out of the window opposite hers with a knit blanket; without speaking, they would lie next to each other on the asphalt shingle roof under Tori's woven blanket, the one from the new Walmart, watching the stars or the sky or the rain clouds move over them in watery undulations.

Unfortunately, Lydia realized she had to still live in her skin. She still saw Jack on their shared high school campus; from a distance he had the same silhouette as the body. Once, he ran over to her, calling her name with a wide, almost feline grin.

"Lydia! I miss having you around. There's no one to play *Mario Kart* with." He slapped her back playfully but just a little too hard.

She smiled. They knew their roles, and Jack wasn't quite the same as the body that would come into her room and into her.

"I've given up my Nintendo habit, I guess. I'll see you around," she said over her shoulder. As she turned, she caught Tori's eyes glazed over in imaginary ignorance. She hated that she knew that Tori was pretending she didn't know. She shot her stink eye and then walked away and down the hill.

Out of sight, Lydia ran to the women's bathroom, cigarette-scented and hung heavy with innumerable clouds of floral body sprays. In the stalls, locked away, she dug her nails into the softness of her bare stomach and raked them across until little microbeads appeared on her skin. From then on, she had a refuge when her thoughts tangled around her or when she was forced to watch Jack walk by. Sometimes, if she'd bitten her nails down, she would break the clip off a pen and drag the jagged plastic across the tiger stripes along the inside of her thighs.

The precise stinging on her sides had mostly receded into a dull, warm ache when she finally made it to her modern history course. It was still a surprise to see Ms. Miller at Lahainaluna High School; she'd taught Lydia and Tori—in different classes—at the Lahaina Intermediate just below the high school campus, and now she was here, a newly minted social studies teacher. It was one of the many things in Lydia's life that made it feel like things could change sideways, but nothing could go away or change. Things could be. They could not become.

Despite that, Lydia liked Ms. Miller because she let her sleep through class (on the days she fell asleep), and because she usually didn't give hard homework and would answer questions. She was the kind of teacher that had big-sister vibes and could be tricked into telling anecdotes, but the anecdotes were at least interesting. It was kind of a shame that she could sleep through Ms. Miller's class and yet usually didn't, since Lydia liked history and didn't particularly like napping. And, as a bonus, that class period happened to fall at the end of the day.

Lydia hung around after class longer than she normally would; it seemed like too big a thing to be surrounded by people, by bodies.

"What's up?" Ms. Miller shook the stack of papers above the desk a little before tapping them into an orderly pile.

"Just waiting for a little bit." Lydia wasn't lying, but mostly she couldn't handle seeing the seniors out and about, couldn't watch Jack walk by.

"Are you still staying at Tori's?"

"Yeah." It was no surprise Ms. Miller knew. Everyone would, sooner than later. If she were lucky, no one would ask Jack why, because Lydia knew the story he would offer would be terrible. Plus, it was obvious Lydia wasn't going home—she'd been to her house once with Bethany and Aaron, when only her stepmom was home, and they'd gotten her school things and a few clothes.

A soap bubble of curiosity broke to the surface of Lydia's mind. "Why are you here?" she asked.

Ms. Miller's eyebrows crinkled. "There was a job opening up the hill and, if I'm being honest, I kind of prefer teaching the big kids. Fewer head lice." She chuckled at her own joke, even though Lydia didn't see the punch line.

"No, I mean why are you on Maui? You're from like . . . Boston, right?"

"Massachusetts. Not Boston. Very different." Ms. Miller sat on the edge of a desk, brushing some eraser ash away. "I needed a job."

"Okay, but why here?" Lydia asked again, not sure why it mattered.

"I guess I needed to get away."

"From what?"

"Nothing in particular."

"What kind of nothing?" Lydia pressed. Ms. Miller wasn't normally evasive. The answer would be interesting, if she could get one.

"Well, I went to NYU. Graduated in 2002."

Lydia couldn't figure out how that mattered, especially since she was sure that NYU wasn't in Massachusetts.

Ms. Miller shrugged. "I was in New York on September 11th." The look in her eyes was not the look of someone who was seeing the things in front of them. Lydia knew exactly what that kind of eyesight felt like, but Ms. Miller continued, "I needed to prove to myself that I didn't just survive. I didn't know anyone personally who died. But my friends did, my professors did. It was like the entire city was grieving, but I wasn't really a part of it. I was just there, watching everyone figure out how to survive. When I graduated, I wanted to find a way to live my own life."

"How do you do that? How do you live after you've survived?"

Ms. Miller stood up then, walked toward the window a few steps, then back. She knelt down in front of the desk and laid her head in front of Lydia for a moment, then looked up with an almost eager sadness. "I don't know, Lydia. You tell me."

The words echoed through Lydia's mind in almost-synthetic tones while she constricted herself against a pillow in the guest room and tried to keep her body from betraying itself, from crying or making a sound she couldn't take back.

If you've had to survive, how do you live?

Then, the more pressing question: she survived. Did she want to?

Lydia fumbled for the knife that she kept in the nightstand under a stack of papers, the knife Tori asked Ikaika for, that she'd cut Jack with, that now she might use on herself. She flicked it open and traced it along her forearm. Without thinking, she pressed deeper, paused before she made the incision. What would she find under her skin that she didn't already know about? She pulled the knife back and saw the clean imprint, the unbroken skin. There were little scars on her lips where she'd kept from screaming, marks left behind by Jack's nails, bruises that were finally fading away. Lydia couldn't make herself open her own skin, even though she thought it might bring a measure of relief. For the first time since she was eight, her body was her own and she wanted to mutilate it. Lydia gritted her teeth and tried not to scream. She threw the knife and it stuck into the drywall. She left it there, staring at the hilt until, finally, someone knocked at the door.

"Lydia? I'm coming in." Aaron opened the door, eyes going first to the knife in the wall and then to Lydia. He pulled the old desk chair over and sat down. It was his house, so it wasn't that weird, but it still surprised Lydia that Aaron rarely wore a shirt at home. Sometimes, when he thought of it, he'd pull a tank top on when Tori had friends over, but since Lydia started staying with them, he didn't always think about it.

"I'm sorry about the wall."

"Don't worry about it." Aaron took a deep breath, pulled the knife out, and clicked it shut. He bounced it in his hand, calm. It was horrible. She was just another rescue. "Come downstairs." He walked out without turning back to her.

When she got to the kitchen, Aaron and Bethany were waiting for her, already a bad sign. Tori was sitting at the counter, looking like she wanted to look occupied, with a textbook open in front of her and her legs swinging freely. When she saw Lydia, she hooked her feet around the legs of the stool. It was weird to see Tori every day, weirder that it felt normal. Lydia didn't want to say it should be difficult to see her best friend—even the words "best friend" didn't feel like they covered it all—but she thought it would be harder to be at her house every day. The very ease of it made Lydia uncomfortable, like life was trying to lull her to sleep so that she could freeze to death. She'd made herself comfortable. It was unwise. She'd repaid their kindness by throwing a knife at the guest room, a knife that she probably shouldn't still have for criminal reasons.

"Is something going on?" Lydia responded a little more icily than she intended. "I'm really sorry I stabbed the house. Really, it was an accident."

Bethany's lips tightened. "How do you accidentally stab a house?"

"I threw the knife at the wall."

Bethany breathed out, a small breath that sounded like it was doing math, like she was trying to make everything add up. "We can fix the wall. That's not why we wanted you to come down. We talked to your dad today."

Lydia felt her stomach drop through her entire body and out her feet, leaving her middle voraciously empty and numb. "What did he say?"

Aaron cleared his throat. "Your father doesn't believe the severity of the abuse, but he does believe that you aren't willing to come home. More than that, he really doesn't want to bring the law into this, and your stepmom . . . she's not in a place to hear anything bad about her son."

This was not news to Lydia. She could still feel Jack's body pressed against hers, the suffocating weight of him, and she knew equally well that he was a perfect son and, in many ways, the kind of white boy who would never see the wrong side of the law, and there wasn't another option that she knew of. She had never tried to find her mom for a reason. Aaron continued, "I've been there when a lot of families have their big falling-outs, and it's never good for the kids to go live way far away if they don't have to. New school, new life, it's a mess. Your dad said he's okay with signing a caregiver affidavit and allowing you to live somewhere else for a year until Jack goes to college."

"So I just need to find somewhere to go?" Lydia ticked through the list of places she knew of, people that might take her in. For a moment, she wondered about Ms. Miller.

Tori finally piped up, a grin on her face that she kept trying to wipe off. "No, stupid. You'd live here."

Bethany cut Tori off before she said another thing that sounded mean but wasn't. Not to Lydia, anyway. "We've prayed about it and talked about it since you first called us from the McDonald's. I might as well say, I was surprised you called us then, but I guess it makes sense. I'm not saying it will be easy, particularly for you. But if you want to stay, you're welcome to."

Lydia opened her mouth to say yes, to say thank you, to breathe again, but nothing came out. She swallowed, tried again. "I don't want to impose. I just know people wear out their welcome or whatever."

Tori looked scared. Small, even. "Do you not want to be here?"

Lydia shook her head so fast that her teeth chattered. "I do, if I can. You guys should be able to use your guest room."

Aaron shook his head, then did a double take at the knife still in his hand. He put it into his pocket. "As far as we're concerned, you're not a guest. Bethany and I . . ."

". . . we think of you as our hānai daughter," Bethany finished, her face relaxing.

The word had the weight of the ocean behind it, around it. Hānai. Adopted, no matter what a paper says. There would be no takebacks.

"We'd like to have you stay here, as long as you want. It's not a perfect family. It's just yours if you want it."

Lydia felt like "I want to. I want to stay. I want to live here."

I want to live.

As soon as the words were said, Tori rushed over and wrapped Lydia's thin body completely in hers, and Bethany's weight added to the warmth. Lydia thought she would cry, but instead she felt herself pass through numbness and into a moment of calm, like the peace of watching the light come over the mountains. Aaron's hand settled on her shoulder briefly before he grabbed his car keys. Bethany stared pointedly at him until he looked over. She grabbed his shirt off the stool where he'd thrown it upon getting home, and he quickly put it on. Then, he squeezed Lydia's shoulder in a way that made her feel stronger, like she was standing up on her own.

"Let's go to your dad's. It's time to get the rest of your stuff."

JULIE USHIO

Setsuko Hawthorne

Setsuko hadn't been out of her condo for over a week, but another letter had arrived.

It was the same as the one she had received last month. An official-looking envelope with red lettering on the front, "URGENT—Immediate Attention." She opened the drawer on the right side of her desk and added it to the pile and shut the drawer.

She knew the contents inside the envelope. A one-page letter with "OVERDUE! DO NOT LET YOUR INSURANCE LAPSE!" at the top of the page, an invoice for $19.95, and a return envelope (please affix postage). She'd read the letter over and over but did not understand why she had to pay for an insurance policy she didn't own.

When she received the first letter, she thought that Harry had bought an insurance policy on her and was planning to kill her to collect. She'd seen it before in movies. That's the way American men were, she thought. Whisper sweet words in your ear, get you to think about romance and love and adventure, then abandon you. But Harry killing her to collect $5,000 didn't make any sense. He had plenty of money, she'd seen his bank statements. Besides, he was happily remarried and living in Colorado.

Setsuko had known from the start that Gloria had the hots for Harry. Gloria had appeared a little over a year ago, sitting behind them at Sunday service, with her bluish gray permed hair, ample bosom, and rose-colored rayon dress. Every Sunday after that, she was there in the same spot, ready and waiting when they turned around to "share aloha with neighbors." At first the three just exchanged handshakes from over the back of the pew, Gloria's big fleshy wet hand encasing Setsuko's cool fingers. After they'd become acquainted over cookies and punch in the community hall following church service, Gloria and Harry started giving one another "Aloha hugs." Setsuko was quick to extend her hand when Gloria turned to her. More like a shield rather than a gesture of friendship.

A few months later, Harry started going to Bible Study on Wednesday evenings. Setsuko demurred since reading aloud Biblical passages and talking in a small group would not have been easy for her. Only later, when Gloria moved up to sit on the other side of

Harry, did Setsuko learn that Gloria was also going to Bible Study. They became a trio, every Sunday, standing up to sing hymns, Gloria warbling next to Harry's deep baritone, while Setsuko seemed to shrink as she quietly mouthed the words. She'd never been a good singer, even in Japanese.

Still, it was a surprise when nine months later, on his seventy-seventh birthday, Harry told Setsuko he was leaving her for Gloria. "I don't know how much time I have left," he said, "so I want to spend it with the woman I love."

Setsuko, though shocked and angry, was actually secretly relieved. There was little to recognize of the handsome Army man she'd married fifty-five years before in Tokyo. Over the years, his slim frame had become encased in layer after layer of wrinkled flesh. When he took off his shirt, he reminded her of the Pillsbury biscuits that pop out of the container, expanding slowly in the moist heat of the kitchen. She should have listened to her mother who told her, shortly before her family disowned her, that she should marry someone she could grow old with.

But when you are twenty, you think you'll never grow old.

Harry let her have the condo and she left his 401k and pension intact. She'd hired an attorney referred to her from the Japanese Service Center who spoke fluent Japanese. Tak Kurashige was bilingual, and because he was referred by the Center, she trusted him.

Harry would have said, "It's because he's Japanese," because everyone Setsuko hired or turned to for advice was Japanese. Forty years ago, Setsuko had been ecstatic when Harry got a job with the postal service and transferred to Hawai'i. After they married, they had gone back to Harry's hometown in Iowa and she had been the only Japanese person in town. She had felt so alien and alone, especially around Harry's family. She knew they meant well, and even though they spoke slowly, in loud voices, she couldn't understand a word they said. So, they just smiled at her and she smiled back until her cheeks ached. But once Setsuko and Harry moved to Hawai'i, she discovered pockets of Japanese people from Japan. Her doctors, hairdresser, and banker were all Japanese. She shopped at Japanese grocery stores and all of her friends were women about her age who'd been born in Japan. Harry said she never trusted any other ethnic group, that she lived in a bubble. He told her that she should mix with other people, try to be more American.

But Setsuko never paid any attention to what Harry said about making American friends. Why should she, when she could live a Japanese life in Hawai'i, free from all the societal pressures that living in Japan entailed?

On Monday morning, Setsuko called and made an afternoon appointment at the Japanese Service Center to help decipher the insurance bills. A tidy woman, she'd become compulsive as she got older. Everything had its place in her life. What wasn't useful was tossed down the garbage chute or donated to the Salvation Army. And even though the insurance letters were out of sight in the drawer, they were like festering bacteria, ready to explode and contaminate her quiet orderly existence.

As luck would have it, Tak was volunteering and assigned to assist her with her problem. After making a few phone calls, Tak explained that the insurance policy had been connected to a joint bank account that Setsuko had years ago with Harry. Eight years ago, the bank had offered a $2,000 insurance policy, free to clients with bank accounts. Harry had enrolled Setsuko for the insurance and increased the coverage to $5,000, sending in an annual payment for the extra $3,000. Last year, the bank had stopped paying for the $2,000 premium (a notice had been sent to them by the bank) and after the divorce, Harry had stopped paying for the extra $3,000 coverage. Setsuko thanked Tak for his help and explanation, and said she wanted to cancel the insurance. After calling the company back, Tak assured Setsuko the bills would stop.

"I haven't seen you since the divorce papers were filed," Tak said. "Have you taken care of everything?"

Setsuko nodded. After Harry left, she'd stripped the condo of the bedding, wall decorations, plates and cookware they'd used over the years. She bought new white towels and rugs for the bathroom, and a soft fluffy white down comforter for the bedroom. Except for a few framed Japanese woodblock prints on the walls, the condo was bare. She relished the simplicity and Zen-like space.

"You should protect your condo, maybe make a will," Tak said. "I know you don't have children, but is there any family you'd like to leave it to?"

The image of her niece popped into her mind, the only family member she'd seen in over fifty years. The twenty-five-year-old woman had shown up at the condo three years ago. She'd come from

Japan with some girlfriends and was staying in Waikīkī. Setsuko was surprised to find out that anyone back in Japan knew anything about her, much less her address in Hawai'i. Yoko, her niece, wasn't really a niece. As Yoko explained, she was Setsuko's youngest brother's granddaughter. Setsuko didn't know her youngest brother Saburo had married, much less that he had a granddaughter. Yoko knew her brother's name (she called him Ojiichan), but Setsuko knew it might just be a scam, that Yoko had somehow learned about Setsuko's family tree.

Harry, of course, had invited Yoko to stay for dinner. Over a dinner of spaghetti and meatballs (Harry's specialty), Yoko seemed a little too interested in the condo, gazing about it appreciatively, as if imagining herself one day living in it. And Yoko referred to Setsuko as "Obaasan" rather than "Obasan."

As if Setsuko was her grandmother, instead of a distant aunt.

"No," Setsuko said to Tak. "I have no family at all. No one to leave it to."

"Well, think about it," Tak said. "A good friend, someone you care for, your church, an organization that might benefit from your gift. I can always help you draw up the papers."

Back at her condo, Setsuko took the insurance bills out of the drawer and tore them into tiny bits. She thought about Tak's words about giving her condo to her church. She'd stopped going there after Christmas when she'd seen Harry and Gloria's photo greeting card tacked to the bulletin board in the community hall. Harry dressed in a suit wearing a rose-colored tie that matched Gloria's floral dress. The two figures reminded Setsuko of matching salt and pepper shakers.

Setsuko parsed out the shreds of paper, sprinkling them into the three garbage cans in the condo. She gathered up the small trash bags and walked out of her condo, down to the garbage chute at the end of her hall and dropped them inside. Give it to "someone you care for." Besides Harry, the only being Setsuko had ever loved was her dog Bunny. Forty years ago, after Setsuko's third and last miscarriage, Harry had brought home a small puppy that looked like a little fox. She knew the breed, Shiba Inu, had seen them in Japan. Over the twelve years that Bunny lived with them, Setsuko adored Bunny. She liked the dog's cool detached demeanor, the cleanliness of her, how she licked herself like a cat. Bunny rarely barked, only howled on occasion when a stranger appeared.

When Setsuko let herself back into her condo, she heard the click of the door behind her.

"Home at last," Harry always said when he heard that sound. "Locked in and secure."

Even though he was gone, Harry's words were always with her, like an echo in the back of her brain. She realized how much he'd sheltered her, taken care of her over the years. Now that he was gone, she had to take the bus because he used to drive her everywhere. Though her grocery needs were small (no more steak and potatoes to buy), she had to carry all the packages up by herself. She found herself missing the oddest things, like straightening his shoes beside the doorway. He'd always just walk out of them, or kick them off, leaving them where they dropped.

Setsuko went to the refrigerator and pulled out dishes for her simple dinner. Cold soft tofu. A bit of salted salmon to fry. A bowl of day-old rice to reheat in the microwave. She went to the cupboard and got out a tea cup for her green tea.

Voices came from the hallway outside her condo door, receding as the people walked to the elevator. It always made her uneasy hearing strangers outside. Last week, someone knocked on her door and she froze. Maybe they had knocked on the wrong door, or were trying to sell something, but they didn't knock again. She never answered the door unless she had buzzed the person in through the security door downstairs.

Setsuko pressed the buttons on the microwave panel, watching the bowl of rice slowly turn inside. Maybe she needed a guard dog. Like Bunny. Tomorrow, she'd make some calls to see if she could find another Shiba Inu.

Then she'd talk to Tak. See if she could leave her condo to Bunny II. And maybe, just maybe, she'd write to Yoko to see if she'd like to come and visit. After thinking about it for a couple of years, it was nice to be referred to as someone's grandmother.

And maybe Yoko liked dogs too.

AMY UYEMATSU

When All They Can See Is Our Eyes

More than 3,000 hate incidents directed at Asian
Americans nationwide have been recorded since the
start of the pandemic . . .

— CBS News, 2/25/21

Sixty years ago I knew the danger
of walking past white kids my age
who would sneer and glare
and pull up their eyes—
still so young, I
was relieved if they didn't
also yell "Jap" or "Chink"

In World War II propaganda
Americans were told
how to differentiate
loyal Chinese citizens
from treacherous Japanese
like my California-born parents
locked up in camps

"How To Spot a Jap,"
a U.S. Army pamphlet
in comic book–style,
explaining that "C's eyes . . .
have a marked squint"
while "J has eyes slanted
toward his nose"

In 2020, the pandemic
brought our eyes
to the forefront again
as President Trump kept
blaming anyone Asian—
proclaiming the "China virus"
or even "kung flu"

No coincidence
we soon became scapegoats
strangers yelling
"Go back to China"
when we're Korean
"Infecting and disgusting"
though Pilipino or Thai

In 2021, COVID still raging,
a Sacramento teacher
lectures via Zoom—
"If your eyes go up, you're
Chinese" she gestures,
"If they go down,
they're Japanese"

As the racist bullying
now escalates to our elders
a grandmother assaulted
and robbed at an ATM
an 84-year-old fatally
smashed to the ground
by a 19-year-old

To those who insist making
"slanty" eyes is harmless fun—
"Can't you Asians
take a joke?"—
whether Miley Cyrus
or Houston Astro
Yuli Gurriel

No such thing as
a little racism—so-called
innocent teasing
and taunts transform
in an instant to
this all-too-familiar
avalanche of hate

Where attacking us for
our Asian eyes
is as American as
"Japs Must Go" signs,
"Gook" and "Ching Chong" insults,
the Chinese Exclusion Act
as far back as 1882

AMY UYEMATSU

Again

— May 2021

1
My love affair with pine trees and stones
comes from something too ancient
for me to comprehend

I've had the luxury of contemplation,
a gift of time composing
my little odes and haiku

But now I have cancer again
with a pain that makes sitting, walking,
sleeping an uncomfortable task

Precious seconds as I recalculate
new ways to put on my clothes,
even cough or laugh

I take comfort in the afternoon's sky
a May blue that's filled with these
wind-driven clouds

A bit more courage to remember
the world keeps on calling
me closer than ever

2
Is it better to know or not know?
If a stroke or heart attack, maybe no warning at all.
If a risky operation, then maybe but no guarantee.

I just found there's no cure.
Maybe months or if I'm lucky, years.
But isn't that true for everyone?

I know there are no pills or treatments.
No prayers or secret escape hatch.
I take comfort in one more day.

3
to leave but not alone

my heart
   keeps   growing

    your hearts
        meeting mine

what is   breaking

and all
   that can't be   broken

   our hearts
      deepen   as one

LADY WENDOLYN

A Re-past in Tūtū's Teacups

Aloha e dear Aunties, e komo mai!
Please come in, rest from your 'Ewa travels.
For you a lei of white ginger, the favored flower
of our beloved Tūtū.
These delicate chains, a connection, an evocation
fragrant whispers of the past arise
as we embrace.

E hele mai, onto the cool lānai.
Our gathering is blessed by makani aheahe, the gentle wind
caressing our cheeks like the many blown kisses
from our cherished kūpuna.
Come, sit close, e kama'ilio of the olden days
with sweet memories on our tongues to
rouse our appetites and season our cups.

Listen to the nahenahe music of Aunty Bina's classic tunes
as the garden fountain streams in rhythmic accompaniment
hushing the echoes of songs that Tūtū used to sing and play.
Melodies that linger; we'll hum for days.
"Love Letters in the Sand" she would serenade
and a joyous Hawaiian waltz of the "Queen's Jubilee"
conjure images of pīkake strands and the Holokū Ball.

Bouquets of Tūtū's grafted yellow and orange plumeria blossoms,
more valuable than any jewel,
are placed on tea tables of lovely flowing lace.
A pageant of colorful mu'umu'u flutters amongst them
as our tea servers prepare dishes with graceful hands,
moving through the garden like floating blossoms of gardenia and
    pakalana,
swaying like the ti leaf stalks that dance with the Moa'e.

Tūtū's antique tea set, specially arranged
winks and shimmers in gossamer afternoon light.
An intricately designed tea service

brought to the islands by sea captains,
held in the palms of generations and handed down
like the family moʻolelo and legends we share.
My favorite is the one about Tūtū having tea with the Queen.

Auwē! Time flies and the tea is ready to steep.
How easily we fall into reverie!
You'll be amazed at the taste of the earthy brew
sipped from Tūtū's teacups, with honey, milk, or lemon.
We gaze into the golden elixir, our captured faces reflecting back
the likeness of Tūtū's eyes, Kūkūkāne's nose and cheekbones.
We drink and sate our yearning.

Do you like the beautiful teaspoons? They were given to me by a
        friend.
Stirring, they clink against the gilded edges of our cups
like Tūtū's tinkling laugh, unforgettable and enchanting.
Teacups sit in hand with steam rising, we hold on to the ethereal.
The fine porcelain feels delicate and fit for aliʻi.
Vessels of soft gold, blue, and green, with matching saucers too!
E hoʻoheno i kuʻu wahi teatime treasures.

What other delights to satisfy and sustain us?
Coconut water ices, an ʻono piece of fancy sponge, pastry with pohā
        jam.
Aunty Mae's chocolate layered dream cake,
or Tūtū's famous banana bread dessert.
Timeless family favorites to compliment the tea flavors
flashback to summer days of watching Tūtū at her stove.
Do you think these recipes came from the palace kitchen?

It is a privilege to be together in this place of our lineage.
An honor to partake of these rituals and legacies
when siblings and cousins thirst and hunger from afar.
To be nourished by our shared stories, food, and breath.
Tūtū's teacups filled to the brim with loving memories,
with knowledge, with mana, and spirit to rejuvenate us.
Every sip a reminiscence, every bite a communion.

We swirl the last drops of our tea to scatter loose leaves
like stars on a bone-white sky
to read the shapes of our fortunes.
The past, present, and future in one cup.
Our treats are consumed but our thoughts remain,
as we idle together in twilight, reluctant to part.
Drowsy with recollection and renewal, we inhale deeply
to hold us until we meet again.

Come, e Mākuahine, take these tokens of my aloha.
Preserved sweets to savor, tied together tightly
with knots of affection and fellowship.
Wrapped in a finely embroidered kāmaki napkin
a keepsake of our time together, this afternoon tea.
A tribute to our ancestors in three courses,
a re-past in Tūtū's teacups.

MAHEALANI PEREZ WENDT

Da Aunties

In those days, Lāwai Valley gossip was an elevated art form and Auntie Elsie its impresario, chief purveyor, artist-in-residence emeritus.

Her heraldry was legend—no one could match the sleuthing and peerless detective work to get the story; none could match the voicework—perfect pitch, timbre, timing, modulation, embellishment; no one could create more suspense, was more chilling or thrilling in recounting the fascinating, lurid and sometimes downright putrid.

"You wen hear how dey find old Mrs. Vilche buried by da backyard cesspool?" Long pause, Auntie's eyes narrow, her voice lowers conspiratorially. "Johnny Galaza was hunting up Kahili, one of his dogs dug up da old lady, pua ting. Body all palahū, falling off da bones an everything. Dey say da husband use the same knife for cut dry abalone. Dey say he going straight to da calaboose." Auntie makes a dramatic slow slicing motion across her throat.

She knew the backstory—the one shouted over the din of baby lūʻau celebrations and cha-lang-a-lang music at Kekaha homesteads; the neighborly one traded over pasture fences to the mooing accompaniment of Herefords in Kalāheo, the one that made Lāwai telephone party lines crackle, pop, and sizzle with electric excitement in the fifties.

She was a native of Makawao, the storied Maui heartland. My Uncle Manuel fell in love with her while working at ʻUlupalakua Ranch, married and brought her home, the rest is history.

"And what—how yo muddah?" She would begin the interrogation after Mom ran off with a boyfriend.

"I dunno, Auntie; she went Honolulu and we nevah hea from her long time."

"She still stay wit dat guy work movie house?"

"Gee, Auntie, I dunno. Da last time we went go see Ma in Honolulu, we meet dis guy, she tell us dis Uncle Leo."

I picture the kindly gentleman with the slicked-back Three Flowers Brilliantine jet-black pomaded pompadour and sporting gold-trimmed incisors. "He cook fry menpachi fo us on the kerosene stove. Where he live, the store right downstairs, das where he buy kerosene. Ma send us there fo buy bread, twenty-two cents one loaf Love's, one pound luncheon meat fifty cents, one bag poi twenty-five cents. When we go store for Uncle Leo, we get dime tip. Downstairs too get one Chinese restaurant, one bakery sell sugar cookies, crack seed store, and Nancy's Grill. Get jukebox at Nancy's, you can buy cherry Cokes."

The recollection of sweet sour salty seed and cuttlefish I bought with ten-cent tips makes my mouth water. "Uncle Leo work Princess Theatre right next to the building where Ma stay. He bring us all kine candy from his job. He get Shirley Temple posters, da kine dey put on da walls. He let us go movies for free. We saw one zombie movie, was real scary. You can stay in the movies all day and see the same ones over and over. The other movie had vampires, was scary too."

"And he get one television, we watch *Lassie* and *Crusader Rabbit*. Uncle Leo give me one movie poster but Daddy swear and tear 'em up. He rip 'em and burn 'em in the outside stove. He was real mad."

Tsk, tsk, tsk. Auntie shake her head. I answer everything she ask. Das Auntie, gotta respect. She get on the phone and call Auntie Sophie. I hear bits and snatches, "poor kids" and "what kine muddah dat" and "I going cook one roast for dey dinner tonight."

But it's still lunchtime. She just put on the rice, the stew almost pau. The smell of baking bread in the oven wafts through the kitchen. She and Uncle raise milk cows and churn their own butter. Mmm.

Her kitchen is food heaven, home-cooking haven and headquarters for snagging the good story. In her kitchen, one is happily disarmed, all caution and discretion taken flight on gustatory wings.

The phone rings. It's Auntie Angeline. They're on the phone a long time, there's a familiar tenor to the conversation—"tsk, tsk, tsk" and "pua tings." I'm thinking, Ma was a good cook. She's been gone long time. She stay Honolulu. I wonder if she ever going come home?

Outside by Auntie's clothesline get Chinese parsley. It's a heady experience hanging clothes out there. She clamps a hand over the phone mouthpiece and dispatches my cousin.

"Annabelle, go get some parsley."

Annabelle stay all ears. She jes like her muddah, she like hear da scoops. She play deaf ear. She not budging.

"Annabelle!" A menace in Auntie's voice and cousin bolts, flies out the kitchen, hurtles her toothpick legs down the front porch three steps at a time; she comes flying back, a bunch of fragrant green sprigs in her hand. She plops breathless into the chair next to mine. So easy for get stuff to eat here. Just go get it, from the garden, the trees, the rivers, the wild thickets and patches. Where Ma stay, gotta go store for everything.

Auntie's kitchen is like Easter flowers, sunny bright. There's a long yellow Formica table with eight matching chairs where everybody sit together. The linoleum floor is a brick-red floral bordered with fleurs-de-lis. There are white gauzy curtains at the windows above the kitchen sink with three decorative corner shelves on either side, bird figurines poised. The windows overlook the pasture, Lāwai Stream, our home in the distance.

There's a white crochet doily on the table, its spidery lattice intricate as the vein work on Auntie's hands. On the doily is a vase with lavender, orange, and pink zinnias. I'm checking this out while eating lunch with Annabelle.

That night Daddy tells me, "Look, Lani, what goes on in our home is our private business. I don't want you talking to anyone about our personal lives."

"What you mean, Daddy?"

"Auntie mean well but you jus gotta be careful what you say to her. Please don't talk about Mommy and me to anyone."

"Okay, Daddy."

The next day, Auntie starts in on the questioning again. She's wearing an apron, a kitchen towel over the left shoulder, holding a wooden cooking spoon in her right hand as she gestures toward me.

"Yo muddah, she stay pregnant, I hea. From dat boyfren work movie house."

Her magnified eyeglasses eyes watch my every movement intently, the eyebrows adding perfect gravitas to effect a patina of worried concern but subtly imperious, demanding answers, incised with suspicion.

That's news to me. I nevah know Ma was hāpai. I been changing diapers long time. I fold them by the dozens. I 'au'au the babies from when my second bruddah was born. I thinking to myself Ma nevah say going get one uddah baby.

Now Auntie leans her corpulent body into mine. I can feel the pressure of her ample bosom as it brushes against my right arm while I study the detail of tiny multicolored flowers patterned on her shirtwaist blouse, the neatly ironed cuffs of her blue bermuda shorts. I notice the varicose veins on her legs are quite prominent. She awaits my answer. She takes the kitchen towel off her left shoulder, polishes the table in front of me, folds it back in half lengthwise and replaces it on the shoulder. She shifts her right hand to her hip, she's tapping her foot, talk about a pregnant pause, she is expectant, her magnified eyes getting more magnificent by the second.

I'm acting oblivious, like I'm spacing out, staring absently at nothing in particular. I really don't know how to answer Auntie. And even if I knew the answer, Daddy told me not to say anything. I'm checking out Auntie's salt and pepper figurine collection arrayed in little nooks and shelves about the kitchen—paired robins, bluejays, cardinals. The avian motif displays throughout the house except in the living room, where the winged creatures have taken on an aspect of angels—kitsch angel figurines, Kress Store angel paintings. The white gauzy curtains lift and flutter in the soft breeze, a heraldry, a summons of sorts.

"I dunno, Auntie."

"Yo muddah, she put on plenty weight, eh, from the last time she was home hea."

"I dunno, Auntie."

"I heard she working in one bar, eh, in Honolulu?"

"What dat, Auntie?"

She doesn't answer but keeps jibber-jabbering with the questions, cooking all kine stuff. We wouldn't be able to eat like this if wasn't for her. Daddy cook canned corn beef with tomato sauce and onions. Sometimes he fry Vienna sausages. I cook the rice. He make Jell-O, Jell-O pudding.

One time our other auntie down the road pity us, bring goat stew. I sitting there at dinner, goat stew simmering thinking eeeeww—this smell like perspiration. Somehow I knew that word, perspiration. I would get slaps if I ever said anything like that out loud about food. I take little bit.

How you like it if your food smell like the billy in the pasture? I tell you, that's not a very good smell. But Ma always tell us respect the food. 'Ai ka mea loa'a. Eat what get. Be thankful, no waste. I think of Ma all da time. I miss her.

One day I go school, Mrs. Hamamoto tell me come see her after class. I wonder what, I did something wrong? Somebody wen tell I tease June that she like Alfred? Or that I call Alfred, "Alfred the football head"? Oh-oh.

But Mrs. Hamamoto just say, "My dear. Sit down. I heard your parents are getting a divorce. Is it true?"

You see, in those days teachers were blithely unconcerned about student privacy. In fact, I'm pretty sure they were ignorant of the concept and would find it ludicrous. They were like aunties. They scold you when you act up. They pull your ear and rap your knuckles with rulers when you *po'o pakīkī*, hard head no like listen. They make you lomi them, massage, walk back and forth on their backs while they lie down on the classroom floor. They lock you up in the broom closet if you no finish your homework or talk back, *'a'ole pilikia*, no problema. Mrs. Jarvis, the fourth-grade teacher, lock my cousin Andy up how many times. She ask about my parents too. The only one no ask nothing is Mrs. Ventura, second-grade teacher. She wear hairnet, get liver spots on her face.

One day Daddy write something down on one paper, he ask me for copy 'em, one letter to Ma. "Dear Mommy, We miss you. We wish you would come home. We don't have anybody to take care of us. Please come home. Love, Lani Girl."

"I hear yo muddah coming home, eh?"

"I dunno, Auntie."

Today she's making pasteles, Spanish rice, the works. She sends me home with a generous amount for dinner. She cooks dinner for us a lot. And when we hang out there with our cousins, Auntie feeds us lunch and snacks too.

"That would be nice, eh, Mommy come home." She hands me a bundle of hand-me-down clothes.

"Yes Auntie. I wish Ma would come home. Daddy say he get hard time take care us by himself." I guess I shouldn't have volunteered that.

One day out of the blue Ma come home. She catch the airplane from Honolulu, land Līhu'e Airport, her fren Julia pick her up. We so happy to see her, but all I remember is her and Daddy yelling at each other until late that night. When he go work da next day as heavy equipment operator, she tell us pack our clothes. She tell us hurry up, no more time for dillydally. We pack everything real fast. I ask Ma can I take my marble collection, I'm a good player, get bumboochas, peewees, cat eyes, crystals, any kine. It took me my whole life for collect my collection. No, Ma say, no can take that on the plane. Gotta leave 'em behind. We drop 'em off at Auntie Carmen's for my cousin Kenny Boy, that lucky dog. He never could beat me. Only way he get my marble collection, Ma force me to give 'em up.

We never see Daddy for long time after that. By then Ma had a new baby, our little brother Jerry Boy.

I guess we moved to the tenements of Honolulu when we left Kaua'i but I didn't know what tenements was then. I went to Royal School, first time I wear shoes.

One day I walking home from school and see Mrs. Yee, my third-grade teacher from Kalāheo School. I don't know what she doing in Honolulu, attending one teacher conference or something. She really pretty, always wear flowers in her hair, one of my favorite teachers. She put my Mother's Day poem on the bulletin board:

> My Mother is so kind and sweet,
> She works for me with weary feet,
> She lets me go outside to play,
> And loves me each and every day.

Mrs. Yee say, "Lani Girl. How are you? We miss you at school. We heard your mother brought all of you kids to Honolulu. You have a new baby brother Jerald, yeah? How nice for you. I bet you love your new brother. I see your father is still working construction at Port Allen. How is your mother? You folks must live around here, huh, close to school. How do you like your new teachers? I know some of them there at Royal School. I talked to Mrs. McKenzie, your fourth-grade teacher. She said you're a good student but are having a little trouble adjusting. I notice you're wearing shoes. How do you like wearing shoes? Feels different, yeah? Have you tried catching the bus yet? How's your brother Duane doing? Please tell Mommy Mrs. Yee said hello. And don't worry about school—everything will be fine.

"By the way, I saw your Auntie Elsie at Matsuura Store the other day, told her I was coming to Honolulu. I didn't expect to see you, but I want you to know your auntie really misses you kids. Your auntie was crying when she talked about you folks. She called your new teacher, Mrs. McKenzie, just to make sure you kids were okay. I hope you can go visit her and Daddy soon. Don't worry, everything will be all right."

The next day at school, Mrs. McKenzie started asking me questions, lots of questions.

MAHEALANI PEREZ WENDT

Mohai Aloha (Sacrifice)

1.
The night you went over the mountain
Above Nua'ailua Bay
The night you fell, drove or were driven
There was a mechanical failure
Or a fatal miscalculation
You took that turn
The truck skidded
We were dreaming of stars
Starbursts, star trailings
White nestling birds
In the clefts of moonlit cliffs
We were dreaming of trees
Their shadowy paths
All the way down
A dark mountain
Stars floated on the ocean
Scintillate lights were everywhere
Stippling the dark sea
You missed the turn the truck went over
The trailer buckled, the hunting dogs howled
Guns, coolers, the trailer shifted
The dogs howled in their cages
There were glistening reefs and caves below
Shattering rocks and waves below
Craggy places spliced open
The moon foreshadowed
Last prayers
Dimmed stars
That night
We did not know you went over the mountain.

So many others went there
You weren't the only one:
The little boy who followed
Tiny white sailboats

To his farther horizon;
The twins whose momentary rancor
Became their uncoupling;
Another who loved beyond reason
Defiled and scattered
By one fell beast, then another—
You weren't the only one.

This is encomium, liturgy, benediction:
You were flung over
Or went off on your own recognizance
You gave yourself
Lele aku, lele wale
We choose
Our lightways, our beginnings, our ends
Somehow love is in it.

2.
How the mind meanders
Calla lilies, their elegant white throats
Their naughty tongues of orange flame
It is disconcerting
When you want to write poems
But menace is written all over
The house next door
The young neighbor guy
Always saying sorry aunty
When I inquire about his dogs
Not the incessant barking
But the long bouts
Of piteous howling
And the sharp yelping cries
I call over the fence
What's going on with your dogs?
As the cries get louder
And I storm over
In this little village
Where everyone is related
Everybody makes nice
They don't burn bridges

They mind their own business
My heart is beating furious
This and that, he says
In his "Code Aunty" deferential tone
Implausible explanations
To fend off my alarm
And possibly ratting him out
I'd like see for myself, I say
With a strained civility
I push past him
And there they are
Chained, skeletal, red striped
What the hell is wrong with people?
Later I call the Humane Society
But when they show up
The animals are already gone
The guy is in prison now
For molesting his stepdaughter
But a new bad boy has moved in
The landlord is not scrupulous, no—
Raucous parties, screaming, yelling
Ka tunk ka tunk heavy boom box action
Roaring motorcycles
Up and down our little village road
All hours into the night
My husband's temperance exhausted
Though he wouldn't do anything
About the dogs
He gravely puts on his Army boots
His camouflage pants
Sharpens his machete
"Sorry, Uncle," they say
When he shows up
In their driveway
Cut the crap or get the fuck out
My husband says
Here in our village
We get ways
For deal with rubbish
Clean out

If you not going have respect
You don't belong here
The ʻāina tells us so
"Sorry, Uncle," they hang their heads
And follow him to our house
"Sorry, Aunty"
Later the cops arrest one
For dealing
Another for stealing
They find a cache of drugs
Sorry sorry sorry
What I want
Is the peace of early mornings
Getting ready for loʻi
The hunters' quiet silhouettes
Commiserating on weather,
Conditions up mauka
The stand of avocado trees quite possibly a wallow
For wild boar, a prolific sow
Their brindled offspring;
A little red one
Came tra-la-la-ing through our pasture
The other day
And what immediately came to mind
Was that the red ones
Sometimes give themselves
For ceremonial occasions
If the prayers are fastidious, taut
Knives only brought out
Well after the ascension
Mohai aloha
A sacrifice freely given
But the honohono orchids
Are interfering with my train of thought
There they are, underneath Tūtū's orange trees
Showing off to splendiferous advantage
Brilliant lavender splays under arbors of orange
The Chinese thrush are distractions too
Hwamei's glorious trillings
Our rooftop a contrapuntal drum

For their playful loulu seed mischief
They are wise ones
They likely understand far better than we
How in the rainy season of ho'oilo
Cars are efficaciously banged, stripped, torched;
How a riding mower is fenced;
And the most expeditious route
To wilderness, forest, hidden caves
From a boyfriend whacked
And murderous out of his mind
Hey! Underneath Tūtū's orange tree
We throw the taro cuttings after 'ihi
There Hāloa grows
Dark green, wild,
Ravenous.

L. YURIKO WILLIAMS

Da Bes'

"Race you up the hill!" I yell at my son, who is walking parallel to me, but on another level of what my husband and I called "the ant hill." I hear a shrill yelp of excitement as my son dashes up the sidewalks adjacent to the apartment buildings.

I am off in a sprint but my body feels heavy and sluggish. My feet, in zori, fall hard against the pavement and in no time, the beach towel that is wrapped around my waist loosens. I slow down, panting.

"Stop by the dumpster! Wait for Mommy before crossing the street!" I yell as I gasp for breath. Catching up with my son on the corner, I reach for his tiny hands to cross the street.

"Remember, the drivers can't see you if you cross from behind anything, like this dumpster. Come out in front first, so they can see you. Then, you have to look in all directions."

I point in three different directions. My son's tousled head turns to and fro as he goes through the motions of looking for cars, but I know that at this point in time, he is not at all streetwise. Would he learn how to cross a street in this dense apartment complex, I wonder, or somewhere else in another residential setting? We are living in a dense apartment complex of mainly transient people, many of whom are students, post-docs, or junior faculty at nearby colleges, single parents, widows or widowers, and an odd assortment of corporate newbies We recently sold what I thought was my dream house in upstate New York and moved to Philadelphia, where my husband was starting over in his career for the third time.

Exhausted from our recent move, I was enjoying the respite at the community pool every afternoon. My son and I had an especially fun time this afternoon with the other children and their parents. Seeing my son scampering up the hill made me think that he looked none the worse for wear. Yes, we had survived the recent move.

As I enter our apartment I hear my phone ringing. I see that it's my mother, who calls several times a week.

"Oh, Mom?" I answer. I hear the usual clearing of her throat, followed by the beginning of what is likely to be a long argument of some kind. She only speaks in Japanese. Her one-sided conversation went nowhere until she finally came to the point that she needed to make. I had promised to go home to Hawai'i as soon as Timmy was out of diapers. Now he is five years old. We are living in an apartment so it would be inconvenient for them to visit us. I am currently unemployed and between jobs, so I have no excuse to delay going home for a long visit. Last but not least, she had been miffed by a remark made by someone in what I thought of as her "culture" group. She was asked why her daughter hardly ever goes back to Hawai'i.

"Yeah Mom, you're right. It might be a good time to visit you guys." My mom continues to persuade me in spite of my not opposing her in any way. She takes on a stern tone as she expresses the hurt and shame she is feeling from the remark that was made to her.

"Okay, I'll start planning our trip. I'll let you know about the flights," I say calmly as I try to end the call. My mother sounds happy as she says she is now waiting for me to call back to let her know how soon we can be there. I let out a sigh. Beneath the constant pressures I feel from my mother, to have married the right person at the right time, to have at least two college degrees, to own a house as soon as possible, to have a professional job, and to have several children, I have a terrible fear of failure in mid-life. Does she know that my marriage is now a bit shaky and that I may never find the career that I want and that my husband is struggling to start all over in another job? On top of these worries, my mother is beginning to find faults in Timmy that she says were due to him being an only child.

I hear the loud clacking of my son's Lego. He is totally self-absorbed in his solitary pastime. Maybe he is a lonely-only I think, and my mother is right to be concerned.

"Guess what?" I ask him, trying my best to sound excited. "You and I are going to Hawai'i to see Grandma and Grandpa!" Timmy stops playing with his toys and turns around to look up into my face. He is all smiles and dimples, but with a questioning look in his eyes.

"Will we get to ride on a jumbo jet?" he asks.

"Of course!"

"Yay!" he screams, his skinny arms flailing as he jumps up and down. I remember how he had reacted in the same way when we bought a huge Christmas tree in New York State during a blinding snowstorm.

"When are we going?" he asks eagerly.

"Very soon, probably in a couple of weeks," I answer, feeling resigned but somewhat relieved to see how happy it makes Timmy feel. I really do not want to go home to my mother, but then Timmy would probably have the time of his life. I had been blessed with precious memories of my own grandparents which I carried with me since I was Timmy's age. Furthermore, I consider this to be a time of transition for me and going home might be the best way to regain some perspective on my life.

As expected, I am not able to sleep a wink the night before our flight. I am grateful to have my husband accompany us to the airport and see us off. Looking back at him after we said goodbye, I notice how gaunt and tired he looks. Timmy surges forward towards the boarding gates with his child-size knapsack full of his favorite toys and snacks.

The incredibly long journey is uneventful and Timmy is able to tolerate the endless hours, asking only three times, how much longer before we reach Hawai'i? About two-thirds of the way across the vast Pacific, Timmy asks me if Grandma and Grandpa will be at the airport. I immediately feel a twinge of anxiety picturing my mother at the airport.

"Yes," I reply, "and don't be surprised if Grandma makes some kind of scene at the airport. She always does that!"

"What will she do?" Timmy asks with a worried expression.

"Well, there'll be something she doesn't like, maybe my shoes, my handbag, what we're wearing, the new freckles on my face, who knows!" I say, trying not to express anger. "There's nothing you can do about it, so just ignore her, okay?"

When we begin our descent, the island of O'ahu appears to our right. I see the same hotels and many more that I do not recognize, as well as massive pillars supporting the new highways. I try not to cry as the plane lands but I am teary-eyed.

Timmy is full of energy and seems to be leading me towards the terminal and baggage area. I wonder how he is able to navigate his way in the airport at such an age. Finally the homecoming scene is before me, people waiting with expectant smiles, in bright floral wear, some with leis in hand, and couples in warm embraces. As always, I spot my father first because he is usually one of the tallest in the crowd. I see him, smiling, happy, his kind face staring at his grandson. I then see my mother, who is incredibly tiny, under five feet, size four shoe size. We greet each other with questions and answers about the long flight. Timmy seems shy but he and my father begin exchanging jokes as we head towards baggage claim. Retrieving my one travel bag is a painless process until it catches my mother's attention.

"What?" my mother asks in a loud voice. "Is that all you brought?"

I begin to recoil. Not that again please, I thought. I remembered a trip I went on during my college years. My parents had seen me off at the airport. There at the baggage check-in area, my mother had thrown a fit, browbeating me in front of the other passengers because she felt that they had a good show of luggage while I stood holding a small inexpensive vinyl bag. I was so embarrassed that I wanted to cancel my trip. Fortunately, many of the other passengers could not understand my mother speaking in Japanese, but some of them did and regardless of the language spoken and heard, my mother's tone of voice had caused quite a scene.

My mother suddenly laughs. "As always, she travels so light!" she chuckles. "We'll give you one of our large suitcases for your return trip. You can fill it with presents and food."

"Mom!" I plead, "I don't want to be loaded down now that I have Timmy. Also, I don't know if Dave will be meeting us at the airport. We may be taking a shuttle from the airport."

"Is that so?" my mother replies in a tone that meant she heard me but is ignoring anything I said.

We walk out of the terminal. I am silent and apprehensive as my father goes to fetch the car. My mother, Timmy, and I wait for him on the sidewalk outside the terminal. In the bright Hawaiian sun, I notice how my mother has aged and how her makeup now looks overdone. The black liner applied to her lower eyelids heightens the aggressive look on her face. Her chin is held too high and I notice the flashy blouse she is wearing with a high mandarin collar, with brightly colored orchids printed asymmetrically across her chest. She glitters with too many pieces of jewelry. She suddenly steps out onto the middle of the busy road, her little hands on her hips, elbows pointed outwards, brow knitted, and her lips curling upward into a snarl.

"Mom!" I shout. "What are you doing? You'll get run over! Get off the street and wait here on the sidewalk!"

"What is he doing!" she shouts. "Where is he? He's so slow now, all the time!" my mother growls in Japanese, her short arms waving wildly.

"Mom, will you please get back here and wait quietly? Standing out there blocking traffic isn't going to make Dad come back any faster! You'll make Timmy go out on the street too and get run over!"

I feel beads of sweat on my upper lip. It is a great relief when my father appears with the car.

When we are back in my childhood home, I experience what everyone experiences going back into one's past. The house looks much smaller and darker than I remember. I am oppressed by the heat and the smells permeating the house. My mother reads my face and runs about, opening all the windows. Timmy is perfectly behaved so that I forget he is even with me. He is exploring with his eagle eyes and spots a tiny wooden house on my bookshelf. He reaches out and takes it off the shelf. The little wooden house has a door but a key is needed to open its door. It is a wooden puzzle with secret doors and compartments.

"That used to be mine, Timmy," I explain. I show him a secret compartment on one side of the house with a drawer that pulls out. The tiny key to unlock the house is in the drawer. Timmy is surprised to find something so fascinating in my bedroom. "Do you like it?" I ask. "It's yours now!"

"Really?" Timmy looks at me in disbelief while scanning my room for other curiosities.

"Just don't lose that key, okay?" We've been home only a few minutes and I'm already reclaiming old possessions, I thought. I had no idea that small treasures like this had been left behind. I look around my bedroom carefully as I change into something cooler to wear.

By the time I am changed, my mother has the table laid full of her special Japanese dishes. There are smells I had missed for many years, nishime that she had cooked the night before, her special chirashizushi that she labored over this morning, and pickled eggplant, which was one of my favorite dishes. But I do not feel hungry at all.

"I'm making you some tea," my mother says in a loving voice.

"Mom, sorry but I don't drink tea anymore. I can't stomach it."

"What? Why not!" my mother says in an outraged voice.

"I don't know. I haven't been able to drink tea since our last move. It gives me acid and makes my stomach hurt."

"Really! This is all due to that husband of yours and what he puts you through. This is what happens when you marry someone who only cares about his work!" My mother continues in her angry tone. Although I am allowed to skip the tea, I feel as if I might start foaming at the mouth. Timmy and my father are having a wonderful conversation together, so I tell myself that as long as Timmy is enjoying his visit, I will be able to deal with my mother. My mother pushes a lot of food which I feel I must eat and begins her nonstop chatter about everything that has happened since I left home.

Eventually I am able to get away from the dining table and sit by a window with a breeze. I try to express my admiration for all the new acquisitions and changes around the house, but fail to notice a display of dried flowers in the living room. As I sit back and try to recover from the meal and the heat, my mother stands in front of me, looking ruffled. I gaze questioningly at her.

"Remember I called to tell you about the protea that I managed to dry?" she asks me, with her head tilted to one side

"Yes!" I reply, trying hard to remember.

"This is it!" she says proudly, pointing to an enormous arrangement of flowers. The light tan arrangement did escape my eyes, even though it had been placed right in the middle of the living room.

"Oh," I say as I get off the sofa to take a closer look. "Boy, this is unusual, isn't it? Was it hard to dry?"

"Hard to dry?" my mother looks offended. "Not everyone can do this! You could end up with a bunch of smelly, rotting flowers. It's a secret passed from one friend to another and even if you know how to do this, chances are you'll fail. I dried these myself, from fresh blooms. I succeeded because I know all about flowers. You have to be really smart to do something like this! So many of my friends tried, but they all failed!"

I am shocked to hear my mother's outburst. Her words had poured out with anger and unexplained resentment. I feel choked to see her need for recognition and wonder if I had failed to give her enough recognition for all that she accomplished.

"Mom, this is amazing. I bet this arrangement would cost a bundle if you were to buy it. That's great you can do this by yourself." I try to sound sincere but my praise falls flat.

I go off to my childhood bedroom to lie down and rest, but the bed feels unbearably warm. I hear Timmy and my parents chatting happily and I hear my mother saying to Timmy, in broken English, how tired his mother looks.

As it turns out, I am not allowed to rest. The three of them have decided to go out to the Ala Moana area to run an errand. I hear my mother say that Timmy could see the beach and also she would be able to pick up her order of cosmetics. My mother sells a brand of Japanese cosmetics to her friends and acquaintances. Although I want to stay put and rest, I am not prepared to have my parents whisk Timmy away so soon after arriving.

"Wait, I'm coming!" I yell as I see my father grabbing his car keys and all three of them heading out the front door. I grab my handbag, jump into the back seat of my father's car, and fasten Timmy's seatbelt. We are off, my mother speaking nonstop about all the changes that have taken place in the past few years. Timmy is enjoying the ride, twisting his head to and fro to capture all the scenery. He is thrilled to be on an island and keeps asking how big or small the island is.

The scent of my mother's perfume makes me nauseous and I begin to feel giddy as I gaze out at the familiar scenery. By the time we are near Ala Moana, the inside of the car is closing in on me. I thought I had learned to overcome my problem with claustrophobia years ago. My vision narrows and I can no longer understand my mother's chatter. I do hear my son asking if he can go up on the pretty stone bridge he sees in the park.

"Dad?" I gasp. "I don't feel well. Are you stopping at the park first? I need to get out for some fresh air." There's a moment of silence from my parents. My mother mumbles something in Japanese and my father looks back at me.

"It must be jet lag, Laurie." he says in a worried and sympathetic way. "You should have stayed home to rest." My father finds parking near the snack concession. I stumble out of the car and walk instinctively towards a small cement building. It is as if I had come to the park only yesterday. My mother searches for shave ice for Timmy. I feel light-headed and wish I could just lie down, anywhere, but convince myself that a splash of cold water on my face would do. I barely make it into the women's restroom where I bend over a sink, my head hanging down. I gasp for breath as the walls swirl around me. Coming home hoping for a recharge of some kind wasn't such a good idea after all, I thought.

Suddenly two local girls come inside and begin a quiet conversation near me. They are suntanned and wearing identical orange-and-lime printed bikinis that appear almost phosphorescent. I had not yet made a complete mental transition to the island scene until I saw them.

"You wen out wit da kine Leslie?"

"Yeah."

"He wen take you out fo' dinna or wat?"

"No. He cum by afta dinna."

"Oh yeah? Where you guys go?"

"We wen drive aroun' an en up on da kine lookout."

"Oh yeah?"

"Yeah."

"You guys goin' steady or wat?"

"No we jus foolin' aroun'. An' you know wat?"

"Wat?"

"We wen sta' out an' we no go home 'til like fo'o'clock!"

"Oh yeah?"

"Yeah and you know wat? My fadda, he wen ape! Good ting Leslie jus drop me off an' he no hang aroun'!"

I fumble through my handbag for my handkerchief. The girls look at me with just a questioning glance and walk out. They looked so healthy and sound, compared to me with my tired and ashen face. My mother would often tell me that I had an *aoi kao*, meaning in Japanese, a blue face, or an unhealthy-looking face with no color. I take out my small travel hair brush and attempt to fluff up my hair. Sadly, it is no longer the thick, shiny mane I used to have, I thought. I remember the good times I had at Ala Moana with my classmates, the bunch of us giggling and looking for new adventures. We fussed over the way our new bikinis fit or didn't fit and worried about hair growing in unwanted places. The main concern back then was whether the unwanted hair should be shaved off.

I am refreshed by the cool ocean breeze as I step back outside to search for my parents and Timmy. I see the three of them at a table, enjoying a huge mound of shave ice colored like a rainbow.

"He likes it!" my father shouts when he sees me. "What kid doesn't like shave ice?"

My mother stares at me and utters her infamous and well-intentioned, "*Daijōbu*?" question in Japanese, which could simply mean, "Are you okay?" However, in my mind I always translated this expression to mean, "Are you healthy and strong?" so that my mother's question always served to remind me that I was weak and sickly.

I enjoy the time we spend strolling along the beach and Magic Island. My father sees that I am talking and laughing again, but nevertheless asks whether I am recovered enough to allow them to complete my mother's errand before returning home.

When we are finally home, I collapse onto my old bed. For a few minutes before falling asleep, I think of my husband who now seems far away, on another planet. Images from our turbulent past year flash through my mind like a bad dream. I hear Timmy talking to my father and sounding like a very happy child. I realize that I can leave him safe in my parents' hands, and an enormous weight is lifted off my chest as I fall into a deep sleep.

I awake to the sound of the Hawai'i news broadcast and a sizzling sound from the kitchen. I feel hungry.

"Laurie, are you awake?" my mother calls. I wonder how she knows that I just woke up.

"Yes!" I shout back. Dinner smells wonderful. My mother surprises me with my favorite dish, fish marinated in miso. Timmy and my father are laughing together. They share the same sense of humor. My father is informing him about all the kinds of bugs found in Hawai'i and tries to convince Timmy that the cockroaches might be smarter than us.

After dinner I offer to wash the dishes. I enjoy the view from my mother's kitchen window. I see the sidewalk leading to the front porch. I see visions of my past, all the boys who came for a date, the soft kisses on the cheek, the beautiful corsages and leis. I remember those who lingered by the front door or came inside for longer chats. There was so much to talk and dream about, not knowing what the future would hold for any of us. My mother would scold me severely after a boy left if she felt that I exhibited *mono-hoshī* behavior. In Japanese this means literally that I acted as if I wanted someone or something, and it was shameful behavior.

I remember when I was presented with an incredible night-blooming cereus early one morning. That was the first time that I ever saw this huge, mysterious flower, which usually blooms for only one night. It was like receiving a trophy from the heavens. As I held the heavy blossom in my hand, my classmate told me that I was Da Bes' then hurried off back into his parked car after seeing my mother rushing out the front door. My mother snatched this flower out of my hands and ran off with it, back into the house while muttering how she might be able to preserve it.

As I watch the sky turn into a beautiful Hawaiian sunset, I allow myself to wallow in my memories.

L. YURIKO WILLIAMS

Samishī

My mother walked my older brother to his kindergarten every morning, but only to a halfway point. The elementary school was quite a distance from the house that we rented so she worried about having to walk for a certain length of time in the sun. She used an umbrella which she brought from Japan for the sun, to protect herself. She couldn't understand why the women of Hawai'i allowed themselves to be so sunburned. As a child who first only communicated in Japanese, I understood her as saying that the people of Hawai'i were being "grilled in the sun" because she used the same verb for grilling chicken or beef over a fire.

I was not allowed to go along on these walks, mainly because I was very absent-minded and did not heed any warnings when crossing a street. I was told to wait for my mother's return inside the house, but I always disobeyed and waited for her return in our yard. Our landlady kept a cage full of canaries and budgies on top of an old wooden desk in the shaded side of the backyard. While I waited for my mother to return, I would always spend my time watching the colorful birds showing their affection for one another in their happy little world. Mother was especially fond of the yellow canaries and would show us how delighted she was whenever they sang. The cage was securely covered each night, but she worried obsessively about the cats in the neighborhood coming into our yard.

After some time I heard the jangle of my mother's keys opening the front door. I took off in a sprint, running as fast as I could to the front of the house. I ran across the rough asphalt surface of the carport when something, a bump somewhere, caused me to trip and be hurled face forward onto the driveway. I broke my fall by putting my hands out in front of me and felt a searing pain in my hands. When I picked myself up, I noticed that the pattern of the rough asphalt was cast into the palms of my hands, which were now bright red and full of rough indentations. Tiny bits of pebbles appeared to be embedded in my skin, but I was able to simply brush them off. Still, I was frightened and cried.

The house seemed very dark as I entered trying to stifle my cries. I was certain that this accident was worthy of my mother's attention. I knew that she would be sitting in front of her mirror upon returning.

As a child I thought of her dressing table as a kind of sacred altar on which she displayed her cosmetics and an ornate crystal perfume atomizer.

My hands continued to sting and burn. I entered my mother's bedroom as I called out to her, announcing that I had been injured and extended my hands, palms up, to show her what had happened. She had a blank expression as she took my hands and looked at my palms. To my surprise, she suddenly made a menacing face.

"Why did you do this to yourself!" she screamed in Japanese. I could not answer. I ran to my bedroom. I knew now that I had upset her and ruined her day from the start, a beautiful morning in Hawai'i. After I stopped crying, I went into the bathroom, climbed onto the toilet seat to reach the medicine cabinet, and found the tincture of iodine. I applied enough of it to paint both of my palms a bright red.

It was a little over a decade since the end of the war with Japan. It was around this time that my memories as a child formed the images that I would retain into adulthood, and it would be many decades later before I could attempt to understand my mother. There was much in Hawai'i at this time that reminded my mother of her Japan. She enjoyed frequenting the okazuya or local delicatessen and shops around the corner. I was self-conscious when I accompanied my mother because I was aware that she stood apart from the local people. I noticed that she spoke in a different way from the local ladies at the okazuya and she often asked questions about the food revealing that she was a newcomer and outsider.

My mother and I would often hop on the bus and ride into downtown Honolulu. She dressed fashionably, turning heads wherever she went. I especially enjoyed our trips to the downtown Woolworth's where I was often allowed to pick out a small inexpensive packet of plastic beads which could be popped together. With each trip downtown and a stop at Woolworth's, my strand of beads grew longer. I thought the plastic pieces were beautiful, especially the light pink beads which I pretended were like the pearls on the necklace that I knew my mother treasured.

My first memories of my mother were that of her need for fashionable clothing and accessories. Life revolved around the clothes that she wore. Even though my father, a sergeant in the army, could not afford the dresses she described as having "New York" on its labels, she always managed to buy a few of these dresses and eventually found a seamstress in a tiny Kapahulu shop who would sew dresses to her liking.

As a child I could not understand why she spent an extraordinary amount of time gazing at her reflection in the mirror. She was at her best when being flattered or being boastful. Throughout her life, she always put on a fashion show for me each time I visited, which would go on for hours as I complimented her on her appearance. She resisted the local Hawai'i style of dressing and continued to dress to the hilt whenever she stepped out, no matter for what purpose, even wearing nylon stockings in the tropical heat. It would take decades for her to dress down. She also controlled what my father, my brother, or I wore whenever we went out together as a family, so that her own appearance would not be affected in any negative way.

She once told me when I was in high school that she had been given advice by her Issei father-in-law when she first arrived in Hawai'i. From his perspective as a plantation laborer who emigrated from a farming family in Hiroshima, my mother was a pretentious woman, needing to come to terms with the fallout from the war and her loss of any social status. On the other hand, she had the greatest respect for farmers and anyone who worked the fields because she had suffered from food shortages during the war. I recall hearing her long conversations with my grandfather. I wondered how she understood his Hiroshima dialect. My grandfather warned her, in a most diplomatic but literal way, that her "nose was too high" and she must adjust if she wanted to enjoy life in Hawai'i. What I hoped for, always, was that she would eventually become a kama'āina.

By chance, my mother met another woman from Japan during her first year in Hawai'i. Like my mother, she had married a Nisei and her husband, like my father, had served in Japan after the war. My brother and I were playing in the front yard when a boy bounded across our yard and dove into the bushes. He was trying to hide from someone. My brother and I were stunned and simply stared at each other, remaining motionless, as if we too might need to hide from something unknown. After a long period of silence and staying motionless, we saw a woman running about and eventually coming into our yard, calling out loudly for Ma-bin, which was likely meant for Marvin. We both giggled loudly because my brother's name was Melvin, which my mother also could not pronounce. The closest she could get to the correct pronunciation was Me-ru-bin. We stared at each other in disbelief. Soon we heard the woman shouting to Marvin in Japanese that he was keeping his whole family from eating dinner, which was getting cold, and he had been forgiven for whatever mischief he had gotten into.

My mother came out of the house when she heard the commotion, excited to hear the woman speaking only in Japanese. Knowing immediately that the woman was not Nisei, my mother asked the woman what was going on. Several sentences were exchanged, after which my brother and I pointed to the bush, revealing that Marvin was in there. Marvin reluctantly gave himself up. He was described as the black sheep of the family, with two other siblings who were not like him. I could see that my mother lightened up instantly upon speaking to the woman from Japan and appeared happy, only too eager to tell my father when he got home about this chance encounter thanks to a misbehaving boy.

My mother and I visited Mrs. Oka. Unlike my mother, I sensed that this woman was very laid back and approachable, but I was still shy and did not speak. They rented the top floor of a small house off Kapahulu Avenue. It was necessary to climb up a steep, narrow, dark stairway to get to their apartment.

We were welcomed in and served tea, but I could sense that my mother was a bit disappointed because Mrs. Oka had a lot of sewing that she needed to complete, which she could not put down just because she had visitors. She explained that she was paid piecemeal for her sewing. There was a tiny space in the corner of the living room which was full of fabric and cuttings, where she sat and continued to work as she held a lively conversation with my mother. They were sharing stories of how they met their Nisei husbands in Japan. I sat on the far side of the tiny living room in silence, curious about the setup of the apartment, which consisted of only the upper floor of a small, two-story house. Suddenly, there was a commotion.

"Haruko! Oh, you're awake? We have visitors, the lady I met the other day, who lives down the street. And, her daughter is here, too." I felt an immediate connection when Haruko replied in English although her mother spoke only Japanese. But I thought it was odd that Haruko was called by her Japanese name, but her brother Marvin was not. I thought of Haruko as a truly Japanese girl because she was called "Haruko" instead of her English name, April.

"Yeah I know! How can I sleep wit' all da noise!" Haruko shouted back gruffly. Mrs. Oka made an excuse for her daughter's response. She said Haruko was not feeling well that morning and she had allowed her to stay home from school. She was several years older than my brother. My mother voiced some concern about the illness, implying that we were intruding and should not be visiting if Haruko was ill.

"No, don't worry. She doesn't have a fever and she will probably go back to school tomorrow." Mrs. Oka sounded gentle and kind. I could not imagine her shouting at and scolding Haruko for any reason.

Haruko plopped herself onto a chair. She had seen me sitting across the room but seemed to be totally ignoring me because she turned her back to me, so that she faced the direction of my mother and her mother. My mother had been staring at Haruko since she appeared in the living room. She then spoke out excitedly, expressing admiration and awe at Haruko's face.

"Oh, my! What a beautiful child!" my mother gasped. "Your daughter will be a great beauty! Her eyes are amazing!"

"Everyone says she looks like her father and not me." Mrs. Oka responded, laughing, as my mother continued to stare at Haruko. This was an embarrassing habit that my mother had all her life, of staring at women she considered to be beautiful, even to the point of causing public disturbances.

"And Haruko has a beautiful complexion, too. Unfortunately Laurie has her father's skin. Look at all her moles and freckles! I can't keep her out of the sun. She loves to play outside, all the time." Then my mother hesitated and said, "And, she always has that *samishī* look on her face." My mother would always refer to my *samishī kao* throughout my life when she felt that she needed to put me down. I never understood why my mother used this expression. As a child, I thought it meant that I had an ugly or homely *kao* or face. But later in college when I studied Japanese, I saw that the Japanese words, *samishī* or *sabishī*, could mean "lonely" and "desolate" and other words would be used to describe a face that was considered to be ugly or undesirable.

"Haruko, why don't you talk to Laurie? She'll be starting school next year. Her brother is a few years younger than you." Mrs. Oka also had trouble pronouncing my name, which she pronounced as Ro-ri.

Haruko bounced out of her seat and walked towards me.

"Try come!" she said, "Mo' betta' on da sta'a." I followed her to the stairway. She did not actually sit on the stairs, but rather on the floor of the living room, looking down onto the stairway. The stairway was extremely dark and narrow, so that I was forced to step gingerly down around her and sit two steps below. As I looked up, her face was silhouetted against the brighter light of the living room behind her. It was uncomfortable for me to sit in this way, and looking up at her, I was intimidated. She reminded me of a cat stalking its prey.

"How cum yo' madda say yo' skin no good?" she said in a rather angry tone.

I was shocked at what she said, but sensed that she really was not feeling well and excused her abruptness. I detected some sympathy on her part for me about my mother saying that there was something wrong with my skin. I did not know what to say and remained quiet as Haruko looked me over.

"Yeah, I see da spots on yo' face an' neck. Show me da arms," she said in a gentler tone. I stretched out my arms and she pointed out a few moles on both arms. I did not say anything more, so she looked exasperated and bored with me. She went off to get some bubble gum to chew and offered me one, but I shook my head to refuse. She sat there chewing and popping bubbles as she stared down at me. I felt awkward and wanted so much to go home.

My mother would stay in touch with Mrs. Oka throughout her life. Mrs. Oka took on a variety of jobs, working full-time and part-time even in some jobs which required heavy physical labor. She also taught Japanese part-time at a local temple. In no time, I saw that Mrs. Oka had become a kama'āina. I always wished that my mother could also simply act and be like the other local mothers but she was not. One habit of hers that always embarrassed me was her need to bow to show her respect for others. It would take her years to break this habit which was so ingrained in her and it would take me just as long to appreciate *ojigi*, the Japanese manner of bowing to show respect.

We moved from Kapahulu and I attended an elementary school on base. There the school was involved in a production of *The Nutcracker* for Christmas which was to be held at the base theater. Many mothers volunteered or were asked to assist in the production. I took an interest in the production because my teacher announced that some of us could be selected as ballerinas playing the part of the sugar plum fairies. Like so many little girls, I had dreams of becoming a ballerina. When I excitedly told my mother that there was a chance for me to be a ballerina, I was confused and hurt by her reaction.

"You cannot be a ballerina," my mother said in Japanese, in a very cold, matter-of-fact way.

I was baffled. As a little child, I would lift my arms in the air and twirl in circles whenever my mother gave me the prompt, "*ba-re-ri-na-wa*?" This meant, "What does a ballerina do?" So I could not understand her sudden discouragement after years of amusing my parents whenever I pretended to be a ballerina.

"You don't have the face for a ballerina," she said harshly. "So it would be a waste of time to take any lessons and you should not think that you will be dancing on any stage as a ballerina."

Nevertheless, when my teacher asked for a show of hands for anyone wanting to try out to be a sugar plum fairy, I raised my hand and proceeded to the designated room. I was surprised to see many children already dressed in tights, tutus, and leotards, with their mothers at their side. We were asked to dance around in a circle to music. There were others like me who had never received ballet lessons and were not dressed as ballet dancers. I felt very self-conscious and awkward moving haphazardly alongside those who had received ballet lessons.

The ballerina rejects were given the role of being flowers to decorate the back of the stage. Looking back, I often thought with much amusement that my lifetime struggles to not be a wallflower may have stemmed from this early experience. At least our heads were adorned with huge petals, and we were allowed to sway to and fro with the music.

When Mrs. Oka started teaching in a Japanese language after-school program, she contacted my mother to encourage her to enroll me in her beginner's class. This took up much of my time several times a week because I needed to walk a distance from my elementary school to a Japanese temple, but I thoroughly enjoyed this experience. The school and temple served as a cultural center.

The temple which sponsored the language program I had been enrolled in hosted a number of festivals and events. The students had an opportunity to dress in kimonos and participate in an annual dance recital. My mother told me that we had been invited to see Haruko perform at the event and Mrs. Oka would pick us up to take us to the temple. It was fascinating to see girls and boys dressed in brightly colored kimonos. I saw Haruko running around by the stage before the program began. While we waited, Haruko came running to us suddenly, breathless and with a worried look on her face. She was by far the prettiest girl in her dancing group and I thought of the Japanese doll which my mother kept in a glass case.

"I wen mess up mai heia!" Haruko cried.

"Haruko, you're much too rowdy!" Mrs. Oka said in Japanese. "That's why your hair has come down." Mrs. Oka refastened a pretty *kanzashi* hair decoration on Haruko's head and rearranged her hair. "Now hurry back! You have to be up on that stage any minute now."

Mrs. Oka had delivered her admonishment to Haruko in a gentle way.

When the dancing began, I was entranced by the music and the children in their colorful kimonos. Unexpectedly, I heard Mrs. Oka encourage my mother to arrange for me to also take dancing lessons.

"Look at Laurie. I can see how she is so interested in Japanese dancing. She's my best student and I'm sure she would do well in dancing, too. Why don't you sign her up for lessons? They all enjoy this festival. Haruko has made many new friends from the dancing group," she explained.

"Hmmm." My mother seemed to look away from Mrs. Oka, responding in a way that showed that she was not interested. But Mrs. Oka continued.

"It doesn't cost much, only a small fee. Laurie could wear the kimonos that Haruko has outgrown. Mrs. Kimura teaches a beginners' class, too. I can pick Laurie up and she can go with us to the lessons."

"Haruko is very attractive. I can imagine how glamorous she will be when she becomes an adult," Mother said, and she used the Japanese word *bijin*, "a person endowed with good looks," to refer to Haruko. "But look at Laurie," Mother went on, "She's very plain looking, and she doesn't even move or walk like a Japanese person, so there is no way she could do well in Nihon Buyō. It would be a total waste." My mother used the word *samishī* again, to describe how I always appeared.

"*So-de-mo-nai!*" Mrs. Oka responded angrily in Japanese, meaning "That is not true!" She seemed shocked at Mother's response and looked at me with pity.

"My Haruko is a real tomboy. She spends all her time competing with her two brothers. She even climbs up trees like a monkey! Laurie is sweet and feminine." Mrs. Oka used the word *ojōsan* to refer to me, which meant a proper, good daughter. "She would excel in Japanese dance, or anything else she wants to do."

"Laurie," Mrs. Oka turned and looked at me. "If you want to learn Japanese dance, you ask your mother for lessons, okay? By this time next year you would be dancing in the recital too!" I looked at Mrs. Oka and nodded but pretended that I was too distracted by the music and dance to be concerned with what had been said. I was relieved that it had grown dark because no one could see that I was crying.

I would for most of my life shy away from things Japanese because of my fear of not being sufficiently Japanese. Perhaps my mother was only preparing me for the military child life that my brother and I would experience, away from Hawai'i, on the mainland and overseas.

My parents seldom spoke of their experiences during the war. My father was a teenager living on the Waipahu plantation when Pearl Harbor was attacked. My mother survived the massive bombing of Tokyo. Both of them had experienced death and destruction. I often made excuses for my mother whenever I suffered from her frequent mood swings, or anger and depression, thinking it may have been due to some fallout from the trauma she experienced from the destruction of Tokyo. She could be tender and loving, and cruel, hateful, and malicious all in one day.

After my father passed, my mother suffered a series of strokes. I was told that she required highly skilled nursing care because of her many impairments and deficits, but I believed that she was still cognizant, if spoken to in Japanese, because she responded to me in short phrases or a series of words. I was baffled to find myself speaking fluently to her in Japanese. At times I wondered if the medical staff pitied me because they may have thought that I was delusional when they saw me holding cheerful, long conversations with someone with so many deficits. In the many long hours I spent with her in the hospital and nursing facility every day, we shared a closeness like that of school girls who were best friends. We made fun of all the doctors, especially the one with the very square face, tried to decide which female doctor was the prettiest, and shared our sympathies for the other patients with all their different kinds of maladies and impairments. We enjoyed spending time with the other patients and their loved ones and sharing life stories. I was surprised to meet someone who grew up on the Waipahu plantation with my father. My mother could not engage in any conversation, but I was able to translate everything for her that was shared with us. I saw how much she had grown to love the local people.

While my mother was still able to eat by being spoon-fed, I drove around the entire island every day, searching for the special foods that my mother liked to eat, her favorite smoothies, azuki red bean and matcha ice cream, hard-to-find Japanese delicacies, and every kind of sushi imaginable. I assisted in feeding her, a task which required many hours of care and patience. The medical staff allowed me to take her out on short trips in her wheelchair. I took her out for fresh air every day, for a change of scenery and would even stop at a nearby fast food because she always loved French fries. Inevitably I became her doting mother, and she became my loving and grateful child, no longer someone I needed to fear.

I was not with my mother when she passed because her death came suddenly and was unexpected. I cried for weeks and was inconsolable. On one particular night as I sat sobbing, I heard her voice calling me, "Ro-ri-chan!" I went to the bathroom to put a cold washcloth on my swollen eyes. I turned on the bright lights and gazed into the mirror. It did not reflect myself. My mother stared back at me, with that questioning look she always gave me whenever she thought that I was being overly sensitive. I looked into her eyes and felt comforted. I realized that now and forever, she was a part of me.

J. FUMIKO WONG

Tired

"I'm tired."

My Uncle Kenji has been saying this every day this week.

He had just let me into his luxury condo on Ala Moana Boulevard. He had walked forty feet, twenty to the door and twenty back to his armchair recliner. He stood with his left hand on his back, took a winded breath in and out, and gestured at one of the chairs. "You can sit."

I place my purse and lunch bag down on one of the dining chairs, as Uncle relaxes into his recliner.

It is the time of the coronavirus, so I immediately wash my hands, silently singing "Happy Birthday to me" at the kitchen sink.

"Uncle, did you eat breakfast?" I ask.

For an 85-year-old, Uncle has great hearing. Even though he is facing away from me, he can still hear.

"Breakfast? I think I did."

"Oh yeah? Good, good." I open the refrigerator. "What did you eat?"

Uncle thinks. "I don't remember," he says.

I have memorized Uncle's fridge. He lives alone, so whatever is absent from the fridge, I know he has eaten. From the look of it, I see half of the watermelon cubes missing from the container I left the previous day. He must have eaten that. The three containers of cut cantaloupe and the two nectarines I left a couple days ago still lie there. The container of Zippy's chili and rice that I left for his dinner yesterday sits in the same position, untouched. I close the door and bite my lip to keep from scolding Uncle too harshly.

"Uncle Kenji, I am sorry I forgot to call you last night." I walk over to him. "I should have reminded you to heat up the chili."

Uncle Kenji looks at me puzzled.

"I don't think you ate dinner last night," I say.

Uncle waves his right hand. "Ah, nah, I must have eaten. Or if I didn't, I wasn't hungry."

Part of me wants to get into the explanation. I've told him this every day. That my mother in her final years was not hungry. But the doctors told us that the elderly often lose their appetites. To avoid a downward spiral of health problems, they must eat three meals a day, or even better, six. I save the explanation for later.

I show Uncle the contents of the Jack-in-the-Box paper bag in my lunch bag. "You have options."

Uncle looks at the greasy goodness and smiles at me.

"There are two tacos, a chicken sandwich, and a Teri Jr. Jack, like a teri-burger," I say. My dad would have scowled at me at this moment. Dad would make Mom eat homemade meals and salads, per the doctor-recommended Mediterranean Diet.

Uncle picks up a taco. "Oh long time, I never have this," he says. I wish he chose one of the sandwiches. One taco is not enough for his lunch. I hope after he finishes, he will eat a second taco.

I hand him a napkin and select the chicken sandwich. The Teri Jr. Jack will be Uncle's dinner.

We dig in. I am pleasantly surprised that Uncle is eating the taco with gusto. I am a fast eater. Normally I will eat one of those chicken sandwiches in about six bites. I consciously slow myself down. I don't want to finish before Uncle. If I do, he will tell me to eat the other things in the bag.

In between bites, Uncle tells me, "Huh, you know, I never been so tired like this."

I nod.

He wipes his mouth. "Is there a flu going around or something?"

"Yes," I say hesitantly.

"Because I might be coming down with something," Uncle says, releasing one of his hands from the taco and feeling his forehead. "But I don't have a fever."

I feel Uncle's forehead. As usual, it is not hot. I put the chicken sandwich down on the coffee table. I have kept a digital thermometer in my purse since the pandemic started.

"Can I use this on your forehead, Uncle?"

Uncle looks at the contraption. "Oh, that's a new thing."

I nod. "Yup, I just need to put it in the middle part of your forehead, like this." I place the thermometer there and press a button. "96.9" shows up on the screen.

"No fever?" Uncle asks.

"Yup, no fever." I show him the numbers.

"That's good," he says, going back to eating.

I put the thermometer away and pick up my sandwich. Today is Thursday, July 16. I took my uncle to get a coronavirus test almost a week ago. But due to the shortage of reagents, the VA clinic's tests would have to be sent to the mainland. We were told to expect results in seven to ten days.

Uncle is about done with the taco. He fishes out the lettuce strips that escaped and are still in the taco wrapper. He folds up the wrapper and deposits it in the small trash can near his feet.

I wait until he swallows his last bite. I do not want to rush the second taco.

I take a tiny bite of my chicken sandwich and wipe my mouth with a paper napkin. Uncle looks content. I take the remaining taco from the Jack-in-the-Box bag and urge Uncle to eat it.

Uncle looks at it. "That's OK." He waves his hand. "I full."

"No, no," I say.

Uncle waves his hand again. "Can eat later."

"You should eat this now," I say, in almost desperation. "It tastes better fresh. It gets soggy if you put it in the fridge for later."

Uncle weighs the pros and cons of taco crispiness and relents. He accepts the taco.

Relieved, I look around the room for conversation starters. Uncle has months of unread, unopened newspapers stacked in the living room.

I eat the final bit of my sandwich, crumple the wrapper and toss it in the rubbish can.

"Uncle, do you read the paper?"

Uncle says, "No," with a full mouth of taco.

"Uncle, do you like to do crosswords?"

Uncle thinks. "Crosswords? Hm, no."

"Uncle, what do you like to do?" I already know the answer, but am hoping for another one.

"Rest," Uncle says with confidence.

I gingerly ask, "But isn't rest for nighttime?"

Uncle says what is obvious to him. "I sleep at night, but I rest during the day."

He must sense my despair. "Only just this past couple weeks. I used to walk outside. But just this past couple weeks, I'm just tired."

I think about my mom. She would have rested or slept in her chair all day if we did not nag her to eat, read, walk, anything. I actually have a suspicion that towards the end, my mom wasn't reading, but just appeasing us with an open book or magazine. Meals were uncomfortable with Dad insisting Mom eat more. Also, what used to be an enjoyable activity, walking in the mall, she grew to dread. Mom loved her brown chair in the living room and protested leaving it almost every time.

I tell Uncle, "You know, Mom saw a lot of doctors. And all of them, her primary doctor, her specialists, all of them said she had to do things during the day."

Uncle keeps eating his taco, slower this second time around. "No, no. Just this week or just this past couple weeks. I am just tired. I am going to rest, to get over this feeling of being tired."

"But Uncle," I say. "All the doctors told Mom you have to move your muscles a little every day. And keep your brain active. Because if you rest, if you just sit in your chair doing nothing, you get more tired. If you do nothing all day, you will get frail. If you just sit in your chair doing nothing, you will be more susceptible to pneumonia."

Uncle thinks. "What if you lie down in bed and do nothing?"

I furrow my eyebrows but look at his smile and smile.

"Nah, nah," my uncle says. "I rest and get better. Then I go do like before."

I try to appeal to Uncle's sense of civic duty. "Uncle, what about the news? An election is coming up. Gotta watch the news and read the paper to know who to vote for."

Uncle chews. "Not a high priority."

I sigh. "What is high priority?"

Uncle smiles. "Rest."

Uncle fishes out the escaped pieces of lettuce and meat from his taco wrapper. He chews and swallows. Then carefully folds the paper wrapper and deposits it in the trash. I make a mental note that Uncle likes tacos. I make a mental note to call him in five hours as a reminder to eat dinner. I make a mental note to bring Taco Bell tomorrow.

J. FUMIKO WONG

Too Big, da Heart

Ho, Uncle Yukio, I tell you. I so mad. Uncle Yukio, one big heart, he get. So all kine people like you know . . . da kine.

You know da guy fixing up his place? He end up living deah! Get laundry detergent and condiments all ova, so I take pic'cha. Uncle Yukio no believe. Even with da pic'cha. An'den naturally wen da bills come, da bills wen go UP. So Uncle Yukio, he tell me, "Why bills high?"

I tell him, "You know your frend. I tink he LIVING deah."

Yukio go, "No no, that Masa son. We go, go check." But gotta tell da home staff a-head of time if take Uncle Yukio out. So I tell, we gon check, but have to wait til weekend. Ho man, Uncle Yukio prolly tell someone. And dat someone tell Masa good fo nuting son. Cuz da buggah go clean up and no mo stuff wen we go.

And ho, so unprofessional, da flooring he make. Latah on, I go ask Masa son, "Excuse, me, what happened here? What is that?"

And he go, "Oh, I steam iron dat spot."

I say, "Oh. Have to do again, yeah?" And da sonnufabitch. He no go take off dat cahpet from edge, he go just cut dat part. And we Kauai yeah, so run out Home Depot. So he try patch, but not with da same carpet. Ho da ugly, brah! So me, I ask my friend, "Yeah, try help." So he wen try fo fix. Befo look so ugly. Now jus look . . . less ugly.

Uncle Yukio he was going sell his place to his friend's sista granddaughtah, for CHEAP. I try explain he need da money, but he get big heart. I go, "So, you want sell house to Russell sista daughtah daughtah daughtah." You know me, I draaaag em out yeah. And Uncle Yukio he jus nod. And I go, "What her name?" Uncle Yukio no can say. Ho I mad. I go tell my realtah talk to deah realtah. And I go call Russell. I say, "My Uncle Yukio does not know your sister's granddaughter's name. What is it?" And I can tell he know he taking advantage. He answer all meek and sheet. I so mad. I tell da realtah I cannot take it. I say I goin still come with Uncle Yukio to da meeting, but das it, pau! Uncle Yukio decide. But lucky! Russell sista granddaughtah pull out dat day.

Uncle Yukio still get THIRTY mo lettahs, BETTAH offahs. So I tell Uncle Yukio, "You know afta dis, das all da money you get. Bank not goin give you loan." Uncle Yukio tell, he know, he know. So now he like sell to da NEIGHBAH.

I tell da realtah I gone walk away, I jus gone walk way.

LOIS-ANN YAMANAKA

The Boss of My Life Is

Me.
They all warned you:
She going write one poem about you—
especially after beloved Eric and Darrell, of our
Bamboo Ridge Press published
"Boss of the Food."
But you neva listen, so—

Remember the time you got mad
and took my minee
that I slept with every night since age two,
walked to the living room with scissors
in one hand and minee in the other, real calm,
ice eyes, and cut a tear then ripped um in half; you
dropped dear minee
to the floor and
pointed the fuckin' scissors at me.
You next.

Or mixing all my perfumes together.
Or using all my lipstick to smear on my mirror:
I HATE YOU LOIS
Or flying the seam ripper from your Singer sewing chest
which stuck in my leg and boinged up and down in my flesh.
Or swinging the bolster cushion, zipper-edged sharp, slash
my face and arms real Edward Scissorhands.
Or throwing the bar stool at me.
Or grabbing the ice pick in your fist
you wen' slash at me.

Maybe you recall the pound of frozen
bacon hurled at my head which I ninja-swayed, *Matrix*-style,
so wen hit the glass door to the lanai.
Same with the crystal sugar bowl shatter, same
ninja skills, same glass door, fine shards

that the cheapo
vacuum cleaner Aunty gave us neva suck up good.

Or the fugitive you wen harbor behind your
locked door.
The sheriffs wen stop me on Clark Street
outside our ghetto apartment cuz you
look like me
to serve *you* a warrant for aiding and abetting.

Or the car we *shared,* the one you took
when was my turn,
so I wen chase you
to the parking structure, stand in front of the damn car, and hold out
my arms
to stop you—
your ice eyes glaring me down, gunning
the car engine—
I neva wait, oh no, I wen dive to the side, real
Charlie's Angels–style,
tuck and roll and all,
as you wen smoke um, burn rubber out of the stall.

Then later when I got supa fuckin' mad at you
for taking the damn car again that I jumped
in the backseat—
remember how I choke you out on the freeway
from behind as you swerve on the freeway
and double-chin your red face
but you was the driver
which I wen only realize when you was almost dead:
Eh, I going die too.
So I let go.

Sista, I could go on and on.
But I not.

You called yesterday when I told you about
this very poem. You laughed and said,
"And after you pau, when you going write the *real* shit?

See, they wen warn you even back then,
"No do that. She going write one damn poem
about you."
But you neva listen.
Til now.

Cuz I *did* already write a poem about you,
but now I doing you one bettah:

Sista, I love you but Truth be told:
I pau.
I wrote one novel.

CONTRIBUTORS

Sara Backer's first book of poetry, *Such Luck,* follows two chapbooks: *Scavenger Hunt,* and *Bicycle Lotus,* which won the Turtle Island Chapbook Award. Recent publications include *Kenyon Review, Lake Effect, Poetry Northwest,* and *Poetry Ireland.* She lives in New Hampshire and reads for *The Maine Review.*

Amita Basu's fiction has appeared or is forthcoming in many magazines and anthologies including *The Penn Review, Fairlight Shorts, Rollick, Bandit Fiction,* and *Gasher.* She lives in Bangalore, likes Captain Planet, and blogs at http://amitabasu.com/

Sonia Beauchamp (she/her) is a healing artist and English tutor on the North Shore of Oʻahu. Read her recent work in *Typehouse Literary Magazine, Hawaiʻi Pacific Review,* and *Literary Mama.* Find out more at http://www.soniakb.com.

Sally-Jo Keala-o-Ānuenue Bowman grew up in Kailua, Oʻahu, and graduated from Kamehameha Schools in 1958. Her articles, essays, profiles, and poems are collected in "The Heart of Being Hawaiian" and "Huakaʻi Hele." She and her husband live in Oregon, where she taught magazine writing at the University of Oregon.

Wendie Burbridge is a Kanaka Maoli writer from Wahiawā. During 2011–2020 she wrote the weekly blog "The Five-0 Redux" for *The Honolulu Star-Advertiser.* Her writing has been published by Bamboo Ridge Press, ʻŌiwi, Fat Ulu, and Autumn House Press. This story is for her Chief and their son, Dakota Huluʻili.

Donald Carreira Ching was born and raised in Kahaluʻu, Oʻahu. His novel, *Between Sky and Sea: a Family's Struggle,* was published by Bamboo Ridge Press. In 2018, he received the Elliot Cades Award for Literature. He is currently working on his short story collection, *Blood Work and Other Stories.*

Lilia Childs grew up in Honolulu and currently lives under a forest canopy in Portland, Oregon. She is a Hanahauʻoli and Punahou graduate.

Jacey Choy was born and raised in Honolulu. She grew up instilled with a deep love of family, the ocean, and the natural environment, which she has carried, and still carries, with her. Jacey spends part of the year on Oʻahu, and too much of the year on the mainland.

Sue Cowing: I live in Honolulu, a stone's throw from Maunalua Bay, where I write poems, fiction, and letters, but mostly poems. Congratulations and thanks to founders Eric and Darrell and all the rest for forty-five years of quality publication, and for supporting and encouraging regional writing.

Leanne Dunic is the fiction editor at *Tahoma Literary Review* and the leader of the band The Deep Cove. Her book of lyric prose and photographs, *Wet*, is forthcoming (2024) with Talonbooks. Leanne lives on the unceded and occupied traditional territories of the Musqueam, Squamish, and Tsleil-Waututh First Nations.

Mitchell K. Dwyer is a writer for the University of Hawaiʻi Foundation, a graduate of UH–Hilo, and a longtime NaNoWriMo participant. His work has appeared in Windward Community College's *Rain Bird* and on 8Asians.com.

For those who stay nīele, **Sharla Jane Aialani Foster** was born on Oʻahu, raised in American Samoa, and currently resides on Kauaʻi, where she tutors at Kauaʻi Community College. She enjoys random conversations filled with sarcasm and humor and continues to wait for her age to catch up to her hair color.

Judith Graham received an MA in English from UH–Mānoa. Her small history book *Hawaiian Voices* was published in 1982, and an extended oral history, *Brother Low Recalls*, appeared on Hawaiʻi Island during 2012–2013. Her work life has varied. She has lived in Hawaiʻi since 1970.

Gail N. Harada is grateful to the founding editors of Bamboo Ridge Press for their vision, perseverance, commitment to Hawaiʻi literature, and so much more. In 2013, Bamboo Ridge published her book, *Beyond Green Tea and Grapefruit: Poems and Stories*. In 2021, she received the Loretta D. Petrie Award.

A circa 1965 Pacific Northwest transplant, **Jim Harstad** is proud to be included in this important issue of Hawaiʻi's most avant publication. T'anks, eh, Bamboo Ridge!

Alden M. Hayashi was born and raised in Honolulu but now lives in Boston. After writing about technology and business for more than thirty years, he has recently begun writing fiction. His first novel, *Two Nails, One Love*, was published by Black Rose Writing in 2021.

no worry about **thomas iannucci** he doin jus fine. no be nīele.

Ann Inoshita received the 2021 Elliot Cades Award for Literature for an established writer. She is author of a book of poems, *Mānoa Stream* (Kahuaomānoa Press), and co-author of *No Choice but to Follow* and *What We Must Remember* (Bamboo Ridge Press).

Darlene M. Javar lives on the Big Island of Hawai'i. She is published in *Bamboo Ridge, Hawai'i Pacific Review, Chaminade Literary Review, Tinfish, Kaimana, Into the Teeth of the Wind, The Distillery, Earth's Daughters, Storyboard 8*, and *East Hawaii Observer*. Recently retired, she is reconnecting with poetry.

Lisa Linn Kanae is the author of the short story collection *Islands Linked By Ocean* (Bamboo Ridge Press) and the chapbook *Sista Tongue* (Tinfish Press).

Jeddie Narumi Kawahatsu is a *yonsei/shin-nisei* born and raised in San Francisco, California. She currently enjoys her time reading, baking sourdough bread, and dancing hula and zouk. Jeddie is most inspired when traveling and forging deep connections with friends new and old.

Sarai Kennerley grew up in Auckland, Aotearoa (NZ) and is of Sāmoan, Māori, and European descent. She earned a degree in Communications at Brigham Young University–Hawai'i and worked for four years as a performer at the Polynesian Cultural Center. She was a writer in the Te Papa Tupu: Mentorship Programme (2022).

Scott Kikkawa writes detective fiction set in Territorial Honolulu and insists this work has nothing to do with his real-life job as a law enforcement officer. Supporting this assertion is the fact that none of his stories contain lawsuits, audits, or micromanagers. He thanks Bamboo Ridge Press for the soapbox.

Milton Kimura has been a Pittsburgher for the past ten years after living the first sixty-five years of his life in Waipahu and then in Honolulu. He keeps busy traveling to opera and symphony concerts, tutoring for Literacy Pittsburgh, and shoveling snow. He is getting better at all three.

Clifford Kōtaro Kobayashi (1919–2014): Pāʻia-born gardener, fisherman, and pediatrician. The grandson of contract laborers, he graduated from Maui High (1938) and studied at UH before transferring to the University of Iowa, where he was a medical school freshman on December 7, 1941. He wrote "In Humble Guise" in April 1940.

Juliet S. Kono lives and works in Honolulu.

Mari Kubo was raised in Hawaiʻi. She has a BA from University of Hawaiʻi and an MA from Boston University. She has lived in Hilo, Honolulu, Boston, Fairfield, and San Francisco, and currently lives in Hilo. Her book of poems, *A Japanese Girl Speaks*, was published by Finishing Line Press.

Lanning C. Lee earned his BA and PhD from UH–Mānoa, his MA from the University of Wisconsin. Part of the first class of PhD candidates in English at Mānoa, he authored the first creative writing dissertation there. He's appeared in BR, his Amazon page: www.amazon.com/author/lanninglee, his website: LanningLee.com.

Jeffrey Thomas Leong lives in the San Francisco Bay Area. For two decades he worked in public health. While earning an MFA at the Vermont College of Fine Arts, he translated Chinese wall poetry from Angel Island, collected in *Wild Geese Sorrow*, winner of a 2019 Northern California Book Award.

R. Zamora Linmark's latest novel is *The Importance of Being Wilde at Heart*. He has just completed *Eh, No Talk Li'Dat*, a multi-authored book on Pidgin, in which he served as editor. "Ode To My Old Self" is taken from a forthcoming novel *And The Winner Is*. He lives in Honolulu.

Christian Hanz Lozada authored the poetry collection *He's a Color Until He's Not* (2023) and co-authored *Leave with More Than You Came With* (2019). He lives in San Pedro, California, and uses his MFA to teach his neighbors' kids at Los Angeles Harbor College.

Darrell H.Y. Lum: Though I was co-editor, blame Eric and Juliet for picking my work! It's nice though, to appear alongside many great writers in "da fat issue." It's testament to their trust in us. With such support, BR will highlight the best of Hawaiʻi's writers for years to come.

Wing Tek Lum is a Honolulu businessman and poet. Bamboo Ridge Press has published his two collections of poetry: *Expounding the Doubtful Points* (1987) and *The Nanjing Massacre: Poems* (2012). He is honored that a third volume, *The Oldtimers*, is now forthcoming next year from Bamboo Ridge as issue #125.

Marion Lyman-Mersereau: Poetry has always been my way of processing experience but I've always loved a good story that is a page turner. I am so inspired by Scott Kikkawa's books, even though I was never keen on that genre before, so I decided to have a go.

Dana R. Lyons is a father, attorney, and aloha ʻāina advocate from Moku o Kākuhihewa (Oʻahu).

Alan D. McNarie may be best known for the myriad articles published during his 30-year career as a Big Island journalist. He has also published two novels: *Yeshua: the Gospel of St. Thomas* (1993) which won the Pushcart Editor's Book Award, and *The Soul Keys* (2015) plus dozens of poems.

Jonathon Medeiros teaches and learns about Language Arts on Kauaʻi, where he grew up. He writes about education and curiosity, teaching his students that if you change all of your mistakes or regrets, you'd erase yourself. Jonathon walks, bakes, surfs, and enjoys spending time with his brilliant wife and daughters.

Fresh from one six-month safari through the Ala Wai, searching for the lost riches aboard the Niña, Pinta, and Santa Maria, **Tyler Miranda** would like to announce one brand-new literary trope: expected irony.

Tamara Leiokanoe Moan is a writer and artist living in Kailua on Oʻahu.

L. Nishioka: Grew up in Kailua, Oʻahu, schooled at the University of Hawaiʻi and employed for 30+ years by the Department of Education. Have been living a life in retirement for 20+ years in Mililani with husband Sax and late dogs—Trooper, Tobi, Rascal—and Kuma— adopted by grandnephew.

Susan Miho Nunes was born and raised in Hilo. Her short stories have appeared in *Bamboo Ridge* and her freelance columns in the *San Francisco Chronicle*. Her children's books include *The Last Dragon* and newly-released *Chinese Celebrations for Children.* She now lives in Berkeley, California.

Born on Oʻahu, **Derek N. Otsuji** is the author of *The Kitchen of Small Hours* (SIU Press, 2021), featured in *Honolulu Magazine*'s "Essential Hawaii Books You Should Read." He is a 2019 Tennessee Williams Scholar. Recent work has appeared in *32 Poems, The Southern Review,* and *The Threepenny Review.*

Christy Passion is a critical care nurse and author of the poetry collection, *Still Out of Place.* She is a contributing author to the Norton anthology, *When the Light of the World Was Subdued, Our Songs Came Through.* In 2022, the Academy of American Poets featured her poem "Waikiki Returns."

Normie Salvador (he/him) is a disabled Filipino-American editor, poet, and occasional playwright. Tinfish Press published his poetry chapbook, *Philter* (2003). His most recent works are poems in *Snaring New Suns* and *Hawaiʻi Pacific Review,* and a short play that won Kumu Kahua Theatre's Go Try PlayWrite Contest (December 2022).

Misty-Lynn Sanico writes any kine in Honolulu. "Scars" is a semi-autobiographical ghost story. Find her online @mistysanico.

Eric Paul Shaffer is author of seven poetry books, including *Even Further West* and *A Million-Dollar Bill. Green Leaves: Selected and New Poems* will appear in 2023. Six-hundred individual poems appear in reviews in America and eleven other countries. Shaffer teaches composition, literature, and creative writing at Honolulu Community College.

Mira Chieko Shimabukuro is a poet, scholar, and Teaching Professor in the School of Interdisciplinary Studies at University of Washington Bothell. Descended from plantation workers in Hawaiʻi, she grew up in Portland, Oregon listening to her father talk story about small kid time in Mānoa Valley, Oʻahu.

John E. Simonds, retired Honolulu daily newspaper editor, has lived with family in Hawaiʻi since the 1970s, when he started writing poetry, at work now on his fourth collection. Grateful for alert neighbors and overloaded healthcare workers, he now wears treaded shoes and a wrist phone during backyard adventures.

Michelle Cruz Skinner was born and raised in the Philippines. She is the author of *Balikbayan* (Bess Press) and *In the Company of Strangers* (Bamboo Ridge Press).

Bamboo Ridge Press published **Cathy Song**'s short story collection *All the Love in the World* in 2020.

Joseph Stanton has lived in Hawai'i since 1972. His books of poems are *Prevailing Winds, Moving Pictures, Things Seen, A Field Guide to the Wildlife of Suburban O'ahu, Imaginary Museum, Cardinal Points*, and *What the Kite Thinks*. His poems have appeared in *Harvard Review, Poetry, New Letters, Antioch Review*, and many others.

Eileen R. Tabios has released over sixty collections of poetry, fiction, essays, and experimental biographies from publishers in ten countries. Recent books include the poetry collection, *Because I Love You, I Become War*, and a first novel, *DoveLion: A Fairy Tale for Our Times*. For more information: http://eileenrtabios.com

Gary Tachiyama: retired, not doing nothing tho. O'ahu born and raised. Like dirty water tilapia, can live thru anything.

O. Wini Terada: Grew up Kalihi. Grad 'Iolani, parents working double/triple jobs, small-kid-time summers at Kalihi Y. Grad UH–Mānoa & Chaminade. Public school teacher, high school English, Pāhoa, Honoka'a, long time Ānuenue in Pālolo; past couple years K-7 computer science. Beloved wife—my savior; wonderful son—my happiness battery.

Bill Teter has been teaching at the University Laboratory School in Honolulu for a long, long time. It was there that Jim Harstad and the real Chris taught him how to write.

Delaina Thomas: LeiHina is now 20 and Napua is 16. They are strong and beautiful, active in cultural, political, and environmental causes.

Ken Tokuno lives in Kāne'ohe with his wife, Diane, a respected artist: "Since retiring from UH–Mānoa, I started to write prose, as opposed to poetry. This is my second short story in *Bamboo Ridge*, along with eight poems previously published. I am honored to be in the 45th anniversary issue."

Lee A. Tonouchi a.k.a. "Da Pidgin Guerrilla" stay da recipient of da 2021–2022 Tony Quagliano Poetry Award and da 2023 American Association for Applied Linguistics Distinguished Public Service Award for his work in raising public awareness of important language-related issues and promoting linguistic social justice.

Born in Hawai'i, **Jean Yamasaki Toyama** is a Beckett scholar and professor emerita of French, University of Hawai'i at Mānoa. Her publications include *Kelli's Hanauma Friends* with paintings by artist Russell Sunabe, *Prepositions* with paintings by Cora Yee, *The Piano Tuner's Wife*, and *Wild Elephants*.

Cheryl Treiber-Kawaoka, originally from Chicago, lived in Saipan before settling on O'ahu with her husband Gerald, daughter Grace, and their dog, Kukui. Recently retired as a visual and theater arts educator, she has been pursuing her love of writing. Her work has been published on various websites including Writers.com.

Heidi Turner is a writer and musician from Maui, Hawai'i. Her work has been published in *Cirque, Hawai'i Pacific Review, The Adirondack Review, The Other Journal, Barren Magazine,* and others. She currently lives in New Hampshire, where she recently completed an MFA in fiction. Find more of her work at www.hidturner.com.

Julie Ushio lives in Honolulu. Born and raised in Nebraska, she has also lived in Colorado and Alaska. She is currently working on a novel based on her Japanese grandmother, a picture bride who lived in western Nebraska.

Amy Uyematsu, a Sansei poet and teacher from Los Angeles, was grateful to Bamboo Ridge Press for publishing so many of her poems, going back to 1986, and delighted to be part of this 45th anniversary issue. Amy's family regrets to inform all *Bamboo Ridge* readers that she passed on June 23, 2023, after a courageous two-year battle with cancer.

Lady Wendolyn (Wendy Sanico) grew up in Pearl City, O'ahu. She was a military spouse who enjoyed traveling the world with her husband and children. But being home in Hawai'i is where she is the happiest. She loves afternoon tea and is a certified tea sommelier and consultant.

Mahealani Perez Wendt has published in Hawai'i, the U.S., and abroad, including a poetry collection, *Uluhaimālama*. Recent work appears in anthologies *Writing the Land* and *13 Miles from Cleveland*, and U.S. special laureate projects, *When the Light Was Subdued, Our Songs Came Through* and *Living Nations, Living Words*.

L. Yuriko Williams was born in Japan and raised on Oʻahu, the mainland, and overseas as a military dependent. She graduated from the University of Hawaiʻi with a major in Asian Studies and Philosophy. "Da Bes'" and "Samishī" are her first works of fiction.

J. Fumiko Wong lives in Honolulu, Hawaiʻi. She would like to thank Lee Tonouchi for his help on "Too Big, da Heart."

Lois-Ann Yamanaka evolved into the Boss of Her Own Life and lives in deep gratitude and praise for Bamboo Ridge Press, especially the OGs and more so the next generation who keep our literature and art alive and relevant as a body of historical, established, and emerging voices.

Mahalo for your support! Bamboo Ridge Press gratefully acknowledges generous donations from the following individuals and organizations in 2020, 2021, and 2022.

Carol Abe
Wanda Adams
Keith Akana
Nancy Aleck
Elizabeth Allen
Cynthia Alm
Robert A. Alm
AmazonSmile
Anonymous (24)
Esther Arinaga
Ann Asakura
Victoria Asayama
Atherton Family Foundation
Marjorie Au
Cristina Bacchilega
Emily Benton
Leomi Bergknut
Doreen E. Beyer
Teresa Bill
Bill.com
Dave Manu Bird
Marlene Booth
Sally-Jo Bowman
Michael Bressem
Michael Broschat
Ann Bunk
Lou Bunk
Robert Buss
The Cades Foundation
Susan Chamberlin
Jeffrey Chan
Lauren Childs
Joyce Chinen
Eric Chock
Ghislaine Chock
Ladonna Chung
Xander Cintrón-Chai
Sara L. Collins
Community of Literary Magazines
    & Presses
Thomas Conger

Kelly Conlin
Cooke Foundation
E. Shan Correa
Joel Cosseboom
Rebecca Covert
Sue Cowing
Linda Cunningham
Tom Cunningham
Cathy Song Davenport
Douglas Davenport
Leighton Davenport
Rachel Davenport
Maria Helena Del Llano-Good
Porscha dela Fuente
Elizabeth Donaldson
George Drick
Suerte Dureg
Christina Dwight
Aaron Ebata
Jason Ellinwood
Ernestine Enomoto
Louis Erste
Deanna Espinas
Susan Nunes Fadley
Elena Farden
Judith Fernandez
First Hawaiian Bank
Alma Rosa Fontanilla
Foodland Super Market, Limited
Robert L. Freedman
Guy Fujimura
David J. Furumoto
Alvin Fuse
Karen Fuse
William Garnett
Caroline Garrett
Claire Gearen
Andrea Gelber
Jeela Go
Joy Gold
Stephanie Grande-Misaki

Susan Griffin
Lesa Griffith
Merie Ellen Gushi
Stu Hada
Keoni Halemano
John M. Hara
Marie M. Hara Family Trust
Mavis Hara
Gail N. Harada
Violet Harada
Ermile Hargrove
Cheryl Harstad
James R. Harstad
Jennifer Hasegawa
Hawai'i Community Reinvestment
    Corporation
Hawai'i Council for the Humanities
Hawai'i Literary Arts Council
Hawai'i State Foundation on Culture
    and the Arts
Timothy Helfer
Lorna Hershinow
Leonore Higa
Hao Chih Ho
John Houk
Craig Howes
Philip Ige
Jeanette Imler
Ann Inoshita
Frances Kakugawa
Lisa Linn Kanae
Susan Karlson
Wayne Kawamoto
Roland Kawano
Scott Kikkawa
Carol Jean Kimura
Milton B. Kimura
Karen Ko
Joy Kobayashi-Cintrón
David Komo
Scott Komo
Susan M. Kosasa Fund, Hawai'i
    Community Foundation
Calvin Kuniyuki
Andrew Kunz
Gail Kuroda

Melanie Lau
Juliet Kono Lee
Lanning C. Lee
Vanessa Lee
Jeffrey T. Leong
Sonia Leong
Kimberli Lo
Phyllis Look
Jason Louie
Dara Luangphinith
Seri Luangphinith
Anna Tseng Lum
Bertha Lum
Darrell H. Y. Lum
Louise and Y. T. Lum Foundation
Mae Lum
Tan Tek Lum
Wing Tek Lum
Mark Lutwak
Marion Lyman-Mersereau
Jennifer Madriaga
Prana Joy Mandoe
Annette Masutani
Jean Matsuo
Gary Mau
Stephanie Mau
Mark Maves
Matthew McGranaghan
Richard Melendez
Meta
Nicola M. Miller
Tamara Moan
Lillian Muranaka
Claire Muraoka
Amy Murata
National Endowment for the Arts
Harrison Neblett
Eric Nemoto
Donna Kimiko Noborikawa
Janice Nuckols
Shyam Nunley
Gail O'Connor
Ethel Aiko Oda
Rainie Oet
Lauzanne Oshiro
Marcus Oshiro

Ryan Ozawa
Pacific Business Forms
Gary Pak
Christy Passion
PayPal
Alison Perrault
Kathy J. Phillips
Poetry Foundation
Nora Pollard
Deborah Pope
Lois S. Price
Michael Puleloa
Makana Reeves
James Reis
Lynn Reis
John Rieder
Nāpunakō Sanico
Misty-Lynn Sanico-Alba
Gayle Sato
Jo Ann Schindler
Noralynn Schubert
Eric Paul Shaffer
Miriam Sharma
John Simonds
Michelle Cruz Skinner
Aviam Soifer
Susan Soong
Helen L. Stewart
Amber Stierli
Eric Stinton
Allen Suematsu
Monica Sullivan
Miko Suzuki
Jeff Swartz

Gary Tachiyama
Gerald T. Takano
Hazel H. Takumi Foundation
Larry T. Takumi
Friends of Brian Taniguchi
Virginia Tanji
Bill Teter
Delaina Thomas
Ken Tokuno
Dennis Toyama
Jean Toyama
Maureen Trevenen
David Tsujimoto
William Tucker
Jeff Uhr
Aldric Ulep
Amy L. Uyematsu
Lani Uyeno
Melineh Verma
Jack Wallace
Sara Ward
Chiye Wenkam
Western Union
Sylvia Wilmeth
Eileen Wong
Haviland Wright
Agnes Yamada
Charlie Yamamoto
Aiko Yamashiro
Ronald Yanagihara
Lisa Yee
Y York
Merle Yoshida
Nancy Young
Lizzie Zerez

© 2023 GKAGIMOTO

CANE
HAUL
ROAD
HAWAI'I

it's a
Shuri
Thing

okidoki

Abunai!

Photo taken by Darrell H. Y. Lum of warnings painted on the rocky path at Bamboo Ridge and given to Eric Chock with the inscription:

To Eric —

On the occasion of celebrating your birthday . . . the birth of a baby girl . . . and a magazine, may we be able to find our way along the path to hook the fish with our name.

— Darrell
1978

WARNING

STRONG
CURRENTS

YOU COULD BE SWEPT AWAY
BE AWARE, READ HAWAI'I LITERATURE

WARNING

WAVES BREAK ON LEDGE

IMPACT CAN BE SEVERE
BE AWARE, READ HAWAI'I LITERATURE

WARNING

SUDDEN
DROP OFF
YOU MAY LOSE FOOTING
BE AWARE, READ HAWAIʻI LITERATURE

WARNING

SLIPPERY
ROCKS

FALLS MAY OCCUR
BE AWARE, READ HAWAI'I LITERATURE

BAMBOO RIDGE PRESS

ULUA SIGHTED

KEEP WRITING
CAST YOUR LINE

YEARS

BAMBOO RIDGE

Celebrating forty-five years of literature and art for, by, and about the people of Hawai'i and the Pacific.